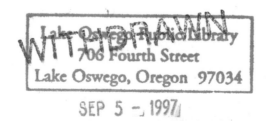

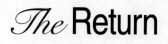

The Return

The Return

Petru Popescu

Grove Press
New York

Published simultaneously in Canada
Printed in the United States of America

Library of Congress Cataloging-in-Publication Data

Popescu, Petru
    The return / Petru Popescu.
       p.   cm.
    ISBN 0-8021-1613-2
    1. Popescu, Petru—Journeys—Romania.   2. Romania—
Description and travel.   3. Authors, Romanian—20th century—
Journeys—Romania.   4. Authors, Exiled—United States—Biography.
I. Title
    PC840.26.057Z477   1997
    818'.5403—dc21
    [B]   97-14270
                                                                CIP

DESIGN BY LAURA HAMMOND HOUGH

Grove Press
841 Broadway
New York, NY 10003

10 9 8 7 6 5 4 3 2 1

To

the Popescus of Bucharest,

and to Iris, Chloe, and Adam

L isten to me. Listen to me.

This voice, my own, is rising from deep down. It's welling up out of a part of myself which I've never seen, since it cannot be seen: it lies somewhere at my core, maybe inside my bones, mixed within my bone marrow, or perhaps spread among all the cells that make up my body. I know it intimately though, for it is the very foundation of my being. It is dark down there, at my foundation. Curiously enough, what we know best about ourselves, we keep in the dark. It is dark like in a storeroom whose bulb went out, and I never bothered to buy a new bulb, because I know every inch of its space and every object that occupies it.

That part of myself conjures up the image of a compact layer of silence, long undisturbed for over fifteen years. I was born and raised in a Communist country. I defected, came to America, lived in freedom, and yet, on a certain level of my being, I kept lying in the dark, underground, in utter silence—until, against all my expectations, I decided to revisit my birthplace. The silence was like a long tunnel between two gateways: one, my escape into freedom, the other, my re-entry into the space of my roots, which I had sworn never to go back to.

When I decided to go back to that space, my silence was finally broken. Noise invaded my foundation, and light flooded it. I peered in, and noticed an astonishing fact. The roots I once severed had sprouted back inside me. They looked different now. We say that we came to America to strike new roots, but the truth is, what we plant in this generous alien soil are the old roots, renewed, with brand-new sap flowing in them. So of course they are new, but still, they're the old ones. In short, America is the place where people reinvent themselves: they don't just get a new future, they get a new past too.

I write these words, and feel that they don't express what I'm trying to say. I reach for more words. I throw out words like darts after a nimble animal, for I'm trying to arrest a certain feeling. But I realize that such a feeling is not in words, it's in . . . smells, sounds, the feel of my hands on certain things, the feel of my body at certain times of the day or night, or during certain seasons. It's a *feeling*. Of what it was like, back then, when I wasn't free, but I was dreaming of freedom. And what it was like when I reached freedom, and got dizzy, almost sick. Freedom was too good, and too different.

My story is not heroic; there is always room for a new hero, but in this story I will be an anti-hero at best. My story is about commonplace Communism (I love that consonance), as I lived it, me, one man out of more than one billion people, the total population of Communism at the time I defected.

I'm trying to slow down. To stop raving and sputtering, and to hit a certain key, whose sound will fill the words I'm using with truth and simplicity. But that key is not so easy to hit, because . . .

What happened back there, behind that barbed wire under which I managed to crawl out to freedom, while other defectors stayed pinned on it, was that our jailers not only held us in, they programmed us to believe that we were not wanted anywhere outside our prison-planet. They took us out of the world, and held us out, separate, until we developed and internalized the fear that we were not of this world, and this world was not for us.

More words. I can't help it.

I guess I still haven't hit that right note.

I need your patience. Whoever you are, I need you to listen, even though some of this might strike you as bizarre, or even incomprehensible. It is that, and more. It is, in its mediocrity, a very extreme experience which, once told, might find its usefulness. I say it again, like I did on the previous page, barely less feverish now, barely more at ease: listen to me.

I was born in a Communist nation, after the Iron Curtain slammed down.

Wait a second. Bingo.

That note. I hit it.

I was born in Communist Romania after the Iron Curtain shut that land out of the world. I grew up there, I had parents, a twin brother. I lost my brother, and then my family. Though I left young, at twenty-seven, I was known in that land when I left it, because I wrote books and made movies. So, I lived there, I loved and lost loved ones, I was formed as a human being. All out there, on my little prison-planet which orbited along, on its own course, crudely self-sufficient.

All of that is contained in one brief line: I was born in Communist Romania.

I hit that note, and I'm holding it.

I grew up loving one land, but that land belonged to Communism. So to remain sane, uninfected, I lived in that land but dreamed of America. I made it to America like the boy in that famous Elia Kazan movie *America, America*. No, I didn't walk barefoot across Anatolia, to Istanbul, and then sneak onto an America-bound ship. But yes, my trek too was long, torturous, and full of perils.

I watched *America, America* in a rickety Bucharest movie theater in the late sixties, when it was released as part of a short-lived cultural thaw between capitalism and Communism. I was a student of languages with English as my major, so I was obsessive about watching any movie in English. The version I saw was censored, but its essence, the dream of a third-world youngster for a land he had never seen, was uncensorable. It dripped out of every inch of celluloid. I recognized in it my own faith in that new land, as absurd and unshakeable as that Anatolian youngster's, who would walk barefoot across the desert to a smoky turn-of-the-century harbor, from where a ship with a tall puffing stack would buffet him away to Ellis Island. There, our hero would step past the Stars and Stripes flying by the gate, drop down to kiss the earth of his new home (that earth was paved!), then walk away into freedom.

In my case, I nurtured my secret dream of defecting against an official dream, that of Our Bright Communist Future. We, the Soviet empire's youngest subjects, were also the most cherished investment in that Communist Future. That Future never materialized—isn't that amazing and singular in the history of human dreaming? After so much toil and sacrifice, the Communist dream crashed without once becoming a reality.

I dreamed of freedom. I needed it like a drowning man needs a breath of air.

Yet, I didn't even know the taste of freedom. Held behind escape-proof borders, some six thousand miles away from the object of my dreams, I grew up, became a novelist and filmmaker, climbed the peaks of national success, all while deep inside me I dreamed of America. America was the silent part of me, then. After I defected, it was Romania that sank deep within me and became silent. And now . . . they are both awake, and making sounds. Making words. Talking to each other.

I wanted freedom, but didn't even know what freedom was. What I needed most was so unfamiliar to me, I didn't even know why I needed it so badly. I just knew that I was ready to trade everything for it. Well, almost everything. Not my life, I'll admit to that. Between bondage and death, I would probably have chosen bondage.

Luckily I wasn't faced with that extreme choice. I first came to the United States as a guest of a respected university. My defection occurred ten months later; it had its own perils, but I didn't face death or incarceration. Other Romanians did—the tens of thousands who crossed the borders illegally. Between 1947, when the Iron Curtain was drawn closed, and 1989, when the revolution blew that curtain open, Romanians took incredible risks to get out of the physical space of Communism. Over and over, they swam across the Danube into Yugoslavia, teasing the bullets of two border-police forces. Even though Yugoslavia was our only neighbor unoccupied by Russian troops, it was not a land of freedom. It was Communist in its own proud way, and it didn't want the Romanian defectors. So as not to be detected by the twin sets of border watchtowers, the defectors hollowed out drifting logs, then snuck inside them and sailed them incredible distances, often drowning or suffocating. Those Romanians unmanaged to cross the Danube undetected had to trek northward on foot, across all of Yugoslavia, to the Italian border. If they survived hunger, exhaustion, and frightening encounters with the Yugoslav police, they had a shot at *that* border, beyond which everyone lived free.

Amazing? I'd say it was. Yet it happened. One of my own uncles made it to freedom by swimming the Danube into Yugoslavia.

Our other borders faced Bulgaria, Hungary, the Ukraine: lands occupied by the Soviet armies, just like ours. So one couldn't escape that way. There was also the stormy Black Sea, crashing onto two hundred miles of Romanian coastline. Those two hundred miles were dotted with cities and villages, each well staffed with police and Securitate men. Lighthouses and watchtowers pierced the moonless nights. Every evening, the beaches were raked, so that a defector's footprints could be easily spotted against the sand. Still, many desperadoes dared the beaches and the waves. One Romanian made it to Turkey by sailing the sea for ten days in a pickle barrel, with all his sustenance in two plastic bags, one filled with water, the other with chicken broth. Had he not been picked up by a Turkish fishing trawler, the scorching Romanian sun would have baked him alive in his barrel. Another, a soundman at the Buftea film studios, repaired the engine of an abandoned Nazi fighter plane, claiming he needed it to recreate the sound of air combat. Pretending to construct a film prop, he rebuilt the whole plane around that battered engine, and without one single lesson, but having memorized a flying manual, he got up in the air and flew to Greece. Others used hot-air balloons, dug tunnels under the border, and again and again swam the Danube.

Many were killed. Some made it to freedom. With their roots inside them, slashed to stumps just like mine, and then growing anew. We all did it. We all grabbed a chain saw and buzzed our way through our past. We burned it. We left it all behind. Slash-and-burn of what we were supposed to be.

And then, we watched the roots sprout up again. Slashed stumps, growing back.

I was first interrogated by the Securitate at thirteen, having been arrested off the basketball court of my Bucharest high school. The Securitate wanted me to rat on classmates who were engaged in subversive activities. They also wanted to know whether my father wrote letters, in code and using devious forwarding addresses, to that uncle in New York who had successfully swum the Danube. We had relatives in America, and that made us bad enough; but my parents were also "bourgeois intellectuals," in a regime of workers' power. Before the war, my parents had been extreme liberals. They had been founding members of "Friends of the USSR," a very radical political movement. My father wrote pro-Marxist essays (naive but courageous for the time), helped hide his Jewish friends during the deportations, and was spied on by the Siguranta, Romania's Gestapo. After the war, shocked by the brutality of the Russian occupation, neither of my parents joined the Communist party. My mother was from a family of harmless winegrowers, and my father had priests in his lineage. Their "unhealthy social origin" was heaped on them, with immediate consequences. My father was jailed without charge. After he was released, our home continued to be searched by the Securitate. Both my parents suffered from job discrimination. My brother and I were automatically tainted by our parents' backgrounds: in school, our grades were systematically reduced by fanatical teachers, while workers' and peasants' children never flunked a test, even if they turned in blank pages. So I had to work twice as hard for good grades, if I wanted to qualify for college. When I applied to Bucharest University, I had good grades but I still had to take tests, because of who I was. Meanwhile, thanks to their political purity, applicants of worker and peasant backgrounds were accepted without tests, no matter what kind of grades they had. That kind of overt discrimination was finally discontinued about the time I defected.

I sound like I'm complaining. But I'm not. Unfortunately, I can't tell my story like a normal individual: this is how I first experienced love, or work, or the loss of illusions, this is how I formed my goals and beliefs. If I experienced, say, love, it wasn't love, it was love under Communism. Communism weighed on all my experiences, distorting and deforming them. The Communist state constantly raided my childhood and youth, and millions of other people's. Everything I did, said, experienced, was in relation to a powerful and nasty "other," which was the Communist state. Barely a few hundred people escaped from that intrusion—the ones at the top of the power pyramid. Under Ceausescu, those few were even fewer: Ceausescu's own immediate family.

At the same time, Communism gave me a sense of importance, albeit in a negative way. Coming from parents such as mine, I was important from the start, as a potential rebel. When I became a challenging novelist and filmmaker in a land where party-line books turned yellow in bookstores and party-line movies played to empty theaters, my importance grew exponentially, which translated into increased surveillance of my work, and of my person. Not one of my books was printed without the censors tearing out some fifty to a hundred pages of my original manuscript. I reworked those pages and put them back in; with infallible instinct, the censors spotted them and weeded them out again. Still, the feeling of my writing came through: it was too rooted in not being free. The title of my first novel declared it plainly: *Captive.* It sold feverishly; the printers ran extra copies and sold them on the black market. I myself bought extra copies from black marketeers, to autograph them for family and friends. My readers' voracious appetite for something challenging, contrary, and different guaranteed my success. Of my films made in Romania, *Path in the Dark,* a depressed love story set in the peeling Communist paradise, became a landlocked blockbuster. Another, a truthful documentary about Bucharest, which I wrote, directed, and produced, was aired only once—it was far too honest for the state-owned TV. In a perverse way, I had it easy, because to be a censor-harassed author meant to be cool. I was *us,* the captives, against *them,* the jailers. I got my good reviews, for artistic judgment per se had not disappeared, but my greatest success was for what I wrote, not for how I wrote it. I was above all an artist who attacked the system.

Thus, shortly before defecting, I became that contradiction in terms: a Commie star. A celebrity in a culture without talk shows or gossip columns.

I was very lucky. Even though my books were savaged by the censors, my writing protected me. I did not have to accept the degradations of Communism to the degree others did. Still, my victory was ambiguous: I was an opposition writer and a patriot in a nationalistic regime that preyed on my patriotism and used it to forward its own goals. I was against Communism and suffered from its limitations, but Communism allowed me a measure of success, and held me up as proof of its broadmindedness. Thus, the system still managed to compromise me, to penetrate my defenses, to taint my stance. I punched breaches in its armor, but as I swam through them, it sucked me back in. Whatever success I did achieve, I was too tortured to ever really enjoy it.

On the other hand, it was hard to enjoy Commie celebrity because it came with that big price: constant surveillance. I woke up every day knowing that during the ensuing twenty-four hours I would be spied on, somehow. My phone was tapped, which I knew from the repairman who came to fix it. We were friends, sort of. I was also warned a few times by lower-rung Securitate operatives who had their own conflicts with the Ceausescu regime, or, being younger, had generational ideals not too different from mine.

I remember that old phone set, the only one in my apartment. Heavy and black, it sat enthroned in our living room like an honored but feared guest. In the Romanian language, nouns are either male or female; the phone is a "he." "He" rang, or let himself be dialled, putting me in touch with the world, guiding my voice to whomever I called, and simultaneously to someone else. An unseen third party, faceless, sleepless, and merciless: the Securitate. The system.

As part of that surveillance, my mail was also opened and read by "steaming": it was held up in hot steam until the glue of the envelope melted, and the respective Central Post Office employee could pull out the letter and acquaint the system with another little piece of my life. Sometimes I recognized "steamed" letters, sometimes I did not. But the thought was always in my mind: before I got to read it, that message—personal, intimate, a love letter perhaps—had been read by the system.

I assumed that many people I knew were informers, yet I couldn't break contact with them. Some were co-workers, even friends. So I watched what I said around certain people, which didn't mean that I was right in my suspicions; some innocent people had undeserved bad reputations; others, seemingly trustworthy, were actively in the pay of the Securitate. That could happen at any time, to anyone. A rejected lover could turn informer. Ordinarily, people were forced into becoming stool pigeons by the need for money. Altogether, we lived surrounded by an invisible aura of surveillance. Our very struggle to remain honest wove a web of betrayal around everything we did and said. We might as well have lived inside a police file.

Therefore, we were important.

In the late sixties, Ceausescu passed a law that reached deeper inside his subjects' lives than all his other laws: the decree for "Strengthening Our Socialist Nation," which forbade abortions and outlawed the sale of contraceptives, under stiff prison penalties. My sexual awakening, my first romances, happened with that added tension: how not to make babies I couldn't afford to father.

Now, sex had always been one of our escapes. Sex was part of our prison privileges; it was cheap and hurried and usually uncomfortable (we had no money to wine and dine our dates, no cars to enjoy the thrill of speed before that of copulation), but still, sex was something fresh, unregulated, apparently uncensorable. Until the man at the helm said: No more! The Romanian nation needed to build up its numbers. One last freedom, that of spontaneous, randy sex, disappeared. People went to jail for buying condoms on the black market. Obstetricians' homes were raided if they were suspected of being clandestine abortion clinics. Village midwives were rounded up. Slighted lovers informed on each other all the more. Thousands of infants were born malformed, from malnutrition or botched abortions. Abandoned, they were locked up in frightening shelters, whose secret was to be pierced after the revolution.

I hated that feeling of surveillance, I hated it passionately. But I also tried to glamorize it. I had to. When I walked down the streets of Bucharest, I felt I was the desperado in *High Noon,* heading for my last gunfight. Not one door was creaking, not one curtain was flapping. And yet I knew that rifles and pistols were pointed at me. At the end of the street, I glanced at the other gunman, the one I was supposed to shoot it out with. He was it, the system. I stood no chance of defeating him, or even of drawing my gun. I'd get shot first, from some rooftop. So I walked tragically, across a doomed silence, the silence before the shooting.

Of course it was all a fantasy, a romantic exercise. To begin with I had no weapon, none of us did: possession of firearms drew even stiffer sentences than possession of gold or drugs, and in the hands of an able "people's DA," a case of that sort could be easily travestied into a conspiracy against the state, punishable by death. Still, my romantic feeling was no less genuine. I was doomed, and center stage. Transfer that feeling to the whole population. Picture being in Romania itself, walking down its streets, and the feeling of being held in the crosshairs of a giant rifle. That was how I felt, how we felt. We did everything caught in the crosshairs; when I say everything, I really mean everything: eating, drinking, thinking, working, copulating, stepping into the bathroom for a pee or a shit or a shower, wiping ourselves, washing up, putting our clothes back on, walking up to the window to look at the stars, finding love, losing love, begetting children, ailing, aging . . .

All in the crosshairs.

I remember my Bucharest apartment in pieces. The room I shared with my twin brother, before he was rushed by ambulance to a gruesome Communist hospital, in which he died. My bed. The kitchen counter where I made my thick, strong Romanian coffee. The window of my study. I used to open that window late at night, to peer out into the peace of an old European street. Above the city shone the moon, to which the Romanians attach so many myths, including how the *varcolaci* (the vampires) were born there, and since they were born hungry, they started eating the moon. As it shrank, the vampires fell to earth, onto the land of Romania. In winter, I looked out on the fresh snow that purified my puckered, quaint Balkan town. In spring, I inhaled the fragrance of premature flowers—spring in the Danube valley sneaks up on the landscape like puberty on a peasant girl. At all times, I felt the crosshairs of that giant rifle, cutting across the moon, across the quiet majesty of the night, and across me.

My study had belonged to my father before he walked out on mother and on me, his one surviving son. Remarried, Dad lived now in another part of town, and often wrote at night: he too was a writer, and had vainly tried to discourage me from choosing a writer's life. At such an hour of the night, with the inspirational moon above me, I should have felt reassured by our continuity, and proud. I should have felt at peace, and clear about my destiny.

But I didn't. I was caught by history in a tragic cul-de-sac, teeming with stool pigeons and jail wardens. Us and them. Us in the crosshairs, them with their fingers on the trigger.

Us and them. That perverted sense of importance.

Then I defected.

The years passed.

I don't know when exactly, but gradually the silence within me started to break. It was invaded by echoes, by remembered sound bites of where I was from, of what had happened to me in my birthplace. Slowly, my renewed roots had grown strong enough to want to face the scene of their uprooting.

Sometime in the late eighties, in California, I started to tell myself things like this:

I want to go back and visit. I want to tread again on those streets, and be surrounded by their dull, drab colors. I want to come close to what's left of the past, so I can examine it, like junk spilled out of an old box. What do we have here? Oh yes, this was our resistance, without glory and for no reward. This was our lack of horizons. This, our loneliness. I heard in my mind a terrifying sound: a cracking wail, like the rupturing of the bulkheads of a sinking vessel. It was the sound of my generation marooned in Communist outer space. I wanted to relive it all. But why?

Why stir up old ghosts? What is to be learned from that? What is to be gained? Why?

To know, of course. But to know *what*?

I could not answer.

After telling myself those things, I felt a deep fear. I feared that I was fated to go back not just to revisit, but to lose my freedom again, to re-enter my old prison. The fear was deep, but even deeper underneath it, I touched an older feeling. Rage. A rage that astounded me, for it felt almighty and blind, and yet purposeless. The past was past, and I was an

American now. Here was the essence of my new persona: an author of books and writer-director of movies, in America. A husband and a father, in America. A successful, rounded, fulfilled citizen, in America.

In my mind, I turned East, towards Romania, and shouted: You hear that, you disgusting gnome, who climbed on the graves of a generation to become a tyrant in a class with Hitler and Stalin? I turned towards Ceausescu, and blurted my brutal cry of freedom all over again: You have nothing on me, nothing. You mean nothing. So why should I want to visit the land that you fouled up so hopelessly?

But I did want to visit it. The rage stormed on inside me, and scared me. It was rage of the purest, most irrational type, even though I could rationalize it with varied evocations of injustice and loss: my twin brother dead, my childhood captive, my books raped by the censors, my mind raped, my destiny scripted without rights, merits, or joys.

There was plenty I could explain my rage with. But rage is rage, rage is craziness, rage is not healed through explanations.

I raged, and I was afraid.

Glasnost came. The Soviets relaxed their grip. The Communist satellites started falling like dominoes. Ceausescu himself fell.

It didn't help. I was still raging.

I had to go there, to open that old pit; it was the only way. Denial had worked many times in my life, but this time it didn't.

Yet before I could take my physical self back there, I realized that I had to chance another important step: I had to allow my memories of Romania to reinvade me. I had to let that private hell come back to me. I'd shut it out successfully, I'd lived without it, like an amnesiac, thanks to many absorbing activities: working, pursuing my ambitions, raising my children, becoming an American. Becoming an American writer, learning painstakingly how to write in English, which was much harder than using English for a job, or a relationship, or just conversation.

Now, I had to remember stuff from before becoming an American. In remembrance there was pain, pain which could not be bypassed. But this whole re-confronting of the past could not be bypassed anymore. Which puzzled me. Like all East European refugees, I'd had access in the West, safely, to all sorts of accounts about Communism. Books and films, political testimonies, academic assessments, intelligence reports. At various times, I had consumed them hungrily, feeling a double understanding: from within, as an ex-player, and from outside, as a liberated survivor.

I knew about Communism. What else did I not know, which compelled me to take this disturbing look in the mirror?

The scary answer was: me.

Finally, I decided. Let's do it. The sooner the better. Let's start.

Part One

Split Feelings

In the breakup of my inner silence, a major event was the arrival of my mother to America, eight years after I had defected. She was over seventy, and her age explained why Communist Romania had granted an exit visa to the mother of a defector tried in absentia. While its citizens were young, the Communist state wanted them to stay put and work, justifying the almost free schooling they had received (of its golden promises, the Communist state had fulfilled only two: cheap medical care, of very substandard quality, and cheap schooling, good because Romania's academic tradition was good). Now that Mother was old and retired, she would benefit the state by defecting, because they would take away her pension, her apartment, her belongings. Mother stepped inside the little place I was renting in Beachwood Canyon, a typical struggling writer's abode, faced me, and declared in her stage-trained voice: "I am staying here, in freedom. If you choose not to help me, I already talked to your uncle Florin in New York, and he agreed to write me an affidavit."

Did that sound like an ultimatum? It was. Mother realized the inappropriateness of her tone (oftentimes she didn't, she had been an actress, and spoke the same way on stage as in life), and sweetened it some: "Besides, you're alone. Don't you think you need me? If you get sick, there's no one here to even make you a cup of tea."

I laughed. Jeez, Mom. I've taken care of myself since the age of thirteen. Now you came to make me a cup of tea?

That conversation was typical of our interactions: hard, rhetorical, threatening, full of distrust. It brought back the Commie taste, instantly. All right, all right, a reader might say, you fled from Communism, that's understandable, but did you flee from your parents too? Yes, I had fled from them too. Ours was a severely malfunctioning family, whose hopeless breakup was precipitated by the death of my twin brother, when he and I were thirteen. Soon after that, my writer dad divorced my actress mother. She and I were left together in the apartment where I'd once had a complete family, and we functioned together even worse. The Communist state had something to do with that—it had violated the integrity of our family from the start, by putting Dad in jail, and searching our house whenever it pleased. That my parents couldn't or wouldn't repair the effect of those intrusions by a different life attitude was a weakness I had judged them harshly for; much of what hadn't worked in our family was still because of them, not because of the state.

Many families had suffered similarly under Communism. Parents and children were separated emotionally, made incapable of attending to each other, sucked away from their roles as family members into the constant madness of an ideologized and policed society. I had to excuse my parents. Right this instant, I had to excuse Mother, or else I would never have helped her. What acted on me was not that this was my mother, but what she said, the key word, "freedom." I would've felt dishonored if I had not helped her.

The next day, I dug into my strained savings and ran around the neighborhood to find her an apartment, making pit stops to buy her plates, bed linen, food, a TV set. While I was doing it, my resentment was wide awake, and my inner silence crackled with loud memories of "duty." The Communist state begot us into lives of duty to the people, and Mother seemed to have begotten me into a lifelong duty to herself. The two were so connected in my emotional memory that I hated her for asking for her freedom now, at seventy! Why was she coming after me, to bring back the past and inject it into my new life? She could've stayed in New York, we had family there. And why had she not attempted to defect long before? Right after the war, burdened with her infants, myself and my brother, that would've been hard and dangerous, yes, but other people did it. Just then, the south side of Beachwood Canyon was being invaded by Armenian refugees from Russia, most of whom arrived with their whole tribes, with wives, children, aunts, uncles, and parents and grandparents who spoke not a word of English and lolled about in their underwear and spiced up the streets with odors of native foods—poor, ridiculous, eager to suck on America's fat. But . . . they came in united families, and cared, cared desperately—that was all too obvious—for their children.

My mother and father had not left Romania while it was still possible, during the three years after the Soviet army invaded Romania. Had they done so, we would've been raised somewhere in the West, and benefitted from everything the West had to offer. And my twin brother

Pavel would not have died, as simple as that, because at that time the West already had the anti-polio Salk vaccine, which Romania finally introduced a year after his death. Everything would have been different, had my parents been different. Or our political system. I was ready to sink back into the litany of personal injustice I'd unreeled in therapy in California, and thought I'd resolved. Just then, as I was hesitating between buying cheaper bed linen (I was poor) or better quality (Mom was a guest, and these would be her first nights in freedom), I was suddenly staggered by an amazing possibility. She and I would not relate in Communism anymore, we would relate here. That could change everything between us!

I glimpsed that possibility like one glimpses a rare bright sunrise in a rainy land. Quick, it was gone. I did not have the courage, or simply the practice, to believe in it. At that time, I was going through a very difficult transitional stage. I'd been briefly married, and was now divorced. It would be several more years before I would remarry and have children. I was writing novels in English which ended up on the floor of my study, rejected by publishers—I still have five of those novels; piled up in my office in Beverly Hills, they rise like a devotional cairn to the arduousness of my literary transformation. The financing of a feature film I wrote and directed had just fallen apart. I was really not in great shape, for there was a free me, born, growing, functioning, and incapable of going back, but as yet not an artistic me—I discounted the movies I wrote in English, even though they were praised, and one was crowned with international acclaim. In truth, I missed having readers, missed it badly. Writing successful books is like constantly going on lucky blind dates, and finding that nine out of ten times the date was a friend, an alter ego, a lover of the same realities. But just now I had no readers, and not much sense of accomplishment: So what had I done with my life?

I eyed the future suspiciously. I felt like telling Mother: Don't come here and add to my hardship, go prance in freedom somewhere else. Instead, I told her: "I found you an apartment, Mother, it's only two blocks away. Come see if you like it."

She stepped into the apartment, and didn't say that she liked it. She approved it, like a queen. Didn't say thanks, either. I left her in her new apartment, a seventy-year-old who was still strong, still youthful, and I could tell, was going to love it out here. She had been married three times in Romania (Dad was the middle one), and now she was looking forward to meeting an American man.

Why can't I write about you mom, as a character, I asked myself, as I drove back home. Why can't I write about Dad, my brother Pavel, *us*? But I couldn't; because all that and the part of me that went with it was buried in the silence. In that grim lake deep within me, which now was beginning to stir. Wind rippled its waters. Birds cried jaggedly, and flapped from one shore to the other. Stuff was happening, and I was petrified.

I had been in little contact with my father after I defected. Communism itself provided the excuse. If I called him, his phone, tapped just like mine had been tapped, went dead soon after I said hello to his second wife. Also, after years of being shunted aside, Dad had made it as a literary critic, then he had been appointed editor of a leading cultural monthly, *The Theater*. He was now a piece of the system, and as such it could hurt him to be in touch with the defector son. So I called him two or three times altogether; then he had a stroke that made him practically mute, then he died. I couldn't go to his funeral. As a defector, had I flown into Bucharest to attend his funeral, I would have promptly been arrested.

So that was the situation. The silence was breaking, but slowly. Meanwhile, the business of becoming American, much of which is making it in America, was still the priority. I met Iris, and much to her credit she didn't mind falling in love with a man still financially unstable. More than that, she got pregnant days after going off the Pill, like a primal woman ripe for mixing her genes into offspring. I directed a movie while her belly was swelling up. I finally broke through the indifference of publishers. There was plenty to keep me occupied.

Meanwhile, back in the Soviet bloc . . . well, there was no more Soviet bloc. Whether he had foreseen the effects of his glasnost or not, Gorbachev could no longer reverse the trend he had set in motion. During all of 1989, the crowds kept stirring, asking for free elections, and paradoxically, no one fired at them. That happened everywhere except for Romania, where no dissidence of any sort was reported. Hungary tore down its barbed-wire border with Austria. In Poland, Solidarity marched for free elections, in Czechoslovakia the students clamored in the streets, in East Germany the population demanded freedom and union with the other Germany. The Baltic Republics pressed for independence. Finally, on November 9, 1989, the Berlin Wall came down. That same month, in Romania, the 14th Congress of the Communist party not only took place as planned, but it reelected Ceausescu secretary general. He seemed so entrenched that only his natural death could free the nation, but he was in no mood to die soon. He gave directives and signed decrees as busily as ever—or maybe his virago wife did it for him; rumor had it that she was the power now, while he had become incontinent and forgetful. Yet his regime functioned on, like clockwork.

I began looking for mentions of Romania in the newspapers, and even got irritated that I didn't find them. Those Western journalists, always scornful of anything east of Hungary! But the Western journalists did not scorn Romania, not just now, they were watching it like hawks—Ceausescu's demise promised to be a big bang. But nothing predicted the bang, or even a squeak for that matter. I started calling *Universul,* an emigré Romanian paper published in the Valley. Its publisher, refugee reporter Aristide Buhoiu, was a name in Romanian circles and had subtle ways to obtain information.

"Nothing's going on," he told me. "But I'm hoping that some public event, like a big soccer game, might spark something off."

"That bastard might cancel all soccer games."

"Don't you think he's so insecure. He just announced he'll be going on a state visit to Iran."

I hung up in frustration. Damn, damn. Had *he* tamed them all, emasculated them all, to the last spark of their conscience? Had he killed within every Romanian soul the suicidal despair they'd shown so often in their earlier history? Where were the kamikaze-like fighters who had taken on the Romans, the Ottoman Turks?

Easy for me to wonder, in America, in safety. I was nervous, I didn't want people to be killed, and I knew that Ceausescu wouldn't hesitate to order demonstrators shot. But at the same time I was harboring hope that a few Romanians, just a few, maybe his immediate entourage, would be so brave as to kill him. But nothing happened. Daily, I surprised myself by praying, in an abstract nonreligious way, for the deliverance of the Romanians. Finally, I called Radio Free Europe. I broadcast in Romanian a series of addresses which I called "Appeal with My Eyes on the Clock," telling my unseen Romanian listeners (I would never know how many heard me) that as the clock ticked on, a change in their fate had to be approaching, it had to be. I didn't make it a direct call to arms, because I didn't want to provide any excuse for reprisals against the population. Yet I said it plainly: the time is ticking, everyone else is fighting for freedom already, what about us?

Then I got a phone call, from the publisher of the *Universul*.

"It started," he said.

"Where?"

"In Timisoara."

A pretty little town with a Hungarian minority. Undistinguished, except that Bela Lugosi, Hollywood's Dracula, was born right outside it.

"Why the hell in Timisoara? Why not in Bucharest?"

"I don't know. I don't have any other details. I'll call you when I do."

It was December 17. As I learned a few days later, people had marched in Timisoara against the closure of a church whose vicar, a Hungarian priest, had criticized the regime in his sermons. The Securitate branded him a "foreign instigator," but the Romanians, usually no great friends of the Hungarians, smelled the lie. They joined the local Hungarians to protect the priest, and ... the high noon showdown started. Crowds came out of homes, schools, factories, and marched down sad streets, shouting all their complaints. They were too hungry and too fed up. Life had lost its value, and when life loses its value, the stage is set for mass tragedies.

So the silence was breaking there too. I listened to it break in Ojai, California, where Iris and I and our kids, my son Adam, six, my daughter Chloe, two, were spending a few days of Christmas vacation. The invasion of Panama played live on CNN, intercut with a bloody, horrifying Christmas in Romania. The uprising in Timisoara spread to other cities, turning into full-scale urban war. Ceausescu, who had gone on with his visit to Iran, jetted back from powwowing with the ayatollahs, but it was too late. In Bucharest, in the streets I had grown up on and now saw torn up by gunfire on TV, the Romanians battled the Securitate's well-armed and well-disciplined troops. And I, with my heart in my mouth, nonetheless beamed with pride: the insurrectionists weren't just a few, they were throngs, armies!

Then something happened that made the world gasp with horror. The first images broadcast from Timisoara showed a mass grave gaping open, a steaming pile of naked bodies of men, women, youngsters, including one uniquely macabre shot of a woman with an infant almost as small as a fetus, lying naked on her stomach. The rumored casualty figures were gruesome: four hundred civilians were said to have died in Timisoara alone, killed in street fights with the Securitate. In Bucharest, battles raged between the population, joined by an initially hesitant army, and commandos of Securitate "terrorists." As other cities and towns erupted, the rumored victims' numbers soared to fifty thousand. It seemed that before going down history's drainhole, Ceausescu had plunged Romania into a bloodbath worthy of the Ottoman raids. I started to call the wire services, asking whether the figures could be verified. They could not.

I lived a week wondering which of my friends and family were among those now dead. I had friends in Timisoara, family in Bucharest, friends and relatives in Iasi, Constanta, Brasov, Craiova, Cluj, Sibiu, cities that had witnessed the Roman legions, and survived the fight against Islam. These beacons of national dignity were now put to the torch by that short and awkward strongman with stiff posture, stuttering speech, and fanatical X-ray eyes. The ridiculous nationalistic dwarf who ended as Europe's last great tyrant: Ceausescu.

I knew the man.

Ceausescu and his wife, Elena, were captured, tried summarily, and shot for crimes of genocide against the Romanian people. As the army sided en masse with the revolutionaries, and the Securitate stopped fighting, the reported numbers of the dead began to shrink. Finally, it was confirmed that over nine hundred Romanians died in the only bloody overthrow of Communism to date, and more than two thousand were injured.

Now, the number of unanswered questions swelled up. What had really happened? Who had been fighting whom? The terrorists, probably a special Securitate cadre trained to fight suicidally, had fired rifles, machine guns, and small cannons; they had strafed and shelled the rioting civilians for almost a week, all over the country. But the captured terrorists shown to the crowds and to TV reporters were less than a dozen. The soldiers that had fallen fighting the terrorists numbered 196. There was no count of the terrorists shot or captured. Where were the bodies, or the survivors? Had they fled the country? Were they in the country, in retreat, in hiding? Had their part in this tragedy been so well rehearsed that their dead were slipped in among the innocent victims, while their survivors mixed among the revolutionaries celebrating in the streets?

I couldn't answer those questions. No one could.

The civilian dead were shown naked, jumbles of bodies thrown on top of each other in dimly lit rooms, nude legs and arms hugging nude breasts and buttocks, as in a macabre masquerade of a sexual orgy.

Something was frighteningly familiar. The Securitate, the haunting bogeyman of forty years of Communism, now loomed over the civil war the way it had loomed over the whole land.

After exactly a week, I finally reached Romania by phone.

My family had survived. The friends I could trace had survived too. But their inside interpretation of the revolution shattered me. One friend, a reporter, had been present at the rally in front of the Communist party building, where people had started to heckle Ceausescu, calling him "assassin" and yelling questions about the Timisoara bloodbath, thus starting Bucharest's own uprising. This friend declared to me that most Bucharesters didn't even know at the time that the Timisoara insurrection had happened.

"Even so, that crowd would have been too fearful to shout anything but slogans supporting the dictator. Those who shouted against him were Securitate. It was the Securitate's hand that brought Ceausescu down."

I almost gagged from his cynicism: "Are you nuts? What the hell do you mean?"

"You lost it out there, in free America." *It* meaning my awareness of history's dark hidden side. He laughed a laugh rusty from years of chain-smoking. "The Securitate mixed in the crowds with tape recorders, and played pre-recorded shouts of 'Timisoara! What happened in Timisoara?' and 'Ceausescu assassin!' As expected, the assassin panicked and fled, sealing up his own fate."

"So the Securitate faked the revolution?"

"You bet. They're still here, running everything."

"What about the crowds in the streets?"

"Those too were Securitate."

"Thousands of people?"

"You think they can't gather big crowds?"

I felt I was tumbling down a dark tunnel, into a familiar hell.

Then I got hold of myself. He was wrong, and I recognized his thinking. It was one of Communism's legacies, to find conspiracy in everything.

I hung up, and turned on the TV. Faces of people cheering in the streets of Bucharest, my hometown. I knew those faces, skinny faces of youngsters with acne, bad teeth, and old-fashioned haircuts, yet lit up by a freshness, a mangy beauty that hadn't succumbed yet to hard work, bad diet, the fumes of a toxic environment, and cultural isolation. They had an unkempt sexiness. I saw a ghostly me among them: I too had been gangly and young on those streets, my hair shaped by an ugly haircut, my eyes wild with hope. The feelings of revolt that I'd squashed within me back then were being yelled by these youngsters now, in the open. But there were other faces too, faces that spelled defeat instead of triumph. Middle-aged men and women sagging from unhealthy diets, uninspiring work, boredom, and apathy. Ceausescu had taken away their best years. Yet even in those, I could see *something exciting.* It was too late for them; it was not too late for their children. The thought that all those Romanians could be delivered again to a conspiracy, to an arranged, contrived new system, was unbearable to me.

In Bucharest, some important buildings had been wrecked in the fighting; among them was the Central University Library. There, on an afternoon when studying just didn't work out for me, I wrote by hand my first short story, "Death in the Window," a kind of Kafkaesque parable. I was eighteen. I read it at a literary gathering, and got my first labelling as a subversive from the dean of official Commie authors, Eugen Barbu, a major cultural thug, and a good buddy of Ceausescu's, too. The scarring of that building didn't affect me; it would be rebuilt. Yet I couldn't bear the thought of those naked dead people, even if they were anonymous to me. But guess what? Other Romanians acted kind of proud. "After so many of us died, now the world knows about us," commented my Romanian barber. His shingle read: Mr. Victor of Paris. "The Huns, Goths and Gepids, Ottomans, Habsburgs, Soviets, all engulfed us Romanians," Mr. Victor of Paris reminded me, "and the world never stopped to notice. But we showed them that we exist, this time around."

Mr. Victor of Paris hadn't been to Romania in thirty years. How easily he climbed into that *we. We* showed them. Was that morbid pride part of the healing of a nation?

"Don't rush back there, to write some newspaper story," my mother advised me. "They would kill you, probably."

"They wouldn't, I'm not that important."

"They would."

"Mother, Ceausescu fell. There is a new government. And the whole world is staring at Romania." I sounded just like Mr. Victor of Paris.

"Just don't go."

I promised her I wouldn't. Though my relationship with my mother continued to be hard and fitful, those days had brought us closer. I had no intention of going, even though the cream of the Western press was in Bucharest, people who would never have honored Romania with their presence before the bloodbath. They reported frantically, mangling the Romanian names, the Romanian words. In Hollywood, friends of mine, screenwriters, asked me to lunch to pick my brain about a big film story. There had to be one. Why was I not writing it?

"Because I wasn't there, to fight along with them," I explained once in exasperation. It was the truth. I felt happy that the Romanians were free, but guilty that I hadn't helped. Now that Ceausescu was in the ground I wasn't afraid at all, certainly not afraid of being physically there.

The big story, for me, was that I felt a bit of ethnic pride burgeoning back in my chest. Oh, it was so timid and hesitant, my pride in being Romanian again, it felt like a fledgling that had survived falling out of its nest. I should've felt more pride, but I couldn't yet. The collapse of Communism had stunned me. I'd never thought I would live to see it.

And I still suffered from those nagging questions: where were the dead terrorists? what had happened to their bodies? They couldn't have just risen to heaven. By chance, I found out that a Mr. Oancea, a member of the municipal council of Timisoara, the town where the revolution had started, was visiting the United States. I decided to ask him about the revolution's unanswered mysteries. Mr. Oancea, an opposition figure of some repute, would eventually run for mayor of Timisoara, defeating a candidate of the allegedly neo-Communist party, the National Salvation Front.

I reached him by phone, in Chicago. He greeted me, "Hello, is this Mr. Popescu the writer?" I answered yes, I was Mr. Popescu the writer, and I wanted to interview him. I was planning a feature on Romania for an American paper.

Mr. Oancea replied in a healthy, booming voice, "Certainly. Mr. Popescu, I'm so glad to be talking to you. I feel like I know you, I read your *Captive* and *Honey-sweet Bullet,* and passed them to all my friends. D'you know how much your banned books cost on the black market before Ceausescu croaked?" For some reason, a claw gripped my heart— I awaited the figure in total anxiety. "Two hundred lei, Mr. Popescu!"

Two hundred lei. A copy of *Captive* cost twelve lei when it was first published, less than one U.S. dollar.

"Mr. Popescu, remember when all those students slept with your books under their pillows?" He sounded positively lyrical. I sometimes met fans from the past, and they all gushed about what I achieved back then. Instead of pride, I felt guilt, for I had run away. I had defected. But had I stayed, I would have been silenced.

"When are you coming home, Mr. Popescu?"

"Home?" For me, home was here, in America. Didn't he realize it?

"Yeah, to see how we live now. And to visit your old grounds. It was hard back then, but I'm sure you must have some beautiful memories . . ."

I flashed back on my first day of elementary school. My twin brother stepping with me into the schoolyard. Dressed with motherly care, carrying brand-new school satchels and lunch bags. An older school boy stood by the gate: his head was fiercely shaved, he wore a drab gray uniform, he was a war orphan. He waved into the noisy yard. Six, seven other kids in drab uniforms, war orphans raised by the state, rushed over and started beating us. In seconds, our noses were bleeding, our faces swollen, our clothes and satchels torn. Raised by the Communist state in the spirit of working-class vengeance, the orphans had seen in us two heirs of the deposed bourgeois class. And none of the teachers intervened. One didn't question the right of the working class to avenge itself.

"Mr. Oancea, what do you know about those graves—those pits full of naked stitched-up bodies we saw on TV?"

For an instant, our connection blurred and the distance was filled with pops and crackles. I tightened up, like in the old days in Romania, when static on the line made me imagine thousands of Securitate spy-birds perching on the telephone wires, monitoring my subversive calls. "Those pits . . ." Surprised, his voice trailed off. "Well, in Timisoara only about forty people were killed, and the Securitate took the corpses to Bucharest by truck, on December 18 or 19. Some Securitate general freaked out, couldn't think of a better way to cover up, so the missing people's families assumed that they'd been shot and buried, and they went searching the local cemeteries for fresh graves. In the Paupers' Cemetery, they saw graves that looked fresh, and they dug them up."

"You mean there were mass graves in the Paupers' Cemetery?"

"No, there was a burial site for unidentified bodies autopsied on the premises. There was a police lab in that cemetery, where they processed the homicide victims from several counties. The old police morgue was too small and inadequate. The bodies that couldn't be identified were buried after the autopsies, that's why the bodies you saw on TV were naked and stitched up—"

"What happened to the revolutionaries' bodies?"

"They were found in the morgue in Bucharest, and returned to their families. But before that happened, the foreign reporters flocked to the Paupers' Cemetery. None of them spoke Romanian, and they didn't understand what was happening, so before they knew what they were really seeing, they put those shots on worldwide TV."

I swallowed, feeling a strange sense of relief. Though forty people had been killed, the system didn't manage to hide them. What we had seen on CNN was not mass murder, just sloppy anonymous death in a faraway land. Eased of a great yet unclear burden, I asked him, "What's this rumor we keep hearing about the 'stealing of the Romanian revolution'?"

"That might happen. In Romania, it hasn't happened yet, but it can still happen. The KGB is coordinating a 'passage to glasnost' in all of Eastern Europe. Who's the leader who came to the fore in Romania? Ion Iliescu. Old guard. Educated in Moscow."

I didn't want to be dragged into a political debate; after all, this man fought in the revolution, and I didn't. But I couldn't resist. "Iliescu was demoted by Ceausescu himself, in '71. Demoted for intellectualism. I was there, Mr. Oancea. That liberal wing of the party was clipped."

"Yes, and Iliescu was elected by a landslide in the first free elections," agreed Mr. Oancea, "but only because the opposition was scattered then. Iliescu's people are Commie old boys without their party cards. I'm excited about something else, Mr. Popescu: I met the king, in Chicago. I think the king can pull Romania together."

I smiled. King Michael of Romania had been forced to abdicate by Stalin in 1947. Mr. Oancea had deep suspicions about Iliescu, but was thrilled with the king, now seventy years old and touring the Romanian communities in Europe and America, trying to finally assume a political role. In fact, one of his aides had just contacted me, asking me to do an interview with him.

I opened my mouth to say that maybe I could do a double story: the old monarch and the fiery opposition activist, side by side. Cute idea. He didn't give me the chance. "You could do something for us here," he said. "God, it's so great to have one of us here . . ."

That fledgling pride responded to his words, like a gentle stroke on frail growing wings. But all I said was: "You think so, Mr. Oancea?"— and I didn't like my tone: it sounded skeptical, almost bitter.

"Of course, and come see us soon."

"I will," I said. "Of course."

The exiled writer wished the opposition activist good luck, and we both hung up. It was spring, 1991.

The conversation with Mr. Oancea had closed a kind of emotional chapter, but it had opened another. As his voice stopped ringing in my ear, and the country where I was born became less real, as my current life reinvaded me, I realized that we had talked about completely different things. I had talked about the Revolution, which I had missed. He had talked about me, as if I was still important to the Romanians, whether I missed the Revolution or not.

I was in my office in our Hollywood home, in the middle of a move to another home, in Beverly Hills. Framed ads from my book tours and posters of films with my name on the credits surrounded me, most of them already packed. Also packed were my books, including my countless English dictionaries, Websters and Oxfords, lexicons of synonyms and slang, glossaries and thesauruses of just about anything that can be put in words. Over the years, as I mastered English more completely, I used them less and less. But I still kept them around, like a navigator never caught without his maps, compass, and sextant.

Come home, Mr. Popescu . . .

I looked at the dictionaries, and thought of a friend, a writer. John Cheever, dead now. He had played a major part in my decision to defect. I had met him in the fall of 1970, in Egypt—he was invited there to lecture, while I, a puppy Romanian writer and journalist, was covering the transition of power from Nasser to Sadat.

Egypt was a fellow Socialist nation back then, with its media censored, its phones tapped, and its streets crawling with Russian advisors—thus for me, traveling from Communist Romania to Egypt was just a swing through the Soviet empire, which now included the pyramids. My meeting Cheever had occurred comically, on a plane ride from Cairo to Luxor. The plane too was Soviet-made, and full of Soviet advisors. An hour into the flight, I looked up from a pad I was doodling on (I didn't take notes; my reports were to be written in Bucharest, along the prescribed party line), and saw a character from another world ambling up the plane's aisle towards me.

It was John Cheever. The renowned American novelist, whom I knew from his photographs, suddenly approached me with an outstretched hand: "Zhenya, is that you?" Out of his element, Cheever had mistaken me for a Soviet poet much lionized in the West at the time, Evgenij (Zhenya) Evtushenko.

I bore no resemblance to Evtushenko, who was quite a bit older than me, except perhaps in the Commie look of my haircut. Indignantly, I announced that I wasn't the Soviet poet. Cheever sat apologetically next to me and introduced himself. I had recently read his *Bullet Park.* Hearing my surprisingly lively English, Cheever became paranoid: Was I some Commie spy set on his tracks? Which wasn't that absurd; we were in the Soviet orbit, even the poet he'd mistaken me for was a Soviet. At 30,000 feet, I sobered him up by explaining that I was a Romanian novelist and that my novels had first printings of at least 20,000 copies; he was floored when I mentioned those figures. Then I told him the subject of *Captive,* and he finally clicked on what I was: a guerrilla artist from an unglamorous colony, idolized by my little nation. I told him how I battled the censors. He told me how he battled his fear of writing, his fear of words that seemed truthful but so often were not, and how that pushed him to drink. We deplaned friends. Through dinner at a Luxor hotel, we envied each other's problems: he my chained youth that defied a tyranny, I his post-success confusion and quest for a personal truth. After dinner, we hired a horse-drawn coach for a ride by Luxor's three-thousand-year-old temples. Under a cool moon shining on the Nile, Cheever asked me if I wanted to defect. I shrugged.

"Don't you want freedom?" he asked.

"I do, but I don't know if I could ever write in English."

I'd stated my quandary, which I'd hardly ever done before. It was dangerous to make such confessions to Romanians, and I would never have done it before a Western writer, whose breed I scorned: they had suffered no persecutions, they wrote free stuff *and* made money, how dare they claim to have a handle on life? Yet Cheever was so obviously considerate and at the same time vulnerable, that I broke my rule. He nodded: "You're right, defecting is one thing, writing in English quite another. Few foreigners ever succeed at it, and you don't know if you're one of them. Besides, back home you're doing something important. Don't give it up too easily."

I gave him a hostile stare: I'd let him see my conflicted self, and he had captured it briefly and accurately. I didn't like that. But when I looked back at him again, he was watching me, all friendliness and compassion.

The Egyptian temples slowly rolled past. We were equals here, against the world's most lasting art, but I didn't think for an instant that we could become friends, or that he would play a part in my defection. I was of the damned, and he wasn't. From Soviet-infested Egypt, I returned to Romania, to my anonymous mission. The English language was a bridge between worlds, but I didn't feel fated to pass it, much less sire children whose mother tongue would be English.

Cheever died in 1982, seven years before the crash of Communism. For a few years after I defected we met and wrote to each other, then our encounters and letters became less and less frequent, as I got sucked away into my new life. But in that spring of 1991, my thoughts rambled, banging inside my brain like caged animals, and bringing up fragments of my buried past shockingly intact. I was afraid of the past, though not of the Securitate, or of Ceausescu, six feet in the ground now, in the soil of that country he so completely possessed. I was afraid of opening the past and facing it. When I felt that way, I usually called to the rescue the images of my children. I saw their bright eyes, I heard their voices saying their names: Adam Popescu, Chloe Popescu. Poe-pess-que. No funny accent—in their mouths, my name sounded almost like Smith. Don't worry, Dad, you're here now, you're ours now. *That* was then, *this* is now.

I felt that reassurance fighting my old rage, the useless empty rage of someone who would never ever have his revenge on his tormentors. My tormentors were old now, or dead. It wasn't worth getting on a plane and flying over there, to find them, to kick them to the ground, or to spit in their faces. But their deaths hadn't healed my rage.

I didn't want my children to inherit that rage. Yet, in a confused and contradictory way, I did. I wanted them to have some part of it, and hold it ready, like a weapon. But they wouldn't need that weapon; their childhoods, their fates were utterly different from mine. They would never feel that they had a hideous pit in their past, into which was dumped their youth, like a stripped body toppled into that mass grave shown on TV.

The street we were soon to leave branched north from Sunset Boulevard, right above the Sunset Strip. A bizarre emptiness impregnated the Strip even when it was teeming. Streaks of cars. Swaggers of bodies. Never touch, never meet. We bought our house from a movie exec, a VP at a film studio; by the time we were moving, he was a senior VP at a different studio. Across the road from us lived a pair of gay realtors; one door up a paparazza who hung out with her cameras at Spago's and Ma Maison; up the road a famous French restaurateur. Higher still, a studio composer/conductor—limos came to pick him up at night, rolling him away and returning him, like a mafia don. The hills' dwellers had crazy schedules, and unpredictable lives. "For sale" signs kept sprouting before their houses. When I jogged up into the hills, swallowing lungfuls of smoggy air, I met neighbors who jogged too: often I'd never seen them before. I nodded in greeting, but few responded. I kept jogging and glancing down, to avoid the rich piles of dogshit from their pedigreed mastiffs or poodles. The dogs greeted each other with excited yelps, friendlier than their masters.

Little by little, we'd found out who else lived on our street, but nothing connected us with them. The sun, the moon, the seasons, the earthquakes, the mudslides passed their cycles over us, leaving us as they found us: without cohesion. We lived each for self and our respective brood, mentally excluding all other human beings from our fierce goal: success. Several writers lived on that street, smart people sitting in their offices and trying to figure art's biggest riddle: the Hollywood formula. So they could climb to the lonely top, and look down on the unconnected cohorts they'd once belonged to.

Our next house, in the flats of Beverly Hills, had been owned by my in-laws, who offered to switch houses with us so we could live near the Beverly Vista School, where my son was already enrolled. I'd accepted with some anxiety about feeling indebted, but I wanted my kids to play with other kids, and I wanted to be close to that school. Moving to Beverly Hills would have been a step up a few years back. But now, "The city's moving northwest," said Mazda, our slick and busy Persian-born real estate agent. I asked him what city he was talking about. The "real Americans," he explained, they didn't want to live in a Beverly Hills infiltrated by Persians, Russians, even a few Romanians, so they expatriated to Brentwood and beyond. I asked him where he placed himself vis-à-vis the "real Americans," was he in, out? Parallel, he responded with humor. Before I had children, I was never bothered by L.A.'s rootlessness, it was good medication for my bad memories. I felt like all the other conquistadors who came here to lose their pasts. Full speed ahead towards the unexplored limits of our energies and skills. I felt solidarity with all those impatient jerks thundering through the streets in their quick cars, I felt the power of our mutual exclusion, and it motivated me, it pushed me forward. My America worked.

I tried to ignore the few things that gave me pause for thought. I was happy, even though selling my writing was hard. Happy with my house in the hills, with its garden nicely landscaped by my wife, one orange tree, one lemon tree, and the far city towers framed by jagged palm fronds. Cages for lizards and snakes lining the garage wall: our son was into nature. My daughter's tricycle, crashed on the grass. Two cars in the garage, an unkempt Jeep for me, a Mercedes 190 for my wife. My wife, a svelte, blond, white-skinned, brown-eyed home deity. She was raised in Beverly Hills, and looked like the ultimate California Aryan. Her parents, Czech Jews, had met and courted in a Nazi concentration camp. They were liberated by the U.S. Army, returned to Czechoslovakia, to Prague, and then the Russians slammed the Curtain down. So they fled, ending up in California.

Growing up with such parents was Iris's karma. Escaping from Communism was mine. Our two karmas had met, made love, and got married. I was in the delivery room at the arrival of each of our children. Adam burst alive out of a C-section, strong, purplish, yelling deafeningly. Chloe came out naturally, a big, beautifully formed infant, eyes open and staring, seeming to smile. While Adam was all intent and masculine concentration, Chloe smiled even when she was attentive and still. She was three now, and when I glanced at her face, I found that smile there, quietly radiant. As if she just got a present.

Here were my new roots.

My wife only knew Romania from my stories, which were of two kinds: sad, and frightening. When I told her about my conversation with the mayor, commenting at the end that if I took a trip to Romania, I could . . . oh well, I could write about it in the papers, or maybe dig up some interesting concept for a book or movie, I was always on a hunt for such concepts, no?—she got a little pale. Not pale-pale, not bloodlessly frightened, but with just a kind of translucent hue under her face, as if her pigment were replaced by an unnatural clarity. Then she remarked that I'd been speaking a lot about Romania lately. She made me angry. Iris spoke about her heritage all the time, why not me too, about my heritage? "I'm not conflicted about mine," she answered, and I raised my voice, arguing back that she was, how could she not be? We were about to have one of our fights, which were reproachful re-definitions of each other, usually started by the respective loving spouse who felt more insecure at that particular time.

But we didn't have the fight. Chloe walked in just then, and Iris asked me to take her to preschool. My daughter's preschool, the closest one to our house, was at a reform Jewish temple.

Chloe and I arrived at the temple a little late that day, and pulled into the last slot of the parking lot. The parking lot was contained between cement walls, and was patrolled by two Latino security guards, named Jesus and Carlos. We entered through a doorway fortified with a bell and speaker. A secretary in the early childhood office waved at me and I waved back, then we hurried along a corridor with religious artifacts in glass cases, towards Chloe's class.

When I married my wife, I didn't give the faith issue much thought. Back home, Communism had persecuted all faiths, and my parents were liberal intellectuals, anything but churchy. One generation back however, my father's lineage was stuffed with priests and bishops, including one Bishop of the Lower Danube. Still, for me, being of different faiths seemed the smallest impediment to a marriage; our mixture of cultures might be fun. Our son, Adam, had gone to a secular preschool, but it was far away and awkward to drive to, so we settled on this temple's preschool for Chloe. A few months ago, I happened to be the one who drove her there on her first day of school and guided her inside this building, her hand in my hand. After delivering her to her teacher and classmates, I walked out past one of the Latino guards (name embroidered on his shirt: Jesus), and sat in my car with my temples throbbing, tumbling inside myself, into a blurry confusion.

When I landed, I found myself surrounded by the ghosts of my ancestors. While their faces had no features, I sensed that they stared at me with a look of deep disappointment. The Christian Romanians in my blood had fought five centuries of Turkish yoke for the right to be Christians. Fought for it, died for it. Some had been martyrs who were hanged, quartered, and skinned alive by the Ottomans. Their carcasses were left to rot and be picked at by vultures; later, their dried-up bones were broken into little pieces and saved in reliquaries, in churches and cloisters. Thinned by struggle and suffering, those ghosts called out at me from the depth of time: Hey, what are you doing to us, up there in America? What are you doing with our cause and our sacrifice? What about the survival of our creed? Were you not beholden to continue *us*?

Simply put, my wife and I were in an interfaith marriage. We'd just had a crucial talk, a few days earlier. My wife sat up in bed, faced me with that honesty which is her best and sometimes hardest trait, and told me, "We can't raise the children in a mixture of two faiths. I don't know how, and I can't do it. It's not that I *want* to raise them in mine only, I just can't do it any other way. It doesn't matter how much that will hurt you, and how much it will hurt me too, because I love you."

Sincerity is a mighty weapon. She was sincere to the point of brutality, yet she talked with anxiety and fear, because we were at the start of a complicated process. I, picturing my kids' identity structured around bar and bat mitzvahs instead of baptisms and confirmations, felt a loss, an uprooting as real as giving up my native land and tongue. Deep inside me died the fantasy that in America I would become even more Romanian than in Romania, for here I could relish my roots in freedom, and then plant them in my kids.

I had discounted my wife's feelings on the matter, as well as her family's. I'd thought that they were all Americans now, living above the call of roots. I made a startling discovery: I wasn't above the call of roots either. My roots were as greedy for replication as hers. Yet if karmas are quantified in pain, of hers and mine, hers was the stronger.

Karma. In Hindu, it really means "the effects." What one lives in one life will have unavoidable effects in the next. True for most people, entirely accurate for my wife and me. I knew it too, knew it before we really got down to the issue. I knew it when I first met her parents.

Iris and I met on a blind date arranged by a film director friend. I was fitfully supporting myself by writing in English. After stints at TV production and acting, my wife wrote screenplays and journalism. We fell in love with urgency, with desperation even. She took me to meet her parents at their house in Beverly Hills. The door was opened by a woman who looked like Iris, just older and with an accent. Tinkering noises came from a garage at the back; then Iris's father appeared, a strong sixty-year-old in shorts and a stained T-shirt. The mother introduced me. The father stretched out a tanned, muscular arm, covered with a film of dust from his labor. As I shook his hand, I read a number tattooed on his arm, strange-looking through that dust and tan. That number leapt through the air, entered my head and inscribed itself behind my forehead. We sat down, but as I watched the man, I saw him through the number on his arm.

We spoke to each other, tentatively, they in their accent, I in mine. Married thirty-five years, Carl and Blanka Friedman had courted in a *Vernichtungslager—Vernichtung* means annihilation in German. Now they sat and chatted with this young immigrant man, me, and in a few minutes, two things became clear: their daughter and I were headed for marriage, and I wasn't Jewish. It's hard to say what I sensed in their attitudes that day, and whether what I sensed was real or my projection, but the tattoo on the father's arm was an extra character in the conversation. It talked. It explained to me the pledge the two had made, to have children who would replenish the Jewish blood lost. It spoke of grief from the past, of loyalty to the future. But that loyalty seemed broken now. Love was breaking it.

Later, I learned that they'd never specifically educated their children to marry within the faith, to ensure continuation. They didn't have to. The pledge to that continuation was right there, carved on the father's arm. Besides, such things are not taught. No one had taught me my faith, in Romania, where my intellectual parents took us kids to church just once a year, at Easter. But, as the saying goes, blood is thicker than water, and what one is, one breathes with the native air.

Did I see anxiety in Carl and Blanka's eyes? Did I see self-searching? Were they wondering if they had gone wrong? The meaning of their life was coming full circle, but it wasn't clear anymore. It was contradictory and baffling.

Still, I was instantly aware of a karma more tragic than mine. My family had been persecuted, my father had been jailed, several of his brothers had spent years in POW camps in Russia, an uncle of mine (the one now in New York, and a Romanian priest no less!) had swum the Danube to freedom. My brother had died because of Communism's backwardness and inefficiency—he and I were thirteen at the time, so I had lived the loss of my twin fully conscious. Of my life in Romania, I'd lived only the last three years with some semblance of dignity, as an author. A tough story, which I was eager to tell to my wife's folks, expecting sympathy for my pain and my courage. But . . .

Was I really so eager to tell my story? To my wife, yes, I had told it, because there is no secrecy in marriage, at least not in a good marriage. But to other people, whether close or distant?

At any rate, theirs was a karma more painful than mine. My folks, my land. I had never been in danger of annihilation. Warfare, captivity, disease, backwardness, oblivion—yes, all that. We had been depleted in numbers, raped and humiliated. But we had never been targeted for extinction.

And that was what decided the issue of the kids' faith, before they were born and before my wife sat up in bed that morning, seized by an obligation to her roots that amazed her too. After all, she had been a rebel—she'd dropped out of college, marched against the Vietnam War, written for *CrawDaddy,* the whole bit. Still, karma is karma. She explained to me, with tears, that she couldn't do it any other way. And I recognized the weakness of my position: I hadn't come to America to replenish Romania's losses. I had come for me, to have adventures, to change, to reinvent myself. I was a pioneer, a settler of alien lands. Not a continuator, except for my direct skills of life, which I would teach to my children, and for my conquests, which I would will on to my children.

Above the corridor that Chloe and I followed was the temple's upper floor, where among other activities there was a weekly seminar for interfaith couples. Iris and I signed up for it, trying to solve our problem California style, by sharing. We shared with eight other couples, all American-born yet as contradictory as we were. Catholics, Episcopals, Methodists, and Jews, talking under the ministrations of two rabbis, one a man with a Muslim-born wife, the other a woman. One of the first exercises in that seminar was to write down the stereotypes we'd heard about *the other.* Jews called Christians "tasteless in fashion, condescending, without soul, square, hypocritical, but also physically pretty, athletic, relaxed, and not too obsessed with themselves." Christians called Jews "clannish, clever, haunted by their own problems, unfair in business, unathletic, but also liberal, influential, and with a sense of humor." At the end of the third session, most of us glimpsed the way to solve the problem: one of the parties had to give in to the other. The one who gave in was the one least dependent on his own tradition, and if he or she made the gift in good faith, they would collect the benefits of their generosity. I made the gift. I'd left my homeland, I'd encountered love, and in choosing love I accepted that it was to be nurtured by giving. Giving is a great trick: you lose at first, then you gain. As a Christian, I could also tell myself, and I did, that my gift was an individual atonement for the indifference of other Christians, during the Holocaust. Meanwhile, the mechanics of interfaith life spoiled the children: gifts at Hanukkah and at Christmas, under the lit candles and under the tree. A tree without any symbols of the baby Jesus, but a Christmas tree nonetheless, nicely decorated by my wife; never before had she had one. To make it easier for her, I took a string of dreidls with bulbs inside, and hung it on the tree among the other lit ornaments; now it really looked like an interfaith tree. I also bought mezuzas and affixed them to the doorposts of my children's rooms. I did that all by myself, without requests from my wife, but I would never have put one by the front door: our home was an integrated territory. That process of acculturation between us included some heated debates, even some cries of pain. I occasionally had to stand firm for respect of my territory, or give notices to insensitive ethnocentric relatives on Iris's side; on my side there was only my mother, who wisely stayed out of it. But we learned to give and receive, and re-give what we had received. And wouldn't you know it, the process that started over a religious issue helped us both with our more intimate issues: Iris, who had a problem with trust, learned how to trust me, her husband. I, whose personal territory had been so violated back home (something I wasn't aware of, I had to hear it from a therapist), learned that my territory was not being violated any more, even if it was sometimes taken for granted. Trust was what we both needed. We got it, and moved towards a loving marriage's next set of fights, for there would always be fights. Such is the nature of love.

But why wasn't I more eager to tell my story? For I wasn't. I was being appreciated for my books and screenplays, but there was no Romania in them, or my childhood, or my defection, no, at least not on a quickly identifiable level. In talks with friends, with my new relatives, with people in entertainment, when it came to where I was from and what I must've endured, they asked the questions, and I answered monosyllabically, almost unpleasantly. So, you're from Romania, huh? Me: Yeah, I am. Commie school, Securitate, tapped phones, defection? Yeah, all that. How did you break out of there? Must've been tough, huh? Yeah, it was. The matter was dropped. More insistent interlocutors asked if I was in touch with my family, if they made it to freedom too, or were stuck back there. Dad died, Mom's here, I responded tersely, and guided the conversation back to anything else, politics, my kids. Or books, films, agents, commissions. Success. Back to my reality, as if what I had lived was unreality.

And yet, since that revolution in which I didn't participate, I was beginning to be puzzled by my own silence. My in-laws played a part in my puzzlement. They were at the age at which one speaks of one's youth anyway; but speaking of their youths meant speaking of the Holocaust, which they did all the time, unimpeded by the pain. Gruesome as they were, their stories didn't seem neurotic. I didn't find in them the taste of shame, fear, rage, or guilt. There was sadness, yes, and some philosophy. But no shame or fear.

To my children, they were wonderful grandparents. When we visited them, the kids zoomed to Grandpa's garage, cluttered to capacity with a workbench, tools, bulbs, cables and extension cords, and other odds and ends from Carl's years as an electrical contractor. He also kept hammers and wrenches, boxes of screws and nails, chains, padlocks missing their keys, clocks missing their hands, all kinds of knickknacks of bronze and brass needing patching or soldering, and even a grandfather clock of carved oak, old, majestic, and in need of a new set of counterweights. For the kids, the garage was a treasure chest: they dragged the old man inside and all three vanished into its fascinating depths. My wife went out, and sometimes I went with her. Or I accepted a cup of coffee, and lingered by the kitchen table with Blanka, who was cooking or baking. Most of my in-laws' interactions happened around that kitchen table. When their friends came, almost all survivors of the Holocaust, they automatically settled into the kitchen. A reflex from their youth: in their shtetl homes the kitchen, with its oven, was the warmest room, and the heart of society. They played gin rummy on the kitchen table, for stakes ranging from a dime to fifty cents, and got excited in English mixed with Czech and Yiddish. Their arms moved across the table to pick up cards or drinks, to show a hand, to deal. In summer, and it's almost always summer in California, they wore short sleeves. Their tattooed numbers moved with the arms, shining a faded blue under the overhead lamp. Carl told me that the first generation of death-camp prisoners had numbers tattooed on their chests, some even on their foreheads. None of them survived, because the evidence they constituted was too damning. The numbers, Carl explained, were initially intended for recovering escaped prisoners; only later were they used for an accounting system.

There was a whole industry of fake papers during the war. "Gentile papers," Carl called them. Carl got his early on, in 1938, when he joined the Czech underground. His ID said that he was an ethnic German:

Cestmir Vencera, Mirek for short. After the war, his wife and friends kept calling him Mirek. The Germans never thought of pulling his pants down, the time's way to check a male Jew trying to pass, for it said in his papers that he was a German, and Germans didn't doubt Germans.

"They were dumb," Carl commented, with a smile of remembrance.

I thought about it, and could not imagine the feeling, could not imagine how a young male would carry, linked to his prideful male organ, the fear of being hounded down, exposed, and dragged away to slavery and death.

"I never had fear," declared Carl. "I was nervous sometimes, yes. But fear? Why? For everything, there was a solution. I knew this SS, that SS, what could make them close an eye. A bottle of schnapps, a piece of gold pulled out of the sewer. I went down in the sewer of Warsaw, after the ghetto uprising. They made us go down, while they waited above; they were afraid. I knew what to get, and who to give it to."

Listening to him, I got the impression that all one needed to survive was a cool head and a good understanding of the Nazis' predictable character. Iris asked him whether he felt bad passing himself off as a German, denying that he was Jewish. Carl shrugged: "What denial? It saved my life." This happened, of course, at the kitchen table. My in-laws sat me there in the first weeks of our acquaintance, so I could hear their stories. They needed to establish a common ground with me, and those stories seemed to be the best vehicle. It helped that my family had suffered under the Communists, that my father and others had been jailed. When my uncle Nicu visited me in California and met my in-laws, he and Carl swapped stories, about Soviet camps and German camps.

Unexpectedly, my in-laws found common ground with me that they hadn't hoped for, and more familiar imagery than they could share with their daughter. I was from back there. I'd physically visited most of those places: Czechoslovakia, Hungary, the western swatch of the Ukraine, and the north side of Transylvania. As a Romanian, I knew well the world of small towns, village fairs, corn fields, peasant weddings, and births at a midwife's hands. I was a city boy, but every time I left Bucharest, on vacation or on some journalistic stint, rural Romania sucked me back, with smoky pubs, muddy roads, foggy forests, even a few surviving shtetls, in Maramuresh. There I saw Jewish men in long shroudlike white shirts, farming with wooden plows. I saw on windowsills real Sabbath candles, handmade, uneven, short, not the elegant varieties sold in

America. I slept in rented rooms where the windowsills were padded with inch-thick buildups of wax, attesting to the ancientness of the custom. I was from across the tracks, faith-wise, yet I belonged. My rebel wife paradoxically got the right guy. As I became a parent, a man I never thought I was grew out of me and stood in the modest light of that kitchen, as if saying to my in-laws: Entrust me, the stranger, with protecting your blood, mixed with mine. That shall be our true and deep kinship.

The stories of my in-laws' growing years were quite different. Blanka Davidovich grew up in Zhdenev, in the sub-Carpathian Ukraine. The town had one hundred and twenty Christian families and twenty-five Jewish ones. Not enough Jews to have a Jewish cemetery; the Jews were buried seven miles away, in another town. She grew up comfortable: her father owned a factory for carbonated water and a beer distributor. Life was simple. The girls milked the cows and did the laundry by hand in the local river, were trained to cook three meals a day, and to obey their future husbands. The men made the money and dealt with the headaches of the outside world. The area used to be part of Austro-Hungary. After World War I, it was joined like a tip to the Czechoslovak squiggle, until 1938, when Czechoslovakia was dismembered by Hitler. Today's Czech Republic became a Nazi *Protektorat,* while Slovakia became independent in name; in reality it was a Nazi puppet. That little tip, the sub-Carpathian Ukraine, was handed to fascist Hungary. At the end of World War II, the area was occupied by the Russians, and remains Russian to this day. Side by side in the sub-Carpathian Ukraine lived Ukrainians, Russians, Hungarians, Jews, Gypsies, some Romanians who had spilled over from Transylvania. The Czechs, who inherited the region through the decision of the treaty of Versailles, were remembered as courteous conquerors: "On *shabbas,* they knew that we couldn't make fires, so if we wanted to smoke a cigarette, they'd strike a match for us. The Czechs were different."

But the Czechs were few: the mayor, doctor, police chief, customs chief, and the teachers at the Czech state school. Sent out to colonize the new territory, they gravitated naturally towards the most cultured local breed, the Jews. Had the Czechs been natives, I wondered, would they have been so free of anti-Semitism? As for the others, when did they acquire hate for the Jews? Did they always have it? I asked my in-laws, on separate occasions. "I don't know," they responded almost identically. "We lived together, played together. We were not told to hate, and I don't think that the others were either. We were the same. But then, it happened."

Then, it happened. Blanka described to me how she once rode the bus to the next village, after the Hungarians occupied the area and enacted the racial laws. Now she wore a yellow star, and could only sit at the back of the bus. At a stop, the bus filled up with schoolgirls who had been her classmates, her friends. They saw her but didn't acknowledge her. They sat in front and talked excitedly about some girlish things, while the girl in the back sat alone behind that barrier of hate. The barrier was invisible, immaterial, yet so real, separating her from her own generation.

I knew the feeling. I thought of the orphans who beat my brother and me in the schoolyard. They, yes, had been taught to hate in the orphanages, where they were trained in class warfare. Look out for the better dressed and fed, they're the "bourgeois," sock it to them. All through my childhood, they socked it to me, wordlessly, or to the accompaniment of party lines: Why are you staring, bourgeois, why are you listening, are you conspiring against the working class? We know your kind—who in your family tunes in to the Voice of America? What are you plotting against us? Step up to the light, so we can watch you. Take your hands out of your pockets, turn your pockets inside out, drop that money on the floor, you stole it from us, didn't you, you stole it from the working class. You're not to be trusted with weapons, books, library permits, passports, with going to college, with singing our songs and touching our flag, with anything. Communism is digging your grave, bourgeois, and you better lie in it quietly. This is your death hour, bourgeois.

I thought about Blanka's bus, and about the Romanian schoolyard, scenes of hate both. That invisible yet indelible barrier of hate. A thought crossed my mind, incredible, fantastic. That was why I wanted to take that trip back. To remove that barrier.

No. No, no. If I kept thinking about it, I could feel sweat erupting on my temples, prickling my scalp. No, I couldn't do it: if I removed that hate, *what would remain?* Then another fantastic thought crossed my mind: if I didn't go back, if I didn't try to tell my story in books or films, it was because I wanted to protect that hate. But why would I protect it? My behavior was incomprehensible. Or else, that of others was, others who had no problems telling their stories. My in-laws.

I listened to their stories, on and on, searching for that standard: shame/hate.

Carl was raised in Slatinske Doly, not far from Blanka's Zhdenev but in a completely different situation. Slatinske was an ugly railroad junction. Carl's father was a railroad man who aspired to make Carl into something better than himself: a tailor. Carl wanted to be an electrician. "Not a Jewish trade," his father warned. To be what he wanted to be, Carl ran away at thirteen, to Prague. He severed his family ties. When his family was deported, Carl was fighting in the Czech underground. He'd gone to a trade school in Prague, graduated, and joined the Czech underground as the Nazis were closing in. He worked as an electrician, exactly what he had set out to become, at the Prague National Theater. Then he was transferred to the Vienna State Opera, whose official boxes glowed with Nazi high brass: Heydrich, von Ribbentrop, Himmler. He was arrested after two underground fighters killed a German in a brawl, and the whole network fell to the Gestapo. He was tortured, tried, sentenced to seven years of hard labor in a camp. The camp was Dachau.

At that time, the ghetto uprising in Warsaw had just been put down, and the Germans needed volunteers to descend into Warsaw's sewers and collect the weapons, explosives, and other valuables left there by the dead ghetto fighters. According to Carl, there was even gold in the sewer. He plunged into the sewer, brought up the valuables, surrendered most of them to none other than Adolf Eichmann. On purpose, to be remembered. The sympathetic memory of the Reichskommissar for Jewish affairs would come in handy: "I expected to meet him again, so I manipulated him." That kind of statement always upset Blanka: "Listen to the big shot," she said, leaning angrily across the kitchen table. "Every little piss SS man could kill any of us then, any time they wanted."

"I'm not lying, Blanka," Carl countered placidly. "I knew what to say to Eichmann. I knew how to control him."

On a second track of my mind, I played back slices of my own family's incarcerations. My father's, in the Jilava jail, near Bucharest. My uncle Nicu's, in various Siberian camps. Even the army time served by my cousin Sandu was jail time: being the son of that enemy of the people who swam the Danube, he was drafted into a sinister work battalion, in which several conscripts died of the cold, or from untreated injuries and ailments. My family's stories were not too different from my in-laws'. Same fear and brutality, and death and disease striking. Same bargaining with corrupt, cruel guards, for an extra piece of bread, a spell in the infirmary, a shovel sharp enough to achieve the work quota. Same bargaining with that ultimate figure, death, which loomed more distant than in Nazi camps, though sometimes not much.

I could've stopped the flow of my in-laws' stories by injecting some similar stories from my side. I would've been listened to. I didn't do it.

"The other equipment I took out of the sewer, I sold," continued Carl. "For a pair of radios, I would get a bottle of vodka. So I bribed some people, to get food or get transferred to another camp, when the floor got too hot under me."

"That was in Muhldorf" said his wife. "That was our last camp. You didn't get transferred, the war ended." She turned towards me: "We knew each other by then, so I made him a pair of mittens—you know how hard it was to steal cotton, thread, and fabric, and make mittens? I gave them to the camp's garbage collectors to take them to him, and he lost one mitten right away. I was so angry . . ."

"You were already angry at him then?" I asked prankishly.

"Sure. He was always going where he wasn't supposed to," she said, like a wife in a Jewish comedy.

"What did he look like when you first met him?" I asked, to appease her.

"Very good." She smiled. "He didn't look hungry, he had hair, few other men had hair then." Her smile widened: "He was clean, and wore a cute blue beret."

"I had the beret from a Frenchman I knew," said Carl. "A doctor. He saved me from death when I had typhus, by feeding me barley and sugar."

My wife was present at that particular session of camp tales. "How did you get typhus, Dad?" she asked, making me feel silently superior: *I* knew how one got typhus, I knew most of the mechanics of dirt, disease, and degradation. They were familiar to me. Not to my American wife.

"From the lice in the camp."

"Always the men had lice," elaborated Blanka. "Before I was in the work detail with the men, I never knew what lice were." I found that hard to believe, but said nothing.

Thanks to the descent into the sewer, which caught the eye of

Eichmann and other SS bigwigs, Carl was transferred to Auschwitz (altogether he was detained in nine jails and camps), but in a privileged situation. He repaired the Nazis' radio sets, radiators, heating and lighting systems, and gave advice about camp security, whose main feature was the deadly electricity running through its wire fences. Every morning, twisted corpses were found stuck on that wire like flies caught in a spider web. Carl told me how he caused power failures, allowing a number of inmates to crawl through the momentarily safe wires, and flee towards the advancing Russians. He worked outside the camp sometimes, under SS guard. He was owed favors, and ate better than the other inmates, and that without being an informant. Because he repaired the radios, which were information lifelines, he had advanced from the status of prisoner to that of captured technocrat.

"I learned this," he said. "The crunch always comes. When it comes, know how to do something. Anything."

He was not unmasked as a Jew even at Auschwitz; all throughout, he was classified as a *Politiker,* and a *Mischling,* a mixed-blood. But Auschwitz was tougher than his other detentions. He was branded on his arm, and although his special status did not terminate, for radios still needed to be repaired, now he would be punished cruelly for any minor infraction. He was beaten all over his body and on the soles of his feet, and submitted to strappado: hoisted by a rope, he was then dropped and held dangling. But he made it, "thanks to Eichmann," he told me. "Eichmann came to the camp and found me tied up, ready to be flogged to death, for listening to the BBC on a radio I made. But Eichmann said to the camp *kommandant* that it was impossible for this *Dummkopf,* me, to listen to enemy broadcasts. Then he walked up to me and asked: '*Du Verbrecher, lebst du noch?*' Meaning, You're still alive, you criminal? And that was it. They untied me and sent me to the infirmary."

As the Red Army got closer, the Nazis began to phase out Auschwitz, their most embarrassing operation. Able-bodied prisoners were shipped out. Carl was marched in a prisoners' column from Poland to Germany, all the way back to Dachau. From Dachau, he was sent by truck to Muhldorf, a lovely little camp by comparison, surrounded by farms; on clear days one could see the Bavarian Alps so beloved by Hitler. As fate would have it, a transport of women had just arrived in Muhldorf, from Auschwitz, in cattle cars. One of the cattle cars carried Blanka.

"By now," Carl remembered, "it smelled of peace."

But not of survival as yet; in fact that was the time for some big hurried mass killings followed by sloppy burnings of piled-up bodies, the last of which were discovered by horrified GIs.

Carl told Blanka that he was Jewish only after they were liberated. "Why should I tell her before? One more thing she should be afraid about?"

"I wouldn't have cared," countered Blanka, "the camp had cured me of fears. Other people were so afraid that they volunteered for nothing, and told others not to volunteer, convinced that volunteering meant death. But I always volunteered. I thought I'd die anyway, and didn't care when and where I would die. I volunteered for the kitchen, where I could steal food. Thanks to that, I'm still alive."

Carl's war was an adventure. Blanka's was a tragedy. The Hungarian occupation shook Zhdenev to its foundations. Blanka's family was faced with giving up their business or sharing it with a non-Jewish partner. They chose a Hungarian, Mr. Stefi Arendatzky, a lifelong neighbor, who immediately stole their property. Blanka's three older brothers were conscripted into work camps, which, survivors say, were hotels compared to the death camps. Armed with fake papers, Blanka went to work in Budapest, an exciting capital for a seventeen-year-old country girl, even during the war. It was a time of fear and yet of some hope. The Russians were beating the Nazis, to which the Nazis reacted with rage, torturing and killing thousands of Russian prisoners. "They couldn't stand that the Russians were beating them," said Carl. "They killed them at the slightest excuse."

In January 1942, it was decided at Wannsee, a pretty, forested suburb of Berlin, that the Jewish question was to be solved speedily once and for all: *Endlosung*. Final solution. Utter extermination. But that took time in rural territories like the sub-Carpathian Ukraine. The Jews were needed for work, and the Hungarians were sloppy. People could still have saved themselves. Most didn't. I once heard my mother-in-law blame the local rabbis for the population's inertness: "They always said don't do nothing, don't try nothing, don't run away, God will take care. A lot he took care." Her stilted English gave a rough and ugly power to what she was saying.

The Hungarians were among the most zealous in speeding up the final solution. By contrast, next door in the old kingdom of Romania, four hundred thousand Jews were unexpectedly saved. Romanian troops had participated in massacres of Jews in Transnistria, and Marshal Antonescu had vowed to fight the Russians to the end, but . . . there was this paradox: Antonescu decided there would be no deportations from the kingdom of Romania itself. The contradictory and enigmatic marshal resisted Hitler, perhaps, as Romanian legend has it, due to his personal acquaintance with Willi Filderman, then leader of Romania's Jewish community. Meanwhile, a few prominent Christians saved Jews—among them was a known literary figure and priest, Gala Galaction, who was close friends with Tudor Popescu, my grandfather. As a kid, I saw that man often, tall and bearded like a Byzantine saint, in the old Popescu house, where Dad was born. That house was razed by Ceausescu during his demented "resystemization" of Bucharest.

But back to Blanka's family: they were caught in Hungarian territory. Less than a year before Germany's collapse, she, her parents, and two sisters aged ten and twelve ended up before the gate marked *"Arbeit macht frei"*: Work makes you free. The gate of Auschwitz. She stepped out of the boxcar and walked towards a Nazi whose gloved hand flipped right, flipped left. Now everyone knows about that gloved hand, swinging towards life, towards death. Everyone knows now about the calls to the showers that weren't showers, that sprinkled poisoned fumes instead of cleansing water. But back then, only the Nazis knew. The deportees over fourteen were fit for work, so for a while they would be spared. Those under fourteen and the old folks wouldn't spend even one night in the camp. Blanka's twelve-year-old sister wanted to stay with her, but she was too young and frail to work, so Blanka told her to remain with her mom. Mom and Dad and the two youngest girls walked left. That night, they were gassed. Had she stayed with Blanka, would the twelve-year-old have survived? No one can answer.

Sometimes, my wife joined these conversations late. I did not hear her footsteps, but looked up and saw her standing at the door of the kitchen, leaning against the doorjamb. For a fraction of a second I saw another woman, not my wife: was it because the transformation in her was so unique? Her body seemed shrunk under an unseen weight, her beauty lost its luster, her lips their fleshiness. She looked old, aged by pain. Her eyes were tragic, horrified. This blond, brown-eyed, vibrant California girl became an icon of her parents' suffering.

When I saw her like that, I felt sadly impotent. How could I give her enough love to erase that pain? What could I do, apart from saying predictable words, or holding her body to body? I did that too, knowing that it didn't defend her against the past. My desire to protect her gripped my heart, and I suffered with her, sincerely. Yet I suffered differently, on the other side of her experience.

Iris absorbed Blanka's and Carl's tragedy, all of it. She learned early on that she was part of it, and always would be. I would have felt the same, growing up with those six numbers flashing on Dad's arm every day, six numbers spelling an amazingly simple duty: don't forget. Iris was accomplished, successful, good looking, a responsible being, in every respect what a woman wanted to be at this end of a century. Thinking and speaking her own mind, a worker, mother, lover, and wife. Yet within the same being, she was all the blood that was lost, saved in an unseen vial. She was the flame of the past, inextinguishable. With her amazing multiplicity of character, she had found me and married me. I guess the logistics of a wedding of such contrasted backgrounds scared us both, for we eloped. I had been invited that summer to Robert Redford's film workshop in Utah, to develop a screenplay, which later became the first feature I directed. Iris came to visit me in Utah. I rushed her to a judge in the quaint little town of Provo, and we got married. The judge asked us to call him "brother," and sure as fire, brother Johnson united us in under fifteen minutes. We came back to Los Angeles and had a big party, without a priest or a rabbi, without a canopy, but with kosher hors d'oeuvres and Jewish songs. I didn't break a glass with my foot, but I was raised in a chair by men in tuxes, relatives on Iris's side, plus one lone friend of mine from Romania, an electronic engineer I'd known from elementary school, who had left Romania the same week as me. Not all of Iris's relatives were there, two uncles had made their displeasure known by not showing up, yet there was nothing they could do, here I was up in that chair. I was watched on my side by my mother and by my uncle who had swum the Danube, and his wife; before the party the priest considerately asked me whether, given the composition of the crowd, he should wear the priestly Roman collar or a tie, and I told him a tie. It went well, and all the card-playing friends of my in-laws smiled misty-eyed. They were moved, and worried. Not only Carl and Blanka, but all of them were giving Iris away. The torch was being passed to us, the breakers of the mold.

Since '89, my in-laws had been taking more interest in Romania than ever. When they saw a rare newspaper article about Romania, they cut them out for me. They asked me repeatedly: didn't I want to take a trip back to Romania? The first since I defected?

"Leave him alone, Mom, Dad," Iris would say before I could answer. "He doesn't want to go, he's scared."

"I don't believe that," my father-in-law would say jumping in to defend me. "Petru's not scared of anything, he's very courageous." I liked to fantasize that he felt so much solidarity with me because he too had married his wife alone, so to speak. Blanka's four brothers had survived, and surely they had looked him over from head to toe. Blanka and Carl were married, and then tragedy struck again: Martin, Blanka's youngest brother, was killed in an accident in a boot camp of the Haganah, the predecessor of Israel's army, which then had a training agreement with the Czechoslovak army.

"I didn't mean that Petru's not courageous," my wife would explain. Sometimes when she said that, she would slip her hand into mine.

Was I courageous? Let's see. I had visited war zones, flown in rickety bush-hopper planes, spent nights in the tropical wild, waking up eyeball to eyeball with dangerous animals, or with inscrutable natives. I'd left my homeland all by myself, without money or valuables, mates or guidance, and knowing the heavy penalties if I was caught and returned. I had taught myself how to write in English. I had attacked Hollywood, the mecca of filmdom, without anything but faith in myself, and an accent.

I thought deeply, wanting to know the truth. Was I afraid? If I met the Securitate agents who pursued me so many times, who roughed me up when I was thirteen, would I be afraid of them? No, I wouldn't be, even though the Romanians in the diaspora swore that the Securitate were still in power, and that they made people disappear. What would I do, if I did meet the Securitate? I didn't know. But I knew that I wouldn't be afraid.

"In June, we're going back to visit too," said my mother-in-law. "We're going back to Prague, and then to Zhdenev."

"To Slatinske Doly too?" I asked, remembering Carl's native place.

"I don't think so. Mirek doesn't want to go to Slatinske Doly."

"We're not going nowhere," Carl (Mirek) interjected casually.

I looked from him to her, and back to him. "Blanka just said you were."

"We're not. What for?"

"We're going to fly to Vienna and rent a car and drive to Budapest," my mother-in-law went on, quietly. "In Budapest, I want to see where I was living during the war. Then we'll drive to the Russian border, and cross to Ushgorod. From there, it's thirty miles to Zhdenev."

"I don't want to go to Vienna," said Carl. From the garage, I could hear the happy noises of my children. Carl's voice was the same, accented but calm. His gestures were the same, the muscular movements of a man always backed up by a strong, healthy body. But his eyes looked away, as if into the past, a past quite different from his bravado-filled stories. Carl Friedman, a.k.a. Cestmir Vencera, the resistance fighter, shook his head and spoke low, as if to himself: "We don't go anywhere. I'm not going."

"He's going, you'll see," said Blanka with wifely infallibility.

"The Russians are in Zhdenev, Blanka," he reminded her.

"So what? I have nothing to do with them."

He shook his head, and I knew that he would go.

Carl kept a spoon, an American spoon, which was given to him by one of the GIs who freed him. He still used it for breakfast and lunch, though it was almost fifty years old. It was made of aluminum, with a hole in the handle so it could be hung on a peg, with the words U.S. ARMY carved on the handle. The spoon's tongue was worn down on the side that touched the bottom of bowls and plates thousands of times, millions of times. Carl had taken that spoon with him, out of Soviet-occupied Czechoslovakia. He brought it to America, where it was originally made. That spoon left America in a GI's hand, and came back in the hand of an immigrant.

Carl's feet were shoeless under the kitchen table. He didn't like wearing tight shoes: his feet had almost been broken in the beatings. He had idiosyncrasies that were all traceable to running away from home, to the war, to the camps. Yes, he was telling his story with words, and with his whole body. And sometimes the two versions were quite different.

That thought crossed my mind again, incredible, fantastic. That invisible barrier of hate, that's why you want to take that trip. To remove that barrier.

No, I thought. No, it wasn't possible.

I knew hate, and my fear of hate, I'd felt them many times in Romania, identical except that under Communism they were political, not racial. I felt the hate so close, sometimes it squeezed me inside it like a corset. Reducing me to the narrowest possible territory, myself. There was this difference though, between Communism and Nazism. Communism was not liquidating whole breeds but reshaping them. Its goal was control, rather than annihilation. Still, millions died in the process of being reshaped. Of those millions, a number of individuals were of my own blood.

"Why does your mother want to go visit?" I asked Iris, as we drove home after one such talk at the kitchen table.

"I suppose for the same reasons that you want to go," she countered.

"I don't know that I want to."

"Then why are you talking about it? You couldn't do it when Ceausescu was in power, but now you can, and you're talking about it. Why? What unfinished business do you have back there?"

"I don't think I have any."

"Good. Then stop talking about it."

I stopped talking about it, and I continued thinking about it.

What was my unfinished business? Was it political? Was it some morbid interest in the dead Ceausescus? No, I wasn't in the least drawn to see their plain graves in Ghencea Cemetery, which were rumored to be covered in flowers now and then, by ex-bodyguards and other faithfuls who would scale the cemetery walls like grave robbers, to bring in their flowers and lay them before the two plain wooden crosses. What a morbid joke those graves with crosses were, too. The Ceausescus had all but destroyed the Romanian Orthodox church.

No, I, a victim of Communist politics, had no political unfinished business. When I thought about it that way, I had no unfinished business at all. What was there for me to find in my ex-homeland, and bring back to America? Renewal, integrity? Forgiveness? I knew that there were certain things I would never forgive, that was one reason why I left. I knew that. I started to focus on that word: *knew*. What did I know, really? I could argue that I knew the past in detail. And yet that I didn't know it at all.

Finally . . .

It happened. I started to remember what I had never forgotten, but just pushed down into that inner lake of silence. With a throb of relief, I allowed myself to look into the lake. And I saw the key scenes. Character forming. Indelibly hewn in my sunken memory. They didn't lie there in order, but that didn't matter. Here was the first scene.

I was thirteen years old, and had just lost my twin brother.

Part Two

Character-Forming Scenes

T wo men in sunglasses, dark suits, and white nylon shirts with dirty collars picked me up at the basketball court of my high school, where I was watching some older kids shoot hoops. It was a hot day in early September, and all the sweat in those men's bodies and the smell of that sweat seemed to have gathered in their polyester collars. In an unmarked black car, they took me to a little apartment—at the time, the Securitate leased small apartments, single bedrooms really, all over Bucharest. These locations were convenient for quick interrogation, surveillance, relaying of tailing teams, rest, everything. The window-shades of those boxes were usually drawn, and their furniture minimal, but all were rumored to have beds. On those beds, supposedly, rested the Securitate officers or lay the bodies of people who had died during interrogation.

I didn't see the beds on my first questioning. I was kept standing in a sort of dining area, in front of an officer who was seated at a desk with nothing on it, not even an ashtray. The officer was built like a prizefighter. His fists had chipped fingernails, and they weren't just big—they also looked swollen, like a heavyweight's after a fight. To make it more obvious that I couldn't get away or resist in any fashion, behind me stood another officer, one of the two who had brought me in.

I wasn't roughed up too much, just shoved around and slapped a couple of times. "Marginally beaten, borscht from the nose," was the expression my friends and I jokingly used later, commenting on my interrogation. We referred to the physical brutality but never to the psychological damage. That was too minor to merit discussion; in truth, we didn't really think that any psychological damage had occurred, which was part of our defense mechanism.

I was only marginally beaten because I'd done nothing, and there was nothing much that they could learn from me. They asked who in my family corresponded with our New York relatives, and I didn't know. They made me promise to report on the creation of any subversive organizations in our school. By that time, the borscht from my nose had dried on my upper lip. I was allowed to wash my face in a dirty bathroom, and towel it with toilet paper, which one couldn't find in ordinary bathrooms. Until late into the sixties, toilet paper was hard to come by in the Soviet bloc— so people used newspaper. The fact that there was toilet paper *there* connected that place with the power of our system. The power rewarded its loyal henchmen with such luxuries.

I promised to tell on subversive schoolboys (Romanian schools were not coed at the time), with no intention of following through, just to get out of there faster. I had briefly fantasized about feeding the names of some high school bullies to the Securitate, but I didn't do it. I would do it some other time, I thought, if the Securitate kept harassing me. I didn't feel bad about that plan. Apart from my family, I owed no one protection.

It would be dishonest to give the impression that I was a precocious cynic, that from my powerlessness I manipulated the situation almost as skillfully as they had manipulated it from their all-too-powerful position, that I was numb of feeling or resigned to what was to be my fate. No. I was both afraid and throbbing with outrage. I felt more emotional than at other times, in more perilous situations, because my twin brother had died only eight months before, of polio, and I still was under the enormous impression of that loss. In its light, my vulnerability was more extreme, and their callousness more suffocating.

The death of my brother had connected me with a vast mystery, and had given me a sort of unspoken, desperate power. A couple of times I looked back at my interrogator with defiance. I answered monosyllabically, forcing him to repeat his questions, to work for his answers. And though I couldn't put my burning stare smack on his face, I put it on his desk and on the cheap cretonne of the shades, as if casting a spell on them, and indirectly casting my spell on the man who was questioning me.

I'd already heard accounts of arrests and interrogations. We all had. Throughout the time I spent there (a little over an hour), I noticed that some things were more frightening than I'd thought they would be, and some were less. The fists of the officer at the desk were frightening; but he didn't hit me, the other one did, and I didn't fear the blows very much because I sensed that they came from a low-ranked man who had no power of decision. But the other, the beefy one, could decide not only how long to keep me in there, but other things too, things regarding my future. So I feared his decision more than his fists.

I also had feared that betraying what I knew would torture me with guilt and shame—I was already sort of a moral type, you see. But it turned out that I knew nothing, and I forgot about my conscience after I walked in anyway. I feared the dirt of the place. The floor looked like it hadn't been touched by a broom in days. Unidentified stains were on the walls, dried-up spills on the desk, and mold everywhere in the bathroom. Newspapers were scattered around on the floor, marked by footprints from the officers' heavy shoes. There wasn't much actual litter, because no one remained in there long enough to produce it.

Seeing that mess, a flicker of boldness sprang out of my fear. The dreaded Securitate were men who had no particular gifts. Quite likely they were stupid, efficient only because of their numbers and their spying devices. I could outsmart them.

But my fear was still bigger than my courage. And there were two things that humiliated me deeply. One was the fact that the officer mentioned, squinching his thick face into a pose of compassion, the death of my twin brother. He knew about it, of course he did. It was, like everything else, noted in the family file.

"A fine lad. Looked just like you, eh? Tall as a young tree. What exactly felled him?"

The imagery he used, intentionally or not, seemed like a cruel mockery of my pain.

"Polio," I breathed, crushed by a holy sense of betrayal. Politics were profane. My brother's memory was sacred.

"But the vaccine?" he pretended.

The last polio epidemic of any proportion had hit Bucharest's child population right before Christmas. There was already an anti-polio vaccine in the "rotting collapsing Capitalist West," but the Communist nations did not want to spend their hard currency to buy it. Our health officials declared that they had the disease under control, even though hundreds of children died or lost the use of their limbs. Finally, the government was forced to drop its rhetoric and buy the damn vaccine. But it was too late for many youngsters, including my brother.

"Too late," I muttered, with a hot raspiness in my throat.

"Weird thing, twins," sighed my interrogator. It wasn't a put-down, it was quite philosophical, and before I could check myself, I nodded in approval, and hated myself for it, for accepting any kind of truth coming from that man.

That was the first humiliation. I was ashamed of having to share my human side with them.

Then came the second humiliation. Because we had talked of my brother's death, the conversation had become almost friendly. At the end, the big officer rose behind his empty desk, uncurled his beefy fist, and put out a thick palm. I was too afraid. I took that thick, humid, meaty slab, and cringed, shaking it as if I were shaking the devil's own paw.

Then it was over, except for my feelings.

I went home on foot, passing buildings and people, feeling like a raped girl who had been dreading that it would happen, and it had. Now the waiting was over: I'd been interrogated. The routine of being treated as suspicious and of being checked on periodically had started. It went on till I escaped from Romania.

The most terrible thing was that I didn't tell my mother and father. I couldn't. We didn't get along, even less so after my brother's death. In today's lingo, I was into denial already, and didn't have a healthy relationship with my parents.

The place I was taken to was close to where we lived, but I chose the longest route back home. I walked down two of Bucharest's main boulevards, Magheru and Balcescu, towards University Square, which would become famous years later as a rallying spot in the anti-Ceausescu revolution. I felt that everyone in the street could guess what had happened to me, just by looking at me. At the same time, I knew that they couldn't see anything. Passing shop windows, I glimpsed myself, a thin gangly youngster, too tall for his age, brown-haired, upper lip hazed by a future moustache. I wore a high school uniform of coarse blue cloth, state-issued, with a blue tie tucked inside the narrow opening of the jacket—the tie was eight inches long, a stumpy, ridiculous thing. All of my outfit looked like a parody of a regular suit and tie. I tried to appear interesting by tightening my lips and narrowing my eyes in a killer stare, but I had to be careful where I trained that stare. There were some real killers around.

I passed the symbols of the system we lived in: bright red flags on the buildings, and portraits of the party's politburo members, unnaturally pink-cheeked and with shiny youthful hair—in reality, those men were two decades older than they looked in their official portraits. Europe's proletariat was an ugly bunch, malnourished for generations, with bad teeth, shoulders stooped by carrying heavy loads, knees broken by work injuries, gaits unsteadied by drinking, moles with hair. But with power came glamour, so our leaders got new official looks, and new official bios as "soldiers seasoned in combating Fascism," and "sons of the people steeled by patriotism."

The truth was simpler: the Romanian Communists had been brought to power by the Soviet occupier. They ruled totally untrusted, and made no effort to win over the masses. They didn't need to, they had behind them the muscle of an empire. Their PR effort was limited to touching up their portraits. Yet, this completely artificial system was obsessed with . . . truth. It monitored the truth with hyper vigilance and one of those instances of monitoring had just occurred to me.

Concretely, I'd been raped, violated. My integrity had been intruded upon by the state. It didn't matter that I hadn't been molested worse, struck with sticks, or penetrated in my privates—my first defilement had been total, my surrender had been total. I knew already how to lay the blame for what happened at the door of the state, and that laying of the blame was a prime feature of life under Communism. This was my first interrogation, and it had occurred unexpectedly, without any preparation, so when I thought back on what happened, my heart beat wildly, and though I'd been cool back there, out in the street I had to fight tears. In a few days, I would attempt to turn all this into a cynical joke ("borsht from the nose"), even into a badge of courage before my peers. But now I was too vulnerable. I felt the taste of shame in my mouth, in my body, in my eyes even: I had a sense of how deflowered and defiled my stare must be, as I put it back on the world around me.

My only consolation was that the whole world around me was being defiled in the same way by the same system, for what had happened to me was occurring all over Eastern Europe, and Russia, China, Mongolia, and North Korea. Across twelve "fraternal" nations, countless youngsters paraded in and out of interrogation offices, then returned to their schools or homes, with the bug of surveillance planted in their brains. Walking back, they passed the touched-up portraits of leaders they had not elected, whom they would never meet, and in some cases would not outlive. And I was just one, in those millions.

And there was nowhere else to go.

There wasn't. The borders were sealed up. There was a small degree of intra–Soviet bloc transit, as evidenced by two airline offices I was passing: one Soviet, the other Bulgarian. We could go to Moscow, and back. Or to Sofia, and back. We could swap smiles with the convicts in other wards, floors, cell blocks. And forget that there was a free, capitalist "out there." But like all kids my age, I was fascinated with that "out there." Passing the entrance of a big hotel, the Ambassador, I slowed down, hoping that some aliens, men and women living in the forbidden West, would show at the hotel's door. I didn't stop, for I would have brought attention to myself—plainclothes Securitate stood around the hotel entrance, staring sharply at whoever walked in and out—but walking past the entrance I felt like some porous object ready to absorb all sensations coming from the forbidden West. Just now, one alien, a woman in a lamé dress, headed out towards a taxi. She had a pleasantly square face haloed by blond hair, and a cutely upturned nose. I drank her in through all my pores. Maybe I should have displayed some dignity, some native pride, but . . . cut off from the world, we'd all become sponges for anything from "out there," whether things or living beings. Everything good, efficient, came from out there, from razor blades and nylon shirts to cars and TV antennas.

And I, who had just been violated by the state, knew instinctively that this was only my first time. I was very young. There would be other opportunities when, freshly compromised, I'd be brought face to face with something or someone from outside of Romania, as if to make even more bitter the certainty of my imprisonment. I would stay here. They would go back there, where they would continue their fulfilled and unmolested lives.

Thus, passing that attractive woman felt particularly humbling after what had just happened to me. My nascent manhood had been deeply offended. Had I not felt so diminished, my fantasy would've brought us together, and a mating would've taken place in my mind, breathlessly exciting though abstract—at thirteen, I was intensely aware of women, but I'd had no carnal experience yet. But as I licked my lips swollen by slaps, I judged myself unworthy even to share the air with that alien. I wasn't her fellow human. I was born to a damned destiny.

It would've been different if I had been jumped by school bullies, or even mugged. But the authority that had slapped me had been the state, the power responsible for our lives. I'd done nothing, I knew nothing, yet I was pre-empted, so to speak, and at the same time made aware that my rapists knew my life with its intimate losses, notably that of my brother, the way a woman's rapist would not be content with her body, but would comment casually during the ordeal about her marriage, or motherhood, or other precious elements of her identity.

So it was a rape, definitely.

The woman from "out there" got in her cab, showing a segment of pretty leg as she sat inside it. And I, shamed, walked faster.

The reason why I could not share what had happened with my parents was that our family was falling apart. To make a quick scenario of the family before my brother died: our parents were two intellectuals a writer and an actress, and we were their twin sons. My parents were from the intelligentsia, cultured, good-looking, distinguished, models of what we, the children, would aspire to emulate. Then, lightning struck: my brother died. Lightning struck again: my father left my mother—at the time of my first interrogation. I wasn't too surprised, I wasn't giving them six more months together. Lightning struck for the third time, this time hitting me alone: my mother threw on me the whole burden of grief and guilt for those events, not gradually but all of a sudden.

All this was happening because Pavel had died. Petru and Pavel, Romanian for Peter and Paul, were our given names. As middle names we both had Stelian, after the saint who protected children in the Romanian hagiography. Well, Pavel's Saint Stelian had not protected him, and my Saint Stelian was not doing a great job either.

A year before, there had been two of us. Identical, mirrors of each other. The sight of us together made strangers stop in the street. And then a polio epidemic hit, and Pavel was one of the first to catch it—in the beginning, the doctors believed that he had the flu. Mom kept him home from school, and I went to classes alone, envying him for being nice and snug in bed. When I came home, we played chess with the board on the bed between us. He complained of numbness in his arms and legs, and I noticed that he moved stiffly. A few days later, I came back from school under a nasty pissy November rain, and found an ambulance in front of our apartment building. A paramedic almost carried my brother to the ambulance: dressed for winter, with his snow boots on, he was stumbling, missing his steps. The paralysis was already setting in. Pavel couldn't bend his knees to climb in, so the paramedic lifted him inside.

Pavel seemed not to recognize me right away. Then he said something like "they won't keep me there long." Stunned, I did not respond, did not hug him. That night, a bout of cold hit the city, and the pissy rain turned into snow.

No wonder I have been obsessed by stories of disappearance since that time. I was not to see Pavel again, but I did not know it. Years later, Iris's mother was to describe to me how she last saw her parents and sisters. She was not to see them again, but she did not know it.

The next day I came back from school, and didn't find Mom or Dad. I stepped into the living room and bolted at the sight of an old woman dressed in black after the fashion of Balkan widows: it was Grandma Pia, Mom's mother, who used to spend a lot of time with us when we were smaller. Grandma Pia told me that Mom had stayed in the hospital with my brother, and Dad would be shuttling between hospital and home. Then she cooked dinner. My footsteps inside the house sounded loud and hollow. I could hear my own breath.

Pavel died three days later, but I wasn't told. One day after his death, a date I reconstructed later, Dad came home with two men with a strange fumigating device, and they disinfected our bedroom—they were from the Ministry of Health. Dad told me that Pavel was putting up a brave fight; but since I had been exposed to him, it was necessary that I be quarantined. No school for now. For the next few weeks, I lived in a bizarre limbo, in the very bedroom I had shared with Pavel, with Grandma serving me my meals and telling me stories about the little port on the Danube where she had been a gymnasium teacher, until she got married and had two children, one being Mom. I did not see my mother again until the quarantine was over and I was declared uninfected. For a full six weeks, I did not leave that bedroom, and saw no one but a doctor, my father, and my grandmother. Before and after visiting me, everyone washed their faces and hands in potassium hypermanganate, a disinfectant solution that was blood-red in color.

During those weeks of quarantine, I slept in the bed Pavel and I had slept in together, and wondered, before falling asleep, if I too might wake up the next day with a high fever, or with my arms and legs numb already. The polio virus had settled in Pavel's medulla oblongata, the lowest part of his brain. When he could no longer breathe, he was tracheotomized and put on a respirator. But that didn't help. I dreamed, over and over again, of his face on the hospital pillow. Of his scared eyes. Because of the tracheotomy, he could not talk. A thirteen-year-old faced with the terrifying nearness of death, and not being able to voice his fright!

I learned the details of his death later, but I suspected enough during my six weeks of quarantine to be scared witless. Daily, I was checked rigorously for vomiting, flushing, or congestion of the throat, and was asked whether I had headaches. Four times a day I had a thermometer stuck in my mouth, while I froze in fright, knowing that a few lines of raised temperature might mean the onset of the disease. In my little prison, I went nuts examining my body, rolling my shoulders and bending and rotating my neck, checking for stiffness of my back or my neck, both symptoms of advanced infection. Since hand-to-mouth contagion was particularly dangerous, my handkerchiefs and Pavel's had been collected and destroyed. Grandma went out and bought me new ones, since at that time no one in Eastern Europe used paper tissues.

My father told me of Pavel's death only at the end of the quarantine—confirmed it, that is, for I already knew. Looking aged and exhausted, he told me that there was no more hope, but he still didn't spell it out clearly: "Pavel is no more." Maybe he figured that I could not hear it said that way. He hugged me briefly, a hug which I did not return, I was numb, inert. My father took my arm: "Come, your Mom's waiting for you."

I was allowed to step out of the house. I breathed the winter air, both exquisite and strange, after the staleness of our apartment.

My father had brought a taxi. Mom was waiting for us at the home of friends, a few blocks from the hospital where she had watched Pavel die. She had stayed at the hospital through the funeral, then stayed on a few more weeks, because she herself could be a carrier. She could not come home to comfort me, to lessen my fear, or just to be with me.

When I entered those friends' home, Mom appeared at the top of the stairs. She became pale: remember, we were identical, Pavel and I, to see me was to see *him*. Then she rushed down, and cried, closing her arms around me. She sounded strange, like an unknown woman: a stage actress almost always theatrical, she was not theatrical now. She'd lost for the moment her sense of being on stage, of being watched. Red-eyed, puffy-cheeked, heartbroken, and real, she cried. We cried together, and that was the last time that I cried with tears for a long time, until other events, other emotions made me cry again as a man, in the ugly, humbling way of men.

The next day, the three of us left Bucharest for a strange vacation. Perhaps Mom and Dad hoped that it might bring us back together—but it didn't work for them, and I had simply become someone else, someone they didn't know, someone I didn't know. We traveled to the Carpathian mountains by train. When I saw the jagged peaks of the Carpathians from the train's window, I felt a kind of liberation. I was scarred for life, but still I was alive and there was so much to life that I didn't know. The sun came out and lit up the mountains. An enormous, superb massif stood before the train, as if alive. Irregularly covered with snow like a wild buffalo whose coat had started to tatter, it seemed to breathe at me one word: survive.

That noble liberated feeling passed quickly. A few days later, we went back home. Here, everything reminded me of my brother. The fact that he was missing from my familiar surroundings was painful, sometimes insufferably so, but above all it was strange. I'd always lived as my twin brother's double, and he as mine. Without him, projected individually onto the world, I moved about as if in a nightmare. The way I looked at our place, at my family, was no longer the same. Our apartment building was still the same, a cubistic structure five floors high, erected in the twenties, during an oil boom that had made Romania an attractive investment. Later, the oil made Romania a prize for the Nazi war machine; as I grew up, the oil was still prized, and pumped out gluttonously by the Soviets. Next to that plundered wealth, Romania's cities and homes, including our building, suffered cruelly from poverty and lack of maintenance. Our building's stairway was encased in a shaft made of glass, proudly modern once, now grimy and missing panes. The tiled patio leading from the sidewalk to the entrance was cracked. No bulbs lit the stairway, the only light came through the keyholes of the apartment doors, when the tenants were in. We climbed the stairs in the dark, past an elevator out of order since before my birth. Because of the housing shortage, by order of city hall, we'd all had to take in an extra family; thus, a pair of strangers had been quartered in Dad's study. The intruders, man and wife, shared our kitchen, bathroom, and toilet. Their radio was on every evening, praising the output of our new factories, but I knew that it wasn't concern for the industrial output that made them turn it on; when they did, it was to have sex. The intruders were activists in a "mobile propaganda unit," often out on the road to brainwash the peasants into joining the collective farms. When they were home, she smelled up our apartment with the odor of her heavy sauces, and he smoked in the toilet, dropping butts in the bowl and on the seat. We could do nothing about them, they were part of the new scene.

Shrunk to three rooms (and that was a lot of space for those days!), our side of the apartment carried vestiges of my parents' life before Communism: framed photos, trinkets from trips to Paris, London, Berlin, furniture once expensive and trendy, now decrepit, old books, magazines, and letters. My parents had been the high rollers of their generation: intellectuals, left-wing idealists, iconoclasts. She an actress, he a lawyer, then a Marxist journalist, they had been daring, dangerous, talked about. My father had been jailed under the Antonescu regime, a jail time that had the panache of political dissidence; while he was jailed, my mother continued to perform at the National Theater, Romania's best. Now my mother was part of a state theater troupe, but got very few parts. Dad, after more jail (Communist this time), was writing underpaid party-line editorials, and was lucky to have even that. Both had failed to sell their skills to the new regime. They were getting by, but they were bitter, depressed, and angry with life and with each other.

Which was to be expected: they'd taken a hard fall from the height of their previous social comfort and self-image. They were not alone, a big slice of Romania's society had crashed in those years, and it would've been hard for any idealists without street smarts to get back on their feet. I, a child, understood that they were powerless. I was there when Dad came back from jail, skinny and smelling bad, and when plainclothes Securitate men ransacked our home, emptying drawers on the floor, hurling knickknacks that fell and broke, carting away books and papers, of which there were so many in our home that each time they raided, the Securitate swore loudly at the clutter, while my parents stood powerless against a wall, until the raid was over. And where were Pavel and I, interrupted from a game or a brotherly scuffle? Against another wall. My father, Radu Popescu, licensed to the bar and a name in Romanian letters, was powerless to stop the Securitate. My mother, who on stage became Medea, or Queen Gertrude, Hamlet's mother, and ruled undisputed at home over us kids, was equally powerless. I was powerless myself. I knew of course how to lay the blame on the state, all of us did, it was in the air. But I was too fragile and vulnerable not to crave my parents' help. I needed strength from them, and confidence.

The night we came back from the mountains, I lay down and slept in the bed Pavel and I had shared before he died. I saw him in a dream, his face soft and alive, his eyes big and brown, eyes which my children have inherited. I took his hand and squeezed it, and tossed violently, banging my head against the headboard, to wake up. If I woke up fast enough, his hand would still be in mine, and thus I would bring him over, I would *bring him back*.

But as I started to wake up, his hand in mine became harder, a hand of stone, the hand of a statue. Then it slipped out of mine, and I woke up without him. He was dead, and I was alone, and the moon tinted the windows and stabbed its rays between the shutters' slats.

The sense of vulnerability that Pavel's death had instilled in me became clear to me that night. It was low, shameful, and all encompassing; even having to sleep in the very same bed was a proof of my defeat. Death could come back to pick me too, whenever it wanted, from the same spot. That feeling sucked into itself every other fear in my experience, until an unnameable dread of what would happen to me in my future took hold of my mind. Then I managed to conceive one thought: this situation was so intolerable that the grown-ups in my life would react. My parents, they would notice how I felt, what I was going through, and would do something.

I waited, with a kind of clinical attention, to see what the grown-ups would do.

Well, they did something very strange. They sort of brought Communism into our home, and combined it with our fresh personal loss.

The one who started was Mother. One day soon after we returned, she suddenly turned her face towards me, and with the kind of solemnity she used on stage, but also the solemnity of Communist pronouncements, she said, "From now on, *you,* Petru, are my support." Parents often feel that way about their children, and even say it, before the child can fully grasp the meaning and workings of what we call a support system. But my mother did it with such emphasis, suggesting so clearly that she had no help from her mate, and that my duties included not just her emotional needs, but relieving all the strains of the times we lived in, that I was staggered. It was as if life stretched out in front of me, and I saw what it was made of: a dour mature duty, with no payoffs.

Mom's grief met her thespian vocation, and she proceeded to dramatize everything in relation to the departure of my brother. Things became before and after Pavel's death. Pavel became a scary standard of perfection, against which she lined me up, and found me defective: when she started remembering him as "her good one" ("God took my good one and left me with you!"), I knew I'd done something wrong. She also accused me of not having loved him enough, on the evidence that I didn't shed enough tears. Expecting my father to leave her soon—since Pavel's death, the rift in their marriage was out in the open—she demanded that I be her constant companion, crashing onto my shoulders with all the weight of an abandoned woman. Her way of enforcing my duties was the Communist state's way of making its captured citizens perform: guilt, plus the threat of punishment. The citizens of unhealthy origin were guilty from the start, and the peasants and workers were guilty for not repaying the party's sacrifices by working themselves to death. Dad fled that political allegory (Mom was the party, I the working masses), but added to it a very important third segment: the absentees of all ilks, always ranted at in party speeches. I needed him desperately in those days, but he was always locked away in his study, or gone for long hours to meet with editors of the propaganda press. He got few assignments for the time he spent out of the house, and when he came home, late, she blasted him. Mom held dinner back until he arrived, so a quarrel before dinner was the rule in our house.

Meanwhile, Mom held me captive in the ritual of honoring my dead brother. Christians of the Eastern Rite honor their dead with numerous services at the gravesite—forty days after a burial, and then every few months at regular intervals, there is the so-called *parastas* (remembrance): a lengthy visit to the grave, with laying of flowers, prayers, and alms to homeless people who live near Romanian cemeteries precisely due to that custom. My mother went to Pavel's grave as often as possible, and I, not Dad, was her escort. We would take a crowded streetcar to the cemetery, an hour's ride away, past the North Railway Station. There we would inspect the condition of the grave, lay the flowers, pray along with the priest, pay the caretaker, and give alms of small change and a home-made wheat-meal called *coliva*. Mom would cry. I couldn't cry. After the storm I'd cried when Pavel had died, I couldn't add one tear. I hated those rituals, but with the kind of denial Communism had introduced, I couldn't admit that hate even to myself: what? hate *honoring my brother?*

So I often came home from school, and found Mother waiting in front of our building, with a quietly proud posture. She was a handsome woman, and in my mixture of feelings toward her there was a sizable amount of filial admiration. She wore one of her better suits "from before." Just like the good new stuff that was from "out there," what was not new but was still good was "from before" the Communists. A watch from before, a car, a gas stove, tablecloths, bed linen, bathroom accessories, silverware, jewelry, clothes were all kept jealously, maintained with care, and even left to children in one's will. The shortage of local goods and the shoddiness of Soviet products had forced the Romanians to become nostalgic antiquarians. Our homes were museums, with today's folk operating yesterday's implements. When something broke down, from watch to gas range to fan belt to film projector, you should've seen the detective work to find parts and secure them.

Mom had always been a great lady, so she had plenty of clothes from before. She was a sight: strikingly dressed, though always behind the fashions. She was still young enough, attractive, desirable even. And she moved about with natural regality, in the proletarian squirm of those days, a contradiction in everything, even in her person. If I was a minute late from school, she would admonish me: "How can you be so late? You knew we were going to see Pavel." Not his grave, but *him*. As if he wasn't dead. For a number of years she inscribed her new appointment books with "To my darling Pavel, Happy Birthday" on the date of our twin birthday, February 1st.

"I'm sorry, Mom. They kept us late at school."

"You always do this to me. To Pavel."

I did that to him. Worse. I couldn't cry for him.

"I said I was sorry . . ."

Her chin started twitching. All right. Give Mom your arm. We walked out into the street together. Side by side, we rode the old streetcar for an hour, squashed between sweaty bodies, past cityscapes adorned with red flags, with leaders' portraits: my horizons. Mom sometimes cried in the streetcar while I stood by. Seeing her so bereaved, the people in the streetcar offered her their seats, and looked at me with reproach: why wasn't I doing something to relieve her grief? I stood grimly by, letting someone else extend help. I was playing into Mom's game of guilt, wanting to feel guilty, to reassure myself that I was feeling something, that I loved my brother. If I couldn't cry, I might as well make myself miserable. Meanwhile Mother, after warming up in the streetcar, rose to full performance by the grave, where she called out my brother's name in her beautiful voice. Her audience was the cemetery priest, who came to read from the Bible with the mien of a bored civil servant, and the always-present homeless. Some of those homeless were invalids, war veterans. They killed time squatting in the sun by the chapel, and when they spotted a mournful party they hurried over, so as not to miss their coliva and alms money. But in the case of my mother they strolled over leisurely, scratching and chatting, sure that they would be in time. My mother would give my brother the works.

Why did she force me to come with her, to face what I still couldn't face? Drenched in her own pain, why was she so myopic to mine? I asked her years later. She gave me a stupefied stare: "What would you have wanted to do? *Not* visit him? Let me go there alone, like your worthless father?" So much like the party! If someone at a political gathering dared ask a sensible question, the respective party activist would direct at them a similarly stupefied stare: "What do you propose we do? *This* instead of *that*? Like in the rotten capitalist West?"

That cemetery scene carved itself so deep in my memory that years later, as I attended burials in the United States, I was nagged by an unclear feeling, till I realized that I missed a sound from my childhood pilgrimages: the rumbling of trains. Our cemetery lay by the North Railway Station's freight terminal. Behind its walls, trains maneuvered and hooted. Against those noises, the cemetery bell clanged loudly, and its voice of stricken bronze tore at my heart. The main alley ran between chestnut trees, their trunks whitewashed to fight off pests, towards the chapel where bodies were left to lie in state. Against the trees rested the shovels and hoes that were used for digging graves. The grave diggers walked by, their shoes shiny with mud. There was decay in the air, but the trees were vigorous, and when the ripe chestnuts slammed down on the ground, their brown kernels popped out, polished and perfect. I tried to keep my thoughts on the chestnuts, so as not to picture what had happened to my brother's body, to the face I knew so well, under the ground. He'd been buried in an old suit of my father's, and carrying my penknife in his pocket. It was awful, odious, cruel beyond belief that he was not here, that we couldn't listen together to the hoot of the trains, for we had fantasized about traveling to Africa, Australia, the American West, and other forbidden places. Had I not felt so angry, so alone and frightened, I would have hugged Mom next to Pavel's grave: Mom, *I'm* here, you haven't lost everyone, and . . . maybe it's time you remembered that I love you. But there she went, saying my brother's name out loud: Pavel, Pavel! She opened the grille to the wrought-iron fence around the grave, and dropped down on her knees to talk to the earth, dressed in fresh flowers. My heart broke, but she was showing off. I fidgeted, and looked around for . . . Pavel, the way I always had, to share with him a quick glance, amazed at Mom's behavior.

The Communist dirges of grief for martyred comrades, which we were forced to sing in school, were identical to Mom's exhortations. The beyond-the-grave voices of Lenin and Stalin, the pledges to dead comrades, were the daily material of our official culture. We the lucky living were not grieving enough, not showing enough piety, not working hard enough, not appeasing the dead by exemplary actions.

So I had to do something to save myself, for no one else was going to save me. I stiffened and raged. In school, and at the cemetery. I raged against Mother, because *my* sadness and fear had never been her priority. I raged against my father for not being part of those trips, and for not having joined the Communist party. He would've then had access to the party shops, stocked with sophisticated medication, and maybe Pavel wouldn't have died. I damned them both for being self-obsessed, and unpractical.

Mom and I continued our hadj to the cemetery. One fall evening, we returned by bus because of an accident on the streetcar line. We got off in an unusual place, in front of Kretulescu Church, a gem of old Romanian architecture, and headed home past the former Royal Palace, a neoclassic pile of sandstone which now housed the National Art Museum. Ahead, despite the late hour, all seven floors of the Central Committee of the Romanian Communist Party building were brightly lit. Victory Avenue, named for our independence from the Turks, ran right past the RCP building. At the peak of Ceausescu's international fame, Richard Nixon, Gerald Ford, Jimmy Carter, Golda Meir, Charles de Gaulle would ride in motorcades down Victory Avenue, next to our dictator—but those glorious moments were still in the future. The Royal Palace's basement had been taken over by the party's administrative offices, and was also lit brightly. In both buildings, the Communists were at work—one could fault them for anything but laziness.

That basement was built high, with a row of little balconies hanging level with the stairs rising past the Kretulescu Church. A short young man with plump cheeks was leaning out of one little balcony. He wore an unbuttoned gray suit and a loosened tie, and was unimpressive except for being punishingly ugly. From between his pasty white cheeks jutted out a thin, foxlike nose, shading a blunt chin and lips that had a life of their own: twitchy, wormlike. I learned later that the man was a bad stutterer, which explained the tireless throb of his lips, as if he rehearsed with anguish his next spoken words. His hair, brown and wavy, was so rich that it soared off his head, like a nuclear mushroom cloud. His skin was pale and blotchy, his shoulders narrow and turned in. Yet there was a fierce defiance in him, instantly obvious. He stood up to the warm fall evening, dwarfishly short, like Napoleon, and his eyes, which he suddenly trained on me, were cold and frightening.

I was looking, without knowing it, at Nicolae Ceausescu. I didn't know anything about who he was, or that he would soon become the main visual fixture of Romania's life. In newsreels, on TV, in still photographs, and in person, his image would be fed to the public daily, giving speeches, inspecting worksites, laying grounds for new factories. Before I would defect, I would see him thousands, perhaps millions of times, until his appearances would blur in my psyche into one uninterrupted presence. After I defected I felt physically relieved from his ever-present foxlike nose, pouting cheeks, and piercing eyes. So, if I overdescribe him now, if I give you so many details of him, it's because I earned them. I got to know the man by heart.

Ceausescu scanned me with eyes so piercing that I felt X-rayed— by the way, one of his nicknames was Comrade X-ray. His hostility touched me as if it were a cold rod. What was frightening about him was that hostility, cold and unhesitant, ready to be aimed at anyone. I'd been raging at my parents for not protecting me, ranging from the loss of my twin to the slaps of the Securitate. But my rage did not compare to the alert and eager hatred I smelled in that individual. Hatred was his essence. I glanced away, noting that he grinned as our eyes broke contact, and there was something complacent in his grin. He'd made other people look away, and I was no exception. Nicolae Ceausescu, whose name I didn't know yet but whose appearance I could never erase, looked at me and Mom. In the same quietly insane way, he looked at other pedestrians passing by.

He was the soul and essence of a Securitate man. He was *it* far more than the officers who roughed me up. I didn't know it, but maybe I sensed it, for I took Mom's arm and we stepped faster across Victory Avenue, while he, like an apocryphal Caesar, remained standing on his balcony.

Ceausescu was then the secretary "in charge of party organization" for the whole RCP. The job sounds dull and clerical, but in fact was a top power position, for he handled the leadership's personal files. He operated as an arch-Securitate, above the standard Securitate and the other police institutions. Ceausescu had acceded to this peak of power as a longtime aide, confidant, and hatchet man to the party's supremo, General Secretary Gheorghe Gheorghiu-Dej.

So maybe, standing on his balcony that evening, he was musing about the changes in his life. Ceausescu was born on the Danube plain in a village of low huts with thatched roofs, the third of ten children in an alcoholic peasant's family. His siblings were cruel to him because he was runty and stuttered so badly. When nervous, little Nicolae spoke a lingo of his own, made of coughs and hiccups, intelligible to no one but himself. The area was one of Europe's poorest. At harvest time, the landowners forced the hired crop pickers to wear muzzles, like dogs, so they would not eat the crops. In peasant homes, sanitation was nonexistent; families urinated and defecated outside, shooing off hungry yard dogs. Husbands tyrannized their wives and offspring. Conflicts were settled by violence. During land feuds, neighbors were known to grab hoes and cut off each other's heads. The lower plain of the Danube, Ceausescu's native land, had learned violence from the Turkish raids, and corruption from the alien occupations. Woe to those born here who were disabled, weird, weak.

Ceausescu was not part of my destiny at the time, yet his life and development hovered over it. The orphans who had beaten Pavel and me in school were of his breed, and when I first heard him talk, I heard in his speech their angry illiteracy. He himself had done miserably in the village elementary school. He left his home at fifteen, during the great Depression, alone. He traveled to Bucharest by train without a ticket, squatting on a car roof. Thousands of Romanian peasants came to Bucharest then, carrying hopes and head lice, but no skills or money. In Bucharest, young Nicolae became an apprentice shoemaker. He met a peasant girl who like him had moved to the big city: his future wife Elena, already a Communist agitator. Both were arrested for distributing tracts for the outlawed RCP. It's amazing that illiterates like Nicolae and Elena chose a path as radical as Marxism, but that was their luck, and their merit. The RCP had less than a thousand members then, of whom half were ethnic Romanians; the other half were Jews, Hungarians, and urban intellectuals. The right wing called it a party of foreigners, and it was, in the sense that it was utterly subjected to Stalin.

That situation gave people like Nicolae a meteoric rise in the party: they didn't have to be literate, all they needed was to be tough and blindly loyal to their bosses. During World War II, many Communists were rounded up and locked away in the work camp of Tirgu Jiu. There, young Ceausescu became the protégé and confidant of party don Gheorghiu-Dej, the general secretary blessed by Stalin. At one time or another, Gheorghiu decided to make the comical stutterer into a top henchman, for after the war, he sent him to Russia, to the KGB's own school for cadre, the Frunze Academy. On his return from Frunze, Ceausescu was promoted to run the "party organization," the party's super-Securitate. When

I first saw him, Ceausescu was Gheorghiu's top enforcer, for he handled the files of the party's elite. He had their past at his disposal, and if he had their past, he could decide their future.

I didn't know anything about the enforcer yet. Like most Romanians, I had to reconstruct his biography later. When I saw him on that balcony, he had long since left behind the poverty of his youth. Now he was chauffered to work, and in his brightly lit office he walked on a thick soft carpet—perhaps because he and Elena had once walked barefoot, they would always love carpets; they collected them and gave them as gifts to foreign dignitaries—George Bush got one when he visited Romania as the U.S. vice president. But luxury would not relax the enforcer. Ceausescu believed in the Stalinist principle of "the sharpening of class warfare *after* the triumph of the revolution" (a principle that Mao was also fond of). Only a state of ongoing warfare justified the party's total control. Only a state of perpetual vigilance against "capitalist menace" justified arrests, searches without warrants, spying, interrogations. In 1948, Gheorghiu liquidated Romania's mid-level peasantry, replacing it with the chain gangs of collective farms. To that aim, he used machine guns and opened gulags. Ceausescu was then deputy minister for agriculture. He helped Gheorghiu murder the peasant class from which they were both issued; then they atomized the other classes, and recast them into an obediently militarized society. But all of a sudden, a key element fell out of that perfect equation. After Stalin's death, the Soviet monolith started to thaw. Youngsters went out into the streets of Budapest, shouting for the departure of the occupying Red Army. The Red Army flattened them under tanks, but a traditional political stance had reappeared: nationalism.

That gave Ceausescu and other younger Communist leaders pause for thought. In the Soviet colonies, the political equation had been: bully your own people, backed up by the Russians, in the name of a sacred Communist crusade. But the Hungarian uprising completely changed the colonies' consciousness. It was also wildly applauded in the West. The United States declared themselves the moral supporter of the Hungarian patriots. And without Stalin, Russia lost its aura of inscrutable righteousness. The Communist world reeled after Khrushchev's denunciation of Stalin's crimes. Ceausescu had noticed how Khrushchev had extricated himself from Stalin's crimes (on Stalin's orders, Khrushchev himself had liquidated the Ukrainian peasantry!), and launched "peaceful coexistence with the West," thus presenting himself as an attractive new option to the United States.

Ceausescu was digesting that lesson. Soon, he would succeed Gheorghiu at the helm, and would expose Gheorghiu's crimes, while claiming that he had always been a moderate, and even an anti-Russian— but for that, Ceausescu needed to lure onto his side the youngest generation, those who could be expected to face the Russian tanks. That was my generation.

Thus, we, the school children, the pubesent boys and girls, the kids, would soon know an easing of regulations. We would get to watch some American movies (carefully selected and edited), we would be dancing the Twist, and we would be told in school that we were *Romanians*—not faceless Communists without nationality, but "Romans historically surrounded by Slavs, Magyars, and Turks," a breed that survived countless occupations. We would eat it up. Ceausescu would entertain Richard Nixon, and keep us raving patriotically, like clockwork. I didn't know it yet, but frankly I couldn't have cared. I first had to deal with the Communism at home.

So. My parents could not protect me from the state, or from fate. But in a way, Pavel's death had also come from the state, for the pitiful sanitary situation was state-generated. As for our individual destinies, they were so influenced by the state's decisions that no other power, including God's, seemed to come into play. My parents could not protect themselves, let alone protect me. The state imposed its model onto our intimate lives: in our home, I watched a kind of tyranny of sadness establish itself, unconsciously patterned on Communism.

My mother became more and more controlling, critical, and unpredictably angry—at the same time, she started to declare her motherly love to me, in a way also reminiscent of the party's. "The party's love for our nation is like a mother's love" was a stock phrase of the regime. Mother told me, tensely, roughly, that she watched me so tightly because she loved me. She disapproved of my friends, did not let me go to the movies, bitched about my school performance without reason—I was a straight-A student, and though I missed over two months of school due to Pavel's death, I made them up and still finished among the top of my class. But she wasn't a pest just about school. Hungering for reassurance that I was there, that she hadn't lost me too, she invaded my life at the time when a young male cherishes most his autonomy and privacy. I had almost none of either. My physical time was my mother's. Forced to wait around for her so that I could be her escort, I missed out on games with friends, on roamings, on discoveries. She tried to make me an appendage, and nearly succeeded. The closeness she no longer had with my father, she refocussed on me. I sensed that there was something very off there, very dysfunctional, yet could not name it; there was no pop psychology in Communist Romania.

In essence, she behaved as if she was married to me, not to Dad. She forced me, not him, to share her problems. She directed her wifely complaints at me, not at him. "He," she said out loud, "was a lost cause."

She *prayed* that I would resemble her, not him, but took no responsibility that she'd chosen his seed, not another's, to produce her children. She used grandiose lines, smacking of the stage, about mother-son bonds, about life and love, duty and expectation. "I gave you life," she would tell me reproachfully, when I wouldn't respond to some other stimulus. Or she described epically how she gave birth to us, the twins. The pain, the pushing. In these loud preachings, my father's part was reduced to a minimum, and his image became one of weakness and truancy. An AWOL dad, even though he was still there.

Was he AWOL? To some extent. On a certain level, I realized, she treated him as a child, a shifty, cagey truant. It was hard not to believe her, so I called back to memory all I knew about my father that was strong and manly. Like the jail time: the man had to have some *cojones,* to deserve being put in jail, no? His opposition to the Fascist regime was real: he'd been a target of the Iron Guards, once beaten by them on the very steps of the Bucharest Law School; beaten along with him that day was his friend Eugene Ionesco, the future famous playwright. Dad wrote too, he spent days chained to a chair, fighting alone the battles of words that frightened many other men . . .

I was desperate to rebuild my father's image, but he gave me no help. He vanished into his work space, received phone calls that summoned him out of the house, disappeared. His evasiveness grew in step with her dominance, and his passivity with her hyperactivity. I watched her acting out, and him doing nothing about it, and felt like yelling: Shut her up, man! Hit her if you have to, or stuff her face with a pillow! I would have applauded him.

But incomprehensibly, he did nothing, although there was no risk, except that she might've hit him back; slapping a spouse was part of the East European scene, many saw it as no worse than spanking a child. Even more incomprehensibly, my dad seemed not to feel the need to talk to me, his surviving son. He did not once bring up Pavel's death, after giving me the brief news that it happened. He explained nothing about the widening rift between him and Mom. I kept expecting him to take me aside and give me some all-inclusive speech about the issues that haunted me, death, Mom's craziness, the Securitate, his inability to fight back the system: that especially, I felt, should've eaten him up—that he couldn't fight back and saw plainly that he couldn't. All I needed to hear was: "Listen, son, fate hit us bad, all three of us, so just now I don't have much to fight back with. But here's some understanding of what's going on. That too is a weapon, and I'll share it with you."

And really, I craved just the beginning: "Listen, son."

A statement of connection, of caring. Father to son.

It did not happen. When we were alone, which occurred rarely, he almost always turned the radio on, to listen to classical music, after a little lecture to me about music's value for a growing intellectual (me), and why didn't I know more about it, didn't I love it? Naturally, I hated classical music then, it was a wall behind which Dad was hiding. And I hated the enigma that he was. But above all, I was stunned that I meant so little to him, that I could be so invisible.

So, I reasoned, this was the way it was in my home. How was it elsewhere?

If I felt betrayed by my parents, I found out that betrayal was nothing new to my family. I need to explain the meaning of the Popescus' name. It reflects Romania's historic identity. "Popa" is priest in Romanian, so Popescu literally means "priestly." The country's nationhood was formed around the Orthodox church, the one institution that resisted the Turks' drive to convert us to Islam, or the Hungarians' attempts to make us Catholic. The name Popescu carries the same ring of prime ethnicity as Smith in England—too common to be noble, it's so popular (there are thousands of Popescus in Romania, most of them not related), that it has become synonymous with the nation itself.

Now with that kind of name, and since Romania had to fight in order to exist, my family had to have a military tradition. The Popescus were in the Romanian army forever, in all the wars, as soldiers, as officers. They chased out the Turks in 1877, reconquered Transylvania from the Hungarians in 1918, and Bessarabia from the emerging Soviet giant in 1922. And they passed on the pride and loyalty of the military, simplified into "God, king, and country," to the generation of my uncles, Dad's brothers.

Well, in the late 1930's that classic creed lost its credibility. King Carol II was a dissipated inefficient ruler, and the home-grown Fascists, the Iron Guard, were gaining ground. The army finally put down the Iron Guard rebellion of 1941—I'm proud that my own uncles defeated the Iron Guards, a clearly honorable cause now. But back then things were very confusing. The Iron Guards had started as defenders of the peasants from the ills of industrial capitalism. The peasants were devout Christians. Unlike in Germany, where Hitler had cowed the Christians into submission, in Romania any political movement except Marxism would have to claim the approval of the church, the institution of survival against Islam. The Iron Guards won over that part of the clergy eager to share in the political pie. Before decaying into sheer anti-democratic anti-Semitic hooliganism, the Iron Guards had the support of most intellectuals—my mom and dad, again, were brave enough to differ. Germany watched closely the evolution of Romania's Fascism. The Romanian army was traditionally anti-German, for it had fought Germany in World War I. But at Munich, England and France had let Hitler swallow up Czechoslovakia, so it was obvious that they could not protect Poland or Romania. In 1939, Hitler and Stalin signed their non-aggression pact, then Hitler moved and crushed Poland. In 1940, Stalin moved too: in June, he absorbed the Baltic states, in July he occupied Bessarabia, a fifth of Romania, and appeared poised to swallow the rest. The Russians had invaded Romania before, in 1812, 1848, 1877, and 1917—the last two times as allies! Since no Western power could help Romania protect its territory, the unsavory option was an alliance with Hitler, against Stalin.

Hitler wanted the alliance, for it gave him access to Romania's oil. Most Romanians viewed the alliance as temporary, just enough to get Bessarabia back. Besides, who was to say that Hitler wouldn't win the war? The Iron Guards felt that the situation had freed their hands: they conducted several murderous pogroms of Jews, assassinated key Christian leaders opposed to them, including one prime minister, then started an armed insurrection. The army wiped them out in a brief but bloody urban war. During the ensuing military dictatorship of Marshal Antonescu, many Jews living within the borders of the old kingdom of Romania were deprived of their businesses, and forced into work camps; yet most of them survived, resulting in a population of 428,000 after the war, the largest Jewish surviving population anywhere in Europe, except for Russia. That was because in 1942 Antonescu refused to carry out the final solution within Romania itself. However, many Jews, and also some Gypsies and other undesirables, were killed in Transnistria, by Romanian and German troops. Transnistria was a "holding area" of the Ukraine occupied and administered by Romania. There, in 1941–1942, a chilling 160,000 Jews, including many children, were killed by execution or starvation or general neglect, on Antonescu's orders or at the initiative of local commandants; the Antonescu regime claimed that those Jews had collaborated with the Soviet army. While in the old kingdom the regime was relatively mild, and Jews were often protected by their Christian associates, a schizophrenic regional genocide raged in Transnistria, and it remained unexposed after the war—I and my generation had absolutely no knowledge of it. The Communist regime put the lid on all information regarding both the genocide, and the salvation.

Fighting in advanced units at the front, my uncles were saved, thank God, from participating in that horror. They dealt with the horror of direct combat. As professional soldiers, they expected Hitler to be defeated, because he was fighting too many foes on too many fronts. Yet, the anti-Russian mood had carried Romania into the unwinnable war, so my uncles fought on the gelid shores of the Volga river, and witnessed cannibalism at Stalingrad, and after being captured, they rotted in Siberian camps. All of them understood that Romania would pay for its alliance with Germany, but no one, least of all my Marxist dad, expected total Soviet occupation. The deal was worked out by Churchill and Stalin in October 1944, in Stalin's Kremlin office. The suggestion came from Churchill, and is written about in his memoirs. "Mr. Chairman," said Churchill to Stalin, "let's not waste time speaking at cross-purposes. Let's settle about our affairs in the Balkans. . . . How would it be for you to have ninety percent dominance in Romania, for us to have ninety percent in Greece, and go fifty-fifty in Yugoslavia?" While this was being translated, Churchill jotted on a sheet of paper: Romania—Russia 90 percent, the others 10 percent. Greece—Great Britain 90 percent (in accord with USA), Russia 10 percent. Yugoslavia—50-50. Etc. As the sign of his agreement, Stalin ticked the paper with a blue pencil. Churchill mused, "Might it not be thought cynical if we disposed of these issues, so fateful to millions of people, in such an offhand manner? Let's burn the paper." "No, you keep it," said Stalin.

Meanwhile, Romania had joined the allies. A quarter-million Romanians died fighting the Nazis. Thousands of Romanians died in POW camps all over Russia. Thousands more came back to Romania, and were jailed again, by the Soviet-backed regime. Despite its sacrifice of lives, the royal army was compromised and humiliated. After fighting in the east, then in the west, my uncles came home and were kicked out of the army, as politically undependable. Their uniforms, olive once but now discolored from repeated washings, were recut into civilian suits. Their shiny epaulettes and golden buttons were torn off; my brother and I got to play with them, the vestiges of their military pride. One uncle, Nicu, the eldest of the thirteen Popescu brothers and sisters, stayed on in Russian POW camps until the mid-fifties. One of my character-forming scenes was his return from the POW camp.

So. Bucharest's North Railway Station, on a summer day.

Here was the family, dressed in clothes from before the war, un-stylish and unfitting since everyone shed weight, some as much as twenty pounds. The station's platforms were crowded with knots of people, tightly staying together, afraid of those they were welcoming, the incoming soldiers: they were no longer soldiers, they were raggedy strangers with wolves' stares. Our family clung together like refugees. So did the other families waiting for a father, son, brother, or husband. They craned their necks towards the end of the platforms, where the tracks wove into and out of each other, and the railway signals lifted and dropped.

One of my aunts, Mia, tried to speak cheerfully, to lift the family's spirits, for no one knew how much of my uncle was going to come back— maybe only half of him? Maybe just a trunk without arms and legs, rolled along in a wooden cart? Mia predicted what Nicu would ask for when he got home. Eggs. In a letter from camp, he wrote that an egg was the rarest delicacy in the camp's diet. Mia was the one married to the priest who crossed the Danube swimming. She stayed behind, with their two sons, my first cousins, hoping that they would be allowed to leave the country sometime, to join him wherever he was (at this time, he was still in one of Tito's prisons, but she didn't know that). She was the oldest of the Popescu girls, four of them. Of the seven Popescu boys, four were soldiers. Because of the war, the soldiers hadn't married; there were no wives in that little crowd. But the sisters were there, ready to fill the place of the missing wives.

My father was there too; he hadn't gone to war. Being of the left, he now seemed like a harbinger of the Soviet occupation. How would he look Nicu in the eyes, if Nicu came back crippled? What would Nicu say when he learned that Dad himself had served a spell in the Commie jail? He was there only months to Nicu's years of camp, but still he came back "smelling of rats." I didn't know what rats smelled like, but I knew how bad my father smelled when he came back.

The heat hazed the shiny jumble of the tracks, and from the shimmering haze a sooty engine finally appeared. The train, overloaded, with men sitting on the car tops, hurtled over the tracks, clacking from its steel wheels. The breath of the crowd, wheezed out of hundreds of chests. The train came in slowly, like in a movie edited for maximum suspense. Even before it stopped, men started jumping off, and on the platforms the waiting relatives, mostly women, sprang forward. Their movement was amazing, frantic yet hesitant, for the men who returned had changed, had lost weight, or arms or legs. On the platforms, hearts started pounding with fear instead of excitement. And . . .

And the crying started. The women's crying at the sight of what was left of the soldiers. Women's hands touched empty sleeves, or crutches. Lips ready to kiss winced in revulsion, but kissed anyway. Hugs were stopped in midair, then the families went ahead and hugged what was left. And more and more people were crying. Those who returned cried too.

Everyone was crying. Wives and sisters and daughters kept embracing old uniforms, whitened by washing, and kept squeezing crutches and empty sleeves . . .

My uncle was among the last to get off. He came down the steps of a car, very carefully, not because he was crippled, but because he was exhausted and fragile. Before the war he'd been a stocky man with a round head, a healthy neck, a confident jaw, and smart eyes. Now he was so thin that he floated in his uniform, and his head seemed ready to drop off the thin fulcrum of his fleshless neck. His eyes had lost their luster; they were dull, their stare was unfocussed. His cheeks were gaunt, his face baked brown by that foreign sun. He took off his cap, a soldier's cap without rank markings, and waved it above his head.

Only then the family realized that he was there, and though he was moving so slowly, he wasn't crippled. He was whole, but a shadow of the man he had been.

The family rushed forward.

So came my uncle back from the war, the last of our family to return. For the Popescus, the war was finally over.

So came the Romanians back, into a country once again occupied by her worst enemy after the Turks. The Russians.

The family trooped out of the station, and piled into a *birja,* a one-horse hackney. At the end of the war Bucharest still had horse-drawn hackneys, and because of the gasoline shortage they were far more reliable than taxis. The mangy horse pulled the *birja* out of the station, and my uncle Nicu glimpsed the streets, the same streets the army had marched on under festive banners, off to invade Russia. Now the buildings were gutted from the air raids, and the roadways were pitted. The traffic was a mess of old cars, hackneys, and heavy, wildly pitching Russian trucks. There were Russians in uniforms on the sidewalks, Russians riding in *birjas,* Russians in cars and trucks, all looking so healthy compared to our returning soldiers. My uncle swallowed, his Adam's apple painfully sticking out of his neck, then addressed the family in an uncertain voice: So . . . how was it with *them*? His chin, which had become pointed, signalled towards the Soviets in the streets.

The sisters chirped that it wasn't so bad. The Russians had never seen toilets that flushed, so they flushed them over and over. Most of them didn't know what telephones or bikes were. They were so funny, ha ha. They didn't mention the rapes, the drunken shootings, the requisitioning of houses by throwing whole Romanian families out into the street. Or the stealing of watches and wedding bands at gunpoint, and the arresting and disappearance of thousands of people. At intersections, the *birja* passed traffic agents: Russian-enlisted women in uniforms, with PPS automatics slung over their shoulders, fiercely waving two little red flags clutched in their fists. Their faces were round, their tightly braided hair balled into buns and squeezed under their caps, their eyes narrowed with the importance of their mission. When those girls raised an arm to stop a line of vehicles, the sleeves of their uniforms would drop, revealing on their forearms wristwatches stolen from Romanian civilians. Sometimes two or three watches strapped on top of each other.

No one commented about the watches, but my uncle was soon to learn to bolt his door against lootings. The Russians behaved like medieval Tartar raiders. They were funny, yes: they broke into high schools, smashed open jars preserving lizards and other little animals, and drank the formaldehyde, mistaking it for alcohol—as a consequence, a number of school principals were arrested and charged with attempting to murder Soviet soldiers. Romania was a wine-producing country and drunkenness was a fairly familiar sight, but not the Russians' kind of drunkenness, their frenzied need to imbibe alcohol as if drink were oxygen. The Russians drank tragically, cried, pulled guns on each other, and then danced and kissed, and again ranted and cried, as if through drink they saw something terrifying within themselves. It was terrifying, and we had become part of it. "United forever," as the banners raised on the gutted buildings proclaimed. "Betrayed forever," my uncle Nicu once commented to me. Yes. That was it. Betrayed by the West, which had promised protection, betrayed by the new allies, who had promised to respect our ways and customs. And betrayed by our own leaders. Antonescu had grossly, misjudged our military odds against Russia. King Michael had bravely switched Romania to the allies' side, but that, alas, had not redeemed us from the Soviet occupation. The Communists had stepped into power without making any protective premarital agreement with the Soviets; they were straight yes-men.

So betrayal had always followed my family. My uncles, the loyal soldiers, were betrayed. My parents, the idealist liberals, were betrayed. I was haunted by a question: who exactly had betrayed them? The respective political leaderships, meaning the state? Or was it the country herself that exacted such faith and sacrifice, then perversely devoured her most devoted patriots? The Romanians explained it all away as "our doomed placement on the map," or as "geography is history," but I found that painfully incomplete. The Czechs had not fought, and thus had saved their lives. The Bulgarians had declared war, but never raised the armies to fight it. Unegotistically, pragmatically, they had not bled through fights among brothers. I admired them. Maybe I just yearned subconsciously for a united family.

At any rate, Nicu the soldier came back, already too old to start his own family. He never married, but became a civil engineer and worked assiduously and without complaints, never paid well, never fully appreciated. But with his chin up, and most often smiling. In time, he would start a special relationship with me. I craved his stories of war and suffering, of the prisoners' comradeship and hope for returning to the beloved land that had sent them off to fight. Even though he'd been the one hurt most, he didn't show it, and when I was with him I didn't feel shame. I should not have felt shame at any other time, I was not responsible for our past thirty years of history, but I could not help it, I was too young and vulnerable.

Shame was an amazing feeling: it was endlessly variable. Like Proteus, the Greek prophet who could slip into any shape imaginable, shame could hide inside any other feeling: pain, loss, fright, confusion, lust, love. It could enter them and become their true substance. I was ashamed that my brother had died and that I couldn't do anything about it. I was ashamed to fear the regime I lived under. I was confused about what to hope for, how to live, what to do, and felt shame for my confusion. My hormones were stirring, and I was ashamed. I loved my parents, but found them weak and unrealistic, and contemptible, and was ashamed. Shame is painful at all ages, but it's the worst in youth. All my other feelings drowned in the morass of shame. After a while, shame seemed deserved. I was captive, I was weak. Look at me.

The shame was present in everything, it was the fabric of daily life. Even things by definition grotesque were rendered more so by the all-encompassing shame. For instance, there was no toilet paper. A common amenity before the war, it had now completely disappeared. We wiped ourselves with little squares of newspaper cut and laid out by Mother in an old soap box set next to the toilet bowl. Before using those little squares, I examined them. They were from *Scinteia,* the Spark, the Communist party's daily; from *Adevarul,* the Truth, voice of the party-controled trade unions; or from *Munca,* the Labor, voice of the collective farms. I wiped my ass with rough paper that hurt and left imprints of cheap ink. With the smiling faces of workers, of Soviet army officers inspecting the preparedness of their Romanian comrades, with "young pioneers," the Soviet boy scouts of whom I was one, with Romanian volunteers in the Korean War, on the North Korean side, of course. I wiped my ass with the leaders of the Soviet bloc, with party boss Gheorghiu, with his hench-man Ceausescu, with Khrushchev, with Chairman Mao, with Kim Il Sung of North Korea—I wiped and wiped with Comrade Kim, for he stayed in power forever. I wiped with Fidel Castro, who made it finally into the toilet paper era. And with their speeches, tirades, harangues, I wiped on, mixing the ink of their propaganda with my waste matter which, lab-analyzed, would've revealed no connection between my diet and our propaganda's claims of prosperity. I wiped with Khrushchev pounding his shoe at the United Nations, with the Bay of Pigs fiasco, with the U-2 spy-plane affair. So did my entire hometown, my whole country, the Soviet bloc. What our minds could not avoid and our mouths could not condemn, finally found its way to our rears. Toilet paper did not reappear in stores until the sixties. As for hygienic pads for women, vaginal douches, deodorant sprays, mouthwashes, they belonged to science fiction.

Our lack of basic amenities may seem unimportant, but it wasn't. Identity included the state of the plumbing. Everything else in our lives was like what we used for toilet paper: cheap, secondhand, odd, shoddy, gimcrack. Our clothes were drab, ill-fitting, our homes cluttered, unaired, ramshackle. Our manners had become rough, impatient, desperate. Want, fear, pent-up anger inflected our words and actions. There was a Communist style of doing things, a Communist tone that had been slapped onto all our activities. That tone was loud yet insincere, like an actor declaiming instead of speaking. Lunch in school or factory cafeterias was eaten to *Scinteia*'s editorial for the day, read out loud like verses from the Bible. Or some party apparatchik would bounce up on the podium (all public places had podiums and mikes, to improvise at the drop of a hat a solidarity rally or a people's trial), and start haranguing the eating crowd. In seaside resorts, a local party zealot might grab the mike and boom at the tanned vacationers, "I hear you chatting about tanning creams, but what about Vietnam's fight against the Yankee aggressor? D'you think your Vietnamese comrades are lying in the sun now? Under showers of bombs from U.S. pirate planes, d'you think they're tanning themselves?" The party zealots were never tanned, but their eyes were lit with ideological inspiration. Their pale lips spat fire into the mikes. When they were finished, no one was chatting about tanning cream any more. No one was chatting, period. What about Vietnam?

Well, what about it? Those people were on vacation, for Marx's sake!

Against that endless deafening ruckus, my amazing little mind found the power to ask some questions. Like, how did Marx come by the concept that only the workers, whose lives he never shared, were to be the leaders of all mankind? Lenin, who was never part of a commune (he could've learned a thing or two from America's hippies), how did he know that Communism was the answer to history's earlier misses? Based on what did Stalin decree that after Communism succeeded, it should intensify its witch-hunt, rather than relax it? How did Mao figure that China needed a cultural revolution? How did those founding fathers know that it was key to make new enemies, now that the old ones were dead? That purges should be organized, conspiracies exposed, old comrades branded as traitors and jailed or shot, so that the party's ranks could be constantly cleansed, and the official thought reproclaimed and rededicated? All those red Messiahs, how did they decide what history's course should be, before they proceeded to put it in practice, at the cost of millions of lives?

How did they *know*?

The answer was simple. I figured it out, and it froze me: they didn't know, Communism ran on faith. The leaders were mystics in disguise, the societies they built were theocracies, atheistic in rhetoric only. Communist states were founded on dogmas that could not be questioned. They were monkish in their frugality and discipline, and puritanical in their view of sex and the arts. The leaders were presented to the crowds as anointed with the working class's faith. They lived lives of mystery, and of supposed sainthood. Not surprisingly, those secular gods were often rulers for life. Both Lenin and Stalin died in office, and were embalmed and enshrined under glass. Mao too remained in power until his death at eighty-three. These pharaohs ruled vast populations amazingly tolerant of hardships, and almost pathologically loyal. Yet when those loyalties finally became spent, those masses carried out change through confused and bloody revolutions. But when the revolutions triumphed, the practical aspects of the change were never sufficiently debated, nor were the new leaders tested for competence. There was no gradual transformation, no maturing of older structures or concepts, but simply a giant inebriated bang, deemed to have achieve a miracle. From private ownership to total state ownership. Just like that, in one blind sweep.

After that, the millions of toilers toiled again, as poor and hungry as before, but content because they'd finally denied blind faith to their old gods. So they were extending blind faith to the new ones, the same blind faith, just worded differently. Until the next big shake up.

What kept them going in between? The new words—another proof that Communism was a mystical society, in which the *word* had absolute reality.

And the words were effective. How many times did I try, feeling that my teenage mind was cracking from the stress, to connect those words to reality, to find their material proof in the world around me. The brotherhood of working men. The equality of us all. Time and time again, I thought I'd glimpsed, in an achievement, in an event, in the person of a leader, the proof that the words had substance, and they were working mysteriously to expand that substance, and actualize us all!

Of course, words cannot acquire reality just through mass hypnosis. But the masses were willing, and the alternative was repression. Hungering for justice, half the planet had rushed to follow the fathers of Communism into a world of words. Into a system that collapsed seven decades later without delivering on equality or any other promise. It took seven decades for the Russians to wake up from that daze, to see through the words, and to realize that they'd been had. As for China, only the students awakened there, in 1989, and that wasn't enough. While start-ing a noisy reversion to capitalism, politically China remains asleep in the bed shaped for her by Mao.

In Romania, Communism was an exportation at gunpoint, compli-ments of the Red Army. Thus, because our revolutionary clamor was fake, what did the party do? It turned up the volume. It built a country of yell-ers pitted against the yelled-at. I remembered those harangues, many years later, as I engaged in some trivial activity; my neck would suddenly tighten, and my heart would pound, expecting one of those raucous voices to yell at me: Comrade Popescu! What kind of nonsense are you engaged in? Stand and be counted! Quick march! To your battle station! Since early childhood, my being had integrated those yells and their message: the need for vigilance and readiness. Any time I was doing something for myself, something unrelated to the cause, my body anticipated the ad-monition: Comrade Popescu! You're cheating on your duty! Wake up! The enemy is about to strike!

Now, to imprint its youngest citizens with Communist dutifulness, the state had evolved a complex indoctrination program. In elementary school, Pavel and I were automatically enlisted in the Young Pioneers, the Red boy scouts. Every week, gathered in the classroom if it was rain-ing or in the schoolyard if it was sunny, we formed a square, and looked up sharply at our detachment leader, a kid of eight, or ten, or twelve—I was a pioneer till fifteen, when, again automatically, I was enlisted in the next level, the Young Communist League. The detachment leader in-spected our formation, raised his right arm in front of his face, and in-toned, "For the cause of Marx and Lenin, be ready!" We chorused with ardor, "We're always ready!" A trumpet bugled a three-note call, a drum beat twenty strokes, and off we were to gather garbage to be recycled, paint a wing of the school, sort out gifts to be sent to "liberation move-ments" blockaded by the U.S. imperialists (North Korea, Cuba, Vietnam), or be bussed to the fields to help the socialist peasants harvest the crop. It didn't matter what it was, it was glorious; the few kids not in our ranks (Radu and Sandu, my cousins, sons of the Danube-swimming defector, were not) never knew what revolutionary raptures they missed. The Red scouts' uniforms were identical to the Soviet Red scouts': white stiffly starched shirts, crimson red scarves, badges featuring the red star, Lenin's profile, and the hammer and sickle. We carried fiery red flags, and sang, "We dance, we play / We celebrate the Soviet first of May . . . ," or, "Smashed chains are left behind our march / The bourgeois evil legacy we'll parch . . . ," or, this a tune from before the Sino-Soviet rift: "Moscow and Peking, forward we shall go/ And make the tyrants know . . ." Etc. etc.

The undesirables, thanks to their banishment, benefitted from a degree of mental freedom. We, the youngest chosen, were at the fore of the delirium. Pavel and I, beaten as class enemies when we were seven, were now "in" at nine, at eleven, at thirteen, so we reacted with zeal to that "we," worked as often as possible into the rhymes and the refrains. "We" was just great—it could mean anything, from two people to two hundred million people, the much quoted population figure of the Soviet Union. The muscularity of those numbers dazzled our minds freshly acquainted with math, while the cadence of the march flushed our cheeks. To hell with being an "I," an individual, here was the revolution's "we," and tramping along inside the "we" were millions of millions.

I finally understood what got the Russians to follow Lenin. After poverty, strikes, famine, the pain and disgrace of World War I, the feeling of being abandoned by the occult Romanov dynasty, the Russians were shown onto a high road with well posted signs: We'll stop thinking! We'll march with the party! We'll forget the sorrow of being one, we are now a mass bound together by class infallibility! There is nothing but we, whoever's outside we doesn't exist! I have to say that it worked, at least as long as we were on parade. The class bond was felt as we poked the nearest comrades with our elbows, and the physical touch plus the unison of the voices and the robotized pounding of feet produced the delusion that a crowd was not a crowd, but a family, a home, a way of life.

As Young Pioneers we got plenty of parades. We carried not only flags, but also the portraits of Marx and Lenin and the native bosses, and effigies of the rogues of the day: JFK was a bad one, he ordered heroic little Cuba back in its place! Before the parades we starched our clothes, shined our shoes, and polished our trumpets. But especially, we prepared by anticipating a feast of the senses. Instead of studies, loud shouting. Instead of teachers' droning voices, drums and trumpets and loudspeakers in Victory Square, where the bleachers of the party politburo were set up to review the passing of half of Bucharest's population. And at the end of the day, fireworks.

So raise high the flag. Our hair was pasted down by wet brushes, our cheeks pink, our knees well-scrubbed instead of brown from crawling or playing soccer. On our way to the parade's rallying points, older people smiled at us: Commies or not, kids were nice to see, particularly when clean and excited. Our flags looked so new, so pure against the peeling facades and shabby storefronts of Bucharest's streets. Our little river of pink faces reached a main boulevard, and flowed into a tributary of adults in blue workers' outfits, who greeted us waving oversized hammers and wrenches, made of cardboard. The tributary absorbed us, then flowed into a much wider stream, rolling slowly along the next main boulevard. The side streets were jammed with other marching columns, ready to pour into the main stream. We saw miners with their pit helmets, with pickax on their shoulders, and slogans: More Red Coal for Our Red Future; in its natural state, the coal wasn't red, but never mind. We saw steel workers, railwaymen, weavers, loggers, builders of dams to harness the mountain rivers into power for our factories and schools and hospitals and collective farms. We saw our brave military, on flowery floats whose engines groaned ominously: under their flowers, they were disguised tanks. Our soldiers stood on them in fraternizing stances with the Soviet army, and with the raggedy guerrilla forces of "anti-U.S. liberation movements." We saw our socialist peasants carrying oversized paper breads, and balloons shaped like giant potatoes, tomatoes, and peppers; they tugged at the strings floating above them, ready to show God that the Communists had built heaven on earth. We saw scientists in lab gowns, teachers, doctors and nurses in hospital frocks carrying posters in which the red injection of Communism resurrected the world from a gray capitalist coma.

Wasn't this gorgeous? Didn't it put its message across marvelously? We had started the morning as kids, but we were kids no more. We were fighters for the bright future among millions of other fighters like us, we were the vanguard of progress.

To organize and keep such a huge show on schedule, exceptional security measures were taken. There were soldiers lining the main avenues, along which the giant snakes of people crawled all morning, towards the distant bleachers. There were police detachments by the truckload, plainclothes police and Securitate combat troops, recognizable by the blue patches hemmed in red sewn on the collars of their uniforms. And there were, or so went the rumor, individual Securitate agents almost anywhere, mixed in the crowds, modestly lifting posters and banners, though under their clothes they carried their automatics, which they would whip out and use against any "imperialist provocation." Bursts of automatic fire could be loosed at any time by those unseen agents, but of course they wouldn't do that if we all behaved, if we gave them no reason to act. But they were there. Or maybe they weren't, but we feared that they were, and that was enough. We behaved ourselves. We wanted to look happy, to feel happy, to think that we were loved by our leaders, and cared for by them. Which was exactly what the leaders wanted us to feel, and to express through our cheers and smiles.

To help us feel cared for, the leaders ordered extraordinary gestures of attention for the public. There were portable restrooms distributed all along the crowds' routes, Red Cross tents set up on the lawns of public buildings and in parks (the Red Cross was the only official display of the cross ever), and ambulances stationed at crossroads, with paramedics ready to handle anything from sunstroke to heart failure. Along the parade route, there were stands after stands with hot dogs, garlic sausages, rolls, soft drinks, fruit, sweets, cigarettes, beer, all low priced, to keep up the crowd's energy with quick shots of carbohydrates, protein, sugar, and nicotine. Gymnasts in leotards climbed up on their floats to entertain us, forming human pyramids which ingeniously spelled Communist slogans. Hosts of balloons and pigeons were released above the crowds. And while the millions marched on—every May 1, the day of solidarity with all the workers on the planet, or November 7, the anniversary of the Soviet revolution, or August 23, our "liberation" by the Soviet army—factories were idle, fields deserted, social services shut down. The trains and streetcars didn't run. Hoes and axes, plows and fishing nets were stored away. The schools were closed too, yippee! Millions of dollars worth of productive work were squandered. But that was why we had a planned economy that included "planned losses." There would be enough for all of us, in Communist heaven.

The payoff for those mass processions was the passing in front of the bleachers. It was about five minutes of super-crowded shuffling, creeping forward, with the lethal midday sun drenching us in sweat, but with our banners, slogans, and flowers up and waving. From the highest bleachers waved and grinned our mysterious leaders. There they were. They existed. And we, sweaty and crowded and tired and smiling and shouting, we existed for them too, for a few minutes.

Our contact with our leaders was so minimal that every chance of seeing them in the flesh, even a phony one, filled in for the normal rapport between a nation and its leadership. I padded my feet across that square many times, as a kid, as a teenager, and I'll tell you that once there, somehow, I felt happy. And yet I hated the men in those tall bleachers—apart from Ana Pauker and, much later, Elena Ceausescu, they were always only men. I hated them with a passion every day, but not on May 1, or August 23, even though August 23 recalled even more strongly the defeat of those Popescu soldiers and priests. But I was part of "this" history. In step with it, I passed the bleachers grinning and cheering.

To the right of the politburo's bleachers were lower ones for the party's mid-range dignitaries, some of whom had stood in the tall ones at the previous May 1 parade but were down here because of demotion or retirement; such table placements were usually the only way for us to make guesses about the regime's inner fights and regroupings. To the left there were other lower bleachers, colorful and different for they contained the foreign diplomats and press correspondents. Their attitudes conveyed interesting messages. When they were friendly, Communism was in a state of detente with the West. When they were grim, the cold war was back on.

Most often though, a phony warmth exuded from the bleachers, while a more genuine one wafted up from us, from below. The parades were our *panem et circenses,* so we, like ancient Rome's poor, were momentarily happy. The bosses in the bleachers, the nation's toughies, had us well in hand. Few of them were workers, Romania's brand of Marxism had been enforced with the best available local material, the dispossessed peasants. Those who bent to exhaustion in fields, or bloodied their feet on the Carpathians' rocks grazing sheep, those had responded with ardor to the call. They came to town, switched from embroidered folk costumes to gray suits and black shoes that tortured their knotty toes, learned how to flick on electric lights, how to shave with razors instead of scythe blades sharpened on stones, how to take streetcars to work, how to read party brochures, how to shout at rallies. In the city they earned in a month what they earned in their villages in a year. The harshly square minds of the Romanian peasants were excellent soil for the new doctrine. Their natural possessiveness and violence were ideal for party vigilance. And their self-hate, unsuspected by romantic bourgeois sociologists, made them determined executioners of their own class. 85 percent of the Romanian peasants were forced to surrender their lands to the collective farms, and the enforcer of that process was Ceausescu. The

West would only wake up to his anti-peasant terror in the eighties, when he bulldozed seven thousand ancient villages, to replace them with "agro-industrial complexes." Of Ceausescu's victims, the peasants were always the first, and the last.

I was sixteen when I saw Ceausescu again, in the bleachers, standing close to boss Gheorghiu, whom he was to succeed soon. He'd grown into his face somewhat, and acted less gauche. His wormy lips twitched less, his ears didn't stick as far out from his skull. He was still very ugly— many other leaders had been prettified by the good life. The portly Gheorghiu-Dej looked okay now, an olive-faced, paunchy grandad of the Mediterranean variety. But Ceausescu was still an animal, or if you will, an alien. His X-ray eyes were not human. Standing so close to our noisy adulation, he stared coldly, yet seemed lost in thought. I would see that abstract look on his face again when he was in power: receiving ovations while he, alone in his mind, planned some new move that would mess with the lives of millions. He had reason to be reflective, boss Gheorghiu had cancer, a secret Ceausescu was part of, and he was next in line.

As his opportunity was about to bloom, Ceausescu pondered the implications of detente for the small nations. Stalin was dead. The Russians (fools) had withdrawn their troops from Romania, in thanks for how loyal the Romanians had acted during the Hungarian uprising. It was just an act. And now Khrushchev had screwed up in Cuba. Romania's nationalism could be revived. Ceausescu pondered the example of Romania's medieval heroes: Stephen the Great, Michael the Brave, Vlad the Impaler had used Turkey's temporary weakness to build reigns of utmost authority, and had profited from the generosity of the West as well. That formula could be repeated, though it was tricky and fraught with personal danger. Ceausescu did not plan to be deposed by Soviet-supported rivals any more than the medieval princes planned to have their stuffed hides stuck on spikes in Istanbul. Most of those princes failed their balancing act. Would he be lucky enough not to fail his?

Rumors were already being spread by the Securitate, presenting the enforcer as an ardent patriot. One rumor had it that Ceausescu had stood up to Khrushchev, resisting Khrushchev's orders to integrate Romania's economy with Russia's. There was another rumor, about an official report of that quarrel lost in Washington by a distracted Romanian diplomat. Thus the Americans realized Ceausescu's potential as an ally. That seemed to explain why U.S. Vice President Nixon visited Romania in those days, while America had previously shown no interest in Romania. Ceausescu liked Nixon: tense, ambitious, uptight, Nixon corresponded to Ceausescu's idea of a statesman.

So, things were promising. If only he could dry up that old gunpowder, and fire it again. Nationalism. Was there enough of it left in the Romanians? Could the party's arch-sleuth heat it up and pour it red hot into the mold of a successful policy, so that he himself would collect all the rewards, including the capital one, rule for life?

Ceausescu didn't know. And I, marching past the bleachers, didn't know that I would be a published writer, that my second novel, a bestseller, would unintentionally help Ceausescu's nationalism, and that I would ultimately have to choose between lending my writing to the nationalist adventure or defecting. I was writing poetry and short stories now. They were at first just an escape into an unreal world, unpoliced by the Securitate or by Mother. Then that unreal world began to fascinate me: once inside it, I had enormous powers. I started to like writing for itself, and fearfully realized that I might become a writer, like Dad.

But I didn't worry about that much, that was the future. Here and now, even though I didn't do it seriously yet, writing helped me. It made it easier to be alone, easier to miss Pavel, easier to tolerate rage or shame. I remember being fourteen, and sixteen, and eighteen, and walking around all keyed-up and bristling with inner rage. My neck was taut, my chest tight, my joints throbbed with tension, as if all of me had mutated into a living scream of outrage. I looked at everything through a grid of hostility, answered everyone in a flat, unfriendly voice, and lived entrenched in my own thought, which was negative and distrustful. But when I wrote, all that changed. I could afford to be trusting, even. And I could afford to understand what I had lost. Before Pavel died, we both fell back onto twinhood, finding protection and being soothed. We were different from everyone else, and we relished the wonder of being identical. I was like Pavel and he was like me, and to have two of us was like a guarantee that we could survive the world. We operated in perfect synch, knowing that what was good for one was good for the other. Against the absurdity of the world, I had that other me.

Now, I had an abstract brother, somewhat sad, somewhat pained, not as warm, not real. Writing.

Surprisingly, my mother encouraged my desire to write. More than encouraged it. She got excited at my first poems, imitations of the classics, and decreed me a born talent. I would be a *great writer*. But of course, I had to do the work. Her encouragement was grandiose, and came with the usual dose of self-directed superlatives. "You got your talent from me," she declared, and if I mentioned that my father wrote too, she would punish me: "That bastard who abandoned you?" Dad had moved out, to the apartment of another woman—later I learned that she was a long-term mistress. A few days into his new life, he collapsed from a perforated ulcer.

He was rushed to the hospital and operated on. I knew nothing about it until one of his writer friends came over to our apartment, got me out into the street under a pretext, and told me that Dad wanted me to come see him at the hospital. I went, fighting shades of déjà vu, expecting to meet my brother's ghost. Looking awful, Dad lay in bed in a small ward packed with literary friends, some notorious. Zaharia Stancu, dean of the agrarian novel and president of the Romanian Writers Guild, was there. So was Aurel Baranga. The country's best playwright (the regime's too), Baranga was then the only one who blew a measure of life into the characters prescribed by official ideology. All these men had risen within the strictures of the regime, far higher than Dad. Different from them but familiar and real to me, my uncle Nicu the soldier was also there, pale, worried; he loved Dad. And a woman, the mistress: youngish, with short dark hair. By his bed, she smoked like a fiend, and moved around the hospital bed with a fierce expression. She too was an actress, and seventeen years younger than Dad. He was out of it, barely talking, spitting a kind of green bile in an enamelled medical bowl, looking like he might not survive.

I expected to meet him face to face. I had even naively pictured him softened by ailment and ready to admit his past inattention to me, pledging that if he made it he would make up for it. When he left my mom, I wasn't surprised, deep down I even approved; he and Mom were not made for each other, all I wanted was my dad *for me*. But he opened his eyes, saw me by the bed, said nothing, just moaned, and closed his eyes again. Angrily, I uttered, "I have to go," and stepped out. The woman hurried out into the lobby after me; she wore pointed high heels whose thukk-thukk I heard as they stabbed the hospital's linoleum floor. Staring at me with burning curiosity, she introduced herself, babbled something about this not being the right way to meet, then asked why I was leaving so fast, was I fearful of my mother? How did my mother succeed in cowing

Dad and me so totally?—she said it pretty much in those words. For a second, I thought I hadn't heard her well. Then my blood rose to my face, and she, maybe fearing that I might explode, took a step back, and mouthed, "Radu told me . . ."

He *told her*. His first name on her lips sounded strange in the fashion of illicit discoveries: I didn't know this creature existed, yet she referred to Dad as to an intimate acquaintance.

I did not explode. I turned and left, feeling almost like when that Securitate officer had asked me about my dead brother. So. He had revealed what went on in our family to his mistress. He had complained about his wife to this other woman, implicating me too, describing me. I thought I could kill him. I don't care if you're sick or even die, I'll never see you again, you bastard, was what I pledged silently. I held that pledge for almost two years. As I crossed the road towards a bus station, a taxi disgorged a giant of a man in front of the hospital, a friend of Dad's, of course. Geo Bogza, former surrealist extraordinaire, then maestro of social reportage, now standard-bearer of propaganda reportage.

Thus, I couldn't protest when Mom told me that Dad had abandoned me, which was both cruel and not entirely accurate. He had done almost worse than that, he had abandoned my dignity to the malice of my mother's rival and replacement. He had transformed me into an item in his complaints to her: Honey, I've got this gorgon of a wife, you should see what she's doing to my son, poor kid . . . and he's so messed up, he lost his twin brother . . . I imagined him talking of me as a stranger would, babbling to that woman so he could reach a completely selfish goal: to get laid. He had described our family damnation to this stranger perhaps in bed, both of them naked. He had transgressed in a fashion that astounded me more than my mother's excesses. As a mother, she was tyrannical and possessive and egotistical, yet faithful, fixed in her life by her devotion to her own blood. As a father, he, the principled intellectual, was a dispenser of semen. I found out that he'd been unfaithful to Mom many times before, and I had no doubt that he would act the same to his new wife. She was younger, but not really young, mid-thirties. She had no children and realistically could not expect children from him, even though they were eventually married; self-absorbed, difficult, impatient, he wouldn't have suffered another baby crying at night, needing a bottle, a pacifier, its diaper changed, not in the narrow space of another Communist-built apartment. Besides, she was an actress, and he was finally coming into his own as a theater critic, an intimidatingly authoritative one, applying the party line with all the fury of his young days. Her goal in a union with him was not a child, but him and the benefits he represented.

But, you will ask, who exactly were my parents, that they lived and behaved so strangely? What strange circumstances had formed them as young people?

I think an answer is in order.

Paradoxically, my parents were formed during one of Romania's best times. In the early thirties, the country was whole, replenished with Transylvania and Bessarabia, which made her one of the biggest European nations.

In social life, economy, and the arts, that growth produced brilliant effects. The economy boomed. Romanians became daring, enterprising, cocky. Heretofore unknown, they made exotic appearances all over the globe, playing, involving themselves in fashions, businesses, or just schemes. They gambled at Monte Carlo. Romanian real estate was a hot investment. Romanian art snapped out of the corset of patriotism, and bloomed into shocking new styles. Poet Tristan Tzara invented Dadaism and drank in Parisian cafés with Ernest Hemingway. A Danubian peasant called Brancusi sculpted abstract eggs that made the Paris critics rave and the Paris museums open their purses. The most beautiful woman of her day, more beautiful than the Hollywood stars, was Queen Marie of Romania. A young generation took over Romania's cities: iconoclastic, liberal, intellectually elitist.

My parents were among those boomers, and both had sprung dizzyingly far from their respective stems. Dad was the seventh of thirteen boys and girls raised on one paycheck by a professor of law. But Dad wasn't going to be another Balkan magistrate, or soldier, or priest, no sir. And Mom, born in a small but prosperous Danube port, and raised in the patriarchal plenty of a fertile vineyard, was not going to marry the local mayor's son. She would become the stage actress and he the maverick lawyer writing Marxist essays that attacked the foundations of bourgeois law.

Herein lies the problem. Rejecting the conformism of their parents, they didn't clearly establish their own moral rules. They lived for the day, and artfully too. Europe was the playground of artists. Europe was not ready for another war, and my parents were not ready for life in war, or under Communism. Hitler, then Stalin, would soon crash down on the good life, but my parents' formative habitat was not constrictive. On the contrary, it cultivated freedom and eccentricity.

When they met, my mother was already married to another man, a prominent magazine editor and poet. As a member of the National Theater, she had star status, and ambled about Bucharest's hot spots dressed like a model, recognized and talked about. My dad had just been appointed defense counsel for a case that rocked Romania: a certain Sile Constantinescu, son of an innkeeper and his waitress wife, had killed his parents and dissolved them in an acid bath, and then poured them into eighty empty apple cider bottles. All in order to inherit the inn. He got the inn, sold it, blew the money, and broke down and confessed to the killings in the bed of a deluxe whore. The case combined the elements of filial duty, the evil of money, and remorse which so appealed to a Balkan audience. Shockingly, Dad pleaded that the grisly bottler was a victim of capitalism's last stage of putrefaction before the Communist revolution. Sile was sentenced to hang, but Dad appealed, now arguing that he had killed because he had been abused as a child; Dad didn't even know that he was anticipating a trend. Mom was so taken with the fiery lawyer that she wrote to Sigmund Freud, asking his opinions on the criminal latencies of abused children. Freud dictated a couple of replies to his daughter Anna. My father got Sile off with life, out of which Sile served exactly six years: in 1944, when the Russians summarily opened the Romanian jails, Sile walked out, and vanished. Later rumors claimed that he became a Securitate guard at Poarta Alba, one of Romania's Communist gulags. After those trials, my father was in hot demand, but he'd had it with bourgeois law and decided to write. My mother filed for divorce from her first husband, and the lovers left Bucharest on the Orient Express, bound for Paris, London, and Berlin. They saw where the world was heading, but they returned to Bucharest. As their train pulled in, the daily papers were screaming about imminent war with Russia. Dad was draftable, but the uncles stepped in to exempt him. Most other men went to war, most other women prayed that they'd hear from their soldiers, but Mom went back to the stage (censored, but still the stage), and Dad, shadowed by the Gestapo, sneaked into anti-Nazi meetings.

As a lawyer, Dad also defended Communists accused of sabotage and sedition. It didn't help him. After the war, the elegant sophistos fell hard, and not only in Romania; 1945 marked the demise of Europe's last great elite, that of the Eastern countries. From Poland to Albania, they took the roads of the diaspora or of internal exile. Paris, Rome, London, Frankfurt filled with them, with their out-of-place airs, their frittered panache, their quiet reproach to history, the way they had filled in the 1920's with the morose great Russian elite exiled by Lenin. But my parents were not made for exile, so they had to face their new circumstances. They had no money, nor any of their past privileges and connections. Their elegant ways were unaffordable, she didn't cook or clean and he couldn't help her, he had to go scrambling for jobs. On top of that, my mother now wanted children and a normal life, bourgeois achievements which required money.

And thus, I came from that elite to end up in the Communist levelling machine. My harsh lesson in dialectics was served to me with an unequivocal message: Submit. You are no different. You are not stronger, or smarter. If you don't believe it, look at your parents. They were among the best, and look where they are now. You might as well join the machine voluntarily, it will give you bread and a place to sleep, and a kind of rough family, the family of the Communists. Your parents, what did they give you?

That was a good question.

Well, they'd given me culture.

My parents were aware that the daily onslaught of propaganda damaged us children. To their merit, even though their relationship was floundering, they tried to give Pavel and me a sense of what they thought was superior in life: culture. One of the benefits of Communism was the cheap books, another the state museums, none of which charged entrance fees. Art was, among all that rubble, one harmonious presence; Pavel and I spent long afternoons looking at classical paintings and sculptures. Our parents taught us French, which we learned without balking too much, for it provided an escape. Still, beyond the diaphanous gauze of culture, the world of Communism was the same: a garden of horrors, a playground of leaping devils.

Then I started writing. Again, writing helped. It was under my control. No leaping devils, no trapdoors springing open.

But writing could also help me make money, which had been the pressing need of our family for as long as I remembered. Now it was a pressing need again: just when Dad started making better money, he left. So, at sixteen, I started tutoring other kids in French, for money. I gave my pay to the last penny to Mother, who took it without thanking me for helping, or praising my precocious dependability. Like the Communist party, she took what was due. And I had duties, not merits or rights. A couple of times I held back a few *lei* for movies or soft drinks. She scolded me harshly. I protested that I had to have some little pleasure in my life. Mom promptly topped me, throwing a master tragic fit, alluding that she might end *her life;* to have to fight with her *own child* for what was right, she found that just too hard to take.

I'd become aware of the importance of money very early, through another character-forming scene.

When we were eight, our parents rented a farmhouse in the mountains, for the summer. One bright Sunday morning, we rode the train to the Carpathians, a great adventure for two little boys.

Four hours later we were at Poiana Tapului, a village on a forested hillside, in the shade of the snow-capped Caraiman peak. We drove to the rented house in an ox-drawn cart filled with perfumed, freshly reaped hay, and met the landlady, who offered to babysit us while our parents went back to the village to buy food for dinner.

Mom and Dad left on foot, Dad with his arm around Mom in one of the few instances of affection I remember between them. Dad was short, dark-haired, and wiry, but with a handsome face, while Mom was a white-skinned sandy blonde whose curves had started to fill up. As they vanished towards the village, Pavel and I were already climbing into the farm's hayloft. From there we saw a calf breaking out of the stable and knocking down a fence, and the landlady running after it with a broom for a whip; then calf and woman disappeared into a gulch about half a mile away. We inspected the hayloft, finding nothing interesting except a small latticed window facing uphill, towards the forest. From there, without any warning, we watched a scene of horror.

Three men in uniforms of the rural Communist police emerged from the trees. Armed with automatics, they herded four other men, who looked like peasants, and were bearded and unkempt and crying. Watched by us, the policemen lined the prisoners against a bushy ravine and shot them in the backs of their heads, one shot each. They searched them, took their valuables, kicked the corpses into the ravine, and threw some dirt and branches over them. Then they quarreled over the valuables—knives, flintstones, hand-rolled cigarettes, and a short stack of money. About the money they haggled so loud and furiously, it seemed absurd that those bits of colored paper required so much time and energy; killing those unfortunates had taken one minute, agreeing on a fair split lasted forever. Two of the cops seemed ready to shoot it out at one point, but then they mellowed out, pocketed a little wad each, and filed past the farm, down towards the village.

Since the hill's incline was mild and long, we could see them for a long time. They finally vanished. Then the landlady appeared, herding the wayward calf back towards the farm, acting as if she hadn't heard the shots. We tumbled down the hayloft's ladder and rushed to her, stuttering in horror and pointing to that improvised grave. Not much later, our parents returned, carrying food—a chicken, milk, cheese in a pouch of oxhide, a dark peasant bread. By this time the landlady had tied up the calf and stepped to the improvised grave, to peer in. She reeled and ran back, her eyes glittering from unspeakable shock, and confirmed in a whisper that there were four dead men in there.

Our father reacted first, with speed. He stuffed a bill in the woman's hand (it looked just like one of the bills the rural cops had haggled over), paying for a night we wouldn't be spending there, then almost roughly pushed Mother and us down the hill. He harshly ordered us kids not to cry, everything was all right, those men were most likely felons who had met their deserved punishment. Mother, always noisy and at odds with him, did not say a word now, and was pale as a ghost. Thus, our terrified little group marched to the railway station, to catch the next train back to Bucharest.

We found out that we had missed the last train for the day. My father hurried onto the highway, and tried to thumb down a vehicle. Trucks were passing now and then, but they were not headed for Bucharest. The sun was slipping behind the Caraiman, tinting the snowcaps pink. My father decided that we would stay in the village that night. As we walked along the main street, we could see the farmhouse, up in the hills, pretty and silent. That overgrown ravine showed above it, a little to the left, as a tangled spot of dark green.

Soon we found a couple who were willing to rent their guest room for the night. The man was a retired postmaster, and his wife a seamstress—we heard the rattle of her old sewing machine, a Singer with a foot pedal, as we huddled in front of the guest room's fireplace. The ex-postmaster made a fire, brought plates and knives and forks and a pitcher of ice-cold water, and bid us to enjoy the food bought by my parents. We sat down to eat, but hardly touched the food.

Dad explained to us that the police had probably smoked out some enemies of the people hiding in the mountains. Pockets of armed anti-Communist resistance still remained in the Carpathians. But those men had looked like regular peasants. Maybe they had refused to join a collective farm. They were impressed on our memories as standing one second, and crumbling the next, as the bullets lodged in their brains. That split-second transition from life to death, from alive and upright to collapsing amorphously, played and replayed on a screen in my brain. I could not accept that those had been people. They hadn't died like people, they had died like popped balloons. But yes, they had been people. God knew what they were now.

And then the voices of their killers, haggling over the money. I couldn't get the money out of my mind anymore than I could those bodies' tumbling into their natural grave. I'd seen money before, I knew its utility. I bought this, I sold that, this and that are too expensive, this and that can't be found in stores no matter how much you pay—these were standard phrases of our existence. Communism proclaimed loftily that money was a vestige from capitalism, soon to disappear; that the Communist human beings would neither value it nor need it—but in practice money was alive and well, and everyone wanted it. Whatever Marx had dreamed about the end of all monetary transactions, it wasn't happening. Money was proving impossible to take out of human life.

But ... money and death, that was a shocking new concept. The cops had frisked their victims first, then killed them, then argued, almost fought, over the money. It was as if the money had a life of its own, more real than the people's. It wasn't money that reacted to people, but people that reacted to money. Those peasants had probably not been killed just to be robbed, yet robbing them played an essential part.

My father had paid that farm woman. Money. Down in the village, he had paid the ex-postmaster. Money. My parents carried money, and maybe that made them as vulnerable as those men now lying in the ravine. The thought was terrifying, but I barely felt its terror: after what I had seen, all aftershocks lost most of their impact. The two visuals, the shooting and then the money, kept turning around in my head. Money was like a devil's substance, emerging from that episode victorious, above death.

We were staying in a room whose furniture was turn of the century mixed with contemporary gimcrack. It was very clean, kept with the kind of respect village people have for dowries and inheritances. The fire was crackling merrily. I heard the deep ticking of an unseen timepiece: it sounded like some big grandfather clock with an old brass pendulum swinging inside a vertical box, dark like a coffin. Our new landlady came in to bring towels, and I commented about that piece. She told me that it was the house clock, and left.

My brother and I investigated the house, but never found the clock, though its sound seemed closer in some rooms and muffled by distance in others. We gave up, and sometime later its sound faded completely. However, at night I woke up and heard it again. It varied in volume, sounding close and then distant, as if it were being carried by some hesitant gust of wind. Again, I remembered the execution and the executioners' haggle over the money, and was afraid of having a nightmare about all that, so I tried to stay awake. We were all lying in the same room, which was reassuring. I was exhausted, but I couldn't get what I'd seen out of my mind. The rural cops were peasants just like the peasants they had killed. How could they do that to people who reminded them of their own brothers, or cousins?

I was learning that European peasants, given an excuse, could be astoundingly cruel; cruelty was in their blood like a virus inoculated during the barbarian raids and Ottoman occupations.

Next to me in the high, hard rural bed, my father snored loudly. That day he had behaved like a regular father. I too finally sank into a deep swamp of sleep. In the adjoining room, the retired postmaster and his wife slept too. Outside, in the houses lining the only paved street, slept other innocent souls. Villagers who had never left their village, whose only contact with the outside were vacationers like us.

Up in that nameless ravine, the four peasants who had resisted collectivization slept a different kind of sleep, deep yet empty. Theirs was the sleep of death. They were not from Poiana Tapului. That much we figured the next morning as we were faced with the calm ordinariness of the village streets. No local household missed a relative.

In the words of a bitter Romanian saying: Lucky the dead, for their ordeals are over.

Not so lucky were thousands of other peasants who had resisted collectivization, and were sleeping now in prisons and work camps all over Romania, prey to that special exhaustion induced by forced labor. Communist Romania's work camps assigned quotas calculated to be impossible to fulfill. The punishments were beatings, or being locked up in cages too small to stand up, sit down, or lie down in. One could only curl up in a fetal position, forehead squashed against one end, feet tortured against the other, and gradually pass out from the slowing down of the blood circulation. They were so feared, those cages, that prisoners came out of them resolved to fulfill their work quotas no matter what. And they killed themselves trying. Many died of exhaustion, in their sleep. Say one hundred prisoners would curl up in those cages, thirty to fifty wouldn't see the morning. This suited the camp authorities just fine. Fresh enemies of the people were joining Romania's gulags every day, and the bunk beds were scarce.

Or they had money, to bribe the prison officials. Money brought in by their visiting families. They paid, and they slept in regular prison bunk beds.

When I researched my last novel in Romania, I gathered my data in my own empirical way, because there was no public information about Romania's gulags. But I wanted to write about surviving the experience. So I posed questions to the ex-detainees I knew, starting with those in my own family, about the work conditions, the punishments, the ways to avoid punishment. The reality that immediately came to the fore was that what saved you was not a shorter sentence, a stronger constitution, friends who wouldn't turn you in to the guards, or luck. What saved you was money. Other things too: prisoners who were attractive traded sexual favors, those who could type often kept the prison books, those who could sing or play an instrument became the camp's entertainers. But mostly money, brought from outside, was what saw the detainee through his years inside. Money had to be brought in almost constantly, to bribe the guards for a mattress, a spell in the infirmary, an extra bowl of food, being assigned to less exhausting work, or receiving letters from the family. Most prisoners would do anything to get their mail, the letters were their mental lifelines. So they asked for money from their families, who most often earned very little: as kin of enemies of the people, they had the worst jobs at the lowest pay. Still, they did the impossible, and the money, the Communist *lei,* decorated with the banners of the Communist state and adorned with the portraits of glorious ancestors or celebrated savants or artists, their bluish, metallic, color reminiscent of the steel of weapons, found their way to the detention places and into the pockets of the officials. Favors were extended, privileges granted, slightly more humane conditions created, and people, often innocent people, got to survive more of their detention, hoping to make it through not completely wasted, to the day when their term was up.

In the process, many camp commandants became millionaires. Their wealth never entered any tabulations, nor was it ever deposited in a bank. This was an economy outside the economy, and it was so cynically and truthfully monetary that it made mincemeat of Marx's lofty yearning for a moneyless society. Had he risen from his grave to see what Romania's prison life ran on, he would perhaps have realized the asinine naivete of his dream. It strikes some people as amazingly vile and revolting that money was such a component in the waging of World War II, in the economy of slave labor, in the production of armaments, and in the individual maneuverings of the officials and commandants, Nazi and others. It is almost overlooked that Communism ran for years on a slave-labor economy. Money came from the outside and went straight into the jailers' hands. You bribed the guard who had it in for you, the doctor who held back your insulin, the nurse who sold your pills to other inmates, the camp janitors who threatened to leave this dead friend of your's lying in your bunk, the Gypsies who threatened to cut you up (many common criminals were Gypsies; organized in gangs, they terrorized the camps). Without money you wouldn't have survived, you wouldn't be here today. . . . My respective witness was here today, talking to me. He or she had false teeth, skin irreparably wrinkled and hardened by work in scorching sun or freezing cold, hands deformed by manual labor, a stoop from carrying loads, a limp from a bone fracture improperly aligned, or spots from a liver damaged forever, or some twitch of the features and sideways twist of the head, repeated every few minutes in remembered fear of a beating, a kind of emotional Parkinson's disease . . .

But money had saved them.

The majority of imprisoned enemies of the people were not peasants. They were teachers, doctors, accountants, lawyers, former mayors and other administration officials, traders, artisans and manufacturers, owners of small and medium-sized businesses, tailors, innkeepers, restaurateurs. In a word, they were "former exploiters" who had employed others, thus increasing the numbers of an exploited proletariat. One would have thought that creating jobs would please the Commies. Wasn't "Jobs!" the cry of the depressed thirties, the goal of all the strikes and rallies organized by the party? Well, whoever had hired others had been an exploiter, simple as that. The purpose of jailing the former employers was to do away with them as a class. From now on, the only employer was the party.

The work camps were death camps in all but name. Aiud, Gherla, Poarta Alba, Capul Midia, Pitesti. They will remain engraved on the secret consciousness of Romania, the one of unrecorded facts and macabre legends, for most of their records were destroyed by the Securitate before the revolution, when Ceausescu's cozying up to the West posed the threat of some such inferno diaries being leaked out. The horrors I heard as I did my research were monotonously similar: beatings on the soles of the feet, on the head, on the genitals, for anything and everything. Hangings by the wrists, by the ankles, burnings with cigarettes and torches. Confinement among thieves, vagrants, rapists, killers. Diets of bread and water, which the prisoners supplemented with rats, snakes, birds, insects, grass, and twigs. No letters. Workdays of fourteen hours or more. Insults. Abuses enforced under threat of death, including drinking urine and eating feces. Routine killings of the prisoners deemed tough or saucy. Promises of early release if one became an informant, often never fulfilled. Vermin. Untreated disease. Untreated injuries. Cynical, sadistic doctors.

They were the same over and over, told in the same tone, described in casual prison slang. One thing stood out: the variety of the offenders' professions, which touched upon sick comedy; it was as if someone had opened the yellow pages and categorized all human trades and endeavors as crimes. Not just the former owners of businesses, the affluent peasants, the priests who preached against collectivization. The opponents were of all ilks. Behind barbed wire you'd find the most amazing assortment of people, jailed because they had the most superficial contact with the West. Like, say, the members of the Braille associations. They were blind and seemed harmless, but . . . they were in touch with capitalist blind people, through their newsletters in Braille! And what about the raisers of pigeons? Pigeons could be used to carry messages. Another big category was the "rumorists," spreaders of defeatist news or anti-Communist jokes. Then the palmists and readers in tea leaves and coffee grinds, the pastimes of many bored Romanian housewives. And the women who didn't turn their jewelry in, after a law was passed that all gold and gemstones "belonged to the people": those bejewelled dames could destabilize our Communist currency, by selling their gold and jewels on the black market, no? And what about the butchers? To counter meat shortages, the butchers were to save the gristle, the innards, the hooves, the bones, the cartilage of all sorts, and prepare it into a revolting kind of meat meal, and sell it to the population. The butchers who didn't do it went to prison as saboteurs. The butchers who did too much of it were arrested as profiteers.

On and on. The list was unending. You would've expected to find the aging Iron Guards on that list too, but no, there weren't many of those. Plenty had managed to flee the country; others, believe it or not, had been welcomed into the Securitate, which would always nurture a vigorous Fascist strain.

Even our honorable army had a sort of detainee system of its own, the work detachments. Romania's draft was universal and obligatory, but those eighteen-year-olds not to be trusted with weapons because of "unhealthy social origin" were drafted into the work detachments, to dig ditches, build bridges and roads, and gather crops. One of my first cousins, a younger son of the famous Danube-swimming uncle, ended up in those detachments. Cousin Sandu (short for Alexandru—now, a resident of Westchester County, New York, he's known as Alex) told me how he served his time with young peasants who had dodged collectivization, with a Gypsy who lived by placing spells, and with several Jewish boys who had applied, against their parents' advice, for emigration to Israel. All digging away at ditches and roads proudly mentioned in the Communist statistics.

Altogether, I believe that over two million Romanians knew incarceration under the Communists, from the harshest and longest to the most transitory. And then there were the ones picked up and questioned, randomly or regularly, the way I was at age thirteen. No one ever bothered to count us. We got it free. We were the freeloaders, so to speak.

* * *

The next morning, as we woke up in the ex-postmaster's house, a bright sun changed my parents' feelings about our almost aborted vacation. We decided to stay down here in the village. For the next two weeks we didn't venture once to the farmhouse we had first rented. We took hikes in the forest, sunbathed on meadows speckled red with poppies, went to country fairs, fished for trout in mountain ponds. And I noticed that life had this incredible regenerative power. In my memory, the killing hadn't faded. I dreamed about it at night, and it frightened me. But in the daytime we all acted as if it hadn't happened; Pavel and I never mentioned it, behaving with each other as if we hadn't seen anything. By the end of the two weeks our parents almost got along, while we kids were tanned, full of bruises and scratches, and happy.

The "house clock," as the landlady called it, kept sounding somewhere nearby, but not at all times—we mostly heard it in the evening, at that hazy hour between dinner and bedtime. Pavel and I cornered the landlady, asked her where the confounded clock was, and she answered that she couldn't show it to us: this was "the house clock," every house had one. It wasn't in any particular room, yet it kept beating somewhere, like a sort of heart. It didn't need winding up or cleaning, and it couldn't be seen, touched, or checked for time—it was the house clock. The landlady was a woman of perhaps fifty, not uneducated. Pavel and I exchanged a glance in which we silently remembered the bodies falling in the ravine; what an idiot this woman was that she could have such idyllic beliefs, while right nearby people were killing people.

I linked up in my mind the dead people and the clock, but didn't know that I did, and only deciphered the meaning of that linkage later. It became clear to me that living where I was born was unbearable, yet I had no choice, for here were the options: that I rebel in some fashion, and end up in a nameless ravine, robbed of my life and my valuables, or that I choose a life like that of the ex-postmaster's wife, stupidly provincial and quiet. Holed up in some rural place, through seasons measured by a house clock, occasionally making a little extra from tourists like us.

I retained the lesson: opposition to the new rule was fatal. But life was possible, in a modest form. Unfortunately, I did not want a modest life.

My brother's death brought me my first taste of notoriety. At school, everyone had known me as a double, but now I had returned a single. And I had been at the edge of death. I must have looked dangerous: the lower grades shied away from my path as I haunted the schoolyard, alone. The girls too had seen me as a double and now as a single. Longing eyes focussed on me from under curly bangs. Given the time's scarcity of romantic characters, I filled on a small scale an unspoken need.

I had a crush on a girl who was interested in being seen with the talked-about celebrity. Her family were monarchists and I the son of left-wingers, so there was a Romeo and Juliet angle to our romance. All we did was take walks in the cold Bucharest autumn, write each other notes (I wrote her poems too), and kiss. When my girlfriend kissed me she closed her eyes in a studied fashion, though all we did was touch lips; using our tongues never occurred to us. We kissed standing upright in a three-by-three foot hallway leading into her apartment; there, we said good-bye after our walks, with our coats on. We were often interrupted by people walking in and hanging their overcoats on an overloaded clothes tree, because that apartment was a kind of conspiracy den, where reactionary gents and ladies gathered to listen to the Voice of America. My first love wore her mother's perfume, a great refinement, and when we kissed its scent overpowered the wet odor of the hanging coats. Sometimes the clothes tree toppled over on us. When we separated, we promised each other that we would stay awake and look at the clock at the strike of midnight, thinking of each other. I didn't, but claimed that I did. This was love.

As the shade on my upper lip darkened, my mother became terrified that she would lose me not to disease and death, but to the hormones stirring in me. Thus, she multiplied her monitoring vigilance, and became absolutely comical in trying to force me to remain at home, and in her sight. She talked incessantly about her merits in raising me, perhaps trying to give me a clue that she needed to be appreciated and reassured, but all I recognized was the old control, now pushed beyond any reasonable limits. Even when I left for school, she ran out behind me and called me back while I padded down the stairs, under some little pretext. If I was already in the street, she ran back inside and out onto the balcony, to call me from there. The poor woman couldn't enjoy that I was turning into an adult. I should've had some compassion, but I'd decided that my compassion would come at a price—if she admitted how she had wronged me with her control. That was exactly what she was most afraid of, admitting that she'd made any mistakes. Her way of breaking my father out of his passivity was by fighting with him; fighting reassured her that they were in contact. Now she fought me, blasting me at the slightest excuse, until I told her, shaking, that if she didn't stop it, I would leave home and never see her again—I'd already not seen my father for over a year. Terrified, she retreated. We had armed peace. But she'd convinced me that she couldn't manage without me, so now I extended, grudgingly, a kind of parenting. She was without a compass, without power, without a man; I had to be the man. Exactly what she had wanted me to be, I was becoming. I started tutoring almost every day, making money. I kept some of it, and gave her no accounts as to how I spent it, but that was the extent of my autonomy.

I was buzzing with hormones. I had to live. The reality of Communism was raw, grainy, undercooked, coarse, churlish; but it was up to me to find in it a measure of pleasure. Maybe I loved that monarchist girl, but I didn't put my hand up her skirt once. I was successfully compartmentalized, and had my carnal pleasures elsewhere. Communism, from Moscow to Tirana and from East Berlin to Peking, was a world of unacknowledged promiscuous sex. The result of the chronic housing shortage was three families to one cramped apartment. People did it in front of their kids. The result of social change too: released from peasant repressiveness, youngsters rushed to town, took jobs in factories, worked locked up against other eager males and females. There was no privacy in homes, but there were city parks with grass excellent for consummating; in streetcars, green stains of grass on youngsters' clothes were a frequent sight. Sex in the open was the only misdemeanor that went unpunished. The party understood. Kids out of wedlock were declared "revolution's babies."

In keeping with that, my classmates and I turned fifteen, and bang, one schoolmate of ours became a sexual promoter. He lived adjacent to a clinic still under construction: there, inside the unfinished building, he brought ladies of the night, and I went with my schoolmates and got laid and paid for it with the money I made by tutoring. The fifteen-year-old pimp found a discarded dental chair, dragged it between the unfinished walls, tilted it back, and made it into our bed of apprenticeship. We snuck over in the evening, gathered on the sidewalk outside, money clutched in sweating fists, then filed in through a hole in a fence and approached the building with hearts pounding. The woman waited already in the chair. Everything happened in the conspiratorial darkness so typical of our lives. The women who serviced us told us to relax, not unlike dentists reassuring nervous patients. Mostly newcomers to the city, they were quickly replaced by others, which our busy little capitalist informed us about with the coded phrase, "Next Wednesday, new movie."

Thus, in a few months he cornered a stable clientele, and prospered. He no longer charged flat rates. The first "go" of the night was the most expensive, and the ones thereafter cheaper in order of increasing promiscuity, which put pressure on the customers, as hardly anyone wanted to follow in the wake of all his friends. So here I was, getting carnal relief in degrading conditions, and going back for it. Why? Because it was satisfyingly base. Because it assuaged my rage at both women and men, which was really my rage at my parents; they'd made sure that I would have no illusions, no hopes, no romanticism about what could pass between a man and a woman.

So, was there a new movie that coming Wednesday? I put on old dirty pants and an unwashed top, because the unfinished building was all dust and debris, went to the clinic, and lay down in darkness with those part-time professionals, gritting my teeth so as not to pant loudly—a few feet away behind the wall waited some of my classmates. A shard of moon threw its glitter inside; the way the chair was angled, the moonshine fell right in the eyes of the woman under me, adding glow to the tip of her cigarette, for many smoked while they did it. I thrust aggressively, which finished me fast, got up, stepped behind the wall to pay our classmate, the pimp. One "new movie," a peasant girl, took a liking to me; she whispered that she'd come to meet me alone, without the pimp, and charge only half price. With the same burning curiosity that took me there the first time, I met her alone, three nights later, in the same spot. There were empty bottles of beer lying about the place, traces of an orgy she swore she had not been part of. She'd been away the last three days to visit her ex-husband in her village. She'd left him because he didn't want to move to the big city. "There's not one hair salon in my village, to get a perm," she explained. As for *this,* it was temporary till she found something better. So what was my story, why did a nice-smelling city boy like me have to come here and pay for it?

Nice smelling or not, to her I was an equal, a being in a state of quest and transition. What stopped me from telling her my problems was class prejudice; later, as a writer, I regretted it: imagine her reactions, her advice, her *empathy*? This young woman felt no shame whatsoever, the sordid exchanges in which some of me entered some of her were just passing things, steps in a new life. This was the big city, where she could get a perm any time she felt like it; no doubt, I was paying for her next perm. She was so disarmingly full of purpose that I felt she might help find my own purpose, whatever that was. Our meetings were like landing on the face of reality, which was hard and smelly and well-defined and sobering.

I was ashamed no more. Clearness of purpose, like a toxic cleanser, wiped off all pretense, all shame. She wanted the big city; I wanted her anonymous flesh. We were both served. I got something extra, her way of dealing with compromise, which was much healthier than mine. She didn't rage after five clumsy matings with five unscrubbed schoolboys, she didn't feel disturbed, she didn't cry, or vomit in disgust. Nah, she knew that life could deal worse cards.

From those encounters I retained a fascination with the edges of life, with characters whose circumstances were simple and low. With the wide-eyed innocence that went with simplicity. Over and over, I met those characters again, in all parts of the world. They were the winners. I was a fool to dream of saving them, as a writer or as a fellow human. They were saving themselves, by starting so low that they could only go up.

That patriarchal prostitution was typical of our end of the world. As it happened, a sort of bawdy house functioned right next door to our apartment building, in a Victorian two-story mansion. The regime rewarded large families; mothers of more than five were declared *"hero mothers,"* paid a state allowance, and given priority in housing. In the manse next door, formerly a private bourgeois residence, the regime had quartered the family of a cobbler with a wife and eight children, seven girls and one boy. They were received bitchily by the other neighbors because their skin looked suspiciously dark and their last name was Bolovan, a Gypsy name. The two older girls, in their twenties, had heavy buttocks, ample chests, and eyes sparkling with come-hitherness. They didn't work, they stayed at home and had male callers. Waiting for them, they sat on the stoop in cotton undies, letting their legs hang down and their slippers dangle from their toes. They chewed sunflower seeds and spat out the shells. No one except the cobbler officially worked. He mended the neighborhood's heels, so when our shoes needed fixing, Mom took them over in person, she didn't let Pavel or me enter the Gypsies' yard.

So I spied on those plump women from the height of our second-story balcony. They too represented life raw and undefeated. Their peasant callers brought them chickens or bottles of homemade plum brandy. Sometimes they were visited by soldiers on leave. There were some city boys too, one a painter who got it free because he did the girls' portraits; he always appeared lugging a bag with brushes and paints and rolls of canvas. All that made for a healthy traffic, but those warm illiterate madonnas had a good sense of scheduling in their heads, for we were never disturbed by a row between two customers. Their mama, enormous from her many pregnancies, could barely walk; when she went to the grocery store on the corner, I watched her from our balcony for half an hour, as her broad silhouette disappeared like a camel's lost in the desert. When she reappeared, taking another half hour, she stepped into the yard and started dropping her packages, which the daughters bestirred themselves to pick up. The father often walked a caller out of the house, and if the hour was quiet, I could hear him from our apartment, hitting on the caller for cigarettes. One younger daughter had a full red mouth, and trained her daring glance at me as I came home from school and found her dangling her feet on the stoop. She was quite pretty. I returned the glance, but that's as far as I went. Communism or no Communism, the social barriers between us were too strong. Her name was Venera, Romanian for Venus.

And none of them felt crushed by history.

When I understood the trade they were running, I visualized my homeland in a rather original fashion: as an emulsion of four fluids, which were heroism, betrayal, death, and sex. Sex kept the others together. Chemically speaking, an emulsion is a mixture that doesn't quite mix. In an oily base of betrayal and death floated gobs of heroism. They were meeting, separating, meeting again, and building up into masses of dark-red blood, marking Romania's various attempts to gain her freedom. In between wheeled the whitish beads of sex, fast and viscous. There were so many of these that they outnumbered the death and betrayal, and dissolved the heroism. And the whole somehow kept hanging together. This was survival. Unless we were dead, we got up from being raped, jailed, or beaten. We found ourselves alive again, and in functioning order, myself included. I went home after my carnal forays, showered fiercely, and worked on my latest poem. *Chiselled* it, as the phrase went in literary circles. What I did not have in life, I could have on paper. Words had power, and I had power over them.

The sense of being a writer was the only thing that Communism granted me with some ease: the option of living outside life, but inside my words. I was not a man or a woman, I was not happy or unhappy, young or elderly, purposeful or lost. I was something strange and whole and inexplicable. I came with my own batteries and my own set of instructions. I was a writer.

Among the friends I grew up with at the time—sharing school books, soccer games, raunchy talk about girls, wondrous curiosity about the stars, and carnal discoveries—there was one who played a special part. I'll call him SZ. SZ was a big-boned boy who excelled at sports, but had became friendly with me, the intellectual nerd. He'd known Pavel. He was dark-haired, rather sullen, not a straight-A student. He read on his own, had esoteric tastes, and wondered about the meanings of life. Similar interests are not disclosed between boys, they are smelled out. I sniffed a kindred type. His father was gregarious and talkative, a lawyer, whatever that meant under Communism. His mother was a friendly little woman with an unmistakable Moldovan accent, which made her endearing the way Southerners are endearing in America.

I was in their home many times, and SZ in mine, before I learned that he was Jewish. I thought we had no secrets, then learned by accident that he'd just had his bar mitzvah. Raised by liberal parents, I'd already had Jewish friends, who were not Jewish to me as I was not Christian to them. Communism had stamped out both religion and nationality, but that had one good consequence: no prejudice, at least not any publicly expressed. No separations. Also, SZ and I were close, so his secrecy struck me.

I paid attention, and awoke to the fact that his people had a tradition of protective secretiveness. That tied in with my own secretive compartmentalized life.

Just then, Communist Romania had begun to allow Jews to move to Israel; in time, it became known that Israel paid our Communist state money for each emigrant. Meanwhile, the Christian Romanians were not allowed to emigrate anywhere; that created some spontaneous anti-Semitism, to be expected because in truth, the Jews had no better reason to leave at that time than anyone else. After the war, they'd had it as good or as bad as the main crowd, and a good number of them had been Communists.

Suddenly, people we knew started to leave, acknowledging thereby that they had always been different. Meanwhile, I continued as a frequent guest in SZ's house, and his family relaxed their protectiveness and spoke freely in front of me. His father told Jewish jokes. I paid closer attention. The Jewish humor poked fun at the Jews, sometimes quite cruelly, but it also expressed a striking group solidarity and lack of illusions. Even the children knew what was what. Instead of behaving in front of SZ with blustering machismo, a common stance in our virile Balkan nation, SZ's father presented him with an attitude of somewhat bitter, somewhat resigned realism: this is what we are, this is what we can expect. SZ absorbed it, and behaved, at thirteen, fourteen, fifteen, like an old soul. He introduced me to Shalom Aleichem, whose writings, truth be told, would never have been published in mass-market numbers without the Commies; but the Commies pledged to respect "minority cultures," and while they didn't let that include religion, they sponsored literature, theater, art, folk dance, and music. SZ once told me that he excelled in sports because he expected Jews to be singled out again, and he wanted to be fit and able to defend himself (he didn't have to, he left Romania the same year I did, and is now an electronic engineer in California).

SZ hadn't had a big personal loss, like I had, but he lived with a diluted sense of many historic losses. His people had been dealt negatives, yet they had upheld their sense of worth and special destiny, sometimes within the circle of a single family. I was impressed. Modestly heroic, that was how SZ's folks appeared to me. I felt I related; I too had been upholding my sense of worth all by myself.

I became fascinated by the Jews in Romania, though at first glance they were hard to spot; they appeared and disappeared in the contradictory and schizophrenic way typical of the Communist state. There were Jews in our own apartment building—right across the hall, for instance, lived Angela Agatstein, the building's former owner. Ironically, she had lived undisturbed in her property during Romania's alliance with Hitler, but as soon as the war was over, the anti-Nazi Commie regime branded her a capitalist exploiter, confiscated her building, and made her a tenant in her own apartment. I had many Jewish classmates, since many mid-level party activists lived in my part of Bucharest; we played together in the street, kicking around a football made of rags, often sending it under the streetcars' wheels. We traded snacks, we whispered, pink-eared, about girls, we stole apples from produce carts, and chased cats. We shared childhoods completely untainted by racial prejudice, though we knew that we were different in some unclear fashion. As my friendship with SZ deepened, I thought I grasped the unspoken difference: they were the same yet not the same, and that's how they saw themselves. They belonged, undoubtedly, and yet their belonging was not as certain, not so confident as to proclaim itself loudly, because it had been derided in the past, and even punished. Mind, Romania's nationhood itself was very recent, and fragile. Romanians too had been punished, mocked, chafed, mistreated, invaded. Their nationalism was almost obligatory, and nationalism is no friend of minorities. On the other hand, due to its lack of pogroms, Romania had always been Eastern Europe's "good-to-the-Jews" country, including during World War II. In practice, the Romanian Jew had much good to say about the country, if he had a tough enough skin or skillful enough persona to deal with the natives' coarseness towards minorities.

Communism, in the same way in which it upheld and yet molested everyone, upheld yet molested the Jews' identity. There was enough awareness of the Holocaust, because the Commies took credit for slaying the Nazi dragon, so when it was politically useful to evoke Jewish suffering, the Jews were paraded out. Otherwise, they were harshly discouraged from behaving as Jews. In their homes, there were no menorahs, no framed marriage certificates in Hebrew, and of course, no mezuzas on the door posts. They didn't celebrate Passover or Hanukkah, at least not overtly enough for friends or neighbors to know about it. They seemed to do none of what they had dreamed of doing freely after the defeat of Fascism.

They were not Jews now, as we were not Christians. Nobody was anybody.

That was normal for an atheist state, and as I said, some of the effects were arguably positive. As long as Communist rule was enforced, there was practically no anti-Semitism. But it was tough for the Jews, because they had waited to come out, and now they were not allowed to. Tough for the Christians too: church-goers were persecuted, fined, framed, fired from jobs, evicted from homes. If they were convicted of anything else, being religious added to the sentence. Owning Bibles (we did) was forbidden, reading them to others was a punishable act, baptism was an offense. Between 1947 and 1968, thousands of children, especially those of party members, were not baptized. Having priests in one's family (we did) was a serious social handicap. Confessing to a priest (we did) could be construed as conspiring against the state. Priests were detained and sometimes tortured. Their homes were raided without warrants, their churches closed on the slightest excuse, the country priests who told their congregations to oppose collectivization were jailed. And yet our new constitution guaranteed the freedom of religion. The monks' and nuns' orders were intentionally and systematically impoverished. The party also made a mockery of the liturgy, by forcing the clergy to include in the service prayers for the health of the party leaders.

But if the mainstream religion had to go underground, ethnic Romanians had more identifications to cling to than the Jews. No one questioned their right to physically be in Romania. In their very names was the proof of longevity and antiquity in the land. The mainstream culture, with its traditions and folklore, was theirs. The ethnic Romanians' culture found secondary means of expression with the versatility learned under the Turks. The countryside churches endured better, and if one had a burning desire to go to church, one could ride a bus to a village, and be reasonably confident that the Securitate wouldn't notice. The Jews had no country synagogues, except for a few in northern Moldova and Transylvania. And one thing which had been traditionally so successful, the Jewish community's trust in itself, had been destroyed. There were Securitate informants among the Jews, like everywhere else.

Thus, the Jews were told when to be Jews and when not to by the Commie leaders, who included a super-prominent party woman named

Ana Pauker, a Jew. Ana had been a famous activist in the thirties, arrested and tried several times. Daughter of a rabbi, Ana was strong, ambitious, flamboyant, and, thanks to the unravelling of events, more and more cynical through the years. In the thirties she'd had a hot affair with Maurice Thorez, secretary of the Third Communist International. When Nazi Germany started breathing down Romania's neck, Ana and most of the party's Jewish intellectuals, the so-called "profs," took refuge in Russia. During the war, she was ordered by Stalin to form a division of Romanian prisoners that would fight along with the Red Army. My uncle Nicu, a prisoner at the time, saw her arrive at a camp of Romanian officers, to sell them on signing up for that division. He'd been locked in solitary confinement that day, for no specific reason, just to soften him up, but happened to watch Ana's arrival through the bars of his cell window. If he'd had any doubts as to what the rapport was between Stalin and his puppets, they vaporized on that day.

First came a staff car filled with Soviet commissars, and then a truck brimming with sacks of flour; up on the sacks, guarded by an armed sentry, sat a huddled figure in an austere gray outfit, the uniform of party activists under Stalin. That figure was Ana Pauker. Fifteen minutes later she talked, and talked passionately, to the Romanian prisoners, about the wonderful Communist system and the Romanians' chance to enter into an alliance with it.

My uncle didn't join, and was punished by being transferred to a Siberian camp beyond the polar circle. That camp was really a village of detainees, which it had been since the time of the Czars. It had no walls or bars, for there was nowhere to run to. His monthly pay, disbursed in accordance with the Geneva Convention, was ten rubles a month. One egg cost fifteen rubles, so he nearly died of starvation. Ana did convince the other prisoners: a division called "Tudor Vladimirescu" was formed; armed with Soviet matériel, it was promptly thrown into combat. At the end of the war, it paraded in Bucharest, chests clinking with Soviet medals.

While Ana's "Jewish profs" waited for the war's end in Russia, at home the RCP was run by "home boys" Gheorghiu-Dej and Ceausescu. The home boys were jailed at Tirgu Jiu and other camps, but were either released or allowed to escape in 1944, when it smelled like the Russians would win the war. After the war, Ana became Romania's de facto party boss. She was not the general secretary, that spot belonged to Gheorghiu, the native son, and he was seconded by two other men, Emil Bodnaras and Constantin Parvulescu. Yet Ana was the Moscow connection. How very advanced of Romania to have a leader who was a woman, a Jew, and an intellectual all in one—but Stalin chose her with something else in mind. He was able to hold the "home boys" in check, while programming her for fanatical loyalty, as he tried to program all the Jews in the parties of the captive countries.

Then suddenly, in 1949, Stalin started his own pogrom against the intellectuals, Jews, and veterans of the Spanish civil war (some qualified in all three categories). He fired them from leadership positions, and framed them with grossly faked charges of spying for the West, ideological deviation, or Zionism, which Stalin preferred to call "cosmopolitanism." Remember how in *Mein Kampf* Hitler had cheered his own conversion from "knee-jerking cosmopolitan" to "anti-Semite"? I guess Stalin owed Hitler one or two reference terms. Between 1949 and 1953, thousands of cadre, many of them Jewish, were arrested, tortured, and made to confess to being Trotskyite, Titoite, bourgeois-nationalist, cosmopolitan, or Zionist, even though the Soviet Union had midwifed Israel's statehood at the United Nations! Most prominent Jews were demoted from spots of influence, and often jailed or executed—luckier than many, Ana Pauker was vilified as a traitor, but only put under house arrest. Stalin used prejudice skillfully. In the grumbling captive nations, instead of the damn Soviets or the damn Commies, the masses were incited to blame the damn Jews. And then, nice and easy, the reins of power were handed to the "home boys." In Bucharest, Gheorghiu was enthroned as the sole general secretary. The crowds, forever hopeful, concluded that the regime was improving. The new leaders were not "foreigners" anymore, they were our own flesh and blood.

At the end of his life and apogee of his powers, Stalin exhibited his own hang-ups about the Jews, who for years had been his devoted followers and comrades. Suddenly, he seemed as pathologically fearful of them as Hitler, as was proved by the "doctors' plot": on spurious proof, nine eminent Soviet physicians (eight of them Jews) were convicted of plotting to poison Stalin, Voroshilov, and other Soviet bosses. The old distrust of ethnics, particularly of Jews, had reappeared, and where? In the very bosom of Marxism! The party started to cleanse itself, rung after rung. The top ones were exposed as traitors, the middle dismissed for some real or purported incompetence. What a film noir for those Jews who had joined out of idealism: the movement that had promised to dissolve such barriers was a fake. In an ironic sense, Stalin was handing them back their Jewishness. Unlike Nazism, Communism did not want to eliminate the minorities physically, but just to convert them, or expel them. Thus, after the trials were over, the Jews who had not been arrested and framed, and in the whole Soviet bloc these numbered in the millions, were allowed to emigrate to Israel. Again the Communist state was totally schizophrenic and unprincipled: not only did it confess to being racist, but it strengthened a capitalist enemy, Israel.

Thus, kids like Pavel and I learned that this classmate and that play buddy were Jewish, and soon to disappear from school, from the playground, from the country. We envied them. We asked them to write and send chewing gum and other little capitalist wonders. Among us kids, the departures produced no disruptions, but among the adults, the reactions were hostile and noisy. Why should the Jews be allowed to leave, after they had been party members, even party bosses—in other words, the regime's darlings? Why them, and not everybody else? That was a good question, but the system would neither explain its reasons, nor worry about reigniting the racism of the common folk. All of a sudden, in bread lines, one heard nondescript middle-aged ladies bawling at other ladies equally middle-aged and nondescript. "You're leaving after you ate *our* bread!" was the stock line. The targeted ones walked away, while their accusers vented their ire to the other shoppers: "We allowed them to settle in our land, didn't we? We gave them a chance. Why would they repay us with betrayal?" The crowd grumbled, pleasantly reinduced to a traditional Romanian feeling: we were the ones who suffered the most, right here, wedded to these harsh lands, loyal to them, incapable of abandoning them.

Mind you, some of the departing Jewish activists had been haughty, unjust, or abusive. But more importantly, they had been visibly privileged. Now, their departure to Israel, Canada, or the United States stirred Romanian anti-Semitism at its root, which had always been social envy. The Jews had arrived in Romania relatively late, in the seventeenth century, seeking shelter from Russian and Polish pogroms. They had found easy terms of settlement which had helped them prosper. As a result, Romania's anti-Semitism had been formed in the context of social competitiveness, expressing itself most often as the ire of the poor and destitute. The Jews were admired for their success (exaggeratedly: there was always sufficient poverty in the shtetls and the ghettos), but viewed as less worthy because they were newer in the land. *We* had been here first. *We* had suffered longer than all others. The stories of *their* suffering were distrusted. About the Holocaust, one could hear such exchanges, between ethnic Romanians, of course:

"Hitler gassed those six million Jews . . ."

"Oh come on, they were not six million. Haven't you noticed how they keep increasing the numbers? First it was three, then four, then five million. Now it's six."

The Holocaust's figures were made ambiguous so that the Romanians' own suffering could be restored to top status. Sometimes, a participant in that kind of exchange might protest: Wait a second, why would the Jews manipulate those numbers, three million or six, the crime was still abominable. I voiced such protests on a number of occasions, and was rewarded with surprised looks: What's the matter with Popescu, is he stupid? My interlocutors would come back stubbornly: *They* did it for their own purposes, mysterious and separate from ours. That's what they're like. Clever. Skillful. I still argued. I argued better than the other side, until the other would shrug: Hey, *zhidanitul* Popescu, what can you expect from him? In all European languages there was that word, *zhidanitul,* meaning "the Jewified." *Enjuive, verjudet, ebreizzato.* To be called "Jewified Popescu" was especially stinging: We Popescus came from Christian priests. We were not just the Smiths of Romania, but also the Cohens.

The social envy against Jews was widespread and obdurate in all of Eastern Europe. The Poles had a saying about Jews: *Vashy kamenitsy, a nashy ulitsy.* Roughly, it translated as: You got the houses, and left us the streets. Not all Jews owned houses, nor did all Poles drift about in the streets, but such was the point of view of the destitute. The more know-how the Jews had, the more useful they turned out to be for an immature East European economy (which was the case of the Romanian economy when the Jews started to arrive in large numbers), the more the social envy took root.

The Romanian upper classes were not envious; they expressed their prejudice in patronizing forms. *We* so generously allowed *them* to settle here. Our generosity should be repaid through repeated acts of commitment.

And now they were leaving! What gall! When some of our schoolmates received permission to emigrate, I asked them how they felt. "I don't want to leave, but Mom and Dad do," was the standard answer. I watched their parents, some of whom I knew quite well. They didn't act guilty. They had been Romanian, but also something else, and that something else was now setting them free. I was dragging along the mortal coil of being Romanian only. And I could not imagine freedom without unending guilt. But I did not become angry at the lucky ones, how could I? I knew them too well from school and the playground. How could I believe that Nonel K., a sweet nerd in my class, had eaten my bread (or sucked my blood!)? It was enough to see his big brown eyes, his fleshy lips that hung open in wonderment, his gangly walk, to realize that he had no power over history, his own included. But when he left, a piece of my childhood went, because Pavel and he and I had learned to ride bikes together, and played soccer, and beaten drums in the Young Pioneers. Farewell, Nonel, I will never suspect your motives, wherever you will be. He left for Israel, but in time moved to America.

Ceausescu's own relationship with Jews deserves a look. In 1945 the stuttering enforcer had had a run-in with none other than Ana Pauker. During the war, after the Communist intellectuals, the "profs," had fled to Moscow, boss Gheorghiu had appointed all sorts of illiterates to top positions in the party: Ceausescu had become secretary general of the Young Communist League, "reservoir of the party's future strength." Then Ana and the intellectuals came back, wearing Russian uniforms. Now, imagine someone of Ana's standards finding as boss of the Communist youth an illiterate egomaniac with mushroom cloud hair. She terminated him, sent him down to a province as a local organizer. But Gheorghiu fought to reinstate Ceausescu, and eight months later he was back in Bucharest. The most pressing problem then were the peasants resisting collectivization. In 1948, the shock-haired Quasimodo was appointed number two man for agriculture, the number two always being the one with his finger on the trigger. One year later he was number two in the army. Soon thereafter he was sent to the KGB academy, and Ana realized how unwise she had been to kick the ground from under him. But it was too late to make peace. Not only did he assist zealously in her downfall when Stalin gave the nod, he also made sure that despite the party's policy of cyclic rehabilitations ("acquittals after death," my dad called them sarcastically), Ana would never be rehabilitated. Pleasing many anti-Semites in and outside the party, he made sure that she would remain a permanent apostate.

Ceausescu could not be blamed for disliking Ana (the dislike was mutual), but being a typical example of the destitute peasant syndrome, he disliked all Jews. They were too complex for his mind. Also, the world paid too much attention to them. As the revelation of the Holocaust shaped Europe's public consciousness, people were cast into five moral categories: the exterminators, the henchmen, the victims, the indifferent bystanders, the rescuers. The victims were at the core of this frightening morality play, central to all the subsequent judgments; they were the setters of standards, like in a latter day Old Testament.

The idea that anyone could set standards apart from the Communist party, which meant himself, was enough to put Ceausescu into a cold rage. But his shrewd peasant mind helped him keep control and even evolve a profitable strategy: the Jews would no longer be allowed in the party leadership (that should please the home boys); instead, there would be a gradual mass emigration to Israel, which was good for his image in the West, and an excellent way to court America. He also made money off that policy. It is said that for each immigrant from Romania, the state of Israel paid him $5,000. The kingdom of Romania came out of the war with more than 400,000 Jewish survivors. Barely 15,000 still live there today. Since most of those who left went to Israel, selling them amounted to many millions. The mass departure was rationalized thus: The Jews were bourgeois, because their families had owned "businesses," from stores to pushcarts. And they left not because Communism was a failure, but because they'd always yearned to emigrate, leaving us here, alone with our pain and destitution. These lines did not come down in directives or in the state press, but were spread methodically by the middle-rung party activists.

The psychological maneuvering was effective: not only did the ethnic Romanians feel that letting the Jews emigrate was unfair, after they'd been so brainwashed about all being equal, but they were made to feel that they were the losers, the last to count, the locked in and forgotten— excellent training for reviving nationalism. Starved for selfhood after the long Soviet occupation, the Romanians bought the nationalism lock, stock, and barrel. They would pay dearly for it.

Do I sound upset at the Romanians? I am. It may not be terribly significant that during World War II the Yiddish theater of Bucharest performed intermittently, occasionally attended by Germans who'd never witnessed an act of Jewish culture in Germany. It is quite amazing that over 400,000 Jews survived the Holocaust in Romania, *during the alliance with Hitler.* But the Romanians neither claimed the merit of that salvation, nor faced the killings of Jews in Transnistria, to which Romanian military units participated. They did not open the records, both good and bad, for fear of being judged. Had they done so, they would've learned that the world was not after them, but even more importantly, they would have felt clean in their own conscience.

True, after the war, no nations were disposed to be totally honest about their participation in the Holocaust. Among the numerous Romanian Jews in Israel the perspective of what had happened was sadly realistic. "Marshal Antonescu saved us, ask any Romanian Jew," I was told by actor/comedian Yakov Bodo, a prominent Romanian survivor. "Without him, I wouldn't be here, talking to you. But that doesn't excuse the Transnistria killings." I felt like turning towards my unseen compatriots, to reach into the distance and grab them by the shoulders: Wake up! Dare to fight distrust, dare to question! Take pride in sincerity! Stop being afraid!

The events I've evoked, which happened in the mid-sixties, did not affect my friendship with SZ. Floating above all that, he and I discussed the real stuff: quantum physics, life on other planets, the fall of civilizations (hopefully Communism would soon fall too!), and better sex than what we paid for at the unfinished clinic.

Having acquired an insight into the Jews' lives, I applied to myself the notion of their complex double identity: what would happen to me if I became a writer and fancied all of a sudden belonging to the world, not just to Romania alone? Thinking independently, acting out of the mold, yet upholding my right to still be from the mold? Would I also be distrusted, mocked in jokes, spat at, and then watched with envy as I trekked out of the native landscape into the world?

Meanwhile, Ceausescu was biding his time. The day would soon come when nationalism disguised as independence would become his cause; he would even publish books about it, ghostwritten in his name, his theoretical contribution to Marxism. Meanwhile, in countless ways, he dusted off Romania's old identity. The national heroes deserved to be slipped back into the school books. The patriotic heart deserved to be stroked. But the purpose was not freedom. The purpose was to enthrone a new soldier-king, our first Communist one. Ceausescu.

O ur high school had a literary society which put out a mimeo-graphed "young talents' bulletin." I was published in the bulletin. Then, when I was barely sixteen, I was published in the young talents' section of a legitimate literary weekly. I started going to public readings. I was published in more magazines, and got paid symbolic sums. I began to develop a writer's pride. I was an artisan of beauty, at pennies a word, publishing a poem every few months. I finished high school, enrolled in the Foreign Languages Institute of Bucharest University. English was my major. Now I had two purposes in life: to write, and to learn English. Writing was for making money (scared of failing, I didn't openly grant it a higher purpose), English was for feeling part of the world—meaning listening to the Voice of America, the "poison-forked tongue of capitalism." That poison tongue and Radio Free Europe were the only sources of unbiased information in the Soviet bloc.

Starting in my second year of college, I worked during the summers as a guide/interpreter for the Ministry of Culture. Guide/interpreters were part-time employees of the state, and chaperoned official foreign guests. I practiced my English with English people, Americans, Swedes, Danes, Dutch, Icelanders, most of whom were writers, journalists, busi-nessmen. I never told those people that I wrote literature; there was a chasm between me the writer, and me the starving student. They ex-pressed shock that in these boondocks, under alien stars, there was orga-nized culture. That we were capable of dances and songs, architecture, painting, and theater. At the end of their visits, I would ask them, "Any paperbacks you're not taking back with you?"

"Excuse me?" asked the respective Englishman, or American, or Swede. "Paperbacks?"

They thought they had misheard me, since I wasn't asking for whis-key, Kent cigarettes, an electric razor, or money.

"Yes, paperback novels, in English."

"Uh . . . yeah, sure."

So they gave me their airplane reading material. For a few bucks, they could buy other copies at the next airport. And my plea was hard to resist. I was eighteen, nineteen, a freshman student who spoke fluent English, though with an audible accent—oh boy, the hours I spent twisting my tongue, to improve my rendition of those bastard Anglo-Saxon sounds! For our foreign guests, I and my accent had a kind of alien charm. So those books were my extra payment, my tip.

Thus, I got to read *The Centaur* by John Updike, *Naked Lunch* by W. S. Burroughs, *On the Road* by Jack Kerouac, *One Flew over the Cuckoo's Nest* by Ken Kesey, *Bullet Park* by John Cheever, *Portnoy's Complaint* by Phillip Roth, *The Confessions of Nat Turner* by William Styron, and many more. I read them and passed them to my friends, but not before pressing them for their quick return, so I could read them again. Some of them shocked me, most of them delighted me—I almost gasped with pleasure reading *Portnoy's Complaint*, what a refreshing outburst of identity, what a book, especially since I read it right after one by that Sophocles of the South, Faulkner, and found it stiff, pompous, and tragic. With each book, I took a dream trip to America. I luxuriated in the inner sounds of English written by men and women of talent. And I realized what a chance I would be taking, if I ever defected. I was now becoming a writer in Romanian. I would have to write in English. But the versatility, the richness, the mental agility of the writers I was reading convinced me that even they, the natives, had worked hard to master English. I couldn't do it. And even supposing that I could, what would I do without Romania? I didn't think I could take my country with me, into the English language.

Romania didn't make sense outside herself. She just didn't. And I would be nothing without her. Without my nationhood and my past.

It was incredible. I, a defiant rebel, I, the son of two bohemian artists, felt organically built out of the ancestral experience of my nation, and honor bound to enshrine that experience into my writing. That was what writing was about, wasn't it? So I reckoned, if I defected, I wouldn't be able to write of Romania for all mankind to read. Therefore I'd be nothing.

Yet I wanted to escape my given limits. I wanted my own freedom to discover who and what I was, aside from just my roots. That deep pain for freedom—pain—I can call it nothing else, was the motor of my life, and it had been so since my childhood.

But still, when brought to stare freedom in the face, I would shudder. All right, I would try to slash-and-burn my roots. After that, what would remain?

Myself.

Which myself?

Another myself. A new myself, undiscovered.

But did that other myself exist?

There was a simpler way to ask the question. Could I make myself write in another language? If I could achieve that, I had a chance of surviving as an author.

But I had never written literature in English. Not even one poem. I studied the pages of yet another paperback—it was Truman Capote's *Other Voices, Other Rooms.* The writing was opulent, decadent, and sensuous—so much craft had gone into writing it. I stared at the compact English words, trying to imagine the travail of that other author, who had composed his words at the world's other end, using a typewriter no doubt electric and high-tech and a million times better than mine.

I lay in bed on those hot Bucharest summer nights, hearing with distraction the jangle of the last streetcars, or domestic fights and then sighs of copulation in other apartments. I heard the street sweepers roll their garbage carts down the streets. Now and then there was the screeching halt of a large vehicle, followed by hurried footfalls, doors opening, slamming again: somewhere, a home was raided, a citizen was taken away for interrogation. More footfalls, drunken ones. Burps, sounds of retching: workers were returning home after a pub crawl. I was surrounded by the music of Communism.

My purveyors of used paperbacks read the most recent works of fiction in English, so they kept me pretty *au courant* with what went on in literary America. To read the classics, I had the American Library, which had just opened in Bucharest, part of the first cultural agreement between the two countries; simultaneously, a Romanian library had opened in New York City. The cultural agreement was a big step in the gradual warming-up toward America. Between my two sources, I was becoming well informed, even developing a snob's taste. Hemingway and Faulkner were impressive, but passe. I found Updike boring. And I knew that Jackie Susann was "trash."

Eventually, my English became good enough for me to translate literary material. The Bucharest publishing houses were looking for translators, and my dad used his old contacts among editors to recommend me for jobs. I lucked out: I was assigned to translate James Baldwin's *Going to Meet the Man,* the first book in Romanian by an American black. I did a decent job, and made some money. The book was published, and I was invited to my first cocktail party at the U.S. embassy. Then I translated a book of essays by E. M. Forster, and got invited to the British embassy. About the same time, my first book of poems was published, with good reviews. I finished a book of stories, started to work on my first novel, but didn't give up my chaperoning of foreign guests. I read George Orwell, Hubert Selby Jr., Norman Mailer, William Styron, J. D. Salinger, Gore Vidal, more Saul Bellow—I eventually translated Bellow's *Herzog,* but it was never printed because I defected. I also read poets: T. S. Eliot; William Carlos Williams, Ferlinghetti, in whose City Lights Bookshop I would step one day; John Ashbery, whom I later met and befriended. I tried to get my hands on those authors' biographies or published interviews, to get glimpses of their destinies. I hoped that I would find in them coincidences with my own. And maybe an indirect answer to the lurching question: could someone of my background aspire to write in English?

Plenty of times, I gave myself the answer: no. With bitter certainty, no. Those writers in English belonged to a shiny race of aliens. I couldn't become one of them, I couldn't compete.

But most of the American writers seemed to have conquered the world with rather simple stuff. Personal stories, their own stories. What made them so hot, that the whole world read them breathlessly, as if to catch up on the latest finds in science? Why were they so *ahead?* I couldn't answer that question.

Today, as I write in English with well earned confidence, as I write these lines in which I am my own character, it seems outlandish that at one time this language was forbidden to me. But then I glance around my office, and see the shelves of dictionaries and encyclopedias without which, years ago, I couldn't write one line. I had to check all my words, again and again. Like an invalid who couldn't take a single step without leaning on a cane. I didn't find English superior to my mother tongue. But it was a universal language, and crisp, concise, direct. It felt *advanced,* the right tool for world communication. Romanian was poetic, folkloric, complex, quaint. Its Latin structure with its Slavic and Turkic additions gave it an essential taste of reality. Romanian was so present in me, naturally, while English seemed so aloof. I feared that I'd never be able to write English with the ring of truth and with a native's richness of juices.

I started to write in English only weeks after I defected, under the pressure of total panic. I chained myself to my typewriter, gasped, ground my teeth, and died on a creaky swivel chair, hitting the keys from dawn till night. Most nights, after a couple hours of troubled sleep, I woke up in the dead of darkness and went back to pounding the keys, into the next dawn. Like a maniac. It worked. I did it.

It took years, of course, but that I expected: toiling for years, in solitude and sometimes in despair, comes with the territory. I'd been writing from age sixteen. I'm still writing. Nothing, no change in me or in the working of this planet can alter that. I got married for the first time, I got divorced, I spent several years single, I wrote movies, I became a movie director, I met my second wife, we got married, we had a child, we had another child. In between all those stations in life, there were the stations in my destiny as a writer. Some were full of ecstasy, others rife with bitterness and despair. While all the other events of my life partook of the normal human adventure, the stations of writing were known only to me, and only I remembered them as different, separate, each useful in a specific way, each unrepeatable under their generic name: writing.

I was writing. I'm still writing. Leaders come and go, I write. Comets show up in the sky, and planes get hijacked, I write. Movie stars pass the million dollar salary mark, then the ten million dollar mark, then the twenty million, I write. Desert Storm starts, Desert Storm is victorious, Desert Storm is over, I write. George Bush steps down, Bill Clinton takes over, I write. O. J. Simpson is a football legend, is a wife killer, is a free man again, is a mystifying enigma for the world, I write, I write, I write.

Continuously.

"You're a rock," my wife says to me sometimes. She means it as praise, and as a criticism too.

"I'm a maniac," I correct her.

"You're a rock," she insists.

"A small one," I hurry to add, feeling the chills of superstition down my spine: will I live after this praise from her, or will I be punished with cancer, with writer's block, with Alzheimer's?

"You're a rock," she utters for the third time, and shakes her head with the powerlessness of humans facing natural phenomena. "And you're driving me crazy."

"I'm sorry."

"Don't be sorry, I love you. You just can't help it."

For some twelve years, I've kept on my desk the photograph of a Polish man who was a fellow writer, what else. I stood it up against my computer one day, and it's still there. I've learned every detail of his face, of his hands folded together under his chin, as if in a gesture of surrender. That man is Joseph Conrad, who learned English in his twenties, never wrote fiction in English until he was past thirty, and became one of the greatest stylists in the English language.

Don't let me jump ahead. I was still in Bucharest, hunting for used paperbacks. I still lived with Mother. Dad, remarried now, had been handed his first important position in the system: publisher of that theater magazine. Mom expected me to take over the duties he had so grossly neglected, in other words to take care of her. I didn't have the guts to move out. I was ready to be on my own, I'd been alone inside me for the last five years anyway, and I was making some money. But if I just hinted at looking for my own place, she pulled out all the stops, changed back into the tearful Medea who crawled on Pavel's grave at the cemetery, and made it plain that my autonomy would come complete with unending guilt. At the same time, she turned herself into a belated wet nurse of my "literary calling." She rearranged Dad's study for me—by this time, we'd won a suit against that pair of activist intruders in our home—and brought me my coffee or my lunch, and set them by my noisy old typewriter. She tiptoed out of the study, in a show of caring humility. But she still told her friends that in my creativity I took after her alone. Trying to win me back, she was the same as usual, big and over the top; still, her recognition of a changing balance of power softened me. I felt pity for her. The woman that had looked so striking was now faded, and her poses were becoming sad. In her last Shakespearean play, *Richard III,* she had played Queen Elizabeth, whose sons had been killed to clear Richard's path to the throne. She had wept naturally in act four, declaiming: "Ah my poor princes, ah my tender babes . . . / Hover about me with your airy wings, / And hear your mother's lamentation." I got teary eyed sitting in the theater, watching her. But as I gave in to pity and guilt, I did warn her: "No more theater at home, all right?" And that was my first overt act of adulthood.

After two years of not seeing Dad, I gave in. In truth, he had been sending Uncle Nicu to plead with me to see him. The old soldier, painfully in love, as I realized later, with my cousins Radu and Sandu and with me, young sons that he hadn't fathered, fought to turn me around as hard as he'd fought in Russia. He pleaded, promised, demonstrated. I grumpily listened, and concealed my wild pleasure each time he uttered, "Your father loves you." Finally, I went to see him at his office. He took me back to his apartment, I strained myself to be civil to the new wife, and . . . my father got off the hook again: he did not come out with explanations as to why he had acted towards me the way he had. Still did not mention anything from the past, did not ask any questions about how tough it had been for me, or admit how tough it had been for himself.

I had to take him for what he was. To keep up with his younger wife, my father became trendy, and acted belatedly as a social climber. His new life was fun: they went out, listened to imported pop music, lived beyond their means. When I came to visit, he forced his wife to make dinner, and during dinner critiqued my early writings. Or we talked politics. Astounding things went on in the political sphere. The Prague spring. We made bets about whether the Russians would invade Czechoslovakia or not, acting frivolously although at heart we were scared for the Czechs, and for ourselves—Romania had rejected the old economic arrangements with Russia, and Bucharest was crawling with entrepreneurs from France and West Germany. I was studying for my finals, knowing that I'd be drafted immediately after, into Romania's compulsory military service. It was in the last year of Romania's free abortion policy, and the other initiates of the dental chair and I were now having affairs with the sweetest of Romanian mistresses: married women, neglected by mid-level activist husbands and flattered to be desired by students majoring in English. They made us gifts of smuggled-in blue jeans, and taught us sexual kinkiness. I wrote fiercely realistic fiction, utterly against Romania's flowery literary style. I attended literary circles and was a terror.

Just like I did, the regime itself behaved like Communism's enfant terrible. All puppet states had said yes to Russia's "new economic integration"—except Romania. When Israel won the Six Day War, Russia and all the satellites broke relations with them—except Romania. Any time the Russians mustered some collective denunciation of China, Romania would not join. Ceausescu was deftly pursuing his U.S. connection through his Israel connection. Romanian economists started publishing feasibility studies about making the *leu* convertible to the dollar. I was translating American authors. In every respect, we were taunting the bear.

In truth, Romania's changes were cosmetic. The party was still all too powerful. All elections ran one unopposed candidate, Ceausescu, and his appointees. The press remained muzzled. The only people allowed to expatriate were the Jews and the Saxons, a minority who had settled in Transylvania in the thirteenth century and still spoke the archaic German of their time of arrival; now those patriarchal farmers were being bought out by West Germany. Their departure left behind Germanic *dorfs* deserted just like the once lively Jewish *shtetls*. There was still no free travel for the ethnic Romanians, yet a few hidden doorways creaked open. For instance, my uncle in New York had worked on one U.S. congressman after another, until his wife and two sons, my two first cousins, were allowed to leave. I was to see them again in New York after my defection.

Still by comparison with the fifties, those were "good" times. Then suddenly the good times were over in the most shocking fashion. The Russians invaded Czechoslovakia. I found myself, along with hundreds of other young Bucharesters, in front of the Czech embassy. Wondering if the Securitate might punish us, we wrote slogans of friendship and solidarity on cardboard. No one showed up to tear them away from us. We clamped them on the bars of the Czech embassy's gate, and uttered calls of sympathy and outrage. Still, no one stopped us. I again had that feeling of being caught in a giant rifle's crosshairs. I heard a strange voice of reason inside me, arguing: What are you doing, this is useless, the Czechs are doomed! Then again: What are you doing, the Russians won't let you get away with this, the Russians won't let Romania slip away! I heard it, but my need to believe in a change was too strong. The hope that this was the break, for me and all of us, was too overwhelming. We left our improvised signs before the embassy and went home, feeling strangely doomed, and strangely proud. We had declared ourselves publicly. But now, what would happen?

What happened was a giant rally the next day, in the vast square between the former Royal Palace and the RCP's Central Committee building. Ceausescu himself called for it. Speaking from the RCP building's second-story balcony, the same one from which he would try to appease the booing crowds in 1989, the little man with exploding hair did something so unthinkable that down in the square a hundred thousand listeners shuddered like one person. *"Romania will not join the infamous invasion of Czechoslovakia,"* he shouted. *"We and all other peace-loving nations will struggle to our utmost to reverse this moment of shame!"* And the crowd, shivering as if stepping towards the gallows, erupted nonetheless in its ancestral clamor of approval. We were ready. We were ready to follow, suicidally, our new hero king.

Reeling and stumbling along the crowded streets, I went to visit my father. I felt that I'd committed myself to a sacred fight for independence and honor. Yet it was also a pact with the devil: our leader was an extreme authoritarian. Twenty years before, he had been responsible for the harshest acts of communizing Romania. He had supervised the jailing and killing of whole generations. He had recently struck us, the young, in our most intimate freedom, by banning the free abortions and taking contraceptives off the market. To qualify for state-issued contraceptives, each Romanian woman had to bear five children first. We had to strengthen the numbers of our threatened nation.

Thus, after having shouted my allegiance to the leader, I felt weird. This, the Grand Moment of our separation from Moscow, was not liberating us inside. The leader had not offered reforms in the system; on the contrary, he had stressed discipline, loyalty, unswerving obedience to his orders. I identified the strange taste in my mouth: it tasted quite like shaking hands with that Securitate bully when I was thirteen.

By the time I figured that out, I was knocking on my father's apartment door. He opened it wearing his writer's attire, a bathrobe that reeked of cigarettes; he spent whole days in that bathrobe, writing. Behind him, in the living room, loomed my uncle Nicu. They looked like they'd had an argument. My uncle spoke, to me, but really to my father. "There are times when even a child cannot be selfish," he said, mangling the words, his eyes aflame, his face twitching. "There are times when even our children must respond to the call of duty."

I was silent. My father was silent. But I could guess what they had been talking about. That child was me. My father had wondered how far Ceausescu would take his gamble. Would he dare the Russians militarily? If he did, Romania would be invaded in a few days, and I and other kids would be killed on those fields that had soaked in blood since Romania was called Romania. They started practically outside the door, those fields. They surrounded Bucharest, turning up nameless human bones every time a plow dug too deep into that bloodthirsty land.

My Uncle Nicu, the Popescus' dean of age, our hero, was buying Ceausescu's crusade. He and Dad had watched it on Dad's black-and-white TV: the leader, gesturing stiffly in front of a clamoring crowd that included me.

And yet, I felt that even my uncle had misgivings. His twitching face spelled inner conflict. He had to preach patriotism to me, for the whole meaning of his life was patriotism. Yet he, the veteran, knew that it was untenable, that we would be sitting ducks.

"We'll see how the Americans react," muttered my father, breaking the silence. "Maybe these children won't have to suffer."

Neither they nor I voiced our skepticism about the Americans offering us protection if the Russian juggernaut started rolling. Why would they? Both my uncle and my father had called my generation children. I did not fail to notice that. But the leader treated all of us as children. And the crowds responded like children, cheering, eager to be played with. Meanwhile, my father, my uncle, and I talked of this momentuous juncture in our fate and realized that we could do nothing to give it direction. My uncle clung to words of love for land and honor in defending it. My father voiced the uncertain hope of American action. I said almost nothing, except for describing the rally. I was the most confused.

Yet about one thing I was clear, and only hours after the leader's raucous voice had pricked up my hairs in a rush of emotion that had felt so genuine: whatever elation we had felt, caught in that crowd in front of his balcony, the violation of our selves by the state could still happen, at any time, in any guise. This time it came in the form of satisfied patriotism, but it was a violation nonetheless, for there were no other options. Here, said the leader, I grant you back the pride of being Romanian; die for it, and for me!

Thus, in August 1968, Ceausescu won the gamble of rekindling nationalism and sticking it into Russia's face. From then on, an unofficial ally of the West, he received lavish praise from U.S. presidents Johnson, Nixon, and Carter. Carter called him a freedom fighter. At home, the freedom fighter tightened the screws, in the name of Romania's survival. The Securitate had carte blanche to inforce control any way it saw fit, because we were *free*! Free of the Russians, and that we were. But free of our fellow Romanians who had learned at the Soviet school we were not. Ceausescu's home rule was even less relaxed and enlightened than the Soviets'. It did not matter. He had told us that we were free. It was a word only, but we gobbled it up.

I lived a strange experience, half the time fooling myself that I was free, or at least freer, the other half remembering that my phone still clicked from being tapped, that in the streets I still saw the same Securitate men tailing me, that I still did not have my passport at home, stored casually in some drawer, and that what I published was still scrutinized for provocative content.

The Russians played it cool. The damage in public relations from invading Romania would have outweighed the gains, so they chose instead to strangle her economically. For years, they had bought 80 percent of Romania's exports. They dropped their purchase orders, and stopped supplying us with oil and natural gas. Ceausescu had to find his oil in Iran, and he soon went to visit officially the still undeposed shah. Looking for new markets, he started developing new products: cars, chemicals, small planes, furniture, appliances—all hard to make and hard to sell for a newcomer. But he zealously persisted, and since the products didn't sell, and the country's foreign debt soared, the effect on Romanian life was somewhat positive: we felt in league with the world. The Romanian merchant marine quadrupled in tonnage, the port of Constanta became a monster, the Danube was dotted with industrial mammoths that used up and polluted the river waters. In effect, the Russians had encouraged Ceausescu's egomania: you want to play in the big league? Go right ahead. Ceausescu did, and discovered how uncompetitive Romania's economy was. He had to fall back on austerity. Caught in the game, the Romanians kept cheering on empty stomachs—the combination of cheers and hunger was inebriating.

At the top, servility reigned. Reality became propaganda, and vice versa. Ceausescu was openly addressed as *conducator,* leader; the members of his entourage competed with each other in inventing flattery for his courage, his original contribution to Marxism, his astuteness in politics, economics, science, even his genius. He was "the best beloved son of the people." The identities of ordinary Romanians no longer melted into the We of Communism victorious, but into the He of the leader. Ceausescu had a thirst for personal worship to which the Romanians responded with a thirst for self-abolishment, with a desperate, addictive dependency on the fateful leader. They praised, and he let himself be praised. Eventually, someone would come up with a flattery so ultimate that it beat the stelae of the pharaohs: Nicolae Ceausescu was *truth itself.*

Petru Popescu

* * *

When I published my first novel, the political situation was still far from total dementia. Yet, it was something of a miracle that *Prins* (*Captive*) was printed. *Captive* was a daring political allegory, starring a young man who challenged the regime's essential traits: the constant control from above, the bureaucracy's festive incompetence, the stifling of the young generation's energies, and the ubiquitous presence of the Securitate, which cruised behind my hero in the shape of a sinister shark-like black car. The story was set in a withering Bucharest, infected with a mediocrity that killed all initiative, and sentenced ordinary people to lonely confusion. The metaphor for this gradual death was that the protagonist himself was dying of cancer. To make sure that my message came through, I selected for the cover a photo of an emaciated young male staring out of a barred window. The subversive cover passed the censorship easily, because the censors and I were wrangling over the manuscript itself, stuffed with political hints or direct criticisms on every page. Missing the proverbial forest for the trees, the censors became so busy "lightening" the pages that the content, a vast rave against the regime, remained. The book, I was told by one reader, conveyed Communism almost physically, like a gag in the throat. One felt like spewing it out, with a loud indignant shout of: NO!

My grim story became popular overnight. I'd guessed the mood of the readers, especially the young ones: we all were that dying young man. We all were monitored, pursued, drained of our vigor and idealism, appeased with cheap fiestas, and then left to die slowly. My cry of angry helplessness was exactly how young Romanians felt at the time.

So the book was out, and its bitter realism felt good. I was pictured on the back cover. All of a sudden, strangers started shaking my hand in the street or in streetcars and busses. One youngster, skinny, freckled, wearing a beret pulled down almost to his eyebrows, expressed that generational appreciation: "You did something for *us*." When we shook hands, I noticed his fingers, stained from industrial oil. He was a worker, a member of the proletariat! Other readers came forth with smiles and outstretched hands, and they were not from the disaffected middle class. They too were of worker or even peasant background. What united us was the big city, and that stifling sense of captivity. I'd pierced through class barriers. I lost my elitism in a hurry, how could I not, and eagerly went to meetings with my readers in working class neighborhoods, or in those villages around Bucharest that had public libraries. I was happy to dress down and speak plain, I belonged!

Due to the unexpectedness of my attack and the directness of my means, I had managed what powerful and influential authors had not: a global rejection of the regime. But apart from my achievement, what stunned me was that I now had *my* readers. Unknown, invisible to me, they communicated back that they understood me, because I had understood *them*. I was their equal, their mate. I felt as if I had received a message of baffling familiarity from Mars, but they did not live on Mars, they lived next door!

It seemed that I had to take myself seriously. I was a real writer now.

My first novel granted me membership in the Romanian Writers' Guild. In our equalized Communist culture, the Guild's gates were open to just about anyone who had published anything at all. Coincidentally, the Writers' Guild discovered my linguistic skills. I was asked to serve as guide and interpreter to the Guild's British and American guests. This was a time when the party allocated fat budgets for the Guild to invite foreign writers and journalists to Romania, all expenses paid; since an American commitment to defend Romania from a Russian invasion could not be secured, the next best thing would be for the English language intelligentsia and press to cry murder if the Russians crossed the river Prut and smashed their way into Bucharest.

So the Writers' Guild invited the revered names in U.S. and British letters to meet their Romanian confreres. Unaware of the real reason behind those invitations, the foreigners obliged. Most came without much notion of what Romania was, and would have been hard-pressed to find it on the map.

The Guild House, ex-abode of a thirties' petroleum magnate, was on Bucharest's finest avenue, the Kiseleff Chaussee, which was lined with handsome oaks and lindens. At the boulevard's midpoint rose the Arch of Triumph, erected to celebrate Transylvania's union with the fatherland after World War I. On each side, broad tree-shaded sidewalks separated the avenue from paved access roads to mansions that had once been owned by grain, timber, or petroleum tycoons. Now they housed foreign embassies, or state institutions such as the Writers' Guild. The location bore proof of literature's importance in the state's propaganda arsenal.

It was one of Communism's stated missions to build a culture for the masses. It took this seriously, wiping out Romania's embarrassing illiteracy. Mass production of inexpensive books on countless subjects was one of Communism's boons (when Communism collapsed, that culture-for-all was replaced with CNN, and with translated potboilers by Sandra Brown and John Grisham). The Guild was wealthy, too: it owned magazines and publishing houses and a pension fund. It had a writers' loaning plan which kept authors in line even more effectively than the vigilance of censorship. Traditionally poor and bohemian, the Romanian writers flocked to the loan office. They found a generous banker in Communism, and that, in my opinion, explained why so few of them were dissidents.

The Guild House, in French Victorian style, rose inside a vast yard closed in by wrought iron fences. It had a wide driveway, and stately front steps. Inside, it was appointed with heavy chandeliers, magnificently coffered ceilings, and sofas of red plush. On the lot next to it stood a fortress with a flat-topped roof bristling with antennae: the embassy of the USSR, right smack by the soft curves of the Romanian Writers' Guild. The omen of that proximity was lost on the Guild's foreign guests, but not on us. Moscow was still the ruler of our destinies, and it was held back only by a fence.

In my professional capacity as guide, I waited for each guest to come down the plane's jetway, then I had him chauffeured over to a top hotel, and chauffeured again to the Guild House. Our most respected literati gathered to meet the visitor for a welcoming chat, with political hints deftly placed here and there by the Guild's party apparatchiks. The guest gave a friendly speech, sometimes reading from his prose or reciting his poems. There was coffee and cognac, and at the end, often, embraces.

I did the interpreting. Most of the barons of our letters spoke no English. Not surprisingly, my own English was getting better; my pay was getting better too. During those interpreting jobs, I felt like I belonged to two worlds at once. To my homeland, and simultaneously to the vast planet that ignored it. It wasn't so hard to put myself inside the mind of, say, W. D. Snodgrass, a U.S. poet who had a sexy red beard and who read us a poem about a knee (yes, a knee), and to see Romania through his eyes: quaint, tragic, self-obsessed, and incomprehensible. Now, the poem about the knee, its deeper meanings notwithstanding, didn't go over too well, and that radicalized the conversation. Mr. Snodgrass began to realize that there was some serious existential despair going on behind the pseudo-literary chat. This occupied land deserved more than parables about knees. But beyond that he understood very little, so he became frustrated and asked what about Solzhenitsyn?

"What about him?" I heard myself reply. "He's Russian and he has delusions of saving the world." I went on, "and that makes great *New York Times* copy!"

Snodgrass turned to me, identifying the young rebel in me. "Why aren't you doing what Solzhenitsyn is doing?" he challenged.

And I countered beat for beat, as if someone in my head was dictating my lines, "Because I'm Romanian, not Russian. I didn't bring this curse on us, Solzhenitsyn and his people did. It's his business to agonize about it and feel guilty!"

Snodgrass stared at me. The barons of Romanian literature stared too. As a junior Guild member, I was supposed to wait my turn, and speak in respectful platitudes. Instead, I'd uttered what was on my mind, with my Romanian chip worn on my shoulder like an epaulette. There could be no doubt that "the curse" was Communism, and yet we were a Communist nation. This meeting was part of a strategy to gain America's sympathy without opening the can of worms of Romania's domestic situation. With one blurt from my big mouth, I had touched all those forbidden topics.

The poet of "knees" seemed concerned with how the elder hosts were reacting. The president of the Writers' Guild muttered that Romania had its own specific problems—alluding to our encirclement by the Russians. Snodgrass took one of the tumblers of cognac on the table and knocked it back. Almost everyone present did the same, as if to find a common ground. I, aware of my solitary position, glanced around the room. An older novelist gave me a grin that seemed friendly; I couldn't even tell whether it was phony or genuine. A Romanian poet read a poem of her own, which I translated while watching Mr. Snodgrass. I saw in his eyes, diluted by cognac, that the close brush with truth was over. He was a stranger in a strange land, and wouldn't take chances. Someone offered a toast to American poets. Snodgrass picked up another tumbler of cognac and toasted back Romanian poets. After a few more toasts, all thorny issues were safely left behind. The next morning, the leading literary weekly carried Snodgrass's picture, and a half page of his poems, in my translation.

I wondered what would've happened had I unloaded the whole truth on the poet of knees: that it made no sense to write Solzhenitsyn-style about Romanian gulags, because Romania was a satellite and no one gave a damn about the satellites' gulags or the satellites period. Czechoslovakia had just given the world a good show, and sunk without a bubble. Besides, we really no longer had gulags; to make points with the West, Ceausescu had freed all but his most obdurate critics. It made no difference, the ceaseless Securitate surveillance turned us into a nation-size gulag. Worse, out of patriotism we acted as our own wardens. Amid Snodgrass's audience were men who had served jail terms, yet recently had been "rehabilitated," and here they sat next to party darlings and even suspected Securitate informants—the Writers' Guild had them too. The game was no longer played as in Solzhenitsyn's novels, whose black-and-white moral demarcations were already obsolete. Ceausescu had found the best way to dupe us into enslaving ourselves: patriotism.

I knew all about it, for I was writing my second novel, *Dulce Ca Mierea E Glontul Patrei*. In translation, the title means *Sweet as Honey Is My Homeland's Bullet*. It sounds clumsy in English, but not in Romanian, for it is a takeoff on the Latin saying *Dulce et decorum est pro patria mori*. Sweet and gracious, it is to die for one's homeland. Half of my title was packed with the traditional rhetoric of patriotism, while the other half punished the first with death by firing squad. In this novel, four cadets of an officers' school served their term against the lethal suspense of a potential Russian invasion. The teller of the story (myself) carried on a dialogue with an older relative, a veteran of World War II (my uncle Nicu, of course). The book described the suicidal absurdity of our stand against the Russians, the suicidal absurdity of all our patriotic stands. And I wrote it feeling torn every day between my patriotism and my true conscience. Every day, I kept filling pages, obsessing along with my heroes about the fundamental question: is it worth dying for a homeland, if that homeland was one like ours?

Thus the American poet who wrote about knees made me mighty angry. Why was he, who had no such dilemmas, so important? What made him so meaningful, why was he sitting there surrounded by us all, like a prophet? The answer was crudely simple. Because he was from America, and wrote in English.

I'd been uncomfortable at those literary ceremonies for a while, and the one honoring Mr. Snodgrass (who later offered me an autographed collection of his poems titled *Heart's Needle*) would be my last. I'd met my share of Americans of the if-it's-Tuesday-it-must-be-Romania variety, which included William Saroyan, who got drunk and became aggressive; John Updike, visibly in a hurry to leave, grand old man Erskine Caldwell, who told me that Romania reminded him of his own Tobacco Road ("That's big of you," I quipped back), the critic Leslie Fiedler, laid back and accompanied by a New York beauty twenty years younger than him. From the Brits, the poised and artistic Francis King was an exception to the if-it's-Tuesday rule: he was in touch, sympathetic, and real. They all came, they all passed the wrought-iron gates of the great mansion, they liked the drinks, the dinners, and the chauffeured excursions to the Carpathians, the Black Sea, and the frescoed monasteries of Moldavia. They talked of their own lives with the carefreeness of strangers on a train. They left. A few dropped postcards to me, their interpreter.

So I quit that job, and went back to my native horizons. I no longer compared myself to these American gods, the pressure was off. I went to meetings with my readers, in bookstores with bowed shelves and missing light bulbs and floors made of cracked tiles. I autographed my books for skinny boys and girls with big burning eyes, and felt important. Forgotten and important. This was my lot, and it was still a lucky one. Thanks to being a writer, I didn't have to compromise as much as most people. I could even punish my antagonists by writing about them. I had a part to play, I had a mission.

Snodgrass's appearance in the mansion on the Kiseleff Chaussee became a turning point for me not because of what he wrote, but because of how he lived. A free-spirited, free-passported poet who had a nice unpressured existence at a prestigious college, fascinating the coeds with his poems and his amazing red beard. Perhaps sleeping with them too. And no angry God reached down from heaven to grab him by his beard and throw him into hell's pit. Which filled me with jealous rage. I visited my father soon thereafter, and described Snodgrass to him as a kind of fool, getting tipsy on the strong Romanian cognac and then departing down the marble stairway towards his waiting car, hopping on one foot and whistling—that was exactly how he had left, stunning some thirty uptight Romanian writers. "Why," I asked out loud, pacing my father's study with long steps, "why would someone like him have it so easy?"

"He must be pretty good."

"Bullshit," I snapped. "How can he be good, by writing about knees?"

"He must have talent. Writers don't have to suffer to be good writers."

As usual, my father was sitting at his desk, writing. He wore his faded robe. Cigarette butts overflowed his ashtray. In the slowly drifting smoke, I could see the twists of his destiny: slow and solitary, deprived of any of the joys I'd seen in the American poet.

I recomposed from memory Snodgrass's poem about the knee, and recited it to my father. Vengefully—there, what about that nonsense?

"It's fun," said my father.

Exhausted, I dropped on a chair. "He's so goddamn lucky, don't you think?"

"That's what life is about," my father shrugged, flabbergasting me completely. He was after all a rationalist and a left-winger. "Luck."

He played with his pen. To the end of his days, he wrote in longhand. I, tapping on my old Olympia, was way ahead of him technologically. I was now way ahead in public recognition too: all of Romania's youth talked about me, while Dad's audience consisted of a tight elite of cognoscenti. He never complained about that. He was my generous and thoughtful advisor, always reading my new stuff promptly, always telling me how to make it better, yet without one iota of control or competition. I was lucky that he and Mom were no longer together. Had they been, she would never have let me reconnect with him. He and I still never talked about the past, just about literature.

"Why should he be so lucky?" I mumbled, defeated.

"I don't know," said my father, but I heard it more like: I'm sorry. Very sorry for begetting you in this forgotten land.

You could have left before the war, I said to him, meanly. Not so meanly, though, for I said it to him in my mind. You could have run away.

"D'you think I'm a good writer?" I asked through dry lips. He nodded silently, while I felt that the meaning of my life had gathered in those two inches of air traversed by the movement of his chin. "What makes a writer a good writer?" I asked.

He replied promptly. "The uniqueness of a few major scenes, which become his main plot points. A writer never has to invent those scenes. They occurred in his childhood, and are deeply imbedded in his emotional memory." Dad seemed to catch himself, for he quickly glanced aside. "That's just one type of writer, of course. There are plenty of writers who write out of pure imagination."

I asked some transparent question about how good I was, about what I should do to become even better. I wanted to know whether there was enough in me to impress the world.

He got it. "Forget it," he said, "you can't guess how good you really are, or how much better you'll be eventually. The answer to that is: keep writing."

"Thanks."

He shrugged, seemed ready to go back to his own writing. But suddenly he stared at me. "Stop complaining. You were enormously lucky." I started to grumble, he raised a hand to stop me. "I know, they tore off pieces, they made you rewrite them . . ." That impersonal "they" could mean, by turns, the censors, the party itself, the Securitate. "But they need you now."

"Sure, they keep tapping my phones, but they need my patriotic art."

"You need them too," my father said equitably. "You want to keep writing and publishing good stuff. You need them to need you. That new minister of youth, he asked you to a meeting. What did he have to say?"

"Nothing much. He thought *Captive* was a good book, but why was it so grim?"

I had indeed been called to a meeting with the new minister of youth, who was also secretary of the Young Communist League. I was still technically a member of that league, into which I'd been automatically drafted in the seventh grade. The minister's name was Ion Iliescu. Pleasant, smart, urbane, and cosmopolitan, Iliescu had impressed me. Ceausescu himself had been secretary of the same league, under boss Gheorghiu, and had behaved like a hatchet man, a stance which his current biographers did their utmost to allow to remain forgotten. But Iliescu had a reformer's reputation and represented the enlightened wing of the party. Was his appointment indicative of some liberalizing process? Was Ceausescu changing? Those were the questions I asked myself while stiffly sipping from the obligatory coffee offered by Iliescu. He had asked nothing of me, but mentioned casually that the meeting's purpose was to get to know each other better. Hmm. What was going on?

"Watch what you're doing," my dad kept advising me in those days, in a tone that contained no omen. On the contrary, he sounded excited, as if a lot depended on my adroitness in those tricky but promising new political circumstances.

Things were indeed in a state of flux. Our press had just announced that U.S. President Richard Nixon had accepted an invitation to Bucharest. "After Mr. Snodgrass, Mr. Nixon," I joked to my father, but the joke fell flat. The announced event contained enormous promise, and though my father was silent, I knew that in his mind the same question revolved: were things about to change? Might the hatchet man of yesterday become today's benevolent dictator, and tomorrow's architect of a true democracy?

A true democracy. Freedom. Oh God.

The thought filled me with a strange emptiness, for it removed one constant of my emotional life—my long dream of defecting. My habit of looking around with a kind of farewell stare: I may not see this much longer. I was fated to end up somewhere else. I would try what Joseph Conrad had tried. . . .

But now, wait a second . . . if we were granted freedom, why would I leave? What for?

My yearning to defect had already been weakened by the success of *Captive*. I had an audience now. I meant something to thousands of invisible brothers and sisters. How could I leave them?

I looked at my father and he looked back at me. I had the clear feeling that my thoughts had been his, at an earlier time. I wanted a confirmation, but I did not dare to ask for it. That feeling of similarity between us was too precious for me, I would not take the risk of hearing it denied. So I would say good-bye to my father, and walk home—usually late at night, after a few hours of debating Romania's fate. Once, on the way back, I stopped in Gradina Icoanei, a tiny municipal park adorned with the bronze statue of some nineteenth-century patriot. I knew that park well, I'd often played there with Pavel before he died. Neither of us had ever bothered to examine that dusty low pedestal, and learn the name of the hero standing on it. It was too dark for me to read it now. I sat down on a lopsided bench and tried to gather my thoughts.

It wasn't easy. I was barely over twenty, and needed to understand who I was and where I was headed. But I felt that neither my identity nor my direction were in my hands. I let a moonbeam hit my face. I closed my eyes, and saw unexpectedly a pageant of history. I perceived history as a revolving continuum, ever-present, the same, and occurring simultaneously in countless episodes, all of which, old or new, were still some-how contemporaneous and current. Just as the earth revolved around the sun and the moon around the earth, our history circled around me, syn-chronous with me, and with itself.

I saw Romania's history since the Roman occupation. A central brick in our foundation was occupation itself. We had been born through an act of occupation, when the Dacians and Romans had mingled to produce the Romanians.

I saw our pagan ancestors, the Dacian kings who carried into their battle against Rome a unique banner shaped like a wolf's head. Beyond the wolf's snarling fangs, the high winds of the Carpathian peaks trum-peted shrilly. On came the Dacians, knocking down mountainsides upon the Roman legionnaires filing through the passes below. The Dacians stormed down the cliffs to finish off the legionnaires with knives not much smoother or sharper than early man's paleolithic flints which were still being unearthed by the plows of Romanian farmers every spring. But . . .

The Dacians lost, and disappeared from history.

I breathed. That spell of time passed, yet somehow I knew that it hadn't disappeared. It remained in its own section of the past, *happening*.

I sat quietly on my lopsided bench. Rome had retreated. Mounted hordes of pagans raided now from the East, flooding Romania every few years, redevastating the land and remixing its population. When the migrant waves abated, the history of the long occupations by Turkey, Hungary, and Russia started, until modern Romania reappeared in pieces, between 1877 and 1922.

Who had my kinfolk been throughout all that? Unknown victims who did not gain the status of martyrs. Who were my parents? Two people who had tried to live freely in an unfree place. They had tried to have fun among a humorless, tragic breed. They had paid for it. For being different.

I was different. No matter how much I suffered remembering our history, I was still different. What was I to do?

Still caught in that past-present continuum, I watched the Roma-nians reappear in history. After their villages were raped, their churches desecrated, their boys and girls deported en masse to become the victors' servants, eunuchs, bodyguards, bedmates, the breed still reappeared. Wondering when they would suffer the next invasion. Throughout his-tory, Romanian mothers and wives added to their prayers special requests like, "Keep the locusts off our fields, and deliver us from the foreigner."

The foreigner, the foreigner.

That sounded so archaic, so full of prejudice. But in this small Balkan land, the natives yearned as desperately to be part of the world as they were afraid of being devoured by it. So in their minds the foreigner gained a mythical status. He was the powerful one, the invader, the smart one, the money-handler, the agent of technology and progress. He was also the plotter, the schemer, the devil who had made it his mission to cheat and undermine this innocent God-loving breed. Thus the Romanian's attitude towards the foreigner, whether as settler, occupier, ally, or member of a minority group, became distrusting, schizophrenic, and unpredictable.

Now history repeated itself. We were expecting the Russians to invade us again, and I, a young man yearning to live as a citizen of the world, might instead become a martyr or an unsung victim. But martyr or victim of what? I was being asked to support Ceausescu, not freedom; Ceausescu who had been brought to power by "the foreigner," then had quarrelled with the foreigner, and now acted as the foreigner *to us*.

I'd felt free after Ceausescu had denounced the invasion of Czechoslovakia. I'd lived a rare spell of being able to look my contemporaries in the eyes with the feeling that neither they nor I were accessories to a lie. But that brief sense of dignity was over. What had happened?

A gradual waking up had happened. The regime hadn't changed. The Russian yoke had been replaced with an indigenous one. Ceausescu was intensifying his personal rule, not loosening it. We were occupied from within. Even that didn't guarantee that the Russians wouldn't invade us too, eventually. Just not now, for Nixon was coming. Nixon's upcoming visit would be used by Ceausescu to enhance his prestige and power even more.

I too had a kind of power. I was a writer now. I had readers. What was I to do with my power?

The moon had changed its position, rising, leaving me in the dark. I finally decided that I could do nothing just now, and rose to continue walking home. But I was muttering a fierce promise through my clenched teeth. I was no longer utterly powerless. Soon, I would do something.

I don't want to give the impression that things had become easy for me. The trench warfare with the censors gave me stomach disorders, sleepless nights, and bouts of depression. For one thing, I could not meet them: in Kafkaesque manner, they relayed their requirements through my editors, who called me in and outlined the size and scope of the demanded changes. I had to deal with that, and hope that some artistic integrity would remain inside the savaged product. I learned how to protect my books from getting utterly castrated, by writing them with maximum subversiveness, so that enough would be left behind by the censors' scissors. I learned to survive in my words the way I survived in life.

The official, party-blessed writers did as much for my notoriety as the public's word of mouth, by blasting my work in the main literary publications. I was often the target of one particular Ceausescu henchman, Eugen Barbu, publisher of the *Morningstar,* an influential political and literary daily. He was a member of the RCP's central committee. This man had first rung the ideological alarm bells on me when I read *Death in the Window* at a literary gathering. Other official detractors took their cue from him. Meanwhile, honored writers who could have defended me chose to be neutral for specific reasons. One, Geo Bogza, a friend of my father's, formulated it. "Who gave you the right to open the file, if we couldn't do it?" he blurted at me, at my father's apartment, after a pleasant dinner during which Dad had glowed about my next novel. Bogza was a "living classic," part of the school curriculum. He and others like him were friends of Dad's. "You grew up in the lap of the statues," critic Magdalena Popescu (not a relative) told me once. Well, it was not my fault that through the fifties and sixties the statues had been merely statues. In Bogza's tone there was the jealousy of an old star watching the rise of a young one.

It was dizzying that all this fuss was about me. Even though the chips on my shoulders were old and many, I was silently growing sure of myself. Too sure. The idea Dad had put in my head, that perhaps I had not been silenced because of some larger game, became one with my hope that the political situation would improve. Maybe the publication of my work signalled that.

I was sincere in my hope, but the regime was not. Cutting slack for a kicking stud like me was done for a reason. The cries of exasperation in my novels fitted with the national mood, and our regime was nationalistic. I got a little puffed up too. I was going to write, dammit, about all the secrets the statues had not dared touch. All of a sudden I was no longer thinking about defecting. No, sir, not a bit. I liked writing. I could live with its mental drain and loneliness. And I had so much money in my account at the House of Savings and Consignations (Romania's only citizens' bank) that I could buy myself . . . a car. Small, Romanian-made, tinny and light, sputtering a thin flatulent noise, it was a Renault 8 manufactured under license and renamed the Dacia 1100, in honor of our glorious ancestors.

Oh boy. What changes that vehicle could've brought to my life. Vacations by car instead of by train. Evening drives with girlfriends. Exciting couplings in the backseat—the Romanian *jeunesse* had learned of the Americans' habit of doing it in the backseat, and was replicating it in those tinny boxes on wheels. But I never squirmed with girls in my little car before defecting, and I took only one long drive along the Danube valley. I was too busy writing. I had no time for anything except writing and my new tribe, my readers. Every week, I was invited to meetings with my readers. I went, and luxuriated in the beatitude of a Communist audience watching one of its own fight the regime in the open. This was an adoration of the shepherds, and I was the gangly adolescent Messiah.

With *Honey-Sweet Bullet,* the older readers took notice of me. My patriotic book pleased the diehards, even the ones who had languished in jail. I was now accosted by older gents and ladies, who looked me over, shocked by my youth, then muttered solemnly, *"Simti Romaneste."* You feel like a Romanian. That stroked the tenderest part of my psyche. "Feeling like a Romanian" had not disappeared, I was the proof of it. Now, those middle-aged readers were really the ones who gave the tone. They were everyone's moms and dads and uncles and aunts. I became just as well-known as a rock star. The printers rushed to reprint me, and reprint me. In the midst of my euphoria, I got nervous: I came from an enormous family, and knew that love in a Romanian family is not relaxed—it's hierarchic, dutiful, authoritarian. It tells one whom to love and how much. My readers had decided to love me. I was being taken over, no longer just a writer; but a model son.

I was being translated now, into Hungarian, Slovak, Polish, Czech, and German—albeit, for an East German audience. Feeling more and more important, I almost expected the big boss to approach me somehow. But he was busy too, playing on a much bigger stage. Still, I would've been ready to negotiate a tough deal between him and me, for if he had the country, I had the readers. In those days, Ceausescu created new political movements, all dominated by the party, of course. In factories, in state farms, in schools and colleges, in the army, wherever the employees or members or students were tightly under the party's thumb, there sprouted giant umbrella organizations meant to prove ever-wider support for the boss. They had names like the Front of National Unity, FUN, the Front of Socialist Unity, FUS (how those acronyms made my friends in the U.S. embassy laugh, and speculate whether FUS stood for "fuss" or "fuse"!). All of a sudden, the youth organization doubled its membership. Its central committee was opened to aspiring young artists, writers, scientists, and entertainers, myself included. In an organization I had belonged to since wearing shorts, I was suddenly hoisted to a top branch, right under that liberal minister of youth, Iliescu.

Needless to say, that was another cosmetic move. Tyrannies often neutralize rebels by throwing knighthoods at them. Still, never had my "unhealthy social origin" been so publicly embraced. My father grinned at me. "What did I tell you? Now you'll have a chance to change things from inside!"

My poor naive dad. The sessions of the enlarged presidium carried no power of decision. We simply were notified of directives from above, and we rubber-stamped them. We soon saw how powerless all the cogs were, except for the master cog, *Him* . In the circles concentrically closer to the dictator, the references to him were more and more impersonal yet clearer and clearer. *He, His, Him*. Or *the Comrade*. In the singular, without a name or adjective to qualify it. There was no need. Among the twenty-two million comrades of one totalitarian regime, he was the *only* Comrade.

I got to see him more often than before, and was fascinated by his stiffness, by the poverty of his expressions and gestures. He talked in an evenly hoarse tone, his right arm and extended hand cutting the air before him as if chopping salami. His hair, dyed now, still flamed about in a nuclear cloud. His X-ray eyes glowed like hot coals, yet showed a strange, empty lack of expression. At times, he almost looked like a robot. Was there something behind those eyes? Did he have a strategy, a plan? Or was he fixed in a state of suspension at the lectern from which he harangued nation, henchmen, even his own family, with no other satisfaction than to stand there, hearing his own empty voice? Maybe he was dead, but none of us knew it. His formidable apparatus kept things going, from one unopposed election to another, from one tirade to the next.

Burial of the Vine, later published in English, was the most rebellious of my novels, and the one after which I could only repent or defect. With *Burial,* I dangerously upped the ante, tackling the main forbidden theme, the party itself, and drawing a fairly transparent portrait of the first pair, Ceausescu and Elena.

Through his claimed independence, Ceausescu had won the West. Now all he had to do was coast along. As the Romanians say, it is the empty keg that rattles the loudest. Ceausescu rattled, and the world cheered the Balkan star. At home, he was for all to see an illiterate peasant at the operatic apogee of power, but abroad he was a freedom fighter and a theorist of deviant Marxism. He engaged the country in ruinous policies, devised insane social experiments, tried to robotize the young generation on the North Korean model, but kept receiving applause, loans, and honors. He slept over at Buckingham Palace, and hung out with the Shah of Iran. He gave Golda Meir gifts of the Romanian anti-aging balm Gerovital, but for good measure let Arafat vacation at the virility-inducing mud baths of the Black Sea.

That Westernizing minister of youth, Iliescu, was the only man in the top team to resist his follies explicitly. He was demoted by Ceausescu in 1971, for "intellectualism." From various minor positions, Iliescu would continue a personal challenge to Ceausescu's delirium, ending up under practical house arrest. The fall of the top liberal signalled that the country's direction had become schizophrenic, outwardly pro-Western, but in fact entirely controlled. Ceausescu had become pathologically restless: he roamed the world, and if state visits were not available, he roamed Romania. To the acclaim of throngs rushed out of worksites and schools, he offered his insights about every field of human endeavor, including art. Most of the time he was accompanied by his empress, the dour Elena, who, rumor had it, ran her own Securitate.

Finally, his self-obsession became ours too, as we could no longer escape his presence anywhere. His picture was front page every day, and our TV news programs featured only him. On payday, people were handed copies of his books, whose price had already been deducted from their wages. His voice filled the radio. There were school contests about how best to tell the story of his life and achievements. He even had the parliament present him with a bulky royal scepter, an allusion to the medieval voivodes who had battled the Turks. And his grammatical errors (they were many) were carried in the press as officially correct Romanian.

In the midst of that, he saw himself as more and more indispensable, and less and less rewarded for what he did.

Next to the pharaoh, his wife was a big-nosed, heavy-boned, wide-footed Isis who seemed to deny any concept of femininity. She, her photo, her physical being, were now forced upon us daily too. But they were not movie stars to fascinate us with their enticing physiques, so they became the demons and clowns of our jokes and sexual fantasies. In every conceivable way, Ceausescu and Elena seeped into our psyches, mine included, and when I looked, they'd become characters in my third novel.

I had started *Burial of the Vine* as the saga of a young man who had been unjustly excluded from the Communist party because he had displeased a local boss. My hero tried to regain his place in society by cozying up to an old schoolmate, now a top "realist socialist" painter. In the process, the hero seduced the wife of the schoolmate, herself an artist. I gave the painter the first name Florea, because Ceausescu himself had a brother of that name. I described his wife exactly as Elena: a big masculine horse given to aggressive outbursts of ideology. I described Ceausescu as absurd, narrow-minded, henpecked and sexually impotent. I made him physically recognizable too: short, narrow-shouldered, graceless, with big hair. Writing those lines I shivered, and shivered even worse when I submitted them to the censors. What would happen if they caught on? Would my betrayal make it to the pharaoh's desk?

That was almost worth experiencing. Imagine the scandal! I was now a best-selling author, *and* a member of the youth league's leadership. Had the book been banned, and I been prosecuted, maybe I would've found my way onto the *New York Times'* dissident list, with Solzhenitsyn and Havel. I had even made fun of Ceausescu's stuttering speech. And I paid myself the kinky pleasure of nailing his horselike empress in my book, for the story was told in the first person. Writing as "I," I described myself in possession of Elena, whom I half-undressed only, on the floor of her own studio, among triumphalist paintings.

This was nuts. Pretty suicidal.

Call it what you will, I wrote the book. I submitted it, and waited, wondering what would happen.

Nothing. Just the standard wrangle with the censors. They tore out various parts, as usual. But my hero Florea stayed in, and so did his wife.

The book came out. I waited. A number of nasty official reviews followed. Of course. My two painters, veteran party members, were described most unflatteringly. She was grandiose, dogmatic, and horny. He was impotent, tyrannical, jealous, and homicidal. They lived in a vineyard confiscated from its owners, where they and other members of the Communist elite drank and debauched themselves, with all their expenses paid. Pretty strong stuff, if I say so myself.

"Would've got you ten years in jail under Stalin," my father said. Then, as an afterthought, "It's your best work. But don't expect praise for it."

I started: "Why not?"

"Because in this novel you're not letting anyone off the hook."

That was true. So it would be an interesting experiment.

The book's first run was 22,000 copies, a huge number for a country the size of Romania. It sold like hotcakes. Meanwhile, party reviewers killed me for my "negativity," my "excessive enjoyment of the grotesque," my "confusion about history," and my "sympathy for the wrong characters." That last one referred to the book's beginning: excommunicated from the party, depressed and destitute, my hero found a job at a Jewish cemetery, where he befriended four ritual body washers. Here, the ex-Marxist watched Jews struggling to continue their ancestral culture. I was sympathetic to the Jews, but also used them as a hint: what were we, the Romanians, doing to our own culture? That being a rare instance of Jewish life openly described in fiction, it helped the book sell as much as the sexual portrait of the debauched Communists. The book ended with my excommunicated hero's return to the cemetery, where a body washer advised him not to knuckle down to history. "Seeds must bear fruit," said the body washer, a defrocked rabbi self-exiled because his own son had joined the Securitate. "Follow the way of the seed, and don't fear the wind. The wind will carry you to heights of fear, but it will finally land you on fertile land."

A subconscious premonition of my defection, that closing line? Perhaps.

The novel, while selling hotly, was selling for the wrong reasons. People read it, but got angry at me. *Burial of the Vine* did not exude that solidarity with a nation molested by history. Instead of accusing the past, it indicted the present. That pressed too many buttons. From the left of the spectrum, I was roasted for presenting communism as a gross farce. From the right, I was crucified for "putting the Jews above *us*" (pretty nervy, that, seeing that I wasn't even Jewish). Many Jewish writers were also mad: while they had never addressed their own issues, I had dared to do so.

But the most amazing thing was that most people missed the caricature of the Ceausescus. The two had become emperors without clothes. I expected to be fried, arrested even. This was the "I would do something" which I'd promised to myself after musing on history that night, returning from my father's. I was panned by the state critics; but otherwise nothing happened. It was a strange success: while a best-seller, the book was a poke in the eye to all values, not just the party-imposed ones, and in that respect it missed. The Romanians had suffered too much to be made fun of. Only the very young truly liked it. The others read it without missing one comma, but complained. Where was the writer who had restored their dignity?

I felt depressed, confused, and guilty. I hurried to finish another novel, *God's Children*. A historical allegory, set under the Ottoman occupation. It was a crowd pleaser, published in 100,000 copies. It sold: I had been forgiven. The retrenchment into history suited the cultural freeze. Ceausescu wrapped himself in the flag every day, and his regime's imagery was more and more historic. If I went historic again, likening him to Michael the Brave and Romania to Christendom's rampart against the Turks, I could become *the* court writer.

The possibility crossed my mind. I responded with an arrogant shiver of contempt. I was too good for that, wasn't I? Yet, as long as Ceausescu had the West fooled, court writer was the job to have in Romania. What was the alternative, dissident manuscripts sent under phony names to Parisian publishers, who would reject them because I wasn't Russian, Chinese, or at least Czech? Besides, I hated the Paris of refugees, and I knew already from my American friends that America was not the land to welcome dissidents. Immigrants, maybe, but not dissidents, not complainers. An act of bravery here would be a complaint there. So, what was left for me to do?

Yet, I knew that I wouldn't do it. And the future looked grim. It was rumored that Ceausescu was preparing a new deep freeze, one so all encompassing that we would live in a state of collective hypnosis. Bound and gagged not only in our flesh, but in our deepest thoughts, hearing Him, watching Him, nodding and clapping for Him.

T hroughout my last five years in Romania, I worked on and off as a
newspaper reporter. That was a contradiction in terms, since our
Communist press reported nothing. Journalists asked the "department of press and publications," a euphemism for our censors, whether
they could write on such and such a subject, and if they received permission, it came with instructions on how to write about the topic. The
live, immediate press, the one that surprised people with news, just didn't
exist. More often than not, our news was old, it was "reported" after its
existence had been rumored for weeks, and sometimes for years.

So I always turned in my stories before deadline, for I knew what I
had to write, sometimes even before the events happened. I went out in
the field, saw the respective places and people, asked my questions, and
jotted down the answers. After that, I wrote my stories in my office in
the prescribed manner, so I couldn't go wrong. I knew the system, and I
was an excellent Communist journalist.

I reached the pinnacle of my reporter's skill a few months before I
defected. One evening, there was an impatient knock on my apartment
door. When I opened it, I saw one of the editors of the party's official daily,
The Spark, accompanied by an unknown man in a gray suit and with a
heavy beard shadow. The gray suit said apparatchik, the unshaven beard
said feverish last-minute mission. The apparatchik said to me, "You've
been selected to be one of the pressmen accompanying The Comrade on
his tour of South America. Pack a few things. The car's downstairs. We're
leaving in five minutes."

"For South America?"

"No, for the Black Sea. Tomorrow morning, the Comrade will be
interviewing the press corps."

I am relating this exchange to give an idea of how Ceausescu used
to summon people to any kind of assignment related to himself. The
decision to include me in that press corps had probably been made dur-

ing the last hour. I'd spent that hour chatting on the phone with a friend. The Comrade's envoys could have asked the Securitate to cut into my conversation, but they had chosen to drive over, and now I had five minutes to drop whatever I was doing and answer the Comrade's call.

I packed a suit and a tie; one didn't wear casual clothes around Ceausescu, he was a stickler for propriety, even if the meeting would take place at his summer villa. I explained the emergency to my mother, while the two messengers paced our living room with uncaring nonchalance, reminding me of the Securitate searching our apartment. Mom kissed my cheek and made a quick sign of the cross over my face and off I was, suitcase in hand, to meet the man who controlled all of our destinies.

We drove all night. At nine the next morning, drained but attired stuffily in my suit, I was hurried across the lawn of a residence perched on an overhang above the sea, towards a kind of gazebo, where Ceausescu sat surrounded by aides. Across the lawn, but from different directions, as if they'd been ushered in through separate entrance gates, hurried four or five other journalists, all older than me. As I was to find out later, I owed being chosen to the fact that I spoke English and French and a smattering of Spanish, and also to Ceausescu's habit of surrounding himself on such outings with people who had a name. The doctor assigned to that trip, one of Romania's best-known internists, had also been yanked away from his routines, patients, family. When we, the press, finished our interview, I saw the illustrious doctor being trotted across the lawn, and behind him came, in a separate little group, three airline pilots in uniform.

The meeting was ritualistic. We were there to be impregnated with the sacred sense of being useful to Ceausescu. He almost did not speak to us. He wore a summer jacket without a tie, rather rumpled slacks and nondescript shoes, and had a light tan; otherwise, I found him unimpressive. I couldn't say that he emanated any overt sense of power, but the behavior of the older pressmen, the majority of whom had "worked" with him before, left no doubt that he was an absolute master, and to be treated accordingly. As there were not enough seats for all of us in that gazebo, Ceausescu looked towards some wicker chairs scattered on the lawn a few hundreds yards away, and *whistled*. Yes, whistled, as if for a dog. But no one showed up, so one of the aides got to his feet. Instantly, the oldest of the press men, fiftyish and quite bulky, jumped up mumbling that the press could bring their own chairs, and sprinted away, followed by half the journalists, in a gallop of middle-aged out-of-shape men dressed in suits and ties. They grabbed the chairs and ran back with them. And that was how human movement in the presence of the chief fixed itself in my mind: everyone in Ceausescu's presence, irrespective of rank, age, or physical condition, ran to him to receive their commands or away from him to fulfill those commands. That was the way it was, an homage to the value of his time and to the importance of his other activities. I watched that running repeated identically hundreds of times during the overseas tours.

Too flabbergasted, I had not moved. I watched him. He stared, his lips breaking into a smug little smile. That contemptible scurry meant that things were the way they were supposed to be. He finally looked towards me. "You don't like *working*?" His face took on a pink shade and his aides stirred in their chairs, expectantly: someone, me, was about to be chewed up. But before I could find an excuse for not having rushed out with the others, Stefan Andrei, party secretary for culture and propaganda, came across the lawn, tanned and walking almost normally, and whispered something into the boss's ear. Ceausescu relaxed.

My colleagues returned with the extra chairs, and Andrei told us a few platitudes about the importance of our job. Ceausescu listened with the same smug, distant expression; he had forgotten about me. Before that brief and meaningless encounter was over, the name of a top television anchorman was mentioned, and the boss's face acquired that reddish sheen again. "Who gave the order to fly him ahead of the team to Havana?" he snapped. "Why should he be bumbling abroad, instead of being here, *working*?"

His cheeks had swelled up. His mouth had become a fierce little slit, and his eyes glowered heinously. He seemed mortally insulted by the notion of anyone not working hard enough, which was why people moved like quicksilver around him, succeeding at looking not just busy but frantic. I gained a perspective into his inner world: it was a workplace, and in it one lonely character toiled uninterruptedly, like Sisyphus, setting the standard for everyone else. That Sisyphus was Ceausescu himself.

We left soon, and now I hurried off like everyone else, feeling in my calves, knees, and toes a special sense of urgency. The mood of the others was catching. And I didn't like it. I found myself diminished, and was embarrassed. I pondered getting some medical excuse, some proof of disability. But how could I not go? How could I say no to such an opportunity to be part of the "central command," even as a docile robot? This was a journey into the brain of the system, and the beginning of it had already occurred, in that gazebo. The tour was to start in Cuba and was to conclude in Chile. I would be seeing places and people nothing short of mythical. Including Fidel Castro, who for years had been the butt of Romania's nasty jokes, as Russia's "puppet among the palm trees," and as the Commie "with a beard of pubes." After Cuba, Ceausescu was to visit Andean lands of legend such as Columbia, Peru, Ecuador. And he was to round up his trip by embracing Chile's Allende, whom our propaganda depicted as Communism's new vanguard in the Yankee hemisphere.

But above all, I was to see our pharaoh in a realistic, unflattering close-up.

And he was irresistible. After a few minutes spent near him, I already felt hooked. Hooked on how the world changed in his presence, on how humanity started malfunctioning at the simple addition of this squat, stiff-gestured, potbellied little gnome who could order anyone jailed and killed with a snap of his sausage-shaped fingers.

A year before, as a reporter, I had stood not too far from Nixon and Ceausescu when Nixon had visited Bucharest. The thought of their combined power had filled me with the awe one feels watching natural disasters. For me, Ceausescu was by far the more frightening. Suppose I shouted a few words only, of dissent, suppose I made the slightest threatening gesture towards our supreme ruler—I would disappear within minutes, forever. The temptation was amazing. I felt drawn to hurling some insult at both of them; one was a staunch Communist, the other a rabid anti-Communist, yet here they stood side by side, like brothers, putting on the facade of detente and respect for other nations' rights. And no one did anything to blow off that facade. Not me either, for I didn't have the guts to shout, You liars, you're full of shit, both of you. It would've been something. But I didn't have the guts to do it.

It is a humiliating admission, but before I defected my life was owned by Ceausescu. To some extent, part of my life was still owned by him even after I escaped to America: I constantly fought fear, and dodged any Romanians who seemed at all capable of being Securitate. I had been tried and sentenced in absentia. My belongings had been confiscated—I could imagine the Securitate ransacking my papers the way they'd once ransacked my dad's. The books I had published were banned, their copies seized from bookstores or withdrawn from public libraries. The prints of my films were destroyed. I could not even travel back to attend my father's funeral, for I would have been grabbed at the airport, minutes after deplaning, by the same men in dark glasses and dark suits who had haunted my childhood.

After I learned of my father's death, I tried to call his Bucharest number, to offer condolences to his widow. But the Securitate wouldn't even let me do that. His phone was monitored. Each time I said my name to the widow, the line went dead.

I gave up, and wept briefly and clumsily in my Los Angeles study. The regime that had toyed with my life for twenty odd years had managed to do so once again, on my father's death, from a distance of over six thousand miles. For years I would carry that sense of insufficient closure: not seeing my dad off on his last trip, to his resting place. I held him responsible for many things, but he was still Dad.

In some corner of my being I remained terrified of Ceausescu and his underlings till the whole Commie world came down, and Ceausescu was pushed against a peeling wall and made into Swiss cheese by bullets from submachine guns. That execution didn't bring back any victims, it didn't repair or correct anything, revenge never does. But somehow the score was evened, a little. The history of that country could finally be restarted.

Back then, I wasn't quite aware of how frightening he was, I guess because we lived in fear of him every minute, so we were used to it. It felt normal. I returned to Bucharest, packed, had dinner with Mother, said good-bye to my father by phone. The next morning I joined the press corps at the airport, and we boarded a huge old propeller plane, a Soviet Ilyushin that had to leave Bucharest two days in advance, in order to drag itself to Havana, with two refueling stops, one in Ireland, the other in Canada. Another such propeller plane carried the lower-rank aides and Securitate. Ceausescu would leave Bucharest a day and a half after us, and get to Havana at the same time. His own plane was a jet.

During the tour, I wrote my accounts of the state visits, layings of wreaths, christenings of new factories, and signings of new treaties by Ceausescu and his respective hosts. I wrote them exactly the way I had always written my clever little reportages: in advance. Before the events even happened. Anticipating everything, and slapping it down on paper.

Since the planes carrying the press and the Securitate were much slower than the boss's plane, most of that trip was spent by us, the rabble, in the air. I wrote my stories in the air. Once I landed in Havana, Caracas, Quito, Bogota, or Lima, I'd get a cab, zoom over to the local embassy of Romania, and telex them home. They were printed in Bucharest practically as the events occurred, as if I'd been reporting them live by satellite, which of course the penurious Romanian press couldn't afford to do. But I knew by heart what our boss would say, and what his hosts would say in response. The speeches were boiler-plates praising independence from imperialism and world cooperation, and making a big fuss over Romania being like a Latin country in that vague East of Europe. I crossed the equator at thirty thousand feet altitude, tapping on my Olympia. I'd brought it along even though it was old and not meant to be used as a portable. Now, my arrogantly casual methods annoyed the other Romanian journalists. Most wanted to arrive in those cities first, settle down in their hotels, and then write. The head of the press corps grumbled loudly about my expedient performance, intentionally doing it in the presence of the cabinet members and senior Securitate officers: how would a Western journalist react if he or she noticed my trick? What if it got reported in, say, the *New York Times*? Of course, the *New York Times* was not on the scene for us. The biggest Yankee newspaper that dispatched somebody was the *Miami Herald,* and that guy checked us out for an hour in the lobby of a hotel in Caracas, Venezuela, and then flew back!

I meanwhile was angry that the impossible schedule left me no time for sight-seeing. My reason to hurry up and write my stuff before it happened was that I wanted to have some time to see those places, after all I was in the Americas! So I told the head of the press corps to stuff it, which could have resulted in anything from a reprimand to being shipped back between two of those mastiff-faced Romanian cultural attachés. I ditched my duties after that particular exchange, and loitered in downtown Havana. Miles away Castro and Ceausescu were hugging before an audience that had left the city practically empty. I could hear the leaders, especially Castro's whiningly incoherent harangue, out of a Soviet-made TV displayed in the window of a department store otherwise so depleted that a Romanian store seemed luxurious by comparison. For a minute, I watched Castro: his beard surrounding shiny red lips gave his face a genital look out of which tumbled fiery rhetoric. Then I strolled off along the famed waterfront, the Malecon: its concrete was melting from the midday sun, and the air was infested with tiny mosquitoes. I was propositioned by at least a dozen women—they did not look like prostitutes, but like normal unoccupied females, who approached me out of dusty little parks and cafés with mustard-colored interiors, offering their company in exchange for anything I wore that I no longer needed. They spoke rapidly in Havana jive and pointed to my shirt and pants; one bent down to touch my socks. Another rubbed her hand over her breasts and belly, while squinching her eyes as if under a shower, making me understand that she would like soap from my hotel, and was willing to come with me and pay for it in kind. In seconds, I realized that their prostitution, if we could call it that, was aimed at obtaining life essentials, and offering themselves had produced some results already. Almost every one wore some article of clothing that was fairly new and that didn't go with the rest of their outfits. And they watched me with a great curiosity and desire to unite with the rest of the world through having sex with me.

I escaped their seduction into a kind of farmers' market, closed for now. Beyond rows of empty stalls, I found a block of pagoda-like structures: a once-thriving Chinatown, now without Chinese people, and without customers.

In a couple of hours, I saw through Castro's pretense of freedom and revolutionary fervor. Cuba's pride hung in threads from the torn shutters of empty stores, and in the tattered pants of kids fishing for crabs off the waterfront's rocks. The only well-fed, well-dressed pedestrian I met was a Russian who gave me directions back to my hotel.

At the hotel, I found out that other members of the Romanian team had been propositioned sexually for soap, old socks, rum, or just *anything,* by the maids.

After my flagrant betrayal of journalism, someone from the Comrade's close entourage was here to talk to me. And now occurred one of those buffooneries that always ripped through Communism's solemn facade. The importance of the Comrade's visit to South America had been grasped by the foreign press . . . thanks to my well-timed reports. In other words, their early publication in Bucharest had tipped the foreign correspondents that Ceausescu was here. A little army of them were now heading towards the area. And, there was a state dinner tonight, and a few comrades from the press corps were invited—I was among the lucky ones. No other mention was made of my unorthodox methods. But that night, at the dinner, I met a certain comrade Lungu (a nice young man with longish hair, something normally frowned upon in the boss's entourage), who introduced himself as the Comrade's head typist. He offered to get me a better typewriter. I refused, but learned that the Comrade read all his communications on sheets retyped by Mr. Lungu in a giant font manufactured in West Germany, 36 points compared to the standard 12. This was done so that the Comrade could read everything, from notes from his aides to official speeches, without putting on his glasses. Lungu's friendliness and liberally shared gossip were another sign that my star was on the rise.

So, halfway through the trip, the entourage started to treat me as the new hot kid, and after another state dinner, I was reintroduced to Ceausescu himself. He looked at me absently, but uttered one line that showed some continuity in his thought process. "Now you like working?" he asked. I just nodded. Starting the next morning, I was literally pushed forward at all functions by eager Securitate men. Dizzy with my own luck, I trembled, expecting some foul-up that would blast me out of the presidential paradise.

But there was no foul-up. My scheme was now imitated by the whole press corps. And I was promoted to the inner circle in a particular way: two of the Comrade's children, his younger son and his daughter, were accompanying him on this trip. All three of us were under thirty. It was a great boost to one's career to spend time with them. With a whole bunch of armed bodyguards, we visited several museums together, and once or twice I helped as an interpreter when the son, groomed as a politician already, met with local youth groups. Technically, I was in the top rung of Romania's youth organization, so I was not misplaced at those meetings, which consisted of rhetoric. The boss's children were brats. His daughter (I called her Miss Comrade) did not even pretend to be civil; she flatly refused to take tea with the children of the president of Venezuela, and of Colombia, and so on, and was the terror of the protocol people. It was amazing that I was in their company: had I been some armed terrorist kamikaze, I could have offed them both. By this time, I was known to all those armed nannies and they allowed me to move about freely. I measured in my head the distance that separated me from a truly ambitious career: it consisted of a few words uttered to the kids, if they were the right words. I could tell how the cabinet members valued the kids' influence: they scrambled and scurried in their presence the way the press did on the Comrade's lawn, carrying those chairs. In fact, Miss Comrade gave me an opening: she told me, in Peru, that she had read one of my books and wouldn't mind an autographed copy. I promised I'd send her one once we returned to Bucharest.

The two youngsters were royalty living atop a pyramid of suffering, but that was not their fault. After the revolution, the son was jailed, undeservedly I think; he had run the administration of a Transylvanian city much kindlier, it was said, than other local chiefs. Among the daughter's options for marriage was the crown prince of Iran, but she passed on him, and the revolution found her a spinster; she was stripped of her privileges and condemned to oblivion. But at the time of the trip they were young, superficially Westernized, and in their bratty way, fun. They openly ridiculed their parents. Still, in their presence people ran. One who didn't was Ceausescu's own interpreter, whose face had become known to all Romania during Nixon's visit to Bucharest. He was sharp as a whip, a multi-language expert, and an aspiring writer. (He survived the revolution, became ambassador to England, and a member of the Writers' Guild!) That man too was surprisingly open, and from him I learned that the Comrade's distant stance towards me was a facade; the boss knew of me, and knew the number of my readers. There was a calculated intent in the way I had been included in the trip.

"You might want to write another historic novel," the interpreter once said casually to me, as we shared a taxi in Quito, Ecuador.

I said nothing. I did not want to find out whether this was the friendly suggestion of a man acquainted with the system, or an oblique directive from the boss himself. My presence on this trip was becoming compartmentalized. With the local pressmen, I could afford to be myself; the Venezuelan, Colombian, and Peruvian journalists were hip and attuned to the events. They knew that Castro's Cuba was a sad mockery, and guessed that we were another. But they were interested in the true dimension of our independence from Russia, for a very definite reason: Allende, the boss of our last destination point, Chile, was in deep trouble. He had messed up the economy, and disappointed his followers. Now rumblings in his military's ranks were said to forebode an uprising supported by the CIA. The sensitive media in the countries we were visiting watched Ceausescu get closer to Allende with the sense of a ticking clock. Would the right-wing Chilean military permit the encounter? Would this occasion for reciprocal Communist camaraderie be allowed to go down in history?

"What would you do," one Mexican journalist asked me, "if while you were here the Russians invaded Bucharest? Would you defect?"

I shrugged, and didn't answer. But I almost hoped that the Russians would. Such a disaster would force me to scrounge my courage together and defect. The Mexican journalist was smart and cynical. He didn't think that Romania could ever escape Russia's pull. "What you are trying is an aberration," he told me, "a beautiful aberration."

"It's a heroic act," I said, unconvinced and feeling sad.

"Like the heroism of Cuauhtemoc, our last Indian guerrilla," laughed the Mexican. "The Spanish hanged him, looted his fortunes, and raped his wives. And now we put his name on beer cans."

This conversation happened in Cuzco, Peru. I'd managed to take a day off to see the ancient Inca capital, the thundering Amazonian headwaters, and the fogged-up ruins of Machu Picchu. We returned to Lima, where the newspaper boys hawked special editions with screaming headlines. In Chile, the army had rebelled. Allende was being besieged in the Moneda Palace. All the journalists who had been hanging out with us had disappeared, trying to make their way into embattled Santiago. The last four days of Ceausescu's tour, which were to be spent in Chile, had been cancelled by the force majeure of the military coup. Late into the night, it was confirmed that Allende had been shot, that a right-wing junta had taken over and it had no intention of honoring Allende's diplomatic commitment to welcome Ceausescu.

That meant going home early, a change of plans that we, fed up with flying, mentally drained by the tension of being next to the Comrade, welcomed heartily.

But we could not return to Bucharest early; we could not because the Comrade had planned a massive rally of the Bucharest population, who were to assemble at the airport, cheering him as he stepped out of the airplane's hatchway to give them a report of mission accomplished. That rally was scheduled in four days, after the visit to Chile. We urgently needed a new country to replace Chile.

That night, the pressmen were among the few in the Romanian party who slept, even though fitfully. Everyone else was running about. By telex and phone and letter, through diplomatic channels and personal ones, Ceausescu's foreign minister felt out the unvisited countries in the area, trying to prod one of them into a last minute act of hospitality. At seven the next morning, the rumor spread that we might go to Bolivia. At ten, Bolivia was out, but Brazil seemed a possibility. At two P.M. Brazil had fallen, but there were frantic exchanges with Uruguay. They did not work out. Nothing worked out. The continent was plunged into deep anxiety and frantic reassessment of policies, with all the South American papers screaming about the Yanquis' involvement in Chile.

That time was possibly my single most enlightened moment under Communism. The downfall of Allende affected Ceausescu much less than the prospect of being deprived of his fun at the end of his trip. As the chances of an alternative visit continued to fade, his franticness increased. His eyes glared silently and his cheeks swelled up in childish outrage. The foreign minister, haggard from lack of sleep, jaws sealed in grim discouragement, kept running to Ceausescu's suite, to report that yet another country hadn't agreed to receive him. The foreign minister's career had taken a downturn. Soon after the tour, he would be demoted.

Momentarily unneeded, the press loitered about purposelessly, watching Ceausescu become more and more demented. He yelled at the foreign minister, at his other aides. There were sounds of broken glass from his suite. He behaved as if his visit was a fiasco, because his final ceremony could not be fulfilled. Through the next day, it became clear that he'd rather chew his bit in Peru than go home early. But there had been no arrangements for "rest days," as they were called, in Peru. The foreign minister fielded embarrassing questions about why Romania's boss was lingering here. The Peruvians were nervous, perhaps wondering whether Ceausescu was weathering some crisis of his own.

Relief came. On our long flight back from Peru to Romania, we would have a "technical stop" in Senegal, in west Africa, followed by a one-and-a-half-day visit to King Hassan of Morocco. They were timed to let us arrive in Bucharest at the appointed hour, to the clamors of a citizenry that for three days had been given no news of its leader's activities.

We flew back, over Amazonia's green immensity, then over the Atlantic's pale blue solitude, into a dirtily humid African dawn. In Dakar, Senegal, President Leopold Sedar Senghor, a Nobel prize laureate, welcomed Ceausescu in tribal garb. He rubbed his leopard skins against the

Comrade's suit, noisily planted a big kiss on him, and read him a poem in French. I could imagine the repulsion of the chauvinist Romanian peasant as he was embraced by the elegantly uninhibited black man—but the great welcoming festival in Bucharest was now less than two days away. After Senghor finished his poem, a fierce guard in camouflage jackets played the Romanian anthem. Not the current, Communist one. The old one: Long Live the King! Ceausescu took it. Wincing, making mental notes about firing the Romanian ambassador to Senegal, but he took it. No one but the Romanians would notice the slipup, and the ceremony was being fulfilled.

The next day we were in Rabat, Morocco. Since these visits had not been prearranged, the press was saddled to work on the speeches and counter-speeches, the friendly op-eds signed by our foreign minister to be carried in the local papers, and the Comrade's answers at his press conferences—we were practically the only journalists present at those conferences. My talent was hard put to invent reasons for being here, or historic ties between Romania and Senegal, or Romania and Morocco. I did what we did in such situations: I turned up the noise. I wrote the most nauseating declaration of friendship between Romania and the peoples of Africa, to be uttered hours later, barely amended, in the Comrade's hoarse voice and accompanied by his routine salami-chopping wave of the hand. It was hard to believe that we were returning home, that I would slip free from the curious spell of his entourage and resume my mundane life.

The plane landed in Bucharest and taxied toward a huge crowd, which cheered like clockwork. The plane stopped, and the boss appeared in the hatchway. In a hoarse voice amplified by scores of loudspeakers, he started his report. The other reporters and I slipped away early. A friend of mine had waited, to give me a ride back home. He gave me a leering grin, and asked me not to forget my old friends, now that I was making it so high up. I asked what he meant by that. He told me that rumor had it that I was involved with the boss's daughter. I said nothing but probably looked nauseated, since he muttered, "So, it's not true, huh? I didn't think so, you were never practical that way."

In appearance, the rumor made some sense: I was one of the few single young men in the delegation, and it had somehow become known that Miss Comrade was reading my books.

* * *

That rumor did not change the fact that I continued to be trashed by the party press. Things looked grim. A new cultural freeze was announced, combined with a rise in the price of paper products. That meant that fewer books would be accepted for publication, and fewer copies of each book would be printed. For the first time in five years, my chances to keep publishing seemed frail.

In my mailbox, I found a letter from the International Writing Workshop of the University of Iowa. I was asked to be part of that year's program, which was to start in October. That wasn't really surprising, since my friend John Cheever was at Iowa as a visiting professor, and I had been interviewed several months earlier by an associate director of the program, novelist and teacher William Murray. Bill Murray, in Bucharest to find Romanian candidates, had told me that he got a "good vibe about me." That made me frown in confusion, for I wasn't up on the latest American colloquialisms.

Still, as I read the letter of invitation, my heart skipped beats. Who knew, I might weather this crisis in my career in America!

I applied for a passport and my request was denied.

Armed with a letter from the Romanian Writers' Guild, which mentioned that the Americans were recognizing me as the most "representative writer of the young Socialist generation," a praise I myself had concocted, I went back to the Passport office. I waited for a whole day to see an official, to explain to him that no doubt I had been turned down in error. They should have been eager to send someone like me abroad. I was living proof that freedom and a rounded education were alive and well in Romania.

I was turned down again.

The more I was turned down, the more obsessed I became. Finally, I decided to get advice from someone who really knew the game. I called Ceausescu's interpreter, who had acted so friendly to me on the South American tour. He suggested that I ask Ceausescu himself.

"He'll remember you from the tour."

"So?" I asked him, my heart beating hard again.

"Tell him some real kiss-ass shit, and he'll give you your passport."

I stammered, "What k-kind of kiss-ass shit?"

He laughed. "I don't know. Be inventive. You're a writer."

He gave me the phone number of one of the boss's aides. I called, applied for an interview, and waited. In preparation, I tried to come up with some dazzlingly inventive line of bull.

The stupid, unfounded rumor of my romance with the boss's daughter had continued. I asked myself whether it was being maintained by that great manipulator of rumors, the Securitate. That would have meant that the young lady truly had an interest in me. That made me panic, for I connected that possibility with my being denied a passport. I'd heard stories about Commie princesses taking fancies to commoners. She could order one of her aides to have my passport cancelled forever. Papa needn't even know. I went into a childish state of terror. Yes. Surely that was the explanation. Miss Comrade, bedecked in Chanel suits but with her fingers stained yellow from incessantly smoking Kents and Marlboros, had ordered me held at hand.

I felt like a child scared by the night. I told myself that I should show my maturity by turning down America, that fancy toy, and by plunging into some scholarly career as yet not forbidden in Romania. Through honest work, I'd make a comeback. After all, I'd already enjoyed fame in my backwater, and had even seen a slice of the world. What more did I want?

Freedom, that voice inside me said.

But I shut it up. To hell with freedom. Freedom was childlike too.

Suddenly, bang, I received a phone call from the presidential chancellery: my interview had been approved. *He* was going to see me.

I was so used to begging and not getting, that any time I received a crumb I trembled with gratitude. That interview was such a crumb. When I got that call, instructing me where to go the next day, my gratitude took the shape of patriotism. There was that other Romania inside me, that solidarity of fate with all Romanians. I felt it stir in my chest. The man who occupied, by usurpation, the country's supreme seat, was a murderous fraud. But the seat still symbolized the country.

The next day, I drove over to the presidential office, which was on the second floor of the Communist Party's headquarters. The "command post." At that time, Ceausescu claimed all of Romania's top jobs: the presidency, the party secretaryship, the top spot in the party-affiliated trade unions, the supreme command of the army, navy, and air force.

My father had never made it into that office. Of my friends and work colleagues, none had. Ninety-nine percent of Romania's population would never enter that building—but a few hundred of them would finally storm their way into it on December 22, 1989, forcing the Comrade to take off from the roof, in a dangerously overloaded helicopter.

My new car, a Dacia 1300 (the Renault 12 model manufactured under license in Romania) was stopped several times at checkpoints, and I drove it haltingly, barely managing not to stall the engine. The car, the proof of my prosperity as a writer, looked like a buggy next to the vast Mercedes and Volvo limousines waiting at the curb for the members of the politburo. But I didn't really notice the sumptuous limos, the marble stairway, or the equally frequent checkpoints set up inside the building. I saw the country. I was close to its highest authority, and knew that I wouldn't get that close again for a long time.

Accompanied by a protocol man, I rode the elevator to a third floor lobby. There were office doors on both sides of the lobby. I felt like I was stepping inside a giant brain, for in those offices were the power circuits that ran twenty-two million lives. Those millions were my brethren, and a few hundred thousand of them were my readers.

I felt that my life had narrowed to a bridge over a chasm, and I had to step over that bridge quickly, without clutching the rails and without staring down at the void. Just look ahead, confidently straight ahead. If I looked down I would get dizzy and take the plunge.

Somebody opened a door. I floated into a vast space.

I was shocked to find Ceausescu's office so bright and airy. I had expected a depressing place, heavily panelled and filled with massive dark furniture. But the paint on the wall was stark white, and the furniture and fixtures were light and modern. An oversized desk almost hid that small man whom I almost knew, yet re-encountered each time with a jolt of shock, because his impossibly flat and empty expression never changed.

He was annotating a manuscript. His latest treatise on Marxism. He hadn't written any of his books, yet he was proofing this one in front of me. He glanced at me quickly, his face hanging towards his papers, so that his look came out at a hostile angle from under his lowered eyebrows. I stopped in front of his desk. He didn't greet me, nor did he ask me to sit. He just inquired why I was there.

I mumbled the reason. Invited to the University of Iowa, I had been inexplicably denied my passport . . .

"Why would you want to go to Iowa?" asked the Comrade, monotonously hostile, reminding me instantly of the way he had first addressed me: "You don't like working?" Worried, I looked at his graying hair. "Why would you want to waste a year in America, when you should be here, *working*? When all of us here, our sleeves rolled up, are engaged in a giant effort of Communist construction? Why would you want to drop out, and laze away in that decadent country?"

He spoke in slogans, which rolled naturally off his tongue. His voice was flat and hoarse, yet I felt that a big powerful feline was closing its fangs down on me, to gore me, to crush me. He was reacting so badly to my request that I could imagine myself leaving his office a nobody. I might find out tomorrow that I was no longer allowed to write anything, not even to ghostwrite editorials praising the leader, like my father did once.

I sweated cold sweat. My brain felt shrunk.

"Be inventive," my friend the official interpreter had advised me.

Some inspiration hit me. I tried not to stutter.

"Comrade General Secretary . . ." He was staring at me from under his lowered eyebrows. "America is indeed a reactionary country . . . but you yourself are an author . . . a theorist of Marxism. So I was thinking . . ." Clearing my throat seemed the hardest thing I'd done in my life. "I was thinking that if I go to Iowa . . . since universities are America's only radical enclaves . . . I could *spread your Marxist thought* among young Americans . . ."

I stopped. I waited, suspended over hell's eternal fire.

The little Comrade suddenly moved. He lifted his face. Instead of oblique and bellicose, his stare was straight now and open. It analyzed me coolly. I didn't realize right away the change of attitude, in fact I wondered if he might sentence me to twenty years of hard labor.

"All right. We shall review your case," he said monotonously.

I turned to leave, but halfway through my motion I realized the miracle. He'd bought it. He'd swallowed my line, my lie. He had reacted to the shameless flattery like a true simpleton, like a rudimentary peasant whose stroked ego overrode judgment.

I walked out, barely controlling my body, for I felt like jumping up and down to release my tension. Several times in my life, it seemed that the flow of my existence narrowed to an impossibly thin and tenuous passage, before being allowed to roll freely again. It was so when my brother died, and I waited to see if I would survive. It was so when I was first questioned by the Securitate. It was so when I tried to guess, from Hollywood, with phone connections to Bucharest forbidden to me, whether my father would survive his second stroke, or die. When I tried to find out whether glasnost had started in Romania. All those were passages, scary, dangerous ones. I also had uplifting, hopeful ones: writing my first book in English, meeting Iris, the birth of my children, my first American movie. That moment with the Comrade was a super-passage. Understanding that I had fooled him, and perhaps fooled the destiny I'd been scripted to, my heart, brimming with anxiety just moments earlier, now filled with mindless elation.

Two days later, I was called back to the Passport office. I was given a "service passport" and a six-month visa for the United States.

My elation stopped me from seeing past the immediate implications of my exit visa. It was as if my life, my whole future, was contained in those six months; I didn't think further, didn't as yet wonder what I would do when my visa expired. My brain secreted the necessary chemicals, so that I would not think of anything beyond my six months in America. I said good-bye to Mom and Dad, separately. They both acted kind of thoughtful, kind of scared, my mother especially, by this heavenly bounty. It came during a time when I realized how precarious my literary career was, and after I'd had a chance to look very closely at the demented brain that controlled our lives. My parents were my emotional dependents, Mother especially. My father too, in a less direct way. Since I'd become successful, he was very fond of going out with me, to dinners, to the theater, to the functions of the Writers' Guild, as if to boast of our association. For a few years we'd had no relationship, but now here we were together, father and son. Also, and for a long time this was hard to confess, I helped him financially. Despite his improved status, he still lived way beyond his means. I thus parented him with money, and he was my literary elder and friend, a profitable give and take.

Mother, much closer to my emotional life than Dad, was also much more anxious. America was full of great temptations. She exacted a promise that I write to her every week, and call her on the phone every two weeks.

I'd missed the beginning of Iowa's fall program. The official date was in October, but I flew out in November. I left Bucharest under an uncharacteristically early dusting of snow. An immaculate veil, spreading a semblance of peace and purity over a precarious, contorted corner of Europe.

As the plane soared, I realized that I'd been right to think of a bridge over a chasm. That flight was my bridge to freedom, but it would turn out to be much longer than I imagined, and the feat of crossing it would take years.

How deep in denial was I, during that flight out of Romania, about the prospect of not returning in six months, the duration of my Communist-issued visa? About not returning at all, or only if and when Communism would collapse, a possibility which at the time seemed completely unrealistic?

I didn't know.

Yet as long as I flew over Romania, I was so tense, I felt as if I were pushing the plane ahead with my own heartbeat. I was subconsciously expecting the Securitate to show up at one of the plane's next stops—it would land in Belgrade and then in Frankfurt before winging over the Atlantic—with orders to bring me back to Bucharest: the dictator had changed his mind, my passport had been revoked. It was an irrational fear, but I lived it to the fullest. In Belgrade, my tension was increased by memories of my uncle Florin, the priest—Communist Yugoslavia was the land that had kept him jailed for several years after he had survived that swim across the Danube. And the Communists' accusations against him involved America: he had completed his divinity studies in America in the thirties, and sympathized with the ecumenical rapprochement between the Protestant and Orthodox Christians. Thus, if the Communists had gotten him, they would have pilloried a triple rogue: anti-Communist, exposed to America, and a priest.

Even in Frankfurt, instead of gaping at the duty-free shops of this NATO nation's spic-and-span gateway, I sat tensely on the plane, trying to read a book and not seeing the print in front of my eyes. Only when a new crew took over, and an American captain saluted the passengers in a growly Midwestern accent while taxiing to take-off, did I start to decompress. I had a few drinks, spending all of my four dollars hard currency. Then I dared to speak to the passenger next to me, an American returning from a business trip to Europe, feeling that the trite words we exhanged were signalling that Communism was opening its clutch, letting me float out like an astronaut free in space. I was defecting already, deep in my soul, but any time I became aware of it I got so scared that I pushed it all back underneath, beginning to build that inner silence which would last over fifteen years. I made pledges to myself: I was a good little Romanian, a good native son who would go back after his six months in paradise.

I spent the next two days in Washington, D.C.; the International Writing Program was federally funded, and therefore I had to show my face in a federal office before travelling on to Iowa. I wandered around in a vacuum of thoughts, except for: 1) an obsessive replay of my three-minute meeting with Ceausescu, and 2) how different America was from what I had expected.

Number 1 should have given me a clue. I was, deep inside, already thinking of defecting; proof was the fact that all of my life in Romania had concentrated in my psyche in that one scene in Ceausescu's office. To go back to Romania meant to go back to the Comrade, to stand at attention again before his X-ray eyes, and give my report as to how I'd advanced his Marxist thought in the land of Lincoln. As for number 2, I was flabbergasted by how *empty* America seemed. It seemed so because I'd landed on a Saturday and everyone in the city was away for the weekend, but even that filled me with angst: how could they all act so relaxed, indeed, so suicidally neglectful? Who would defend America, in case of a surprise Soviet nuclear attack? What kind of country was this?

It was a free country.

And its freedom was a function of its size, my body told me. Of the wide spaces which existed everywhere—space, space, unending, far horizons in all directions, endless ocean coastline outlining endless hearthlands. Glimpsed from every conceivable angle, from the top of tall buildings, from the windows of a bus, staring down one of those long streets, the longest in the world, they were in the *Guinness Book of World Records*, space was always there, generous, lavish, wasteful. Walk aross the street: space. Walk across the suite of your hotel: space. Even in the bathroom, sitting on the john, what I had around me was space, space, unlimited. The bathtubs were big, the elevators capacious, the restaurants vast. Even the people looked oversized. The men were tall, the women were tall, generously made, plenty of flesh, plenty of muscle, of strong bone, big faces, big smiles, gestures that seemed big to me even when they were modest and restrained.

Space. Unpoliceable space. Space inside the people, unpoliceable space. It was obvious from the way they spoke, without afterthoughts, anxieties, skillful ways of phrasing themselves, or clever allusions, or insidious political jokes. Watergate was happening, and all of America joked about it, without any fears. On my first night in an American hotel, I watched Johnny Carson make jokes about the trouble Nixon was in, and it was clear that Nixon was to be afraid of Carson, not Carson of Nixon.

It was, well, awesome.

From D.C., I flew to Cedar Rapids, and was welcomed by William Murray, the Irish-born novelist and an assistant director of the program. He drove me to the university town of Iowa City, across more space, open, flat, and powdered with snow. That night, I had dinner with the program's founder, the poet Paul Engle, and with John Cheever, and a number of the invited writers, most of them also from foreign countries. After dinner, I was dropped off at an all-night supermarket, where I intended to stock up the fridge of the apartment rented for me by the program. I saw on a shelf cans of tuna, a rarity in Bucharest. I piled six of them in my cart, and pushed them and my other purchases to one of the four Iowa girls working the registers, all very blond, very big, very smiley, and with ribbons in their hair. She greeted me with, "Got a hungry kitty at home, huh?" "What kitty?" I countered, nonplussed. "Who are you buying that tuna for?" she asked, pointing at my cans. "Myself," I answered. At that late hour, only four or five customers were lining up at the registers; in the quiet of the store, they could all overhear our conversation. "That tuna's for cats," she said, scanning my person in surprise. I didn't look like a bum reduced to eating pet food, but like a European gent with a cultivated English accent. But . . . I didn't know there was pet food in America. I mumbled an explanation: I was from Romania, you see, this was my first time in an American supermarket. All the store was scanning me now, just like the woman at the register. "What do cats eat in Romania?" a woman asked, with true curiosity in her voice. "Mice, or scraps from the table," I said, feeling the blood rise in my cheeks. "Ooohh!" chorused several voices: the register girl, the woman who had asked the question, and a few more in the line behind me. This was the collective "oh" of America receiving the immigrant Popescu; it happened there, many months before I would officially defect, and it contained the enormous surprise of the civilized world meeting someone from the wilds where cats still ate mice.

I took the tuna fish for cats back to the shelf, and someone helped me replace it with tuna fish for people. In my first years of settling in this new land, I had to take back the wrong tuna many more times, figuratively speaking.

So. What was America about, when Popescu came into it? Nixon was being threatened with impeachment. The hippie sixties had become part of the mainstream. Clouds of marijuana smoke drifted across the land. There was no AIDS, so not having sex on a first date was kind of unusual; if girls went out with you, they usually went all the way, a mindblower for this Commie boy. A teacher of creative writing at the University of Iowa came to his classes barefoot. The women were beautiful, but for me the shock came from how well fed they looked, how nicely formed, how gracefully proportioned, as if God had spent his personal time measuring their dimensions and harmonizing their shapes, before releasing them onto this continent to gratify those unsuspecting, undeserving American males. In the university setup at least, most guys wore dirty clothes and didn't shave to show how unconventional they were, and that didn't stop any one of those pretty, well-fed women from hopping into the sack with them. No one knew where Romania was, no one knew where *China* was. Orgasms were discussed at parties. The greatest writers of America came to lecture at the university, and for my life I couldn't understand why they mentioned their agents so obsessively. Gays held dances in the rented basement of a Baptist church—out of curiosity, I went to one with a student friend named Alan Gurganus, who was later to become a successful author. It blew my Romanian mind to see men wooing other men.

Being a guest at Iowa meant receiving room and board and expenses; I budgeted my expenses so as to be able to travel out of Iowa City often, whenever possible on the cheapest means of transportation: the Greyhound bus. I wasn't the only one, most of the program's foreign guests came from poor countries. For many, seeing America was a one-time wonder, so they too used Greyhound. Among them were two fellow Romanians, poets married to each other, Ana Blandiana and Romulus Rusan. They returned to Romania at the end of the term, and continued struggling with the Communist censorship. Rusan published an enormously successful travel diary called *America of the Greyhound*. Blandiana, talented, determined, and striking-looking, was among Romania's few literary dissidents. In December of 1989, she emerged as a prominent female revolutionary, then became a fiery opposition leader.

Using the bus, I went to Chicago to meet Mircea Eliade, a Romanian who had fled in the forties and was now a renowned cultural anthropologist, and the novelist Saul Bellow, whose *Herzog* I had translated into Romanian. Although it was being printed as I left, it unfortunately never made it to the bookstores because of my defection. I travelled through snow flurries to New York, to meet for the first time that mythical uncle of mine, the priest who swam the Danube, whose sons, Radu and Sandu, were my first cousins.

The priest had been in exile since 1948 and had missed the childhood and youth of his own sons. Because he was an arch "enemy of the people," he had to buy them out of Communist Romania, and when they arrived in America it was 1964 and they were grown men. His dialogue with them had to bridge a gap made of many unshared events and places. The link between the absentee father and the now mature boys was his wife, my aunt. She spent her life making possible the integration of a family so strangely reunited. My strongest impression of my uncle was that in the middle of our first visit together, he had to drive to New York harbor to save a party of Romanian stowaways from the holds of a Panamanian ship; he then rushed to Washington to plead their fate with various congressional committees.

He showed me a book, published in America, crediting him with helping save several hundred Polish Jewish children during World War II. I was proud, and relieved. Barely arrived in America, I was already learning bits of Romanian history that the Communists had never mentioned. A sad one was that a part of the Romanian clergy had been infiltrated in the thirties by the Iron Guards—I'd thought that my church, a victim of Islam, had been spared such infamous alliances. Other pages of history, as gruesome as they were fascinating, were open to me now. I learned additional information about Communist repression. It was overpowering, even though I had lived Communism directly, to see its cruelty quantified on paper by Western political analysts. As I subconsciously flirted with the idea of defecting, I found it disturbing to meet people like my uncle: his chief interest was Romania, about which he asked me countless questions, sucking in the information like a sponge. Not only had he not forgotten the past, but he had built his life around a land he would never see again— he died in his eighties, two years before the revolution.

My cousins, on the other hand, had arrived in America only too willing to forget. In Romania, they had grown up in circumstances far harsher than mine. They were denied the right to go to college, and Sandu served his army term in a work detachment not much better than a Nazi work camp. Barefoot in frozen water, he and other conscripts, all enemies of the people like him, had planted rice, or built dams against the capricious floodings of the Danube, the river his father had swum to freedom. They worked days of twelve to fourteen hours. They washed in wheel barrows, the only objects around that could double for sinks. With cold water, of course. Many fell ill, and some of them died. Sandu recalled one event with a smile: during a rare Sunday furlough, he and several mates entered a movie theater in the nearest little town, in order to dry off their wet greatcoats by spreading them against the theater's heater. And thus, wrapped in smelly fumes from their wet uniforms, they watched an old Hollywood movie: *Trapeze,* with Burt Lancaster, Gina Lollobrigida, and Tony Curtis.

Well, my cousins who had it so hard were now American citizens, handsome, well-dresssed, and prosperous. One was married and his wife had just given birth to a son; the other was getting married—both spouses, one a blonde, the other a brunette, were good-looking and tall. When I was with my cousins, an interesting thing happened: I stopped thinking as a writer. I thought as a man, who had his life in his own hands for the first time. Right there, lying in my palms, clutched in my fingers. And I had to do the right thing with it.

Sandu, who had survived the work detachment, was the more outspoken and expressive. He put it to me in a nutshell: "Be tough, cousin Petru." Some advice, if I knew how to follow it.

There was such a visible transformation in my cousins. They'd triumphed over fate, and over their old selves. They had more to teach me than any literary friends; those, of course, could give me better advice about how to write in English, but mastering English was hardly the only important issue now. I was about to trade not just one language for another, but my small world for a big one, and no freedom at all for more than enough freedom. I was about to trade in the "we" for the "I," for the first time in my life. To gain my "I," to have it, to be the master of it.

Looking back from America, I felt like I'd never ever made a personal choice before. Even my books had been dictated into my subconscious by a chorus of other people: my family, my friends, my landsmen. If I were to stay here, this would be my first truly personal choice.

Between daily revelations about how I had lived and why I couldn't live like that anymore, I hurried back to my Iowa obligations. I took part in seminars, attended writing classes, gave lectures, or listened to the lectures of important literary figures. Just hearing these toilers of the word presented the question Cheever had asked me a few years before, on the shores of the Nile: Would I ever be able to write in English? If I didn't, would I feel like a cultural suicide? Was cultural suicide worth committing, in exchange for freedom?

These questions ramified into others, tough ones, about choices for my life, the only life I'd been granted. How much was there for me to learn here, apart from the language?

Before I could answer, some decisions were made for me. A British publisher offered to print *Burial of the Vine*. I met an American woman who would become my first wife. And more and more, I learned that the censorship in Romania was tightening, guaranteeing to make me unemployed when I returned.

The final act of my decision to defect was played out in Europe. On my way back from Iowa, I stopped briefly in London, to meet my British publisher. Then I flew out, not to Bucharest but to Paris, adding thus a station on my Golgotha of return. Officially I was still going back, still asking for prolongations of my Romanian visa. In Paris I got down to my last pennies. I stayed in a fleabag hotel, and read on the faces of the employees of the Romanian embassy, whom I asked to renew my visa yet again, the specific controlled amusement of Securitate men watching a slave of the system squirming toward freedom but not taking the plunge. What held me back was everything: fear of the future, ties to the past, but especially a sense of betrayal. I was betraying everyone, including my readers.

The redemption from that feeling came abruptly, from the Commies themselves. I was zigzagging around Paris, between the Sorbonne library, emigré gatherings, and my sad hotel on the Rue des Écoles, doing nothing, wasting time. Out of the blue, I was invited to a function at the Romanian embassy, and went. I bumped into the foreign minister, same one as during Ceausescu's visit to South America. He was soon to be fired, but that day he was still Comrade Minister, and he accosted me loudly, in a crowd of compatriots, "Thinking of not coming back, *Comrade* Popescu? Well, if you're about to make that error, know that Socialist Romania won't collapse without you—or without anyone. Socialist Romania is firmly continuing on the path of its achievements."

This from a man who was not an idiot; he was an ex-journalist, a member of the Writers' Union, and even rather friendly with my dad. And here he was, unloading the party line on me, exposing in effect my unde-clared decision, and at the same time trying to make brownie points: the place was packed with Securitate, and he would be on record that he'd warned me, and upheld the line.

Living under Communism had rained many humiliations on me, but I now swallowed one of my biggest. I stuttered a not particularly proud answer, about how decisions about my fate were my own, and he should mind his own business. Then I tried to step away and get a drink, but couldn't—there was a thick crowd around us, for his sting-ing words to me had given a new life to the party. The smell of a man-hunt was in the air. I wondered whether Mr. Macovescu, the foreign minister, had brought with him bodyguards who waited for me in the next room, with hypodermic syringes at the ready to sedate me and ship me back home.

I suddenly decided: I would leave, right here and now.

I stepped out of the embassy, which was technically Romanian ter-ritory, back into France. My heart pounded like a drum. I made it into the street.

Having no money for a cab, I had to walk along the Seine's bank towards the Quartier Latin, to my hotel. I looked at the river: the water seemed made of separate molecules, absurdly held together, and I felt that I too was made of molecules, and would disintegrate in the next few minutes.

Know that Romania, Socialist Romania, won't collapse without you— or without anyone. . . .

Suddenly, that disgusting apparatchik's line did not hurt anymore. Suddenly, it brought liberation. They were not going to collapse without me, for sure they were not. They would go on. They were not in the busi-ness of caring, about me or about millions like me, they owed nothing to anyone. And I, for once, felt like I owed nothing to others, for I was an

"I." Finally, I was an I, my very own. I wouldn't collapse without them. Sad, shattered, confused, I had claimed my liberation.

The events kept racing, at a frantic pace, and for me there was nothing easy about confronting the challenges that kept cropping up in my new life.

My first marriage was a victim of that initial turbulence. My spouse was a fine person, who was brave for entering a union with the mess that I was. For almost immediately after I defected, my long-denied traumas surfaced, and to handle them I was to spend hours on a psychiatrist's couch. The marriage might not have lasted for other reasons, for we were very dissimilar in personalities and backgrounds. But I was so shell-shocked by the world I'd just left that Communism took its revenge even where it wasn't involved at all. I discovered myself to be jealous and irascible. I communicated poorly, and not because of language problems. I was immature; living in captivity breeds little maturity, except what is needed to handle captivity itself. I had to learn so much so fast, from how to balance a checkbook to how not to be suspicious of other people. In that as in many other things, I felt at a constant disadvantage. If ever I was a difficult, moody, conflicted artist, it was during those beginning years.

I needed a concrete direction of activity. I applied to several film schools, and was accepted by one in New York and one in Los Angeles. The one in New York was the film department of Columbia University. The one in L.A., which I chose to go to, was the American Film Institute. So that meant moving to Hollywood.

It was amusing that I would start my acculturation to America with film, and it also felt like a reparation, for I had been shut out of the industry at home. It had happened right before I left for Iowa. I'd written the feature *Path in the Dark,* one of the best realistic movies of Communist Romania. Its box-office success theoretically opened the gates of Romanian film for me. But my next screenplay was declared "unfilmable" by the party-installed movie czar, novelist Al Ivasiuc, and by his hench-woman, producer Roxana Gabrea. It was a drama about Romania fighting World War II on both sides, personified in two brothers, a left-winger (my dad), and a royal army officer (my uncle Nicu). Included, of course, were my subversive musings about the cruelties of history, the difference between official and human morality, etc. Ivasiuc was said to have ties to the Securitate. Whether he and Gabrea were acting by orders from above, or whether their opposition was just collegial sabotage, I never found out. I tried with another screenplay; same verdict, handed down by the same individuals. The confidence with which those two acted made me draw my own unoptimistic conclusion: I was not welcome to work in Romanian films.

In Hollywood, I found myself in a completely different situation. By the very fact that I was here, I was welcome. Hollywood, always nonchalantly non-literate and itself a world of immigrants, saw nothing wrong with an alien like me writing American films. The film industry never once questioned whether I was capable of understanding and portraying America, or anything else, for that matter. If I was willing to work, and show a good attitude despite bad deals, insulting executives, or cynical producers, I was in! That felt like a miracle. One month into my training as a director at the American Film Institute, I was writing an English-language movie, to be released by United Artists. Producers, execs, agents mangled my name and couldn't place Romania on the map, but they didn't question, or even ask for, my credentials. This was beyond trust, or belonging. This was Hollywood!

I was transformed, truly overnight, from a writer who was reality-obsessed to a writer who created unreality, in Hollywood's particular way: with a flair for the dreams of the audience. If I guessed those dreams right, that would take my characters and stories into celluloid mythology.

Film, that insane business, helped save my sanity. For I had no time to agonize over my loss of homeland. Deemed tough enough to take it, here I was taking it. In the future, I might be a writer of books again. Here and now, I received a valuable free lesson about America: it rated many things above writing. In America's list of favorites, movies and sports came first, followed by various forms of self-actualization, by travelling, by sharing in social causes, and only after all those, by reading books.

That tore apart my old scale of values. I'd operated on the belief that writing was all-important. To quote a quip of my dad's: In the beginning was the word.

But not here. In California specifically, in the beginning was the camera, and the star-actors before it.

Into my life came the film people, all seemingly uprooted, and none the worse for it. I directed short movies at the American Film Institute, and went to lectures by the heavies of show biz, the way I went to lectures by the heavies of letters in Iowa. From star Bette Davis to scriptwriter Robert Towne, everyone who was someone came to tell their own stories of uprootment, for which they were rewarded not with guilt or loneliness, but with success. As for the film students, that was exactly what they were about: leaving all of themselves behind, to become pieces of Hollywood. Perhaps because the sixties were over, that rhapsodic command to be one's own self was much muted, especially in the concept-hungry think tanks of the Mecca of film. Gimmicks, clever "takes," brilliant executions of something known or not too far out, were the order of the day.

I was getting a taste of what it meant to be creative in Hollywood, which was to sit around trying to guess the executives' moods, which were in turn based on the market's moods, captured in data gleaned by the best market analyzers, and yet utterly unreliable. The real standard was how much money this or that movie had been making, and whether it was felt that the market would absorb other movies like it. Which finally brought everyone to the defeating conclusion that nothing could be predicted or explained, and one had to rely on a single subtle, volatile, and invisible quality, which was the talent personified in those fickle childish movie stars.

I was in class when I got word that a rising director, Australian Peter Weir, was in town and looking for me. We met at the Chateau Marmont Hotel, where John Belushi later died. Weir had heard of my exotic gifts from a film agent we shared in London. He asked me if I'd be interested in co-writing *The Last Wave,* and we started a script conference right then and there. I, on the second track of my mind, couldn't cease to marvel at the lucky fates of this Australian native son. He'd made movies financed by the Australian Film Commission. I tried to imagine myself making movies with government subsidies, but *without censorship*—that could never happen in Romania with all its two thousand years of European culture, but it could happen in the land of kangaroos and former convicts, they made uncensored movies out there, *in English!* Around us, the Chateau Marmont, in whose pool swam movie stars, seemed to sing a song of independence, a rhapsody to the artist's right to be unique and self-obsessed. Those people were just like me, but no one had contested their right to be not only free, but wealthy and known and happy! That song whispered to me directly: Soothe thy pains, heal thyself of your roots, forget the past!

It took time. But it seemed that I was getting cured.

Everything was part of the cure. Putting aside writing books for a while. Making up film stories, and taking them to the studios, in "pitch" attacks on the minds of the studio bureacracy. Going to crazy parties. I wrote several well received scripts, I wrote and directed a studio feature lauded by the critics, I made money. I flew to Amazonia, looking for a big story to follow my directorial debut, and, wonder of wonders, I met the very man who had found the source of the Amazon.

He was an American, what else. He told me his story, and I, with my new daring ways, proposed to buy the rights to it. I must've learned to talk a good game, for he agreed. And suddenly, I was faced with a story so big that it would be too narrow to tell just in pictures. First, it had to be told in a book.

The old me, starved to write books again, found a big book story in the Amazonian wilderness. It became *Amazon Beaming,* my first American book.

I felt cured all right. Cured of my roots, cured of the past.

Or so I thought.

But in the spring of 1991, I wasn't so sure anymore. Now I wondered.

Sometimes I felt like I'd already decided to revisit Romania, which freaked me out. Did I really want to take a look at my erstwhile hell, now that it was cooling off? To touch its smoking coals and smell its charred air? Yet, the more I thought about it, the more I wanted to visit Romania after the revolution. Yes, that was it, I wanted to see it transfigured by that sacrifice of a thousand lives. That was enough of a reason. Or was there more than that?

I didn't know. What would I bring back with me? I didn't know.

After I faced the fact that I had made the decision, I told myself that I wanted to see the people. My relatives, my colleagues of the pen, my friends, my enemies. Then I felt that I didn't want to see them. I was afraid that too much time had passed, that we had become too different. My relatives had aged, some had died. It seemed that what I wanted to see most were the places and the things.

I wanted to see the schoolyard, to feel its cracked pavement under my feet, to walk onto the game field and touch the metal poles supporting the basketball hoop. I didn't know if I could still identify it, but I wanted to see the building where I was first interrogated by the Securitate. To step inside it, to ride some creaky elevator up to the third floor (I remembered that apartment as being on the third floor), to walk out of it and stare at some anonymous door, perhaps the one I was pushed through by my captors almost thirty years ago. Then ride down again and walk out untouched, clothes unruffled, confidence intact, smile high.

No, no, that would be childish. I wouldn't waste my time with that.

I would go to my brother's grave and put my hand on the tombstone. I would finally stand by my father's grave, and pray by it. I would touch . . .

Just by thinking the word *touch,* a tide of memory inundated me. My palms, my fingers, my fingertips, all my senses crackled with myriads of physical memories. One such memory was of the little park next to our house, with that statue of a forgotten patriot. At his feet, a semi-naked woman of greened-up bronze raised towards him a wreath of laurels: Romania, thankful to her loving son. As a kid, I sat down on her knee, or stroked it, feeling the heated roundness of the metal in my palm. I felt it again, just now. Maybe I'd stop to take a look at that statue, if it was still there. I would touch it.

As if I'd given myself permission in my mind, I started to fantasize about touching everything. The tablecloths in restaurants. I was sure they would be the same, cool and starched. There was a clock on a boulevard corner, next to the University building, a favorite place for young men to wait for their dates. How many times had I waited for a young woman there, how many times had I absentmindedly touched the clock's stone pillar, or leaned against it, hearing the slow peng-peng sound of its hand counting the seconds against the din of the traffic. All of a sudden, I was seized by a memory so bittersweet that I couldn't identify what it was at all. Smell, sight, sound? It was all of them, it was *fall.* A Bucharest fall, smoothed by a light drizzle, with city contours and lights and colors in soft focus. The smells of the wind in my nostrils. The breeze-rippled water of the main pond in Cismigiu Garden, landscaped after the Luxembourg

Garden in Paris. A sumptuous tract of trees, lawns, and statues, natural decor to countless love encounters and love separations. I remembered the feel of my fingers on the back of a bench in the garden, a bench of cracked oakwood, carved over and over by pocket knives inscribing names. Gogu and Raluca, Ion and Sanda, pairs of lovers of yesteryear. No, I never carved my name on a bench there. I was too cool.

I would touch local newspapers again, careful about that damn Romanian ink, always ready to stain my fingers.

I flashed suddenly on a composite sensation of all the human hands I shook back there, especially of the female palms. Some of them returned my shake with unexpected strength—they squeezed my hand briefly but hard, then pulled back rubbing their palms against mine, as if promising a passionate encounter. Sometimes that encounter occurred, sometimes not. Now, here, I remembered my body printing itself in that time and space, and my face braving the wind and warming up the air. There was nothing left of that, nothing. I was there so many years. I lived there so deeply. And yet there was nothing left.

I was so young. There's nothing like the youth one leaves behind, sealed up in a forbidden land.

I would stop and stand in streets where I walked with my twin brother.

I would stop where I stopped one night, drunk with wine and with pride, after I first met my readers and autographed their books. One told me that I would go far, which could mean both distance and achievement. Unconsciously prophetic, that young man whom I never met again. I no longer remembered that street's name, but it didn't matter. I could find it. I used to know my hometown blindfolded. In fact, yes, that was what I wanted to do, I wanted to *walk* around my hometown, just as I had done so many, many times before.

All this felt too sweet and poetic. Where was the pain? Where was the hate?

They were both lurking back there—I realized it as soon as I mentioned their names. Pain and hate, like two dry, faithful spinsters. They were there.

I could take the train to the Carpathians, and get off at Poiana Tapului. I'd heard that it had become quite a resort, with hotels, motels, a freeway. I could look for that ravine where those peasants were shot. Were their bodies found and buried? Or did the forest take care of them, turning them into cleaned-up bones? For an instant, that ravine loomed inside me, as sad and important as my own brother's grave, or my father's, and I knew now why I'd been so imprinted by those pictures of mass burials on CNN. Because my childhood was one of graves. Because I grew up in between graves, and killings.

We were so lucky that none of us were killed that day, that we went down to that village all together, and slept in that rented room, where I heard the house clock. . . .

I realized something terribly simple: I just needed to *be* where I once was, where I once lived. For a while. Being in that space meant bringing back the past and undoing it. I needed to see who I had been, close up and face to face. As if leaning into a mirror which would reflect back not the me of today, but the me of the past. That could only happen there. I suddenly felt again that sense of solidarity I was so adept at feeling, perhaps because I was a writer. This time, I felt solidarity with all the people who returned, at some time or other, to a place from which they had to flee. I was like millions of people who had lived for years with that haunting need to return.

I thought of my in-laws. They were in that number.

I reminisced about fragments of our conversations. Yes, that was what they talked about too. Revisiting places and things, before revisiting people. Places and things, the school, the river. The trains, the busses, the brand of cigarettes, the color of bread, the feel of a certain cloth, the price paid for a first-time jacket or necktie. All that was gone, but it was there. All that, the hate couldn't touch or spoil. All that was themselves, not other people, but themselves.

I wanted to be with myself, with my old self.

And yet . . .

I shook bodily, wondering if there was still some High Noon waiting for me back there. A tragic encounter. A Moment of Truth so harsh that I could come out of it maimed, in my body or in my emotions. Was there such a High Noon? Would I survive it?

I threw that question at the future, knowing that I could not get the answer, nor could I prepare myself for it. I felt prepared, I felt unprepared, it didn't matter. I had to do it.

Petru Popescu's parents, Radu Popescu and Nelly Cutava, in the 1940s

The twins, Petru and Pavel, two years old

The twins in elementary school—Pavel is in the fourth row, far right, Petru in the fifth row, second from the left

The twins with their parents, one year before Pavel's death

Carl and Blanka Friedman in Prague after the war

Traditional Romania: a peasant shrine by the roadside (photo: Emmanuel Tanjala)

The Romanian landscape, pretty and deceptively tranquil (photo: Emmanuel Tanjala)

University Square, Bucharest's Tiananmen Square (photo: Emmanuel Tanjala)

The empty dream: Ceausescu's mammoth building looms at the end of his Victory of Socialism Boulevard (photo: David Stork)

Ceausescu ("The Genius of the Carpathians," "Truth Itself") and his wife Elena (photo: UPI/CORBIS—Bettman)

The cover of *Captive*, Petru's darkly subversive first novel

Bucharest after the revolution: everything's changed, yet the breadlines are still there, and so are the soldiers (photo: David Stork)

Petru before defecting: talking to fans in a Bucharest literary cafe

Petru, soon after coming to the United States—a Native-American dwelling, and freedom!

Bucharest, December 1989: the Christmas Revolution (photo: Ara Ghemigian)

Prague, 1991: Iris facing her uncle's grave, dug out of the forest

Ceausescu's grave, a few months after the first pair's execution: laden with flowers! (photo: David Stork)

Iris and the
Irish volunteers
at the orphan's
home in
Nicoresti, 1991

Petru in
Bucharest, in
1991, with two
of his uncles:
Nicu, left, and
Petre

Petru with
former
schoolmates,
1991

Prague, 1991: Carl and Blanka in the National Theater, where Carl worked as an electrician, his cover in the Czech resistance

Petru with his mother in Los Angeles, 1996

The Popescus of Hollywood, 1994

Part Three

Prague

M y mother received the news of my trip to Bucharest with panic. Her reaction was straightforward: "Don't go."

When it became clear that I would go, she became furious: "Why would you go? See, *I'm* not going!" Which brought back my own anger, on cue. This trip was important for me, yet my mother was reacting with her usual self-centeredness. If *she* felt no need to go back and visit, why should I? Angry, I shot back, "Don't worry, I'll be back in less than two weeks! I'll be here to take care of you again!"

Tears welled up in my unsinkable mother's eyes.

I said I was sorry. She wiped off her tears.

Remember? Mother arrived in California, put me on notice that she was going to choose freedom, then asked me for an affidavit of support. I told her that if she wanted the affidavit, she had to listen to a few things I had to say. Then I let my past feelings come out in the open, and bruised her pretty badly. I spewed out all my childhood's anger, in fairly well articulated phrases, for I had rehearsed them at over a hundred bucks an hour on the couches of California shrinks. Where had she been when I was growing up? After Pavel had died? When Dad had left? Did she know at all who I was, what made me tick? Could she help me handle my old pains, and rages, and fears?

Mom rolled big eyes: "You felt all those things? All this time, *you hid them from me?*"

I burst out laughing. Even though her incapacity to see things from anyone else's point of view pained me as much as always, I momentarily dropped my anger, and let myself enjoy the situation's dark humor. Mother was here again, and with her came an incredibly familiar presence: Communism, unconsciously incarnated in Mother. While I cried out about old injustices, she rolled her eyes, shocked not that I had suffered, but that she had not been informed! That I, while trying to protect myself, had lived in a reality of my own, outside her control.

Then she found the explanation for all that, and said it out loud: "You didn't feel all that, back then. You're feeling it now because you live in America . . ."

"What are you talking about?"

"This is what people think they should be feeling, in America."

"Mom, for Christ's sake, listen to me . . ."

I broke into a painful diatribe about everything that had happened. About how she had made it impossible for anyone to penetrate her own wall of pain. About how my sangfroid in tragedy was numbness, and my apparently unimpeded functioning was paid for inside with enormous emotional torment. My mental balance was maintained by . . . writing. Mom looked at me with her still-pretty brown eyes, and it was clear that she understood very little. And didn't want to hear more about it, lest all that would become an acknowledged element of our relationship. She was very scared of that. She started to talk of herself. "I was in such horrible pain back then. More than you'll ever imagine . . ."

"I did imagine, Mother. More than that, I saw it. That's why I did my best to . . ."

She talked over me. "I needed someone who would be stronger than your father." Jesus! I thought. Me, at thirteen? "And you looked, you acted so fearless . . ."

Who wouldn't want to look and act fearless? But at what price?

It was obvious from the first day of her visit that Mom herself was full of fear. Fear of age, fear of loneliness, but especially fear of having to return to the land where that raving maniac was still in power. She'd also asked my uncle Florin in New York to write her an affidavit, just in case she couldn't enlist me. I was mollified by one word she said: freedom. But I forced her into a kind of pre-marital agreement. I typed out a document stating that she could no longer ignore my feelings or invade my territory, as she had done in the past, and made her read it and keep a copy of it. Rather naive on my part. If she had no idea what my feelings were as a child, how would she guess them now, when I was a fully formed man, with far better defense mechanisms? Anyway, the long and the short of it was, I wrote down the conditions of our new relationship, then I wrote the affidavit.

I saddled myself again with Mother's unending chores and problems, and again I re-parented her. But this time I didn't feel robbed of my own importance and urgency. I was annoyed, but often enough I felt re-integrated, made whole again, when I exerted my right to say no. No, I couldn't do this, no, I was too busy today, no, I had children now, I had other priorities.

She, despite her promise of becoming autonomous, discreet, and unnagging, soon went back to her eccentricity and self-importance. When my children were born, as Iris and I lived the sleepless times that come with new babies, Mom would still call on the phone not just to read me some gas bill that she "just couldn't understand," but also to ask my suggestions for rhymes. Mom, far from settling into grandmother routines, went to English classes, wrote poems, and mailed them to pen pals all over the country. All men, all widowers or bachelors seventy and up. Out of that unseen plethora of bachelors, one, an old bohemian named Tommy Lewis, came to visit Mom in L.A., dragging a trailer behind his van all the way from Arkansas. He had asked her to move there and share his trailer. She'd declined, but swayed him by phone to come visit her in California. Thus Tommy came, saw Mom once, and that was enough. He moved in with her.

Mom was alive and well, a political refugee in America (thanks to my affidavit), and consumating a common-law marriage with a super-Anglo, who had previously been a hotel manager in Hawaii and used to gamble serious sums, or so he claimed, in Honolulu and Vegas and other casino cities. He'd once raised a daughter who was now a mother herself, so he was free of obligations and quirky and full of wanderlust. Just my mom's kind of partner, the one she always wanted. They had little money, but no time pressures, no family pressures, no pressures period. Love was sweet and life-in-love perfect, even if it started at seventy.

I got an unexpected reward out of Mom's presence here, even if it came with the headache that she had always been. Now that she was not under the thumb of Communism, Mom reblossomed. Her indomitable appetite for life, as indomitable today as her appetite for anger and tragedy had once been, forebode well for me. I would live as long, hopefully, I would show as much vitality. Mom drove a second-hand Toyota through L.A.'s crazy traffic. Mom travelled to Tijuana with her old guy, to buy stuff for their increasingly cluttered apartment. Mom forgot my wife's birthday, angering her, or didn't answer the phone for days, getting me all panicked, imagining her sprawled on the floor dying, while in fact she hadn't heard the phone—she was losing her hearing but refused to use a hearing aid. Once, after pounding on her door for an hour, and seeing through the window her unmoving shape in bed, I called the fire department to break down her door. As they started to do it, Mom suddenly moved; she'd been taking a nap. Mom elicited out of my mother-in-law, the modest, dutiful Blanka, a statement of admiration: "She's so full of life, so young! I wish I was like her!" Chronologically, Blanka was younger than my mother.

Iris worded it rather differently: "She's always lived for herself first! So selfish, I wish I was that selfish!"

Of course, Mom was invited to all our family functions. Also to my in-laws'. She always made her entrance with effect, even if she did or said nothing unusual. It was in her way of walking in, of looking around to see not just who was there, but how they responded to her presence. Granting to all a smile, still proud, still regal. Then quickly looking around to spot me in this new crowd, in this foreign setup. When she found me, she gave me a smile, smaller, more real, as if spelling relief. For I was her anchor here. I knew it, everyone knew it (she denied it, of course). However, after Tommy appeared and was invited with Mother to those fourth of Julys and Thanksgivings, Mom searched the crowd for me with less haste. She behaved less nervous, less possessive. She enjoyed belated hippie days with her beau, and who was I to say she shouldn't? It was great. Mom was still Mom.

It had taken so many years to see her here, something of mine finally saved from the past—she was that, despite the price tag she came with.

Anyway, why was Mom so frightened of my trip to Bucharest?

"Aren't *you* frightened?" she had asked me.

"Of what?"

"Of them. . . . You know how they are."

"Just how are they?"

She sat up—I was having coffee with her, in her apartment. She raised her voice. "They are envious, destructive! Always looking to break, to undo! They could do anything to you, put something in your soup at the hotel!"

"Mother, come on. I just interviewed their first freely elected president, for the *Los Angeles Times*. I'm going there as an American journalist. Iris is coming with me, d'you think they'll make us both disappear?"

The *L.A. Times Magazine* had asked me to write a story about Romania after the Revolution. "Factual, but also as personal as possible," I was urged by Brett Israel, the editor of the magazine.

"Petru!" Mom had nothing to convince me with, so she tried to impress me with her gaze. "Petru, wait a few years. It's not good to go now. I *feel* . . ."

"What do you feel?"

"That now is not the time."

I reacted with my old anger, for I felt her fear trying to root itself in me. And I thought it came from her selfishness: God forbid, if something happened to me, what would happen to her?

So I gave her a scowl. "Look, I gotta do it. Sorry."

"But look at *me!*" Full speed back to her own way of understanding things. "Do I have to go back there? I've no intention of ever visiting that place again."

I held back a tirade. She hadn't written my books, waged my war with the censorship, or enjoyed my notoriety. What did she know about being on those pale youngsters' lips, and in their hearts? I was going back to revisit that feeling. For the first time, I felt I had an explanation about why I wanted to go back. I wanted to revisit that generation. I wanted to see how they had done without me.

I remembered how, as a teenager, I battled the fears sowed in my psyche by my twin brother's death. And they were many. Fear of death and of disease, expressed in bouts of hypochondria, torturing because I could not stop them just by thinking logically. Nor could I reveal them to others, for I was too embarrassed. Other fears. Fear of the Securitate, of failure, of selling out. Fear of love and marriage, fear of commitments and responsibilities. Fear of becoming mediocre, corrupt, second class as an artist or as a human being. That last fear was quite justified, I lived in a world which was itself mediocre, corrupt, and second class.

Fear, forever and in all imaginable forms.

Yet despite my fear—and here came my personality's most intriguing contradiction—I was obsessed with questioning, searching, piercing through taboos, breaking laws and regulations. That made for a type of behavior that seemed oh so daring. As daring as humanly possible.

Sometime before I was eighteen, before official maturity, I formed the conviction that I had a mission. And missions were only over when they became completely fulfilled. My mission was to be a writer, and as long as I fulfilled it I could not die, or become cynical and corrupt.

Naive as that thought was, it helped. It helped against my fears.

Did I still have that sense of mission? It was hard to give an answer, for I almost never thought or spoke about it. I spoke of plots that were commercial, of books and films that were timely (timely in rapport with the market, rather than with the readers' consciousness), of publishers with the knack for creating best-sellers, of studios with well-filled production coffers, of agents with strategy and chutzpah. In the light of that type of thinking, why would I fly back to Romania, with a stopover in Prague? I should be in New York or Hollywood, pitching and shmoozing with super-publishers and super-producers.

Or out in the wild, researching. Or at my computer, banging out my next book, which in between working hours I would keep under lock and key, for this crazy Romanian had really wild innovative ideas, and they could be ripped off. . . .

Two weeks before starting my trip to Romania, I had finished touring Britain and Ireland to promote *Amazon Beaming*. The British edition had come out ahead of the American one; in less than a month, I was to go on a similar promotional tour around the United States. I'd scheduled Romania sandwiched in between those tours, as if they were the proof that my new life would go on, unaffected. Our children were to stay in Los Angeles with my in-laws, while Iris and I travelled to Prague, then to Bucharest.

So. It was mid-September 1991, and we were on a flight to Eastern Europe. We had left Los Angeles at ten the night before. Now it was dawn after a brief uncomfortable sleep at thirty-five thousand feet while the plane pierced through a few hours of darkness, then found the sun again, shining on the iced wastes of the Arctic. Around us, the first-class section was waking up for breakfast. The men buttoned up their shirts or tightened the belts they had loosened for the short night. The women passed brushes through their hair. Both rose and lined up before the restrooms, to wash their faces and shave or repair their makeup. A red-eyed stewardess served steaming airline coffee, whose aroma mixed with that of chemically perfumed towelettes. In a few minutes, the passengers straightened themselves out. They looked again like an affluent elite, cultured, purposeful. Their gestures showed confidence, their voices were low, their interactions subdued. Added up, this first-class cabin was worth a few million dollars in residences, stocks and bonds, and other properties. None were headed for Prague or Bucharest, I was sure of that after just looking at them. They didn't have the vibe. They would deplane in Munich, last stop before Eastern Europe, my terra Orientalis incognita.

Next to me, an attractive woman smiled from a halo of blond hair. Iris had slept about an hour, which was more than she usually slept on planes, and her face glowed with energy. Her smile widened, and I saw in it, after two kids and ten years of marriage, the girl I'd met on a blind date in Hollywood. She took my hand. I felt that my whole body, and my knowledge of her body and her knowledge of mine, in short, our life together, was concentrated in our joining hands.

"Any dreams?" I asked.

"I don't remember anything worth mentioning."

"Five more hours." The flight got bumpy, and she squeezed my hand. "You scared?"

"Not really."

"No, I mean . . . of what we'll find there."

She smiled. "Not yet."

The flight got bumpier. I wanted to go to the bathroom, but I waited for the turbulence to subside. I'd explained to Iris repeatedly the law of Bernoulli, according to which the air streaming over the plane's wings creates more pressure below the wings and less pressure above them, thus pushing the plane upward. So as long as those screws called engines were turning, the plane rolled ahead on the air, secure like a car's wheels on a freeway, just shaken benignly by the freeway's little potholes: the updrafts and downdrafts of air variously warm or cold. She understood the principle, but never completely lost her fear.

The turbulence was over. My wife kissed me, and we trekked to our respective bathrooms. I returned first, sat down, and thought about what I felt. Almost nothing. Certainly not fear of what I would find. I carried my American passport in an elegant little folder of leather, in an inside pocket positioned right over my heart. Loaded with passport, addresses, and traveler's checks, it hung there like a holstered pistol. Folded inside my passport was my letter of accreditation from the *Los Angeles Times*. In my suitcase, stored in the plane's hold, I'd packed several copies of the British edition of *Amazon Beaming*. A lot of artillery. If any ghosts from the past approached me, I'd have plenty to blast them with. No, I wasn't scared of meeting my ghosts.

I tried to dig deeper, to find some fear. Finally, I hit some. As I zoomed across time zones towards my long unvisited roots, me, an American who once confused fish for cats with fish for people, I touched it. It was fear for our marriage. I would show my wife my roots, naked, now completely revealed by the collapse of the Ceausescu regime, by the Revolution and the confused painful times that followed. I'd show her, naked, a certain version of me. She'd already told me how fearful and self-conscious she felt when revealing certain pieces of herself. How would she react, what would she think? How would I react to her reaction? Suddenly, a compressed memory of fears for our marriage opened inside me. There had been many. We knew nothing about how to be married and stay married, because the experiences of our respective parents applied so little. The Friedmans had started speaking English to each other as soon as they reached America. The rough, vocabulary-poor English of immigrants, so as to make it easier for Iris and her brother. That and a stable home was what they, two Europeans of the old school, had to offer. Otherwise, they were not talkers, not "connected," not touchy-feely, not politically correct, not very versed in capitalism, certainly not in the beginning, not hip—except for that hipness which I rated as one of the best, the hipness of taking America by the horns. Iris came out of that background as the most baffling combination of know-how and naivete and distrust and daring, in short as strong and yet as various and worried as I was. As for my parents, they were not even here, to claim their parts as role models. We both married alien breeds, the "other" as Kafka would've called it; we didn't know the first thing about a workable marriage, but we knew how desperate we were to keep it going. So we plunged into the Great American Fear of the Future, the next great fear after the cold war. And fear works, just like denial works. We made it, with fear as a daily component. "Let's not get too close to that guy," my wife sometimes whispered to me, at nine in the morning, jogging on a Beverly Hills footpath past a bench with a very healthy-looking bum heaped up on it, staring, awake, silent, undecipherable. Like a Pilgrim's wife: stay clear of that thicket, who knows what's lurking in there. The Great American Fear of the Future keeps us fit, keeps us working and making money, keeps us the mightiest country in the world.

I felt the fear just now. About our marriage. Because danger did lurk in the thicket. Regularly, this or that kid, this or that sweet young pre-teen in Adam's or Chloe's class became a haggard-looking casualty of a divorce. We saw them, walking to school with the limp lopsided gait of a child wrangled back and forth in a custody battle. Losing interest in play, moving like a zombie on the soccer field, getting bad grades. We knew the parents, they had adjusted, gainfully employed, young still, winners. What pulled them apart? Why? Why? That clear fluid love, like ocean water, transparent when cupped in naked hands, furiously dark when crashing against the coast, how could we protect it? There was no recipe.

Iris returned and we watched the world news on the screens affixed to each seat. In a while, the pilot came on, announcing that we were entering the airspace of Germany.

My wife had never been to Prague, Bucharest, or anywhere else in Eastern Europe. As for Germany, until recently she felt beholden by history to avoid anything German, from products to the people. Yet, she drove a Mercedes, from the factory that once provided Hitler's own cars. Mercedes sells a lot in Hollywood, and seems particularly successful with the Holocaust survivors' second generation. It's a way of saying, "I'm not afraid of that place, or even prejudiced against it, here, I use the best of its products." I'm familiar with that mental process. I wouldn't touch Russian vodka in Romania, but I drank it without qualms in California. And when we took a cruise to the Black Sea three years ago, I experienced a cathartic sense of triumph over the Soviets on a wharf in Odessa, when two Russian kids followed me begging me to buy hot Soviet watches.

"Komandirskie," for officers, they insisted proudly, sticking a hatful of them in my face. The watches were adorned with tanks and rockets drawn in silhouette under the brand names. They looked monstrously big and ticked loud enough to be heard at a distance. I bought two, for five bucks each. I strapped on the bigger one, and felt that I wore on my wrist that scene from my childhood, with Uncle Nicu returning from the war to find Bucharest occupied by watch-stealing Soviets. That memory's meaning was reversed that morning as I, an affluent American tourist, deigned to buy two watches from those little Russian thieves.

A Mercedes car costs a lot more than a pair of watches. But the feeling's the same. Let those perfect German machines carry Jewish

Hollywood executives, and let those Soviet watches count the time for me, the ex-Soviet slave who broke out of Soviet time.

I talked with Iris about what she had to do in Prague. Her mother had asked us to look up a family that had been kind to her after the war. Mirek and Blanka were living in a one-room apartment downtown. They had been married only a year, and the arrival of a baby—Jan, my wife's older brother—was a frightening miracle for Blanka, for neither her mother nor any other experienced relative was on hand to guide her into motherhood. But there were the Kahouns, a Christian family living across the hallway. Mrs. Kahoun became Blanka's surrogate mother, teaching the former camp inmate how to bathe the baby, how to feed him, how to burp him. They had a daughter, Indra, a few years younger than Blanka. The Kahouns and the Friedmans became friends. They would have continued to be friends, had the Russians not clamped down, but the Russians did clamp down, and most of the Jews who were not party members saved themselves by fleeing, while most of the Christians hesitated and got caught in the net. I was shown a picture of the Kahouns, one of those sepia group portraits of a husband and wife with faces wrinkled by war hardships. Between them, blond, fresh, daughter Indra. Blanka asked us to find Indra. The older Kahouns were surely dead now, but Indra had to be around.

"How will we find her?" asked Iris. "How are we going to find her in a city of a million and a half, without even a phone number?"

"They did not have a phone; they were simple people. The father worked in the post office. I'll give you the address: Truhlarska 7." Blanka turned towards me, and I nodded; I'd been to Prague, its downtown was small, finding a particular street posed no problems. "They lived on the fourth floor," she added. I nodded again. We'd look up Indra Kahounova— in Czech, women's names are lengthened by a suffix indicating the female gender, which can produce comical results: Meryl Streepova, Oprah Winfreyova. Very possibly, Indra Kahounova married and changed her name, yet Blanka assumed that she still lived in that fourth floor apartment, on Truhlarska 7.

"What errands do you have for us?" I asked Carl, who sat and listened to that exchange in silence, at the kitchen table of course.

He started, as if pulled out of deep thoughts. "Me, nothing. Go walk around the National Theater, I worked there as chief electrician, before being transferred to Vienna."

Blanka had another errand. Right after the war, her younger brother died in a military accident. He had signed up with the Jewish Haganah, which had an agreement with the Czech army to train conscripts locally, before sending them to battle the British forces still occupying Palestine. Martin, training in a camp near Prague, was killed in an explosion. Blanka wanted us to find his grave, in the cemetery of Strasnice. I remarked that the writer Kafka was also buried in Strasnice, could it be the same cemetery? She shrugged, she didn't know. She'd barely heard of Kafka.

Thus, Blanka gave us two emotional missions, while Carl gave us none.

Wait a second. Prague should've stirred my own emotions. Prague was the Florence of my Commie youth, I visited it several times, the last time after the Soviet invasion. But all I felt while discussing these tasks with my in-laws was a smug sense of being familiar with the place. I'd be Iris's guide, I'd help her in her nervousness. I tried to stretch my imagination to the next stop, Bucharest. Would I finally stand at the grave of my father, whose funeral I was banned from attending? Would I see the house of my childhood? Maybe not, maybe it was destroyed in the street fights of December 1989. These questions did not elicit an emotional response, they didn't even make noise inside me. For some reason, they fell flat.

Very well. First, we would look up Indra. And Martin's grave.

And after that, 650 miles to the southeast, in that sun-baked valley of the Danube, in that harsh matrix that gave me to the world, what would I find?

Jesus, was it only 650 miles away? So little distance?

That's all. So, what would I find there?

I didn't know. At this instant, I really just didn't know. The anxiety for my marriage had dissipated, and I sat purposeless. Why was I travelling back there?

I didn't know anymore.

We deplaned in Munich, and scurried to another terminal, to another plane. The airport was crowded, teeming with humans in a cold cage of concourses, escalators, and suspended walkways. Procedures took longer, people addressed each other formally, there were unnecessary complications in everything. There was chamber music filtering in from somewhere, lit billboards for Gothic monuments and baroque palaces, classical paintings used as backgrounds for Rolex watches, Bavarian beers, and Visa cards. There was a strange, tasteless hodgepodge of Europe and America, the past and the present. We passed under a departures board, flashing with East European names, and . . . instantly, as if by magic, everything changed.

I didn't even know when it had changed. Iris and I were still surrounded by Europeans, but that feeling of hodgepodge increased exponentially. The travellers were dressed compositely in clothes that looked expensive and cheap, current and dated, often on the same person. Unstylish long hair hung down from under hats and caps. The color of the human skin veered to the olive, the pale, the swarthy. Haste turned into controlled panic. As we waited behind other passengers, the line was filled with heavy breathing, suspicious glances, and bodily collisions not followed by excuses. As the names Sofia, Bucharest, Budapest, Tirana, Belgrade continued to flash, the temperature seemed to rise, and the smells became spicier. A man cutting in front of me pressed two fresh loaves of bread against his three-piece suit, flour from their crusts sprinkling him like a light snowfall. Other men ran with cigarettes stuck in the corners of their mouths, puffing and gasping simultaneously. Women followed them, swinging overfilled duty-free bags, as if from a last minute plunder. The passengers' rushing seemed caused not by the imminence of departures, but by a far older and more dramatic sense of migration.

I heard words in Russian, modulated with a German accent from above, from a loudspeaker. We'd entered the orbit of Russia. Suddenly I sprinted ahead of Iris. Leaving her behind me, responding to some archaic instinct of first securing the passage, then pulling along my woman. I became aware of it, and turned with an apologetic smile. "What a stampede, huh?"

"Really. What's wrong with these people?" she asked, sounding very American. I took her arm, thankful that she hadn't guessed that I'd almost been swept away by the ancestral impulse.

"Maybe we should've brought some food," she said, pointing her chin to the man with the bread. He was heading for the gate marked Prague, just like us.

"He just likes Bavarian bread," I said protectively.

"What the hell is this?" Iris asked.

This was a crowd of some twenty boys and girls who looked between seven and twelve. With café-au-lait complexions, matted dark hair, and gold-capped teeth, I glimpsed their glitter as their lips parted, a cheap glitter I remembered from childhood. Gypsy kids, they often had gold-capped teeth. Gypsy kids, huddling in the Munich airport, without parents. They looked like they had in my childhood, when their parents let them loose from their caravans, on forays into Bucharest. A tall and wide, almost square-shaped, German woman herded them across the terminal; to keep them under control, she wore a whistle around her wide neck. A German man also tagged along. He looked like an airport official. I stepped into his path: *"Entschuldigen Sie, was passiert mit diesen Kinder?"* ("Scuse me, what's with these kids")?

"Back to Yugoslavia," he said in guttural English, rejecting my German. I felt a peculiar sense of relief: they were not from Romania. "They're coming from everywhere, Hungary, Bulgaria, Romania," he added, as we walked abreast. Iris caught up, asking where the children were being taken. He answered, his English weighted by Germanic thoroughness: They would be put on a plane to Belgrade, and handed over to what was left of Yugoslavia's social services. Which meant that they would be back here in two months at the most. They would find a hole in the border to slip through. And the police would chase them and round them up again, which was damn expensive; the damn was the only personal inflection in his little speech.

There was a time when one of us would've protested: Why are you sending them back, they're *kids,* why can't they stay here? That wouldn't cost you much more than to keep chasing them and rounding them up.

As if to preempt such a protest, the German official talked on, explaining that most of these kids had criminal records. They smoked and drank too—he raised his rounded fist in imitation of a bottle, went glug glug. Ahead of us, the nurse turned impatiently. The man mumbled, "Excuse me, the plane is leaving soon."

The little horde had stopped, enjoying being the subject of attention. I spotted one boy, small, very dirty, with blond hair. A shot of Slavic genes into his Indic ancestry. We made eye contact. His stare was blindingly bright and alert. He sized up my wife and grinned, enjoying this clearly sympathetic female not for her kindness, but for *her*. I noted the consistent discrepancy between the kids' appearance, small, frail, misgrown, and the streetwise adultness of their movements. The girls showed no more innocent softness than the boys: they walked sashaying their skinny hips, bumping the air with their narrow chests, and, cocking their heads to the side, appraising the adults with whom they crossed paths. I watched one girl sweep her narrow palm along the rim of a baggage conveyer; this was it, that "Gypsy sweep" Pavel and I were repeatedly warned against in childhood. They let their hands hang down, the easier to swipe loose objects. They looked exactly like this when a *shatra,* an itinerant clan, cut its noisy path down a Bucharest street. Now here they were crossing the borders as refugees, and crossing them back again as extradited aliens.

The whistle blew, the little horde hoofed away, with the two adults following. We stayed, as if on the edge of a broken illusion. Only a few years back, we used to drive around L.A. with our car stuffed with loaves of bread and bricks of cheese, trying to assuage the hunger of the homeless. Almost all turned down our bread and cheese, asking for booze or cash instead. They got angry too; once, a cripple shockingly rose from his wheelchair, and ran after us waving his fists. Then we started to look for credible charities. We gave to foundations for Romania's orphaned children, not knowing whether our money ever made it to Romania. We gave to Christian dinners for the homeless, some of them organized by my wife's temple. We gave when we didn't have, we gave when we had enough, we kept giving, never knowing whether we made a difference.

I watched the Gypsies being swallowed by the vertical jaws of a metal detector.

The emotional upswell mysteriously absent in me till that minute suddenly rose, and grabbed me by the throat. I gasped, then ground my teeth. I couldn't afford this, my trip hadn't even started. I needed that cynical smugness, man, where was it? All gone, just from seeing a little rabble of transients? One childhood memory ignited, and here was my heart, tearing my chest under my American passport?

I spoke out loud: Dammit, maybe the Germans and Yugoslavs should combine efforts and give these kids shelter, rather than fight off their incursions. Wouldn't a few hundred social workers cost less money than all this shuttling across frontiers, tying up in the process judges, policemen, customs officials? Iris wondered in reply, maybe that solution was tried and found inefficient?

The Eastern Europeans in funny clothes had watched the little column of children, and us arguing about them. They looked at us with curiosity, but stepped aside to let the kids pass, faces closed, set in. They had their own destinies, their own children to take care of. As we all moved through the detector, I saw myself, back then. I glimpsed the person I once was, a human caught in a moving segment of history, aware of the events, of their sad implication, yet forced to move along with them. Then, I did speak out. I wasn't indifferent. What came of it?

As I stared at my past, the real purpose of my trip seemed to come to the fore. What did I hope to find? Some proof that what I'd done back then wasn't useless or meaningless. Some proof that being born under eastern stars had counted, that even today it added up, amounted to something. Some reason for pride in those years, to take back to America. *Pride,* which in my Communist vocabulary was nonexistent, pride which certainly wasn't among my trip's stated goals. I felt dizzy from the clearness of that word, and from the snug fit it made with this shameful scene.

If that was my real goal, my trip had to fill a tall order. I felt very tense, as we walked up the jetway into the next plane to sit in a first class very literally like Europe: small, cramped, noisy, and already filled with cigarette smoke.

I told Iris of my insight into myself. She asked, how did I survive my first ten years in America, when I didn't have any notoriety? "Is that all you think I'm about, being important?" I almost snapped. She smiled: "Nothing wrong with that, in fact I think that's your form of goodness."

I was silent, feeling crushed under the weight of an impossible gamble. Not only to face the Commie past, but to bring something uplifting out of it, otherwise what was the point? Yet I felt it was impossible. Iris noted how the people around us smoked and drank. To her right, a Czech man had reordered complimentary red wine three times, and slipped the little bottles in his attaché case, to take home. I muttered tensely that life was lived to the extreme here, to compensate for the tightness of borders. She looked out the window at the shiny Bavarian Alps, and commented on how pretty they were, so I told her that barbed wire ran across them, and border points studded them, and there were graves of unknown soldiers scattered all over them, except perhaps on the very peaks. Some graves were from Roman times, others from the two world wars. In front of us was the Czech border, to our right the Austrian border. Farther ahead, where my Romania lay, the number of countries had doubled since the Soviet Union's fall, so the numbers of borders and excuses for conflicts had doubled too. Americans think of Europe as vegetating peacefully between Napoleon's reign and World War I, a continent of comical monarchies. What a misperception. Napoleon had barely been dethroned, and Europe exploded again and again. 1821, Romanians, Greeks, and Russians battled the Turks. 1848, social revolutions against the monarchies, which the monarchies put down by lending troops to each other, Prussia to Austria, Austria to Russia, Russia and Hungary to Austria, etc. In 1855, the Crimean War. In the 1860s, the Prussians battled the Austrians, their former and future allies. In 1870, the Franco-Prussian War. In 1877, the Romanians chased the Turks out of Europe; new frontiers were drawn, not satisfactorily for anyone. The soldiers returned to their farms, found that the promises of social improvement had not been fulfilled, and re-exploded in uprisings bloodily pacified through armed force. Then the Balkan powder keg blew up, in 1912 and 1913; Romania was ripped by both explosions. In 1914, as if all those dress rehearsals were not enough, the first armed conflict to deserve the name "World War" tore the lids off all the reservoirs of Europe's hate. And for over four years, they all fought and killed, fought and killed, fought and killed.

For what? Some nations re-gained ancestral territories, like Romania. Or their independence, like Czechoslovakia. Were those gains enough to justify the losses? They had to be, judging by the celebrations that ended World War I. But a new historic course had been shaped, and it already pointed to World War II. So what was the lesson? Was there a lesson? Of course there was, but its meaning escaped me.

I drank one of those little bottles of red wine, and told Iris of my previous visits to Prague. I had been there at twenty, briefly, before the Soviet invasion, and then a few years later, as an author published in Czech and Slovak. That second time, Prague was occupied by the Russians: I saw them in the streets, through the déjà vu of my childhood in occupied Bucharest. I ran around that gem of a town with a Czech friend, and it was still a gem, though the invaders were visible and the natives grimly talked of defecting. I kept staring at the upper floors of the buildings, because the ground floors had been ravaged by the Russians. Where during the Prague spring there had been discos, jazz bars, coffee shops with long-haired patrons, private stores, avant-garde theaters and art studios, now there were sealed doors, broken glass fronts, eviction notices, and lease signs. Instead of capitalism re-blooming, now there was the drab return to normal. From the second floor up, Prague looked less changed, though even there it missed the glamour of youth. Before the occupation, blond girls with high cheekbones (my wife has the same Slavic cheekbones) hung out over old railings, waving to their dates, young men driving well-kept vintage cars, which those skillful tinkers the Czechs kept rolling all through Communism. Now the girls were gone, and their wooers in antique cars were gone too. It was as if youth had left the city politically and physically as well. Instead, there were morose windows, darkly sooted walls, gargoyles. Very Kafkaesque.

A few days before, packing, I'd asked Iris what she knew about Kafka. I'd anticipated a California answer, and she didn't disappoint me: "Kafka? He wrote real off stuff, and had a weird thing with his father, right?"

I laughed, it felt good somehow that Kafka could be summed up like that. In my youth I had walked in awe past the Kinsky Palace, in the heart of Old Town Square, where Kafka's prosperous father Hermann had his store. The muscular, well adapted Hermann stared out of his shop directly at the statue of Jan Huss, the fourteenth-century reformer of Czech Christianity. Kafka grew up on that square, hearing daily the bronze bells of nearby St. Tyn Cathedral. That seemed to me a good metaphor of how to survive and compartmentalize (my central issue in those years), because only two blocks away rose the Old-New Synagogue, also in pure Gothic style, and next to it was the cemetery where Rabbi Lowy, the raiser of the Golem, was buried; Lowy, coincidentally, was the maiden name of

Kafka's mother. The Kafkas (the name means crow in Czech) were bilingual in German and Czech, but Franz wrote in German, the language of wider culture. Through the Kafkas' social standing and thanks to the Jews' success in Prague (nicknamed Little Jerusalem in Kafka's time), Franz went to the best available schools, and got a doctorate in law at Prague University, one of Europe's oldest. But instead of becoming as prosperous and prominent as Hermann, he worked in a workers' insurance company. Diagnosed with tuberculosis, he did not fight in World War I, but retired on a state pension, and was cared for in Europe's best sanatoriums. Apart from his ill health and his personal demons, he lived a privileged life.

When I was in my twenties, it was obligatory to read Kafka and to be blown out by his metaphors of totalitarian systems. The distant, unseen authority residing in the Castle. The faceless justice system from *The Trial,* which revealed itself to be not about justice, but about a strange unexplained punishment, hovering above the novel's hero until in the end two faceless men would arrest and kill him. These were great themes, but Kafka had died before Hitler occupied Czechoslovakia, and he had only the vaguest idea about Communism. Having studied his biography in detail, I developed a theory much at odds with Kafka the political prophet. His father, unimaginative and unsupportive, tried to shape the boy into another assertive, contentedly assimilated male. The boy refused, and bore him a grudge shown at length in the "Letter to My Father." Unlike his over-energetic father, Franz Kafka's mother was passive and self-effacing. Franz had a longing for his maternal ancestors, because of family tales about their rabbinical learning—yet he never met most of them, was uneasy as a Jew, and even declared himself an atheist. Distrusting women, Kafka twice betrothed and then broke off with Felice Bauer, whom he put down cruelly for her slightly crooked teeth. Other sweethearts resided abroad; he wrote to them obsessively, memorizing the mail collection times, but never married any of them. He liked, in turn, the Socialists, the Anarchists, even the Zionists, but never became active in any of those movements. Altogether, because of parental neglect and illness, he lived an unhappy life. Whether he described alienation in society, or projected his own alienation onto his characters, it was a chicken-and-egg kind of issue. In all aspects of life, the man refused what was close but imperfect, in preference for what was ideal but unreal.

And that choice, I was convinced, was not politically motivated. I lived under Communism at the time, and it was suffocatingly real. Its very lack of freedom was almost physiological. The corruption, duplicity, compartmentalization, and other responses of the self to the state's intrusions did not exist separately from physical reality. In fact, it was the physical reality that most often defined them. We couldn't move across borders, physically. We couldn't *do* certain things, *have* certain things, *give* certain things to others, all those being concrete stances and actions. Quite interestingly, if we had money, even the non-convertible Commie currency, we could afford certain things, which created their own measure of freedom. A car equalled freedom to move, to travel. A house of one's own equalled freedom to be private, to exclude the state from one's own immediate environment. More plentiful food for one's family, or objects one could give to others equalled the freedom to feel prosperous, and generous, instead of being the deprived and powerless slave of the state. Etc. etc.

Being meticulous about his inner torture, but vague about its meaning, Kafka was a gold mine for the critics; but contrary to the fashionable interpretation, the occult justice system of *The Trial* seemed to me uncharacteristic of either Fascism or Communism, uncharacteristic of totalitarianism, period. Totalitarianism was precise, not vague. Its limitations were practical, utilitarian, and logically, if cruelly, motivated. It didn't breed alienation, for it forced its slaves to be one with itself, it *invaded* them.

I thought Kafka's agony about "otherness" relevant to himself, and perhaps to Prague. That city was so "other" to itself, through its repeated fragmentation of cultures and faiths, and its renewed submissions to foreign masters, that it created a feeling of futility, of elusive accomplishment. I, as a tourist, absorbed it consciously. The short-lived Prague spring was no more. Authority was back, placing a self-defeating contradiction on everything I saw. On the churches, tolerated with a kind of perverted pride by an anti-Catholic regime. On the Jewish memorials, marked in all the tourist brochures, but standing mutely without Jews. On the ambiguous sense of being Czech or Slovak, historic identities contaminated by the Germanizing of the culture and the Sovietizing of the politics. Where was the real Prague? Where was the soul? Well, like in Kafka, it was there, but you couldn't see it. When you thought you'd heard it, its call was over. If it lingered on, it was behind sealed doors and windows. Each time one of those opened, a puff of mysterious meaning wafted out. But when you caught a handful of it, it steamed through your fingers, and vanished.

Thinking about Kafka in my youth, I responded to a much needed impulse to think about myself. To try to separate how much of my pain came from Communism, and how much from myself and my own problems. I decided that a lot came from me and from my parents. On the other hand, Ceausescu's nationalism, which I had perceived at first as a breath of patriotic fresh air, made me feel less and less comfortable. I didn't need his nationalism to feel Romanian, in fact I aspired to find my own balance between feeling Romanian and all else I wanted to be part of. Again, Kafka's case was enlightening, especially here, in his own hometown. He was a Prager, yes, but not a Czech; not an active Jew, but not an atheist or an agnostic; an Austrian subject, yes, but not a German, even though he wrote in German. Throughout his life, it could be argued that he was never enough, never the right thing, never the genuine article, even to himself. But on the other hand, not being enough was his way of not being something imposed by others. Of resisting the definitions of others. Of preserving autonomy and freedom, no matter how modestly and unaggressively. If he was a spirit in pain, he was a free one nonetheless. And after he died, he became in his books so much to so many. He had talent.

I too had talent. As much, less, more, that did not matter. Talent was its own nationality and its own passport. I owed to my talent as much as I owed to my mother and father, or to my people.

I finished telling Iris about how Kafka had helped me sort out my problems, adding that I still picked him up and reread a few pages now and then. Just to remember how I felt in those days.

"Instead of that kind of writing, I'd rather have entertainment," she said directly, almost harshly. She sounded not quite like her, and strangely older.

I remembered a time when she talked frequently about being a child of survivors. About old feelings of unease that she'd stifled because they seemed trivial in comparison to her parents' suffering. That was an agitated time in her life; hoping it might help her, I bought her some books by survivor authors. She leafed through them, closed them, never opened them again. I asked her why. She explained in that same harsh tone, "I don't need the b.s. of authors about something I already know. About that, I need solutions, or nothing at all."

I was stunned. Then I agreed with her. For the same reason, back in Romania, I couldn't read Solzhenitsyn. I knew that stuff. I lived it.

"Is that Prague?" my wife asked, leaning so far over against the window that her forehead rubbed the glass, slightly frosted on the outside. "Not what I expected."

I bent over her seat, weighing against her body. A sea of opiate, greenish smog. Then the high rises of Prague's suburbs. Jesus! In the seventies, the Czechs had great architecture, or so we thought. *Almost like in the West.* The towers I saw now were ash-gray, with roofs browned-up by a kind of industrial seepage collected in big dirty pools. From the windows hung the tired flags of clothes put out to dry. I saw little patios with plants that looked like they'd died of thirst many generations back, before some lost, final war. Twisted paths cut past the tiling of intended passages, directly across the dirt, worn out by a population too tired to look where it stepped. I saw broken sidewalks. A comatose streetcar. The colors were all dusty dilutions of brown, yellow, and gray, and the contours of things were all lost in that particular Third World soft focus: dirt hanging in the long unpurified air.

Thank God this is not Bucharest, I thought. I knew it had to look more desolate, due to Ceausescu's devastation. If Prague started like this, my wife's eyes, and mine too, would have the time to get acclimated.

The descent seemed to take forever. We floated over rusting car hulks, and rusting railroad tracks. It's not all going to be like this, I said more to myself than to my wife, the old city itself is great. And we floated down slower, deeper, slower, deeper. I remembered Ruzyne Airport as a clean, modern, antiseptic place, all functional shapes and well-oiled technology. That was before I'd seen Western airports, of course.

"I'm nervous," my wife whispered, her hand seeking mine.

I responded in a positive California tone, "Why? We'll meet your parents' old friends, and find your uncle's grave too. Your mother will be happy, and you'll get a glimpse of her life when she was young."

"Come on, give me a break."

I nodded, let a few seconds pass. "I'm lucky," I whispered in her ear, "that I married this survivor girl, who for the sake of renewing the lost blood will never divorce me."

She squeezed my hand, and kissed me. We touched down, and the pilot said, Welcome to Golden Prague.

Prague was called golden because under the medieval Bohemian kings many of its roofs were gilded. And because, under the same kings, a little street ran steeply uphill to the Hrad, the royal castle, and in that street's little houses lived alchemists, the scientists who tried to turn ordinary matter into gold. They lived at the kings' expense. Like propaganda artists, they did nothing all their lives but try and try to turn sand, wood, even garbage, into gold. When they died without finding out how to make synthetic gold, they were buried at the king's expense. And their street was called the Golden Street *(zlata ulichka)*.

Cities, like people, are only attractive relative to what else we know. More prosperous and advanced than Bucharest, Prague was, as I said, my Commie Florence. But this time, I'd seen Florence, beginning with the airport, Prague was not what I knew. The inside of the terminal was dirty, with torn and stained vinyl and linoleum, with wooden fixtures from the sixties, heavy and chipped, with missing lights, old-fashioned escalators, jammed luggage conveyers, and a puckered crowd of taxi drivers and money changers hustling us in German, English, French, Czech as soon as we stepped down the jetway. Knowing the layout of the airport (amazing how that memory flashed back instantly), I pulled Iris past customs officers who stamped our passports indifferently, into the baggage claim area, where I fished up our bags and then led the way out. I had to fight off a little gang of volunteer porters. Neon signs for Western products had invaded the place, making its lack of maintenance even more glaring. And at the bottom of a stairway, staring up with the certainty of hunters setting their traps, there was a band of Sikhs, looking just like they might in an American airport, with the same blond hair and beards, and the same turbans, maybe just a little dirtier. I pushed Iris past them, and waved my arm at a line of taxis. A Mercedes 190 hurtled out of the line in an aggressive un-Czech fashion. A lanky young driver popped out. Saying he spoke English, he threw our bags in the trunk, and before we knew it we were on our way to the Intercontinental Hotel. He drove off into a gridlock, which he manuevered through by constant honking, even though his voice and manner were otherwise courteous. Schizophrenic feeling: Prague with the manners of New York.

"Bad traffic because Ruzyne too close to Prague, only eight kilometer," he explained. Here it was, absurdity from the start: instead of being

convenient, the closeness was a handicap. The driver introduced himself as Frantisek, Czech for Frank. Iris looked wide-eyed at the interior
of the car: it had been reupholstered in a kind of fake fur, gray and wispy,
like that of a creepy mask for Halloween. Iris kept staring; the driver
thought that she was disturbed by the radio broadcasting Czech music,
and obligingly turned it off. I looked outside, and didn't recognize the
place, or the people. They moved as if their wrong button had been
pushed, bustling and swaggering without any of their old decorum.
Frantisek slowed down behind another car and a man standing in the
street thrust his arm through the window, fluffing out a wad of money,
yelling that he was offering a good exchange. "Careful, that's Polish
money, worth nothing," warned Frantisek, and stepped on the gas. The
money changer, experienced, pulled his arm out intact, and vanished. I
looked at the driver: thirtyish, thin, his face already wrinkled. He drove
astoundingly fast, eager to be finished with us, to grab another fare. He
didn't seem worried about Prague's police, and maybe there were no
police, the way everyone drove, ran, shouted, crossed the streets against
lights, again in the most un-Czech fashion. I asked Frantisek how things
were. "There's no money," he shot back, sounding truthful but perhaps
hoping to ensure a tip. "Freedom needs money," he added.

I saw a daily paper laying in the seat next to him. With my global
Slavic, I guessed what one headline said. The giant Skoda factory was
being sold to BMW. I pointed at it: "You sell Skoda, you'll make money."
"The government will, not me." I saw a sign repeated again and again on
the front of buildings: *Na prodej.* For sale. "Everything's for sale," grunted
Frantisek, "and still there's no money. Aarrgh," he waved his arm with
disenchantment, and I caught the whiff of his armpit. He didn't smell bad,
he just smelled like "home": faulty showers, paprika sauces, and tobacco,
even though I didn't see him smoking. A kind of cheap spice.

Frantisek turned, asked what part of America we were from, seemed
to believe that I was as Californian as my wife. Iris mentioned that her
parents once lived here. "You look like a Czech girl," he said promptly,
without flattery or condescension. Objective. A little start of pride made
Iris sit straight. "What you doing in Prague?"

"Visiting," I said vaguely. "Do you know Truhlarska Street?"

"Sure. Big street." He looked back at me quickly. Now he could figure we weren't just visiting. So be it. We're here to visit my mother-in-
law's old friends, ha ha. The people across the hallway. The old *babichka,*

ha ha, she showed Blanka how to put her nipple in the mouth of her first baby. I suddenly shivered, truly shivered. What the hell was this? Who was I justifying myself to, in my mind? I used to do that all the time when I lived under Communism, constantly prepared explanations in my mind, about anything and everything, just in case I'd be taken away and interrogated.

I did it again, just now! I did it with my American passport in my pocket!

All right, boy. Slow down.

"Truhlarska's not far from the Intercontinental hotel," said Frantisek. He looked back at me, drew a little map in the air, with his finger. "We go to the hotel down Revolution Avenue. After the hotel,"—why was he looking at me so closely, to see if I nodded in recognition to those names and places?—" Truhlarska is to the left, before Na Porici . . ."

If I remembered right, young Franz Kafka worked on Na Porici. That was where the workers' accident insurance building was. "I can take you to Truhlarska," said Frantisek. Then, with insight, "You want to go to Na Porici too?" Was I going nuts, or was he prying? "But there's nothing much to see on Na Porici . . ."

I put a stop to his inquisitiveness: "Look, just now we need to go to the hotel, and freshen up. . . . What's this?" I asked, pointing out the window, to take control of the conversation.

"Letenske Sady, the summer gardens," he responded, without giving them a look. Big dusty spreads of chestnuts, oaks, birches. I knew those gardens. During my second trip to Prague, I had walked with a Czech girl down the footpaths of Letenske Sady. We came across four Russian soldiers. One was peeing on a tree. The others started shouting at us, I didn't understand what they said, but I could figure the meaning. I didn't really know the girl, we had smiled at each other in a museum, and kind of picked each other up—but you should've seen her shout back at the Russian soldiers. She gave it back to them with interest, while I, aware of their number and of the silent darkness of the park, lived a few minutes of panic. My Czech firecracker loosed her foul mouth at them, and then we walked off, and I scolded her. I told her that she could have been raped. "Pfff!" she exclaimed with disdain. She led me out of the park, through suburban streets that looked spooky, till we climbed to her apartment and were the masters of each other's bodies for one sleepless night.

A kind of something saved in some deep memory cache awoke inside me. It was not smell, or color, it was not physical, yet it hit me with the strength of a physical impact. It was a feeling about that forgotten little event, and it could be summed up in these words: I was the one who walked in that park, and I was young, alive, and real. What made that feeling so strong? Time. Giving the memory a kind of aged power, like a shot of alcohol.

I pulled myself back to the present. We were rolling over Svermuv Bridge, with the green waves of the Vltava below. I asked Iris how she liked the look of the streets. "From the second story up, they're fabulous," she said quietly.

I suddenly guffawed with laughter. "You got it, baby. That's the way to enjoy this city." I kept laughing, till she gave me a worried look. Then she leaned forward to ask Frantisek how long he'd been a taxi driver. "Two years. I studied to be an electronic engineer, but now I'm driving a cab. Here's your hotel." A high rise that reminded me of the United Nations. Refurbished sixties, with a collection of flags above the entrance. "If you want to hire me for whole day, I give discount," he announced, then popped up the trunk, and pulled out our bags.

High tea was being served in the lobby, on glittering Czech china. Up in the room, the wood panelling was dark and heavy. One bed lamp did not work. I walked out onto the balcony, and saw far to the west, peeking from behind a twist in the river, the spiked silhouette of Hrad Castle. I felt like I was in an elevator that had reached the bottom of its shaft. We were here. This was it.

My wife stepped barefoot to my side. "I just tried to call home but didn't get through. The circuits to America are busy. Can you believe that?"

"I can believe that, and worse. Shall we try to sleep?"

"I can't sleep, I'm too jazzed up." She threw her arms around me and hugged me hard. "I feel that I need to hold onto you, otherwise you'll disappear, and I'll never find you again, or get out of this place. What are you thinking about?"

"I'm thinking what if we descend to the lobby, and the first taxi driver that presents himself is no one else but Frantisek? It may be coincidence, or . . . who knows?"

She smiled. "You gotta get rid of this paranoia."

"Sure, that's why I'm here. And it's so easy."

We were back on the seesaw of marriage, getting scared in turn, reassuring each other in turn. We showered, changed clothes, tried another call home, but the outer lines were still busy. We went down, asked the concierge to get us a taxi. He stepped out and whistled, and a little Mercedes pulled up. The smiling driver was Frantisek of course.

Frantisek explained that he had waited, confident that we'd soon reappear. All Americans arriving in Prague after transatlantic flights checked in at the hotel and tried to catch some sleep. But they failed, their systems being scrambled by too many time zones, so they came down again looking for taxis. Iris asked him about the cemetery where her uncle was buried. She knew its location—Strasnice, a little bedroom community adjoining Prague. Frantisek instantly clicked: the Jewish cemetery of Strasnice? Sure, today he would drive us around Prague, and tomorrow he would take us to Strasnice. "Wonderful," smiled my wife. She turned towards me: we would go out now and look for Indra's family. And tomorrow we would look for her uncle Martin's grave.

"Wait a second . . ." I heard myself, I sounded gruff and displeased. "*I* have some things to visit here too . . ."

What the hell. This was the old valley of tears of *my* youth. The Commie zone, my territory, my bailiwick. And she, she was taking it over.

She touched my arm, gently. With the proper reverence for what connected me to this place: "You want to look up your Czech friends?"

My Czech friends. . . . They appeared in my head, fast and at random: Petr Pujman, an essayist and critic, son of the classic author Marie Pujmanova. Petr used to work for the Czechoslovak Writers' Union. Under the Russian occupation, we bummed around Prague at night, drinking, spewing out our hatred of the occupier. Some fifteen years older than me, Petr was thin, good-looking, always sharply dressed, and lively, a fine gent caught in an invaded land. He told me that he would never leave, that he could have no home anywhere but in Prague. Had he stayed true to his pledge? I didn't know. Marie Kavkova, a scholar of Romance philology, a kind of grand dame of Czech letters who had translated my *Captive* into Czech. Unrelated to Kafka, despite the almost identical name. Ivan Klima, whom I met when he was still editor of the Czech Writers'

Journal. Others, with whom I shared sailing on our tragic Ship of Fools, Communism. I feared meeting them, I might find them old, bitter, wasted. And what would I tell them? Hello again, I write in English now, and live in Hollywood?

No, I didn't feel like seeing those friends. I felt . . . what did I feel? A kind of nothingness. And . . . anger. I was annoyed that my wife was chatting away with Frantisek. I resented her openness when she explained to him why we wanted to drive to Truhlarska Street, or to Strasnice tomorrow. Wait a second—I was here first! I suffered here first!

"I don't want to go to Truhlarska yet! I want to see some other places. All right?"

"All right," agreed my wife. "You all right?" She stared me in the eyes.

"I'm all right."

"All right then. And if you feel bad, it's all right to feel that way too."

"I'm all right. Sorry."

"You're a bit of a jerk," she said softly, and laced her fingers through mine, letting me know that I was already forgiven.

I nodded, while Frantisek, with brows raised, observed our interaction and wondered if his employment was in question. I told him that I wanted him to drive us to Na Porici. Where Kafka once worked—but I didn't mention Kafka. Reassured that he was hired, Frantisek lit up:

"Na Porici? Good idea, great antiques in the little streets there." He held the door open for my wife, and then for me.

I was still angry. But I knew my own cycles. When I got angry, it was from fear. Pretty typical male reaction. To avoid feeling fear, males switch to anger, an encouragingly active emotion. I was angry, which meant that I was afraid. But what was I afraid of? I was over that ridiculous fantasy about Frantisek being an unlikely agent of the Czech secret service. So, what was I afraid of? I didn't know.

We drove off to Na Porici.

On the way, Frantisek explained that Czechoslovakia had become a vast antique mart. The buyers were affluent Germans who paid ridiculously high sums for old Czech jewelry, glassware, and furniture. That gave rise to a peculiar kind of crime: burglary for antiques. "Gangs break into churches now," explained Frantisek, "cut up altar pieces, chairs, icons, and sell them to the rich Germans. Go to Frankfurt, to West Berlin, visit the boss of Volkswagen, what has he got in his dining room? A church piece from Prague, or Brno. Used as a serving table, or wine rack."

I asked what the police were doing to stop the theft. He replied that the police took bribes from the thieves. The police had to live too, how could they survive on their miserable salaries? He entered Na Porici, and expertly shot to the curb and into a parking spot being vacated. "Here you are. Little streets ahead, back, all antiques."

I could not identify Kafka's old insurance building, but I stood in the street looking at the people. It was hard to accept what I felt, that everything was so familiar, yet had become so alien. It was just after five P.M., and people were spilling out of trams and busses. They walked through creaky doors, stepped into ancient elevators. Pots clanged in kitchens, I could hear them through the open windows. Voices called out. Minuscule balconies display dented toys, mattresses, more clothes drying on lines, peasant-style wine decanters and pickle jars, mops and brooms, small tomatoes spread on sheets of cardboard, left there to ripen under Prague's cool sun. Many of those apartments had no refrigerators. Men in under-shirts leaned over the balconies, enjoying post-work cigarettes. Women pushed the men aside to look down and yell at straying kids. Girls stepped out into the street, heavily made up, in punk outfits. Their toenails, painted black, peeped out of platform shoes. They met boys with their hair so short they looked like skinheads. In my time, rebellion was advertised by long hair. Now it was short hair, and earrings on both girls and boys, and all kinds of metal hoops in their noses and lips.

My eyes were readjusting to the irregular look of an East European street. The sidewalks were not straight, and the buildings' fronts bit unevenly into them, like humans leaning impatiently out of a waiting line. The people on the street shared the same look of irregularity: their teeth were crooked, their bodies were stooped or askew and many had beer bellies. They were dressed in mismatched tops and pants, mixing trendy jeans with Soviet vintage windbreakers. Here and there I saw a Hugo Boss jacket, a Versace handbag, lost in that wrinkled look of Communism, which I'd forgotten. Communism was gone, but the look lingered. People passed me, speaking in a lingo I didn't recognize: it retained the singsong intonation of Czech, but it sounded full of unslavic words. Between the pedestrians' bobbing faces, I read the shops' signs: Video. Fax. *Comicsy. Cyber-misto*. The Czech language, defended by generations of patriotic scholars against the German and Hungarian cultural colonizations, was now thrown open to technobabble.

I saw the older Czechs, the ones who had lived under Communism. Drabness hadn't left their clothes or faces, and it never would. Many looked to be only in their forties, but they were balding, sagging, stooped, murky-eyed, toothless. When their eyes met mine their glances were soft, cushioned, beyond tame. They were dead. They looked like they had nothing to do with the boisterous youngsters, yet they'd parented those youngsters. Their faces, their eyes, hummed a resigned song: we were cheated. And it's too late for us. Though we're still moving, our life is past.

I hurried to catch up with Iris and Frantisek, and heard Iris asking the taxi driver, "Your people look so depressed, what's the matter with them?"

"They're . . ." He searched for words. "Finished, you know? Used up. They worked hard for Communism, and then boom, Communism is gone, and what do they have, their pensions? Not enough for bread. And their kids grow, want big things, expensive things." He shrugged. "Used up."

"How old are your parents, Frantisek?" asked my wife.

"Fifty, my father. And forty-four."

"And they too are used up?" I asked from behind.

"They too," he confirmed, turning to me. "You don't believe me?"

"I believe you."

We stepped from the main street's sidewalk to the cracked pavement of a back lane, part of that antique mart mentioned by Frantisek. The pavement's fault lines disappeared under wares spread on tables and on tarps unfolded directly on the ground, and under vendors and buyers and strollers. Iris lit up, started touching heavy old fabrics, richly tasselled pillows, macrames, chintzy tea sets, fur coats. She grinned at me. "By the look of all this, Communism wasn't so penurious."

I quipped back, "Sure it was. These are the leftovers from the party elite."

She walked ahead, dipping her eyes into Victorian, art deco, functional fifties. I followed, noticing turn-of-the-century golf clubs, World War I binoculars, driving gloves from the twenties, gramophone records. And Soviet bric-a-brac: Red Army medals, Lenin awards, Class I, II, and III,

Comsomol belt buckles, heaps of red flags with hammers and sickles, and countless mock-ups of the first Soviet space satellite, the Sputnik. Man was always a mass-producer, and always made his products cute. From a few extra chips on the edge of a hand axe, to Lenin's baldness fitted so creatively onto the shiny roundness of a pipe bowl, cuteness was a constant. Scanning the flea market, I felt human evolution, ingenious and wasteful. I stepped up to a row of tables heaped with used books. I saw a leather bound edition of Marx's *Das Kapital,* side by side with *The Critique of Dialectic Reason,* by Sartre. Then *The Complete Bolivian Diaries of Che Guevara. The Wretched of the Earth,* by Frantz Fanon. Mao's little red book. Bertolt Brecht's political plays, in two volumes. Essays by Georg Lukacs and Marcuse, a coffee-table album of Angela Davis's visit to East Berlin—Angela was on the front cover, Afro and all, shaking hands with an East German party boss. I gave a start: solid, bound for eternity, here were the complete writings of Nicolae Ceausescu. I looked away as if he'd burned my eyes, to a handwritten notice in English: These books belonged to the library of Charles University.

Now they were for sale, at a few Czech crowns per book. The Czech crown was worth about twenty-five cents.

Few people stopped to look at the Marxist books. By some coincidence, they were all men. I looked around for a vendor, but didn't see one. I moved from table to table, my mind spinning. All the ink, the printing labor, the editing hours, the sales campaigns, the toil and sweat invested in leftist propaganda through the past century, it was all here. And all gone. I looked around. The casual faces bending briefly over these tables had already been replaced by other casual faces, pausing, looking quickly, moving on.

I felt an unspeakable sensation. Triumph of a sort—here was the stuff you shoved down our throats, you lying Commie bastards—and defeat. For none of this would have withstood a century had it not been for the idealism of the initial believers. But where were the believers? The ghost of my father seemed to float over the tables. The desire for an equal world, born with Christianity and transferred into the naive sociology of Marxism, hung above those tables like dust. Here were the gospels of a vanished monks' order. And so many of them had thought and written in exile. Far from home, they produced dreams for millions. Strangely, they came to power about the same time as another factory of dreams, Hollywood. Where I now lived. My father was part of the old dream factory, and I of the new one.

And Hollywood was present, right here: I saw a sprinkling of show-biz memorabilia inspired by the Communist saga. A poster for a film on Che Guevara's life, starring Omar Sharif. A cast list of the Broadway production of *Che,* marked with the year 1969. Another poster, of *Reds,* starring Warren Beatty and Jack Nicholson. Che was long gone, so were most of the Communist leaders present on those tables. This book sale was a graveyard. I could dance on these graves, if I wanted to, but one of them was my father's. He was one of these people, not a leader but a dreamer, yet still one of them.

A pang of fear: in two days, just two days, I would be boarding my flight to Bucharest. I would be able to stand by Dad's grave.

I looked at the writers lying there. Sartre, one crown. Brecht, one crown. Others, all one crown. Fright invaded me. Was this why these men wrote so obsessively? To lie here now, all thrown together at one crown each? Was this why I did it? To be forgotten too, in ten, twenty, forty years at best? No, no. I would not be forgotten. Tell me that I would be remembered, even if isn't true.

"Kind of sad, isn't it?" my wife asked suddenly. I started. She was standing to my right, contemplating that dead sea of dreams.

"Nah," I pretended. "This had to happen. It was happening already when I defected."

"Then you must be happy that it's finally over."

"I am. Of course I am."

I was lying. Unredeemably male, I was posturing. I wouldn't admit that in this disaster a piece of me collapsed and died too. Worse still, that my life work, my prayer, my disease, and my medicine—writing—could be as ephemeral as these writings here. These "weapons of denunciation and accusation," as Che would have called them, Che who thought that revolutionary spirit was the only proof of authenticity in art. Well, what was authenticity in art? I'd heard it defined in so many ways. What made writing authentic, sincerity? There were millions of sincere books that were forgotten days after they were published. No, sincerity alone didn't make it. Depth of thought? "Universally human" emotion? Inventiveness, applicability to society, what? And what was the mission of writing in this era of entertainment? But what had been my mission, on my sealed-up little planet, before I left it? To protest tyranny? I did that. To call for freedom? I did that. And now, what?

I looked aside, and saw a woman. Warm and healthy, imprinted by motherhood but still thin, nimble. Something alive, true, and concrete, a woman. My wife. She and I, the beginning of a new genetic line. Wasn't that more glorious than writing books?

I guess my emotional turbulence showed in my eyes, for my wife gave me a look of sympathy. "You want to show me anything around here, anything you know from before?"

"Sure. Uh . . . let's walk."

I took her arm, and escorted her back into the main street. Frantisek got into his Mercedes and followed us slowly, while I enjoyed the smug little pleasure of being followed by the car like a king by his coach. We walked towards the Old Square. I looked up at the old houses, at the churches' stained glass and gargoyles, waiting for spirituality to re-descend on me, on us. But it didn't. It was spirituality back then, when I walked the streets counting my pennies for a cup of *kava,* and spirituality was forbidden, making it cool and hip. The thing to talk about, to seek, to feel. Now it was not spirituality, it was something else, and I just couldn't figure what.

Slowly, with grimy grandeur, Prague fell upon us like a heavy, open-eyed trance. We orbited towards the statue of Jan Hus, the soldier-priest who attacked the decadence of papacy a century before Luther started the Reformation. That meant freedom, in his time, and Hus was burned at the stake for it, as a heretic. I explained that to Iris. She replied with her innocent brutality, "Today's freedom is in consumerism. Hey look," she called out, pointing with her finger, "guess what made it into your boondocks?" I followed her finger with my eyes, and saw in a little apartment window a bilingual sign, handwritten on yellowed paper: *Kostel na Scientologie,* Church of Scientology.

We drove back, to Truhlarska. Frantisek asked Iris questions about Hollywood. How much was Sylvester Stallone really paid? The Czech press reported twenty million dollars, but Frantisek was convinced no one would pay an actor that much, no matter what kind of box-office draw he had. Then he asked Iris why she was not an actress, she could easily be one, pretty as she was. Meanwhile, my strange funk had returned. It came out as we found the house on Truhlarska, and she commented that the Kahoun family must be at home, there was light up on the fourth floor.

"That's the second floor. The fourth is two windows up."

"What are you talking about?"

"This is Europe," I explained tensely. "The ground floor is never counted, and the first floor is always the one above it. Usually in a building like this there's also a mezzanine, which isn't counted either. So what you think is the fourth floor is really the second. I'm sure when your mother told us fourth floor, she meant it European-style." I looked up at the fourth floor. The window was dark. "There's no one at home."

"Let's go look." She jumped out of the car, with a spiritedness that could lead to a fight. I realized that I was good for one too. Easy.

I couldn't stand being so out of control. Throbbing, I led her into the building.

The rounded front entrance opened into a kind of inner patio, walled in by other buildings, sadly pierced by little windows. I felt that the whole soul of Europe, opaque, sad, constrained, had been graphically gathered in that patio. All right. Here was the second entrance, from the patio into the main building. Two cracked steps led to a completely dark doorway. It was about six P.M., but here it was the dead of night. I heard Iris breathing unevenly behind me. "Where are you going?" she asked, as I ascended the stairs.

"Don't worry. There must be some light switch somewhere."

"Can you stop? I can't see a thing. I'll trip."

"Don't worry." My palm went to the wall, my fingers groped over peeling patches of paint, feeling it fritter away under my touch. How many entrances like this, how many dark steps like this, and buildings like this had I groped into, before defecting into brightly lit America? As if my fingers had grown radar, I immediately found the switch, and flicked it on. A tepid light oozed down from a bulb I couldn't see, turning the stairwell in front of us into a hanging spiral haze. The light uttered a buzzing sound.

"Hurry up," I said, "this light's on a timer, good only for two floors."

Now we could see the apartment doors, made of old darkened wood—oak, I thought. In another time, this building had some stature. The light went out. Proud of my instinctive knowledge of the place, I shot an arm back, grabbed Iris's wrist and pulled her after me, against her muttered warnings. Loudly, I counted the floors. When we got to the fourth, European style, I rapped on the closest door. It opened, but almost no light flowed out—was there yet another power cut? I faced an older man; from behind him, feeble daylight from his apartment's windows silhouetted him, dark, round, amorphous. I asked in German whether the Kahoun family lived here. He muttered in Czech, pointed to the opposite door, and closed his own.

"This is it," I said reassuringly. In the dark, I stepped past Iris's face, eyes glittering faintly. I rapped on the Kahouns' door, convinced that they were not at home. But the door opened. Still no electric light. Against the day's fading glow from unseen windows inside, stood an old woman.

"Indra Kahounova?" I asked.

She made an indistinct sound, perhaps of agreement. But my wife read its meaning fully—this was Indra, the daughter of the Christian woman who helped her mother learn to be a mother. Iris rushed forth, gushing in English who we were, gushing her parents' name. As my eyes adjusted to the darkness, I could see more details about this creature—she seemed in her sixties, about five feet tall, and very frail. She had white hair, but not a lot of it. Her eyes looked too large in her face, and then I guessed that they were normal size, but she, the woman, was very thin, emaciated. By now, the name of Blanka Friedmanova had clicked; the woman replied in Czech, *"Ano, ano* (yes, yes). Blanka and Carl, who departed *na Palestinje"* (to Palestine—there was no state of Israel then; everyone called the place Palestine). With help from my hazy Czech, she asked Iris if she was Carl and Blanka's daughter.

She was. And she stepped to hug Indra Kahounova.

It was only a few minutes later. We sat in the apartment, which was still unlit. But there was electricity. Indra turned on a desk lamp to look for a little stack of pictures of Iris's parents, and in doing so finally revealed herself. She had barely any hair left, but otherwise I could tell the resemblance to the blond girl I saw in the picture showed to me by my mother-in-law.

There was no phone in the flat. Indra told us that she had arrived from the hospital just today. She went often, and stayed a few days at a time, for chemotherapy. She had leukemia.

We made ourselves understood in a strange linguistic hodgepodge. I helped with my German and minimal Czech, while she spoke some German but no English. Iris spoke only English, yet somehow the two of them communicated faster than I could help with my tortuous translations. Indra told us that her parents had been dead for fifteen years, and that her own husband had died five years ago. Iris asked if the neighbor we'd just met had a phone. She wanted to call her mother in the States and get the two women to talk to each other. Indra seemed to be afraid to use the neighbor's phone.

I looked around. The place was small, modest, cramped, obviously the home of a single aging person. I saw things that I recognized: appliances from the seventies, from the time of my escape. But the heating unit was from the late forties, when the Friedmans escaped. The succession of their departure and mine was marked in this apartment by the silent testimony of objects.

Indra, I could tell, was once a good-looking woman. Her skin was white with a touch of ivory. Her eyes were deep brown, bright and expressive. Her lips, withered now, had been full of the comeliness of youth that I remembered from the young Indra in the photo. She was twelve or so when the newly wed ex-camp inmates occupied the apartment next door. It was a time of hope. Indra seemed to describe that time, for she talked faster now, with animation. She imitated Blanka, pregnant with my wife's older brother, acted out a pregnant woman puffing up the stairs, then made gestures of motherhood, babying an unseen child. She laughed in a thin voice, reminiscing about Blanka's confusion: the young survivor was thrown into birth and breastfeeding and changing diapers without the usual guidance of her family's older females. Those females had perished.

"I've got it," said my wife with a flicker of inspiration in her eyes. "We'll take you to our hotel, Indra. We'll call my mother from the hotel."

Indra understood hotel, and burst into rapid words sounding like an objection. I managed to figure out that her son would be coming here sometime later, to visit her. She didn't know exactly when, but he would arrive for sure, and she didn't want him not to find her. It seemed that he lived some distance from Truhlarska. How could we warn him, since there was no telephone? I found the solution: we would write him a note. Indra wrote it herself, asking him to look for her at the Intercontinental Hotel.

Five minutes later, we were in Frantisek's car. Indra sat between us, and Iris held her hand tightly. Indra didn't seem to mind. She had covered her hair, thinned by the chemotherapy, with a wig. The wig was gray and stood high, like an obsolete beehive hairstyle. I watched Frantisek check on us in the rearview mirror. He seemed thoughtful, totally aware now that we were no ordinary tourists. At the hotel, I paid him for the day and hired him for the next. "Strasnice tomorrow, right?" he asked.

I nodded, and followed the two women into the hotel, still prey to my strange mood. I thought of tomorrow's search for Iris's uncle Martin's grave, and my anger flared up again. Wasn't my wife something. She had no sympathy for the culture of my youth, but boy, was she clear about the importance of her own pilgrimage! This woman Indra, she knew only from family stories. That man Martin, she'd never even met him. I was jealous. I was jealous of the spontaneity of her feelings.

I hadn't called anyone in Bucharest yet. No friends, no relatives, no literary peers. Petre, youngest of my father's brothers, lived in Bucharest with his wife, and a son and daughter, first cousins to me. They didn't know that I was coming to visit, after so many years. No one knew, kin or stranger, friend or foe. No one. As if I were planning to take the trip incognito, like a ghost, like an invisible man. How could I do that? Why didn't I write, phone, make arrangements? Petre and his wife Ella and my cousins Riri and Tudor might not even be in Bucharest. I might miss them, I might not see them at all. I didn't even know if I could secure a hotel in a city notorious for its lack of accommodations.

What was the matter with me? How far had I pushed the denial of my past?

I was mad at Iris, and then at myself. Also, I was scared.

At the Intercontinental, there was a phone for overseas connections in a booth made of solid oak. Inside, it was harshly lit from above by a large bulb, its filament glittering in a dome of matte glass. Under that light, Indra looked even smaller, even thinner. Her wig showed its fakeness in full, and her complexion could not hide her sickness. I noticed that she had only a few short eyelashes—perhaps a result of the chemotherapy. Commie chemotherapy, brutal, like everything else here. Out of her nearly lashless eyes, Indra cried, and I knew that my mother-in-law was crying too, six thousand miles away. Iris stood vigil by the phone booth, looking in, listening to the mysterious sounds of Czech—Indra spoke quite loudly, standing on tiptoe and pressing a thin hand on her chest, as if to help maintain the volume of her voice. Iris's cheeks were shiny, but she wasn't crying anymore.

Then she remembered me, turned, mouthed almost inaudibly, "Thank you."

"For what?"

"For being with me here." She pointed her chin at the bewigged little woman in the phone booth. "We have Czech money, should I give her some?"

Earlier, in the street, after I gave Iris a little lecture about who Jan Hus was, we had been approached by a young black marketeer in a shiny German-made ski jacket, who offered us crowns for our dollars at an incredibly good rate. He spoke pretty fluent English. I was reluctant, but Iris poked me: More of your old paranoia? This is a good deal. So I acquiesced, and he pulled us into one of those vaulted Prague entryways, quickly took a hundred dollars from me, and counted out Slavic bills printed with the meditative face of the astronomer Copernicus. He advised us to stuff the bills deep in our pockets, then walk away and start spending the money at least an hour later, just in case some plainclothes Czech policeman had happened to notice our transaction. We hadn't spent any of it, for our next stop after the old town square was Indra's apartment.

"I don't know," I said. "Giving her money might offend her."

"Bull. Didn't you see how they live?"

I had no time to reply. Indra stepped out of the phone booth; just then, a stranger approached our little group: a shortish young man, in jeans and an old windbreaker, balding already, and smiling unsure of himself, almost shy. He was Indra's son and he'd found the note.

He spoke even less German than Indra, but was very polite and unassuming, and seemed worried that his mother was here instead of at home. We tried to convince them to have dinner with us, but they refused, he explaining that she needed her rest, she'd just come back from the hospital. They sat with us, however, in the main lobby, on two old sofas, and we treated her to a soft drink and him to coffee. They acted terribly modest, as if being in this hotel was such an undeserved experience that the best they could do would be to leave it as soon as possible.

We talked, in the manner of strangers who share a great deal of real experience, but lack the words to express it. Indra's eyes shone almost feverishly. She told us how amazed she was by what had happened. That we were here. That Blanka remembered her. She asked Iris if her mother was still pretty. We dug in our pockets for the pictures we carried, fished out a few that showed my in-laws photographed with our kids, one of them on vacation at a ranch, another with our son in a riding cap and holding a crop. Blanka was handsome in both, and dressed like the cream of Beverly Hills. Indra recognized her right away and started crying again, while her son smiled and smiled. We asked whether Indra needed medication sent over from the States. The son shook his head, informed us that they had the best medication here. And free, socialized hospitals. One good thing the Communists did. So they didn't need anything. They didn't want anything. That gentle denial had me clenching my teeth.

We have the best medication and the best hospitals, the physicians had said back then, a few days before Pavel died. Now, I kept my skepticism to myself.

We pulled out the money we exchanged in the street, all but a few bills, and heaped it into the hands of Indra's son—both Iris and I did this, at the same time, with embarrassed smiles and protestations that it was a gift from friends. We were sorry that we had nothing else to give them, so we hoped they would accept it and forgive us for coming so unprepared. The young man gave me a long look, then put the money in his pocket, and said *"Dekuyu"* (thank you) several times. Gently and softly, but deeply, it seemed, really reading the friendship in our gesture.

My wife embraced Indra. I didn't dare embrace her, she looked so frail. But I tried to kiss her hand, in the gallant Balkan fashion I learned as a teenager in Romania. I touched my lips to the skin wrapped over her thin vulnerable bones. It felt warm and feverish. Then I shook hands with the son and felt in his palm the hardened calluses of manual work. We got up, and danced strangely towards the exit, the women hugging again, we shaking hands. I offered to get them a taxi, but the son refused. He would drive Mama home, he had his car here.

I didn't get to see the car, but I imagined it to be some, economical homemade Skoda, the national set of wheels. The two of them disappeared past the square corner of the hotel's wall, he walking with small minced steps, and she, at his arm, seeming to be literally lifted off the ground by the strength of his arm. She was skin and bone. I wondered how much time she had to live.

But she had lived today more than a pleasure, she had lived a meaningful completion of fate. I had seen it.

We turned back towards the lobby, finally completely exhausted. I insisted that we enter the bar, to have one of those excellent Czech beers that even Communism couldn't deteriorate. We perched on two tall bar stools. I plunked down the rest of our Czech money, and noticed the prunelike frown of contempt on the face of the bartender. The old-style Commie bartender, with gray hair slicked back on his big round skull, with heavy jaws wrapped in rippling fatty tissue. Built like a bouncer, with the jowly grin of a pit bull. He crumpled the money, plopped it back onto the bar. "Deze no good," he said like a bad guy in a movie.

"Why?"

"Polish money, not Czech, deze. Dey not wort notting now, dey just been devalued."

What? I felt like a hammer had struck me between the eyes. I grabbed the crumpled bills, straightened them, examined them. How could I be so stupid? Even in that dark entryway, dizzied by the quick rattling talk of that little crook, I should have noticed that these were Polish *zloty*. I should have known the difference, I was from this end of the world. Besides, the man whose face was printed on the bills, Copernicus, the savant who first figured that the earth revolved around the sun instead of the other way around, was Polish, not Czech.

"You change money in de street?" asked the bartender knowingly.

I nodded, crestfallen.

Now I understood the increasingly shy smile with which Indra's son took the money. He noticed its lack of value at a glance, but didn't tell us, so as not to embarrass us. He put the valueless bills in his pocket and thanked us as if we had given them a truly generous gift!

Goddamn. I could of course get angry at my wife. Revile her for her naive greed: "This is a good deal!" But I was too angry at myself, angry because I was taken right here, in my old territory. And because a hundred dollars worth of crowns would have helped Indra and her son, just a little. Helped them at least buy a good supply of bulbs for Indra's poorly lit apartment.

I took out my reliable U.S. traveller's checks, and paid the bartender for a beer and a coke. We sat down. "We must send them something. We must help them somehow," I repeated, wishing hard not to forget, not to lose their address, after we returned and got sucked into the flow of our lives.

"My mom will write to Indra. I'm sure she'll send her something," said my wife.

The bar had a dance floor, but no dancers. A combo of young musicians played "Havana Gila" for a table of red-faced, misty-eyed, and sweaty middle-aged men. They swilled tall Czech beers with exaggerated gusto, as if to prove that they still belonged. Almost all the little tables were taken, some by adults, some by youngsters. I noticed a boy and a girl, both in black, with a very big dog, a royal Dane, lying quietly by their table, not even pricking up his ears at the blaring music—maybe the dog was a regular customer here. Natives and foreigners, the mix was even, and I could tell the natives again, by their postures, the urgency of their talk, the oddities in the way they dressed. Most of the patrons talked intensely, not minding the music, or perhaps favoring it as a cover. It smelled of deals, of promises made by uneasy traders, of partnerships started in haste, between strangers. It felt like the set of a latter-day *Casablanca,* but the set was real, the players were real.

I took my wife's hand. "Let's get out of here. Just for a few minutes."

She followed me, although we were both ready to give out. But somehow, this day could not end in a scuzzy bar. I led her to Charles Bridge, and explained the stories of the statues on it. Then I made her climb Nerudova Street, and we stopped halfway to the Hrad, on a passageway with ramparts of old stone. Hrad, the castle, the jagged eminence of the city, the reminder that this place was built by soldiers and scholars and saints. People of discipline, of rigor. People who could abstain from the material, who could endure loneliness, and leaning their heads back at night, as we did now, would opt only for a dialogue with the cold twinkling stars.

Then we walked down again, into the night that grew thicker, into streets that even today, with freedom blaring out of bars and cafés, felt occupied.

At the hotel, we got in bed, turned off the lights, and Iris slept. I did not.

I was still prey to that envious anger, yet I didn't really know what it was about, except that it involved my wife. Today, on the first day of my return, her parent's story had made her more emotional than my story—so? I too had felt emotional meeting Indra. I thought about the Friedmans' family gatherings, which consisted exclusively of relatives on Blanka's side. She had three brothers in America, who had produced a host of children and grandchildren, so during those functions, Carl and I became co-opted husbands. In the beginning, I'd felt overpowered by the number of those relatives, by their cultural homogenousness, by the way the older ones told stories, one after the other, about themselves. Why didn't I tell my own story on one of those occasions, I wondered lying awake and listening to the noises of the hotel. Why? Was my story not worth telling? Of course it was. Was it more humbling, more demeaning than any story of theirs? Certainly not. Then why did I remain silent, even though somewhere inside me I felt I was shortchanging myself, and not just me, but also them? For my story was not in conflict with theirs. In fact my story and theirs validated each other.

Finally, I drifted into sleep. I slept tensely, restlessly, starting at the noises of the night. Like in my youth.

The next day. Only twenty-four hours before my flight to Bucharest. We got up early, and ordered room service. While we waited for it to arrive, I dug inside myself, and pulled out another me. This other me, calm, mannered, a little reserved but not unfriendly, called Bucharest and talked to a writer friend, Augustin Buzura, currently president of the Romanian Cultural Foundation. Making it sound all very normal, I announced my visit. Augustin Buzura drew in his breath, wished me welcome "home," then asked what the purpose of my visit was. To write a story for the *Los Angeles Times,* I told him. I thought I detected a slight anxiety in his voice before he responded, "A story on *us*? Good, very good." I asked him how things were, and he told me they were fine; the country was in a state of "great leap forward." He acknowledged that the hotels were not yet part of this leap, and offered to find me a place to stay. "See you tomorrow," was the way we both ended the conversation, almost in unison, and we hung up.

Then the same me called my uncle Petre. We had not spoken for over fifteen years. Petre had once had a high, vibrant, echoing voice; his voice sounded the same, but was weighted with an extra sound which at first I couldn't define: as if someone had poured a layer of ashes on a piece of steel. Age, most likely. That other me noticed calmly that he sounded incredibly like my father; just then, Petre exclaimed, "God, I wish your father were here." "Me too," I answered matter-of-factly. "Will you stay with us?" he asked. I thanked him, no, I had accommodations arranged already, besides I wasn't alone, I was traveling with my American wife. "We can't wait to meet her," he said promptly, in the name of all the Popescus still alive. "I'll call you tomorrow," was how I ended our first talk after so many years.

I hung up. I listened to a hair dryer being used by my wife. And I thought of the meaning of that word. Tomorrow. Twenty-four hours. One thousand four hundred and forty minutes. Eighty-six thousand and four hundred seconds until tomorrow.

* * *

Frantisek was waiting for us in the hotel's lobby. Very friendly, he wished us good morning, then rushed to hold open the taxi's doors. In seconds, we were driving to Strasnice.

Later, I couldn't recall what I talked about with Iris, except that it was light and meaningless. But when we came in view of the old cemetery I suddenly felt like I'd received a physical blow. To the left of the cemetery's gate was a kind of shed, wooden, old, rural almost, out of which a round old woman sold flowers to put on the graves. The flower shed was so much like the one I remembered by the gate of the Sfinta Vineri cemetery, where Pavel was buried, that I had to grind my teeth to suppress my emotion. This was going to be a tough one.

It *was* a tough one. I knew it as soon as I stepped out of the taxi. The air smelled of warm wax from lit candles; they were sold next to the flowers. It also smelled of trees lush with summer. Some were chestnuts. We walked in and up the main alley, and I stepped on a fallen chestnut. It was as if I'd stepped on my childhood. I felt underfoot the spiny green skin splitting, exposing the brown polished core. I looked ahead at the burial plots, in the hope that I could stay calm, and be helpful to the main protagonist, my wife. Although there were no crosses because these dead were not Christian, there were elevated tombstones among closely growing trees, just like in Bucharest. None of that restful openness that one finds in American cemeteries. Here the dead were busily kept together. I gasped: it was all like back then, during those pilgrimages to Pavel's grave, with my mother. I thought of my mother, and I lost my breath.

I thought: I forgive you, Mom. I forgive you for those pilgrimages, and for a lot of what happened back then. . . .

The feeling wasn't quite convincing, but at least I had said the words, silently, to myself.

I was so taken by surprise that I forgot about Iris. My wife, staring out towards a narrow vista of graves, many rather overgrown, was experiencing something else, not forgiveness but the pain she had felt in her own mother, years before, during her American childhood. Her chin began to quiver. She looked in her purse for Kleenex. Then she swallowed her tears. We were facing a small low structure with a rotting wooden roof, not much bigger than the flower shed outside.

Frantisek had preceded us by a few steps. He entered the little building, exited it, and came straight to me. "The caretaker is here," he said. "You can talk to him. His name is Mr. Radvanski."

I took my wife's arm, but she slipped from my grasp. "I'm fine," she whispered.

We entered the caretaker's office, and found that it smelled like an old buccaneer's hideout. A sixtyish character with a scraggly white beard, a shabby skullcap, and dirty fingernails sat at a desk covered in old newspapers, finishing a lunch brought from home, a dubious stew in a dented tin container. Mr. Radvanski wore a black vest over a white shirt with short sleeves. His right arm had been tattooed in a concentration camp. We stepped forward to explain our presence. He claimed that he spoke German, but my German and his were completely different. I called in Frantisek, to translate. Meanwhile, my wife put on Mr. Radvanski's desk a note written in Czech, by her mother. The note explained that young Martin Davidovitch was buried here back in 1946, and described from memory the location of the grave.

Understanding what we were after, Mr. Radvanski played out a little scene of annoyance, about Americans who came expecting to find graves that their relatives had abandoned more than forty years ago, and wanted to find them quickly too. How could he find Martin Davidovitch's, even if we knew the year of his death? It was impossible. I answered that we were not in a hurry, and would assist him any way we could. As Frantisek translated, I looked around: the office was a part-time or maybe full-time home; there were clothes hanging from pegs, and a bathroom without a door exhibiting a razor on the edge of a sink. I had the feeling that the cemetery was under no one's particular authority, and that the caretaker wanted something more tangible, money, to help in the search for the grave.

"Mr. Radvanski," I said with the help of Frantisek, "you know the name of the dead and the year of the burial. Surely you must have a registry of the burials and a map of the plots."

"It's impossible to find," he said, then corrected himself: "It's not easy."

"But we're here to help." I waited a beat. "And if we find it, it's the wish of the deceased's sister to leave some money with you, for the care of the grave."

Bingo. He set himself in motion, dropping on all fours and extracting a stack of old ledgers from under the desk. He pulled one out, blew the dust off its spine. I glimpsed the year 1946 inked in cursive on the spine and on the cover. Radvanski opened the ledger. Dust wafted out. He stopped at a particular page, scanned the entries, and found Martin Davidovitch. Then, from the back of the ledger, he pulled out a master plan, stretched it on the table and pushed his lunch aside with his elbow, all in one motion. The burial plots were marked by numbers.

I looked at Iris, and she looked as if she was holding her breath. The caretaker groped in a corner and came up with a hoe. He leaned it against the desk, lifted the ledger, decided it was too cumbersome to carry along, and simply ripped off the page. He picked up the master plan and the hoe. He took the lead. Well, this was it. A walk to the grave, and we would be out of here in under half an hour. My wife explained to the driver how her uncle Martin had died after joining the Haganah. Frantisek offered to bring the car inside, to follow our party up the main alleyway. Radvanski was well ahead already. I saw him passing between two trees. He disappeared.

Frantisek had started the other way, towards the car. For an instant, Iris and I were alone. The sadness of ten minutes ago seemed gone. We looked at each other, not quite sure where we were, not quite sure that this was happening. There were no pathways cutting through the grass, which looked wild and healthy, shaded by big palmated leaves and pierced by sharp clumps of fern. The trees were so thick that we wondered whether to backtrack. We had probably lost our way, and left the cemetery. The caretaker had taken a shortcut.

Iris tripped, and I shot out an arm to hold her up. She pulled her foot out of a tangle of weedy grass; where she had stepped, bared by the intrusion of her foot, we saw the pale grayness of a stone slab. It was a grave. She had stepped on a grave invaded by grass.

Now we got it. We were still in the cemetery. But this part of it had been overgrown not just by ferns and weeds, but by a whole forest.

We saw Radvanski again. He was bent down, with the plan of the graveyard draped precariously over a cluster of ferns.

I heard a soft mechanical noise, out of place here. It was the Mercedes, Frantisek was driving it up the main alleyway. The alleyway too had been invaded: I saw saplings rising in the path of the car. But they were not fully grown trees, because over the years some irregular human traffic had continued along this path.

That calm me was trying to reappear. Forty-five years, it commented. Enough for a forest to grow.

My wife burst into tears.

Frantisek maneuvered the taxi to within ten yards of the grave, driving gently, fraying no more than a few saplings. When he got out, he found the three of us, the caretaker, my wife, myself, on our knees, pulling at that tough weedy grass.

We were pulling it off the wrong grave though; we realized that when we uncovered it enough to glimpse a stranger's name. I felt a pang of guilt, now that we had partially cleaned it, maybe we should clean it completely. But there was no time to clear the graves of strangers. The hoe brought by Radvanski was ineffective: it was so heavy that instead of cutting off the grass it chipped the tomb slabs. We moved over to the next grave, and ripped with our hands, burying them in underbrush to our forearms. My wife was crying quietly. Behind us, Frantisek was not sure whether to join us or not.

This time, we had found the right grave. Panting, we cleaned a gray slab and the tombstone that went with it, and stood up. Here was what was left of that young man: an inscription in Czech, one in Hebrew. There was a candle dish, of glass, cracked in two. The glass of candle dishes often splits if the wick burns all the way to the bottom. I knew that from experience, from Pavel's grave.

I gathered the two halves of the dish, joined them up, and then fit them in a special round dip in the slab. My wife lit a candle. She was still crying. She was crying for the years of repressed, residual pain of her mother, and for the years of casual, unexpressed pain of her father.

I understood that.

Then I remembered the previous night's stifling feeling of envy. Now, it had vanished. Quietly, I listened to Iris's crying, sad for her sadness, yet hoping that she was finding relief. I felt the kind of love one feels at such moments, when the differences, the itches, the bickerings of marriage are forgotten, and a spouse, a mate, is redeemed of all imperfections by the revelation of true character. She was pure in her pain, she was selfless. And I could only love her.

I realized that she was sad, but not conflicted. Nor was her mother conflicted, six thousand miles away. Iris had come here to understand the past and honor it, not to fight it. But I, in some depth of my soul, was fighting the past. I had left conflicted, and now I returned conflicted, on an American passport, after over fifteen years of freedom.

About what was I conflicted, though? For the last twenty-four hours, I'd seen the waste of Communism, and just now what I'd seen felt sufficient. I could fly back to Los Angeles already. In one day, I had moved across so many ripples of the past and the present that I felt I could leave this place pretty reinforced. Or at least meaningfully reminded of what I had been once, and of what I was now.

Yet, obviously, my trip was not over. In the next few days, something would happen, to resolve my conflict, or perhaps to enshrine it in me as a permanent feature.

I thought of Mother, but my conflict was not with her.

I decided simply to put off solving that riddle, and be here, and now. With the candle flickering and the stone cleaned, the grave had assumed a kind of somber beauty. Surrounded by that forest, it seemed not abandoned, but hallowed by a special loneness, in the midst of nature's regeneration.

Now would have been the time for me to play investigative reporter, and get from Mr. Radvanski the story of how Prague's Jews, those who escaped the Nazis, had fled again en masse, to escape the Communists. Leaving behind their dead. How the relatives' visits stopped, and the forest started advancing till it engulfed the graveyard. How Radvanski stayed on here, every day seeing fewer graves and more forest. Now would have been a good time for that. But I couldn't do it.

Following my mother-in-law's wish, I gave Radvanski five hundred dollars and made arrangements for him to keep the grave clean. I told him that the family would send more money, and visit again, soon. Throughout this, my wife continued to cry.

Frantisek waited by the car in a pose of sincere respect. He'd heard about this lost cemetery, I was sure, it was close to Prague and Prague is a small place. But it was a different thing to see it, and to see mourners like my wife bringing their homage to this macabre wilderness. Iris's mother had asked her to photograph the grave. She tried to do it now, still crying, but her eyes blurred and she handed me the camera.

Frantisek held the car door open. But we needed to walk. We told him that we would meet him by the entrance, and he drove the car in reverse, giving a lift to Radvanski and his map and hoe. Iris and I stepped out of the trees, into the graveyard's maintained sections; here there were clean footpaths and reasonably trimmed vegetation. Totally unexpectedly, I saw Kafka's grave. There could be no mistake; in letters carved on a stumpy little obelisk it said Dr. Franz Kafka. Underneath on the same stone was carved Hermann Kafka, the father Franz loved and yet reviled, and lower still, Julie Kafka, the mother. Hermann and Julie had survived their sickly, not-yet-famous son. Prague's most known citizen in this century, whose life belonged nowhere. He belonged here now. There were two funereal wreaths at the foot of the grave, copious expensive ones. They were both wilted already, but I could make out the contours of German words—a club from some German burg with cultural tradition was honoring here the strangest writer in German, the man who epitomized "otherness."

From this unexpected encounter, I drew a kind of cold encouragement. Writers had unusual fates. I had to let mine unfold. My past lay ahead of me, yet it lay there as part of my future. Right. My wife dried off her tears. Frantisek graciously held the car door for her. As long as they are not enemies, humans respect each other's pain. Right. I would call my mother from the hotel. Just to ask her how she was, and tell her that I was well, that we were well. How many more seconds till Bucharest?

Part Four

Bucharest

The Romanian plane was a BAC 111, a small British-designed jet that used to be manufactured under license in Romania some twenty years ago. I'd flown this kind of plane to Cairo, where I unexpectedly met John Cheever. This plane was the same one, no kidding. The one flown on back then had dark red carpeting and blue seats. This one had the same carpeting and seats, both utterly threadbare, as if not a single *leu* had been put into its maintenance since my defection. It had a clean, scoured look, two stewardesses, and six passengers.

Six passengers. We were two of them. As we stepped into the plane's emptiness, Iris whispered to me, "Where the hell are we going, to the North Pole?" Then she restrained herself, looked at the other passengers: a Romanian couple in their late thirties, with two daughters in their early teens. Iris commented that the two girls were pretty: "Do all Romanian children have such nicely hazy eyes, as if done by a Flemish master?" I said nothing. I felt incapable of talking.

The girls' parents had the cautious look of career diplomats; maybe they were diplomats, flying home for a vacation. I heard them talk: unmistakably, they were Romanian. I could walk over to introduce myself, but I was numb from how empty the plane was. Was it always so empty? I wanted to ask questions. But for some reason I couldn't talk. We took off abruptly. The plane sounded like a car without a muffler.

Lunch was distributed as soon as the plane finished climbing, in yellowed plastic containers that looked as old as the plane. We each got a sandwich made of a slashed bun, inside of which were two little slices of ham that looked like red autumn leaves pressed against each other. Two specks of pickle adorned each leaf. I closed the sandwich, closed the container over it, and looked up at the nearest stewardess. A tall artificial blonde, not bad looking, but wearing her makeup spread thickly on her rather grainy skin. She took back my lunch without a word, and I glimpsed her eyes: swampy green, stagnant, life unawakened yet to its power. Two years after the revolution, this woman seemed to sleepwalk. The other stewardess, a skinny brunette, moved with the same dormant pace, her energy on hold. They both wore perilously high heels, instead of the flat practical footware of Western flight attendants.

The two stewardesses sat next to each other in crew seats facing the passengers, with their lips stubbornly spliced together. I didn't care, I'd found my voice and was giving Iris essentials of Romania's geography and history. From the flatness of Hungary, the land started rippling with hills, then built up into the bluish Carpathians, still snowcapped on their highest crests. Villages, white-walled, red-roofed, hung higher and higher on the slopes. Purity glittered roughly in twisting rivers. I showed my wife Transylvania, and explained that this elevated paradise was the Dacians' old home. I pulled her over to the window, to show her the moun-tain passes where the Dacians wore out the Romans by pushing whole cliffsides down on them, where the Romanians did the same to the Turks and other intruders. I recited a quick poem of compressed history to my American wife, and she asked if I'd known any of those spots in my childhood. Sure, we passed over the Prahova valley, with that village where Pavel and I heard the house clock. The plane's rattle decreased, the pilot announced his descent, and my wife whispered in my ear:

"It'll be all right, you'll see."

"I know. Absolutely."

The Carpathians fell behind us. The plain of the Danube flattened ahead, dusty, harsh. Roads of mud were replaced with roads of asphalt. Bucharest was before us, we would land in six hundred seconds. One of the stewardesses sleepwalked towards us, to make sure we had returned all our trays and cups; the other studied her nails. I saw the low brown barracks of an infantry boot camp, and squirmed excitedly against my seatbelt: this was the camp where I served my army time, the inspiration for my second novel! The plane turned, and I saw far to the south the city, and even the Kiseleff Chaussee, with the Writers' Union building standing at midpoint! I felt like yelling: I was there so many times! I lived right down there! I caught a stewardess's confused glance, and I controlled myself. Easy, boy. Four hundred more seconds.

* * *

We landed, we deplaned, we walked into the airport. My first sen-sation was that I was drowning. My first and last, for through the next five days, that sensation resurfaced over and over again. Drowning in my native sea, Romania.

"I'm so pleased, indeed moved, to see you again among us," said my friend Augustin Buzura.

We hugged, then stood facing each other inside the Otopeni Inter-national Airport, in front of the customs booths. But that didn't make our stances relaxed. Augustin, Gusti to friends, a quiet man who wrote slowly unfolding books, very complex and philosophical, had not aged much. He was accompanied by his assistant, a vivacious tanned young woman, and by another man. "I was lucky that Mr. B. here could come along," Gusti added. "He talked to the customs and they let us welcome you at the jetway."

Mr. B., a brown-haired man in his thirties, was an attaché at the Romanian embassy in Washington. Mr. B. flashed a smile, kissed my wife's hand (oh that irresistible Romanian custom of kissing a woman's hand), explained that he happened to be on vacation in Bucharest. Hav-ing heard of my arrival (just how exactly, I wanted to ask him), he thought he might come to the airport and make himself helpful. He did, rushing ahead to waive the airport tax for us. We passed customs so fast, one glance at our passports, one thundering of stamps, that I didn't get the joy of staring those bureaucrats in the eyes from beyond a U.S. passport. On the other side, our bags were already being pulled off the conveyer by an amateur porter who looked barely out of high school. An army of por-ters, taxi drivers, and tourist guides was waiting by the baggage claim area, outnumbering the arriving passengers. I took a deep breath, but still felt like I was drowning in these forgotten native stimuli. I could not tell whether the airport was smaller, or I'd grown bigger. I was deafened by the sounds—so much Romanian, a language rarely heard in the streets of L.A.; here I was drowning in it, and it was rough, purposeful, alive. The faces it came out of were the ones I remembered, but there was something changed about them. It was the roughness. The voices shouted and cursed, with no concern for decorum, or fear of punishment. Free! I thought. Sev-eral men were quarrelling, looking ready to fight each other, and their lack of concern for the law stirred in me a rush of approval, yes, yes, no fear of the law, of police, of authority! That's what I wanted to see!

I momentarily forgot about my wife, and spoke straight Romanian, insensitively. I looked up at the sky. Harsh, blue, hot, real, that's what I wanted. It would keep me from becoming emotional, which I didn't want to be, at least not from the start. Our porter piled our suitcases on a cart, blurted at me, *"La care masina, sefule?"* (To which car, boss?) Gusti had a car, but Mr. B. interjected that he had a better one, air-conditioned, Iris and I could ride with him. His English was very confident. We emerged from the terminal, and I almost broke an ankle stepping into a ditch, a long unmarked fault in the pavement. "Is this from the revolution?" I asked Gusti, grinning. I knew that there had been battles at the airport, which the Securitate had orders to defend. "This? No," Gusti laughed, "I don't know when this fell apart, but it's certainly not from the revolution. The whole town needs fixing."

"They have almost no budget for public works," said Mr. B. "It happens that the mayor is from an opposition party," he added, turning to include my wife.

She didn't get the meaning of that. "So?"

He continued, smiling. "The opposition campaigned accusing the leading party and President Iliescu of being crypto-Communists. So they won Bucharest and some other cities. And now they're doing nothing about getting them in shape. The other day, a journalist asked the mayor why Bucharest looked this way; the mayor said: We don't have time to rebuild, we have to fight the crypto-Communists. Petru," he addressed me directly, "didn't the city look better in your time?"

My time was under Ceausescu, and I didn't recall letting him call me by my first name.

"Would you like to ride in my car?" asked Mr. B. Not only his English, his manner too was terribly confident.

"I think we'll ride with my friend Gusti." Iris, lost, nervous, slipped her arm around my waist. Little pearls of sweat glittered on her forehead. I was sweating too. The scorching heat of the Danube valley in September, no breeze from the river, no wind from the mountains, just the cobalt blue sky, breathing a blue heat. "Any ideas about a hotel for us, Gusti?"

"Better than ideas." Gusti's face shone, he looked sincerely pleased with himself. "I got you staying at Palatul Elisabeta!"

"You're not serious. My God!"

Palatul Elisabeta, the palace of Queen Elisabeth, wife to King Carol I, Romania's first monarch after the retreat of the Turks. Carol and

Elisabeta were Romania's first German-born kings, imported by the Romanian politicos to give status to the brand-new independent nation. The palace was a heavy cake of a building where many historic acts had occurred, including the abdication of King Michael, forced to leave his throne by Ceausescu's mentor, boss Gheorghiu.

"Yep," hummed Gusti, savoring his effect like a piece of chocolate. "I got you in at Elisabeta. You can write on the table where the king signed his abdication."

"Jesus. Sure, I mean, thanks. . . . Is the place . . . all right?"

"It's a palace," said Gusti self-evidently.

A convoy of horse-drawn carts appeared from a side road, filled with freshly mowed grass. I realized that everywhere, by the airport's runways, by the freeway, sprouting out of the broken concrete, rising wildly from marble enclosures that once shined with flowers, there was tall weedy grass. Everywhere. Peering out of the plane, I had noticed clumps of it growing out of the runway's potholes. Grass, standing straight and simple in the windless afternoon, it bespoke of decay and the breakdown of the urban services.

"What's with this grass?" I asked. "Why doesn't the city cut it down?" I remembered Ceausescu's grass. Trimmed to perfection by unseen armies of city workers who took care of it at night, when the city slept.

"Same as with everything else," said Gusti's tanned assistant. "No one's taking care of anything. We're in a mess." Her English was good too.

My wife had been looking at the carts. "It's so rural here," she said with sheer amazement. Luckily, Gusti and Mr. B. were supervising our bags being loaded into Gusti's car. Iris breathed quickly to me, "Where are we going? Who's this big bureaucrat?"

"Sshh, he's a friend and runs an important institution. He knew my father. He's a good writer, actually." But suddenly I saw Gusti through her eyes: next to the dapper diplomat, he was modestly dressed, clumsy, hard to classify. I felt that she was both right in her reaction, and wrong not to see beyond the surface. But then I felt that I myself was one minute on one side, peering from the larger world into Romania, and the next on the other side, staring from Romania out into the world. And that was how I used to live back then, switching perspectives back and forth every minute. God. How did I not go nuts?

We got into Gusti's official ride, a battered native Dacia. I was glad that Gusti's assistant, Carmen, was talking to my wife. I couldn't make conversation, I was too eager to look out of the car, to absorb the free-way to Bucharest. We zoomed towards the Kiseleff Chausee: Elisabeta was situated a couple of blocks from the Writers' Union. So many pieces of me lay along this tree-lined thoroughfare, even the hospital in which Pavel died was close by, on a parallel freeway. As a schoolboy with hesitant down on my upper lip, I took dates along the chaussee's footpaths, and tried to kiss them by the huge bronze head of the Latin poet Ovid, exiled to the Black Sea shore in 8 A.D. This was where I talked anti-Communist talk with my friends, under trees we hoped were not studded with microphones. Kiseleff Chausee was exactly as I remembered, but narrower, and very dusty. The dust rose to blanket the foliage of the big old trees, thick and golden like dirty pollen. Dust from the emissions of a big industrial city uncleansed by rain or by city workers. And grass, again, tall grass! And the mansions I knew, which housed this and that official institution, this and that foreign embassy or trade mission, loomed beyond the grass, the same but with an extra hue of yellowing decay, like a tossed newspaper on a sun-flooded porch. The contrast between the stylish architecture and the decay was incredible. The car hurtled over countless potholes that weren't here before, not in my time. My city had a grim propriety and distinction that made it suitable for the motorcades of Charles de Gaulle, Golda Meir, and Richard Nixon.

Something snapped out of my hand, with the movement of a live creature. It was Iris's hand, which I'd been squeezing. I looked at her, and she raised her palm, red from my squeeze, touched it to her lips, smiled at me. The car turned left. I heard myself speak, explaining to Iris the ornate style of Elisabeta, nineteenth-century country baroque adapted to Romanian taste, the Brancovan style. The palace was heavily walled and buttressed, like a low, stocky fortress.

We got out of the car. I found it hard to believe that within thirty minutes of arriving, I was faced with Romanian history in one of its most critical moments. Here, armed with handguns, party boss Gheorghiu and his acolytes (Ceausescu was probably in their number) forced the still very young king to abdicate. Soon thereafter he left the country, and the Communist propaganda presented to the nation a movie of freight trains passing the frontier, allegedly filled with the king's personal possessions. A lie: the king had left practically as a pauper.

How isolated this place felt. Bucharest pulsated right outside, but the tall trees and the stone walls made this an island of emptiness. Gusti

explained that the palace was regularly borrowed by the city hall administration to accommodate special guests. Very well. The city might send
me a student as a guide, which was my job twenty years ago, ha ha. I
mentioned that I wanted to phone my family. Gusti frowned, for that we
had to go to his office, at the Foundation. The phones here might not be
working.

"What d'you mean, the phones might not be working?"

"You see, the place is not regularly used."

Mr. B. had followed us in his car, a small BMW, but a BMW nonetheless. He drove in, and found us huddled over this problem. Elisabeta
had phones, but they were so old, some might even be hand-cranked.
Meanwhile, no one stepped out of the front entrance, no one moved inside, beyond the gloomy windows. I looked at Gusti, and got back a look
of utter candor. I said, "Gusti, I'm here as journalist. I need to call people,
ask questions . . ."

"Sure, sure. The palace is being overhauled. You may have phones
put in in a day or two."

"I need a phone now, not in a day or two." I started laughing nervously, stupidly: here was the Kafkaesque bit, encountered not in Prague,
but here. Mr. B. saw my concern as well-founded. "You know, Petru," he
said reasonably, "this place has the advantage of being civilized and quiet.
The hotels—most of them haven't been privatized yet, and they're still
run by the old Ministry of Tourism." He made a face.

"I'm sorry, I must have a phone. What's the nearest hotel?"

"The Flora," said Gusti.

My memory clicked: the Flora used to be a pretty, well-run spa hotel, with a nest of Securitate monitoring the guests, because the Flora
specialized in foreigners, from businessmen to Olympic sports teams.

"It's the Flora," I decided.

"I'll drive you there," offered Mr. B.

Gusti shrugged, fine. He gave a look to Elisabeta. He himself was
impressed with the old place, he'd stay here without griping. He'd thought
I'd be happy here. I put my arms around his shoulders, he was shorter
than me but built powerfully. I hugged him, as if the hug could punch a
hole in the time separating us. "Let's meet tomorrow, I want to talk to
you."

"Me too. The Foundation has a publishing house."

"Come on, we'll transfer your bags to my car," said Mr. B.

I breathed. Out of this capsule of old time.

And into the next.

"Mr. Popescu, my name is Dora D. Mr. Popescu, I never thought I'd ever get to see you again, ever!"

Dora D., the assistant manager at the Flora, had achieved in under one minute more than I ever achieved trying to tell Iris who I had been in Romania. She looked up from behind the hotel's registration counter, recognized me, and her face, full and pale, filled with little dots of redness. She put her hands on the counter, as if to steady herself. She was probably my age. I was beginning to notice how certain Romanians aged: instead of becoming wrinkled, carved-up with time, they gained a kind of meat-pie roundness—I quickly thought of that meat-pie look engulfing the stewardess on the plane; she'd let it take her over without any resistance.

But Dora D. was full of pep: *"Si doamna?"* And the lady? My American wife, I explained. She switched to English: "Welcome, Madame. He *lullabied* my youth!" She pointed at me, and though being called "Madame" plus the picture of me lullabying Dora years ago should have been funny, for the last half hour Iris had been in a serious, reappraising mood. She put her passport next to mine, and we signed registration slips, while Dora D. chirped on about the hotel not being in great shape, because *he* never spent one *leu* on anything after the mid-seventies, except on a giant folly called the House of the People (I'd heard of it, it was supposed to have more square footage inside than the Pentagon), on his personal guard, and on his trips. (He traveled like a fiend; two days before the Bucharest uprising that brought him down, he visited Iran.) "But we'll do our best to please you and Madame," she finished, and I felt that I was drowning again. Sinking. Flailing my arms and legs, yet not able to swim up above the emerging sense of my old self. It crawled up on me like quicksand, but never quite merged with who I had beome. I switched back to English to talk to Iris.

I was on a unique roller coaster of emotions, and I realized that it wouldn't stop, not until we departed.

In front of us, Dora called the hotel's maintenance man, who showed up with a cardboard box of bulbs. Following him and avoiding the elevators, because "they get stuck," we climbed to the second floor. The maintenance man fit new bulbs in the empty sockets of the second floor's sconces. Dora unlocked a suite and stepped in first, like an army scout, to check the fixtures. Again, two new bulbs filled two empty electrical sockets. The suite was ample, dusty, with chairs and couches as threadbare as the seats on the plane. The bedspreads were faded from rewashing. A chair I brushed against with my hip collapsed, it had only three legs. The sink and tub had been scoured, but Dora promised to have them scoured again within the hour, if we could wait that long before taking our showers. She was unembarrassed, this was beyond embarrassment. She answered the unuttered question that kept revolving in my mind: what really happened here?

"He killed us, that bastard. He put a noose round our necks, and twisted it. Now we're back breathing, but we're too weak to do anything but breathe. And we're being drowned in Gypsies."

"In . . . what?"

"Gypsies. We have three million of them now. He passed those laws against contraception, remember? Well, the Romanians evaded the laws as best they could, they aborted illegally, even went to jail for it. But the Gypsies, they took full advantage. . . . Ask me for anything else you might need."

"Thank you."

She closed the door. I opened the balcony door, and looked out at a mammoth building that rose about half a mile from the Flora. A twenty-story citadel with a square central body and pawlike lateral outbuildings, a Stalinist sphinx beehived with offices. Built in the fifties, it was patterned after Moscow's Lomonosov University, and used to be topped with a Kremlinesque red star, which was missing now. Each of the capitals of the "friendly countries" had one such building. Romania's was called Casa Scinteii, the House of the Spark, the Spark being the daily paper of the Communist party. The House of the Spark housed 90 percent of the printing presses of Bucharest, 90 percent of all the offices for publishing books and magazines. And, last but not least, the state censorship offices, mildly designated as the Direction of the Press. Thousands of people worked in that building. When they went to work in the morning or left in the late afternoon to go back home, their marching throngs lent the open space around the sphinx an air of mass refuge. It was Stalin's own conception to have all press, literature, and propaganda, centered under one roof, and the building came complete with several restaurants, a barber shop, and even a medical clinic.

In that building, though I never found out where exactly, my manuscripts encountered their censors, whom I would never get to know by name or appearance. Their paths crossed with mine in the city, for they, just like me, went to movies or shops, or strolled in the streets. They might recognize me (I appeared on TV, I was a public person), while they would remain invisible to me. The state's obsession with security also mandated that the censors would speak to the authors indirectly, through their editors. So I never even heard the voices of the surgeons of my books.

But I did go inside the sphinx when I delivered the literary criticism and reportage I wrote for many of the publications gathered incestuously there. While I chatted over coffee with this or that *redactor* (press editor), in an operating room in the same building, my latest book lay under sedation, being surgically eased of its diseased tissues. There was no telling whether it would survive the operation; a lot of the Romanian literature of those decades came dead out of the hands of surgeons, or barely breathing.

So here was the sphinx after the revolution. Right in front of me. Its red star was missing, and a statue of Lenin in front of it, on a pedestal of rosaceous marble, was missing too, though the pedestal was still there. There was a big sign above the entrance, I could easily read it from here: THE ROMANIAN STOCK EXCHANGE. I looked at my watch. It was almost five P.M. At this time, long lines of employees should have been filing out of the building. But there was barely any movement now. A car pulled in at the entrance, two people came out of the front door, got in the car. The car pulled away.

I stepped back into the suite. Iris was unpacking. I helped her, and commented on how Mr. B. had materialized at the airport as if on cue. Before dropping us at the Flora, he suggested that we should have dinner with him before we departed, at Bucharest's only Chinese restaurant. Was he checking on me? The foreign office used to be stuffed with Securitate. "So what if anyone's checking?" asked my wife, surprising me. "You're a big deal here. They need you."

I shrugged, what could I possibly do for this place? She shrugged too, and moved to something important: the suite had two phone sets, and neither had a dial tone. Dora had told us that if there was no dial tone we should wait a few minutes, it would return. Half an hour later, it hadn't returned.

I had an amazing realization. Maybe I was in the crosshairs of that giant rifle again—but even if it were true, the rifle was no longer loaded.

Iris took a lukewarm shower. Minutes after she was done, one of the two phones came alive, just like that, for no apparent reason. I called my mother in L.A., where it was now eight in the morning. Mother audibly sighed in relief: she hadn't slept all night, she was so worried. I told her all was fine and everyone super-nice, but the phones were bad, they could cut off at any minute. She urged me hurriedly: "Find out what happened with our vineyard."

"Mother!"

Of our past bones of contention, that was a big one. Less than a year before I defected, she'd pestered me and pestered me to help her buy an acre of vineyard twenty miles north of Bucharest. It was a way to invest the unexpected royalties I'd made. Mother argued that such a little *pied-à-terre* (she used French when she was nervous about the outcome of a request) would give me the quiet I needed to write, away from the city bustle. The vineyard came with a narrow little bungalow. In fact, Mother planned to play vintner herself. She had saved money from her pension, but could never have saved enough to buy the place by herself. I gave in like a nagged husband, knowing that I'd never spend time there, and paid half of the price. After I defected, the vineyard was not confiscated because it was co-owned, and Mother rented it to a tenant; when she in her turn defected to the States, the tenant occupied the property.

Now she wanted me to see if we could repossess our vineyard. She'd already mentioned it in L.A., and we had quarrelled. I'd been a fool to sink money into that place, and she'd acted totally impractical, not having sold it before leaving. Now as usual, I had to clean up her mess. The phone started to crackle, preventing another quarrel. I told her that I'd look into it. If there was time. I hung up, and the phone rang again. Dora D., from reception. She asked if we had enjoyed the snack she'd sent up, composed of tomatoes, *telemea* cheese, and thick Romanian coffee. Yes, it was very nice, thank you.

"Are you going out, Mr. Popescu?"

"Uh . . . yeah, I guess."

"Do drop in at the reception to see me, it's important."

"What's going on?"

"I don't want to tell you on the phone. But please."

She hung up, leaving me with a bit of curiosity which quickly turned to paranoia. What did she want? We'd left our passports at the reception, which made me feel like I'd checked my gun, and now I was unarmed. Whoa, easy. Iris phoned her parents. "They're treating him incredibly here," I heard her say. I stepped into the bathroom and took a shower. Now, the water was ice-cold. When I came back, Iris was dressed and pretty, and smelling of good perfume. "You had two calls while you were showering," she said. "From two newspapers."

"What newspapers?"

"I should've taken down the names, but they both said they'd call back. One spoke pretty good English, he asked if you planned to give a press conference."

I was seized by a superstitious fright. "I'm not giving any press conferences. Let's go out, I'll show you the city."

"Fine. Just relax, okay?"

"I'm relaxed."

"Really? Look at yourself in the mirror."

I had buttoned my shirt unevenly. I rebuttoned it. "Let's go," I said tensely.

We stepped out, and heard hammering noises coming from the shaft of the elevator. I grew more and more nervous as we approached the registration desk. Dora was there. She gestured with one finger raised, flew back into the office behind the desk, and reappeared holding an object in a plastic bag.

"I sent home for it," she said with a smile, and placed it on the desk.

The plastic bag was transparent. Inside, I saw a stack of printed pages, eroded at the corners, as if gnawed at by mice. Dora scooped inside and brought out the stack by holding it with one palm underneath and the other pressed over the top page. She revealed the top page so brusquely that I was startled. The letters on it were faded, almost erased, but I still could read the title: *Captive*, my first novel.

Two other people were working at the reception desk, a man and a woman. Both young, in their twenties. They stared. Iris stared too.

I cleared my throat. "It looks like it fell under a train."

"It didn't. Friends of mine borrowed and re-borrowed this copy. Some made mimeographed copies of it, even though they might have been fined or jailed."

"Jail?"

"A month in jail, I think. There was a law about books by defector authors."

"Then you could've gone to jail too?"

"I could have." She gave me a prankish grin, like a street urchin. "Would you?" She handed me a pen, she wanted an autograph.

I took the pen, and started writing her name. Carefully. The aged paper was so fragile that the pen punctured it. I rounded out the letters: To Dora D. . . . What else could I write? In memory of the days we shared? Of the fight we waged? I could not write something so grand, even though this book circulated like a tract, like a manifesto.

I looked at the two younger receptionists. "Did either of you ever read this book?"

"I heard about it," said the young man.

"Everyone read it," said Dora. "Everyone my age, and even younger. Those who didn't read it didn't read anything," she stated passionately, glancing around to include my wife, as if Iris understood Romanian.

I wrote the only other words that came to my mind: Thank you. And signed my name.

We stepped out of the lobby to look for a taxi.

"I was about to ask you: how the hell did you come out of this place the way you are?" said my wife in a soft voice. "But after this woman brought out your book, I guess I can't ask you that anymore."

I understood, and grinned. "I guess you can't."

"Your readers saved you from going crazy," she said.

"Yeah. Maybe I saved them a little bit too."

"They surely saved you."

Damn. Since we had landed here, Iris had talked in such a calm, normal voice. And she'd worded my reality so accurately and precisely. I felt again that envious anger—why was she so calm and insightful? Maybe the two days in Prague had brought her an important completion, I thought, flagging a battered old Dacia, which crawled slowly up to the hotel's entrance. Could two days make a difference?

But what about me? Where was my completion?

The taxi driver was in the mood to chat, and so was I. So, brother Romanian, what's up? "The Turks are coming," he said, and I bolted up from the shrivelled vinyl of the back seat. The Turks: plunder, fire, rape, castration. Iris shot me a mystified look, and I translated to her that most loaded phrase in Romania's history. "There they are," the taxi driver pointed out the window. Both Iris and I looked out, I almost expecting to see turbaned hordes brandishing crescent-shaped swords. No. I saw little lunch counters with signs for Coca-Cola and Marlboro cigarettes, and pushcarts with bread, vegetables, fruit; some of the pushcarts were equipped with umbrellas against the sun. "Turks from Turkey," he explained, "come out here, take licenses, and sell." An impotent shrug: "What can you do, you want cigarettes, you want fresh bread instead of the unbaked shit they sell you in our shops, you come home late and find nothing to eat in the house, you go to the Turk and buy bread and a chicken on the spit, or cold beer. The beer's from Turkey too."

We were caught in traffic in the vast, round Victory Square. Minus the red flags, it looked exactly like when I marched across it on Commie parades. All around the square, the passersby clustered around little vending spots operated by the Turks. Next to a metro station's entrance, a gaggle of girls gestured alluringly at the motorists, leaving no doubt about their trade. Their crimson lips and kohled eyelids could be spotted from across the square. I asked the driver how old those girls were. Nineteen, eighteen. Sixteen. Jesus. Where were the cops, the social workers? He grinned, there were no cops, no social workers. But there were scores of political parties, and hundreds of political leaders. And thousands of *bishnitsari* (from *bishnitsa,* a Romanian twisting of "business"), aggressive young con men, hanging around at airports, in hotels, on street corners. There were a few by that metro entrance too, next to the brashly made-up girls. Two steps away stood an anonymous Turk, selling, making money.

"So why can't we be in NATO?" asked my driver indignantly. "Look, the Turks are in NATO!" "Why don't our people work?" I countered. "Which 'our people'?" he snickered, "the Gypsies?" I asked him why everyone had the Gypsies on their minds. He turned so indignantly that my wife shrank back against the seat. "How could we not have them on our minds? D'you know that the Gypsies have their own political party now, and even a king of their own? An old *baragladina* they dug up God knows where, King Cioaba!"

Cioaba meant shard. *Baragladina* was a historic insult. I stopped translating, to hell with you, you Balkan Archie Bunker. A pity that the revolution found you too old to start a new life, but not old enough to be resigned to your fate. I know what irks you, your best years were wasted under *him*. Sorry. I'll give you a big tip.

But proof to the fact that his words had effect, I stuck my head out, and as downtown Bucharest grew around us with stores, cafés, movie theaters, offices, all packed, I looked for Gypsies. I saw many, many more than in my time. Their look was almost Middle Eastern, the tan of their skins deeper, with a purplish under-hue, while the Romanians' ranged from a rugged peasant olive to an elegant urban ivory. As we passed *bishnitsari* hassling the pedestrians, I saw that many were Gypsies. They weren't at all subtle: *"Allo, sefule, un'te duci?"* (Hey, boss, where ya headed?), *"Ai dolari, sefule?"* (Got dollars, boss?), *"Vrei hotel cu fete?"* (Want a hotel with girls?).

To my left, I glimpsed the wide windows of downtown's main bookstore, Mihail Eminescu, named after Romania's most famed poet. Four of my books were launched there. I told the driver to slow down, so I could look at the place where I'd given my first autographs. I took in the dusty windows; instantly, a bunch of *bishnitsari* sprang forth towards the car. *"Allo, sefule!"* I tapped on the driver's shoulder, and he stepped on it.

I told my wife that I was going to show her something very special. The school where we crouched under our desks with our hands over our heads, during the Cuban missile crisis. She and other American schoolgirls were doing the same thing, six thousand miles away. By the way, down this very boulevard I marched shouting Ho, Ho, Ho Chi Minh, just like she did, but to her he was a hero, and to me a Moscow-supported bastard.

When we got to my high school, the sun was setting. The gate was open; I walked directly onto the concrete of the main yard. Ten steps around the building, and I showed Iris onto the basketball court, where I was picked up by those Securitate. I clutched the iron pillars supporting the hoops, and my palms remembered the feel. When I looked around, the neighboring buildings jumped through the air into my field of vision: turn-of-the-century, with spiked old-fashioned roofs, on which I heard the rain patter so many times as I hurried off into cool autumns. Incredibly, they hadn't changed. What a mindblow. So I stepped out of the school-yard, and pulled Iris by the hand, leading her about a third of a block away. We stopped in front of a little old church. Pavel and I passed it every day, walking to school. I told Iris how we used to cross ourselves with our tongues, that was part of our hidden link with God.

I saw her chin begin to twitch. "I'm all right," she said. "But when you talk of your brother, I see both him and you, and that does something to me." She took a breath, cleared her voice. "These old buildings are beautiful."

"Thanks," I said, gratefully. Something, something here was beautiful.

"Really. Why don't they make these the showpiece of the city?"

"Because people here don't think that way."

We walked back to the taxi, and I told the driver to head towards Tomas Masarik street. My street. On the way, he summed up the country's situation. Two political configurations were battling for power. One was the PDSR, the leading party; its acronym stood for "party of social democracy." It was led by President Ion Iliescu, the man I knew as a progressive minister of youth, before Ceausescu demoted him for "intellectualism." The PDSR was full of "old Commies," said the driver. The CDR, or "democratic convention," was the umbrella organization of the opposition, mainly grouping the city folk and the intellectuals. The "Commies" knew how to run things, they'd done it before. The opposition had little experience with the economy, with administration, or simply with power. The opposition favored "surgery": rapid privatization, rapid everything, even at the cost of thousands of people losing their jobs. The PDSR advocated "therapy": the country was too traumatized, change should be gradual. But the economy was worsening, prices were rising every day, and the people just didn't work. "The truth is," he concluded his grim overview, "they should not have killed him."

I thought I'd misunderstood. "Him? You mean, Ceausescu?"

"Yes. They should've given him a chance to mend things. He would've done it."

I was flabbergasted. "You wanted Ceausescu to stay in power?"

"Why not? He was smarter than this whole new bunch. In his time, we had everything."

"But look at how he impoverished the country . . ."

"He didn't want to do it," countered the driver with stubborness. "He was forced."

"By whom?"

"Eh," he said—a strange syllable that hinted that I should know, and if I didn't, all talk was useless. "Go to Ghencea Cemetery, see how his grave is covered in fresh flowers every day."

"Who covers it in flowers? His henchmen, perhaps?"

"Eh," he answered. "Is this your street? Here you are."

I would have stepped out into my street full of reminiscence, but what I'd just heard had fallen inside me like a hard lump. I helped my wife out of the taxi, onto a sidewalk humped upward by the roots of old trees. The taxi hurtled off. It took me a few moments to digest that lump, and look at the street I grew up on.

It was narrower than I remembered it. And the buildings seemed lower. But what shocked me was the dimness. I could see one sole street light, flickering at the end of the block, like a fibrillating heart. I pointed the building out to my wife.

"This is it."

She reacted as if she were trying but failing to avoid a blow. "Are we going inside?"

"Sure. Come on."

I led the way along the narrow paved passage leading to the entrance door. The wall to my left, separating our building from the house of those lush sisters, was much lower than I remembered it: I could look over it into the sisters' front yard. No sisters. A plaque on the wall of the house indicated that it was now a business of some kind. I moved on, to my building's entrance door. When I got close to it, I noticed that I could almost touch its upper sill with my forehead. But that didn't make sense: I had left the place as a grown-up. I was as tall when I defected as I was now.

Then I got it. All these years, my memory had been playing tricks on me. I'd been remembering the size of the building with my child's memories, not with my adult ones. I remembered the wall outside taller, and the doorway higher.

I entered into profound darkness, like during the power cuts of my childhood. But here, I didn't have to grope along the walls. I didn't need light, I could move inside blindfolded. I took Iris's hand, and she followed me trustingly and wordlessly.

My feet remembered. One, two, three, four, five, six, seven. Seven steps up. I stopped in front of the rickety old elevator.

I opened the elevator door and the light inside came on. I pulled the grille aside, to let Iris in. She hesitated just a second, then stepped in. I followed her, drew the grille shut, pressed the button, feeling in my fingertip the amazing sensation of that button's stiffness and roundness. It was the same as my fingertip remembered it, after more than fifteen years.

The elevator had a small, foggy mirror. I used to check myself in that mirror as I rode down, off to meet a girl, or my friends, or to read at some literary event. I remembered a crack in the bottom part of the mirror. It was there, the same.

This was my past, but just now, it was my present too.

The elevator cruised up to the third floor—the second in this illogical old world—and stopped. I guided my wife out, and she laughed nervously: "Since Prague, I feel like I keep stepping into dark hallways, and pounding on dark old doors."

"That's not a bad description of the way we lived."

And I put my hand on the door handle of apartment 7. I let my palm and fingers recognize it, then raised my hand to the doorbell. Despite the dark, I found it without fail, and pressed it.

There was nothing else to say now, except: I remember.

Through that strange overlapping of past and present, the time advanced, the events occurred, and somehow I made it through them. Living here today was the family of a certain George Novac, former coach of Romania's national soccer team. Novac himself answered the door. In his fifties, he wore his hair cropped, like an ex-athlete. I stepped in, and he took a long look at me. A heavy hush fell between us, and Novac's family heard it from the next room, the living room: an attractive blond woman peered into the hallway. From behind her peered a skinny teenage girl with her father's features. Novac hesitated, then said softly, as if to himself, "I don't believe this." Then, to his wife, "*Draga* (sweetheart), it's Mr. Popescu."

He and I knew of each other. One of my uncles, Tudor, used to be the doctor of the national soccer team when George was the coach. But I had no idea that after my mother's departure George and his clan had ended up in our vacated apartment.

Our vacated apartment . . .

I couldn't recognize any of it, for it had been completely repainted and refurnished. The paint was recent, a bright white enhancing the lighting, which for the first time in the last three days was strong, normal. The place was nicely furnished. The difference between the dimness outside and the brightness in here, the relative abundance of the household, the family's decent clothes, their stances, surprised but otherwise casual, all of that felt like yet another shock, one more among this land's incomprehensible contradictions.

Mrs. Novac stared at me with curiosity. The daughter advanced a few steps, stopped, and rubbed her hip against the side of her father's body. Indicating that she was Daddy's girl, and that we had intruded into a relaxed family time during which she was the center of attention.

Mr. Novac knew that my mother now lived in L.A. How was she? I mumbled that she was well, thank you, noticing how perilously scratchy my throat felt. Mr. Novac remarked that she used to be an "impressive" actress. I flashed a glance back at Iris, and she gave me a guarded little smile.

"Mr. Novac, Mrs. Novac . . . it may seem strange, but would you allow me to come in and walk around for a minute? To move from room to room—if you don't mind, of course. I lived here for twenty-five years."

"Please come in."

"Is it all right if my wife comes in with me?"

"Most certainly. Sure."

We stepped into the living room. All I recognized was the shape of the room and its size. Oh, the doors were the same. Repainted, but still the same. I walked out of the living room, opened the door to the kitchen. When I was a child, it hung low, rubbing the floor; today, it still rubbed the floor. The kitchen had different smells now. But the same positions for the stove, the refrigerator, the pantry. I stepped down a little hallway leading to my former bedroom. The hallway, a brief space between door-ways, was dark. Because it was dark, it felt even more like back then.

I stepped into "my" bedroom.

My bed was no more, replaced by one belonging to the Novacs. I'd had nightmares in my old bed, and yet, as the years passed, I slept in it more and more soundly, and when I became a man I brought women to it. What had become of it, I wondered; I had experienced tragedy and happiness in it, dreamed ennobling thoughts of art and enjoyed sexual athletics. And now it was gone. But the wall against which it had been set was here, and I remembered it intimately: I used to stare at it till it became the screen of my fantasies. The wall was the same, just brightly painted over.

I leaned against the wall, with my knees flexed, lowering myself into my stature of back then, and looked at the bedroom's window. From this same distance and at the same angle I used to look through the window, at a stretch of sky riding the roof of a house across the street. There was that roof, the same. Made of tin. Above it, a rising moon put a rusty path of light over its surface, just like in my childhood.

The door to the balcony was the same too, arched and narrow. I moved through it, out onto the balcony. My face hit the quiet Bucharest night, the smells of trees, and the faint reek of a sewer. The same one, it always started to reek in late August, filled to capacity with the garbage of summer, uncleansed by the few, unreliable rainfalls.

My wife had stepped out after me. "It's good. Do it," she said, like a character from another life.

"Do what?"

She put her hand on my cheek, wiped something off. I felt my collar, the front of my shirt. They were wet. I'd been crying.

I stared upward: the stars looked bare and immobile, the same. I looked back at the street. Another smaller street opened into it, like a brook flowing twistedly into a river. This was one of the oldest sections of Bucharest, with its byways meandering around irregularly, in a confusing maze. That chaotic layout was caused, we were taught in high school, by the rapacious development of capitalism. Well, that made for some uniquely picturesque views, which I rhapsodized about in my Romanian novels.

Someone was walking below, whistling a tune. It sounded almost like a tune from the operetta *Sylvia,* by Kalman, which my schoolmate SZ used to whistle when he walked up my street, to pick me up for a stroll on the town.

We stood on the balcony of my old apartment, Iris and I, and I couldn't stop crying. I'd cried for at least five minutes, and it didn't look like it would stop. If it didn't stop soon, I would have to walk back inside, making a show of myself in front of the Novacs. So what? They had seen worse, I was sure, even the girl, who looked pretty much like the protected type. They were here during the revolution.

My throat was terribly raw. My wife tied her arms around my waist and rested her head on my chest, against the damp front of my shirt. There was a chair on the balcony. She pushed me into the chair, whispering softly, "You know, if it hadn't been for that war, we might have met in Europe. I could have been a Czech girl, and you could have been a Romanian writer. Would we have married each other?"

"Most likely not." I spoke haltingly. "Because of the . . . faith difference. . . ."

"Then I'm glad we didn't meet here. What are you thinking about?"

I tried to explain that I was thinking in turns about Dad, Pavel, my mother. Then I focussed on the one still alive, Mother. Had she been here, I would've told her: Guess what. I think I know now. I think I know how much you suffered. And I forgive you.

The words I'd spoken in my mind in that Prague cemetery. Now I felt them.

261

* * *

The Novacs were very patient. They allowed me to move around, and sit or stand in my old physical space, in order to remember this or that piece of the past. My last experiment occurred in my former study, where I pushed a chair to where I used to sit when I rattled away on my old Olympia, and sat down on it. Placing myself in the latitude and longitude of the writer I was then. A tree rising from the Gypsy sisters' front yard tapped on the window pane. There was a hesitant breeze outside. The painted wall before me became a mental screen on which I saw the long road of writing, stretching before me. I made an effort to think of America as I thought of it back then. As an impossible goal, a forbidden destination. That's how I thought of it in this room, which was my workplace, my monk's hut, my hermitage. I left it a Romanian writer. I was visiting it now as an American writer.

And it was only right that the writer of today would sit and pay homage to the faith, and madness, of the writer of then.

Novac stepped in. In his hand was a glass, which he offered to me. Ice cubes clinking in an auburn-colored fluid. Whiskey.

"We're in an incredible rut," explained Novac, as he and his family and the two of us sat in the living room. Iris was sipping iced water, I was finishing my whiskey. This was my old abode, and I spoke my native tongue, intercutting it with translations for my wife, but I was not the host here, I was the guest. "We don't know where this new road will take us, or even whether to start walking on it at all, because, you know, given our geographic position . . ."

His wife cut to the chase. "What if the Russians recover their power? We're still here, under their foot. All they have to do is stomp down, and crush us."

"Wait a second . . ."

I'd never had a harder time in my life with what I had to say. I didn't want to offend, to seem like I was judging. But on the other hand . . .

"But Ceausescu kept the Russians out, didn't he?" my wife asked. "All that had happened here for the last fifteen years, happened without the Russians."

Novac breathed, as if liberated by the fact that someone else had articulated it. "True, but the Russians and the Americans were enemies, so America supported Ceausescu. Closed an eye to what he was doing to us. But now he's dead and America is friends with Russia. So the Russians can sweep in here any time they want."

"No they can't," I said. "It's a new world, and the Russians want to be part of it."

"Maybe it's a new world, but the Russians can still invade us whenever they please."

Here it was again, the Big Excuse. The same old one. It wasn't a lie—like Mexico, Romania couldn't just stop sharing borders with the superpower next door. But it wasn't the truth either, because there had always been a superpower next door: Rome, the Ottoman Empire, Habsburg Hungary, Russia. The way Novac described the situation, the Romanians had sunk into a pit of indecision, fearing that if they acted they would be punished—from outside by the regrouping Russians, from inside by some nefarious old demon seeking a new institution in which to re-incarnate itself. A new totalitarian party, a new Securitate.

I'd heard it before, over and over. Even before I defected. If we weren't Russia's neighbors, we'd do this, we'd do that. The truth was, the Red Army had been withdrawn from Romania in 1959. Ceausescu had hamstrung the country all by himself, and the Romanians knew it. He had used the same excuse: the Russians might invade. Easy, brothers, or the Russians might invade. Don't rock the boat, don't question my rule, or the Russians might invade. Suffer my yoke, toil, starve, die, or the Russians might invade. When it became obvious that the Russians would not invade, because Romania was either too hard to swallow or too unimportant, the Romanians should have realized that all that kept the tyrant going was the system's unquestioning adulation. They should've balked much earlier. They didn't.

I made that point, and Novac accepted it. "We were stupid. Ceausescu commanded, and we obeyed. He told us we were an important nation, and he slept over at Buckingham Palace, while we chanted hurrah and tightened our belts. Stupid."

All right. Stupid or not, it was over. What now?

"There's some freedom, undoubtedly. But look at what comes with it: crime is out of hand, the papers are publishing police blotters, all we read about is rape, murder, corruption, trafficking in illicit goods. We don't know what the power is up to . . ." The power, I knew by now, was the leading party and the freely elected president. "We have privatization laws, but they're being implemented at a snail's pace. The peasants carved out their private plots of land, but they don't have titles of property, or money to buy equipment or fertilizer. And how do we know that the power's not flirting with the Russians?" Novac seemed to become aware of his grim tone. "Maybe things are not as bad as we think. But you know, when it all comes out into the open, all the junk comes out too."

"But wait a second, most people are not working, we could see that just by driving over here. The streets are packed like on a Sunday, the cafés are full. Those Turks roasting chickens on spits, they're making money. Don't the Romanians want to make money?"

Novac shrugged. Money wasn't enough, not for what everyone expected after a revolution. What exactly did they expect? I asked. He opened his arms: simply, everything.

"The Gypsies are prospering," Mrs. Novac interjected sardonically.

Iris had been sitting patiently, her forehead wrinkled. I realized that, despite the constant bombardment of explanations, what she saw and heard was still mysterious to her. "How did things come to this?" she asked; it felt as if an alien had asked a most appropriate question, which the natives seemed incapable of asking. Yes, how exactly did things get like this?

The Novacs hurried to respond, interrupting each other, a sign that they'd obsessed about the answer before. It had all started with that anti-Russian stance: saying *nyet* to the Russians, Ceausescu made the Romanians feel as mighty as their superpower neighbor. Then, through a series of PR extravaganzas, the flashiest being Nixon's visit to Bucharest, Ceausescu faked an image of strategic importance to America, which the Americans welcomed as both useful and cheap. Flirting with Ceausescu required only the renewal of the most favored nation clause, and closing an eye, momentarily, to his human rights abuses. Economically, the Americans didn't bail him out, and Ceausescu was too grandiose to admit his debacle. Was the trade between Romania and Russia dead? No problem: the Romanians would produce everything, from needles to tanks. And the little nation developed monstrously, becoming a forest of smokestacks, a grid of dams, a hemorrhage of industrial waste. Steel, plastic, cement, tractors, paper goods, mining equipment, agricultural machines, cars, were all produced locally. Full industrialization, just when the world had started to de-industrialize. The products were shoddy, impossible to sell. Foreign debt soared. No problem: to get cash and repay the foreign debt, the agricultural products would be sold abroad. But since the world already had plenty of lettuce and tomatoes and chickens and beef, Ceausescu could corner the market only by drastically undervaluing his product. He had to sell entire harvests, the nation's daily bread, year after year. Mass malnutrition set in. The party press started publishing medical advice about the perils of eating too much protein.

My wife leaned forward. "But what was in his head? What kind of goals was he after, to bring you to this?"

Again, the Novacs interrupted each other. "He created a cult of national independence," said Novac, "even if we had to do everything ourselves." His wife snickered: "What independence? He was simply so puffed up, that if anyone challenged him, he had to have the last word. When the trade with the Russians collapsed, he should've made peace with them. They would've forgiven him, and we wouldn't have starved."

Novac protested fiercely. "They would have axed him in a nice little coup d'etat."

"So? He still wouldn't have ended up shot like a dog. He was an idiot, an idiot." She turned to my wife. "Don't you think, Mrs. Popescu, that the truth is more complex than that! Things here are simple."

I could tell that my wife liked Mrs. Novac. Romanian women were more direct, more real than the men. "So what was it like during his last years?" she asked.

To answer that question, Mrs. Novac closed her eyes, to recall the basic feel of that time. "It was horribly dull. Till the late seventies, we still watched *Mannix,* or *The Untouchables,* an older American or French movie now and then, a pop music concert from time to time. It was livable. But when the Americans finally questioned Ceausescu's human rights record, and he told them to back off, and then he lost the most favored nation status, that was it: off with *Mannix,* off with *The Untouchables.* Since we had to save power, he cut down the TV programming to two hours a day. The 'tele-journal' started at 8 P.M. and lasted about half an hour. It was all about what *he* had done that day, of course. Then there was an hour of "spontaneous" interviews with workers saying how good they had it under his reign. At 9:30, there was a half-hour show: "Romania in the World," most of it about him again, and at 10 P.M., that was it. Curtains."

"All restaurants and bars in the nation closed at 10," remembered Novac. "Except for one bar for foreigners, at the Athenee Palace Hotel."

"Why?" asked Iris candidly, not guessing the reason for that restriction.

"The restaurants didn't have much food either. So, the less they stayed open, the fewer customers they had to serve."

Iris squirmed in her chair. "But that's . . . sick!"

"Very sick," agreed Novac. "Now you understand why we're so confused?"

"I would've thought the contrary. That you'd know precisely what you want to do, or not do."

"No, *draga.*" Mrs. Novac patted Iris's arm. "I know you were born in freedom. But let me tell you, when you get up every day and the first thing you hear is that another staple food has doubled its price, or you read in the paper about a new law choking off another little breathing hole, you just get so numb, you sleepwalk through life. I only felt awake when I watched a foreign videotape. They started smuggling them into the country in the early eighties. That was it, that was all we had to connect us with the rest of the world, with a normal life."

In America we fought to ration our children's videos. Here, they were a lifeline.

"People sold their cars to buy VCRs," reinforced the husband.

"Of course. Who would hold on to a car, when the gasoline was so scarce that you only drove once a week? The VCR kept you sane, every night. You watched a tape, went to sleep thinking about what you saw, woke up remembering it, went to work, asked your office friends about what they had watched last night, compared shows. . . . It took us through the day, and then came the evening, dinner, and a new tape."

So as not to offend the Novacs, my wife lip-synched at me: Like in jail.

They didn't notice. Mrs. Novac explained how marriages stayed together, thanks to the VCR. It saved the Romanian family.

"But it wiped out reading," Novac interjected. "What kid would read our classic patriotic poets, if they could watch *Die Hard,* over and over?"

I tried to laugh. "At least we share the same problems. What about the reading situation now?"

"Our free press is terrific," said Mrs. Novac. "It'll keep us from returning to Communism. And we love American authors. Sandra Brown. She's a great writer, you read her books?"

* * *

We left late. Novac accompanied us down, adding his weight to ours in the creaking elevator. We stepped out. Over the top of the side wall, I stared at the adjoining house: dark, lifeless. I asked Novac about the Gypsy sisters. They were evicted just before the revolution, he explained, after a neighbor ratted on them for stashing dollars. The house became a public library.

"It would be good if someone like you did something for us *out there*," said Novac, though with some doubt in his voice. "We have a terrible image. We're portrayed as unadvanced, devious, lazy, the worst of the bunch. But I see what's happening, I still travel with our soccer teams, to the neighboring countries. They're not any better. They too have Commies, everywhere. I don't care if you have friends in the government, someone should help us."

"I don't have friends in the government."

"But didn't you know Iliescu?"

I did know him, and had even interviewed him after the revolution, by phone, for the *Los Angeles Times*. So? The Romanians had elected him president, in free and fair elections, according to the Western observers. The opposition hinted that the vote had been rigged, but produced no evidence. And then the opposition refused to enter a coalition with the new president.

Novac interrupted heatedly, "Iliescu didn't want to enter the coalition."

"So the opposition obliged?"

"The opposition," he countered, "recognized in him the old apparatchik. The opposition includes former political prisoners, and the cream of our intelligentsia."

"Very well. But they were defeated at the polls. Speaking of image, how does it look when the cream of the intelligentsia neither accepts defeat at the polls, nor agrees to help?"

"The intelligentsia's helping us keep our eyes open," he said stubbornly.

I felt that something had closed inside me. That little window that gushed tears only hours ago, it was shut now. That purity, that immediacy of emotions, was gone. Instead, Novac and I were arguing politics. Heatedly, like true Romanians.

We parted friends, though. I led Iris towards University Square, looking for a taxi. The streets were dark, the pedestrians rare, and my wife nervous. I reassured her that I knew every inch of these streets, and

could handle any situation; meanwhile, I chivalrously held her arm, helping her over pitted sidewalks which my feet remembered from two decades back. Her forehead was carved in thought. She finally spoke: "I'm
glad you're not planning on moving back here. I can just tell how you
would be welcomed, if you came back dragging along a Jew wife."

"Three hours ago, you thought I would get the red carpet treatment."

"Maybe you will. But the nationalism of these people, it's just too
much."

I didn't think I had the energy to reply. But that was the kind of re-
mark which *I* could say, but wouldn't let an outsider voice, not even my
wife. I took her hand, and poured out a little tirade: I knew nationalism,
and I knew its dangers; it was showing its horrible face right across the
border, in the former Yugoslavia. What we'd heard from the Novacs was
something else, it was that sense of injured nationhood, dating from long
before the Soviet occupation, from the Ottoman rule and earlier. From
the centuries when ten, twenty years of peace were the average spells of
respite between invasions. And if a longer foreign rule lasted, it meant
unremitting destruction of everything native, the culture, the economy,
the people. The Turks, for instance, taxed Romania annually for over half
of her wood, grain, livestock, horses, textiles, honey, and wine. In addition, thousands of native youths were seized every year, the girls to
end up in harems, the boys to become either janizaries, converted
Muslim soldiers, or eunuchs. Those chosen to be eunuchs suffered
mass castrations, and then were buried to their waists in pits of limestone, to heal; only 20 percent survived, to be chained and marched to
Istanbul *on foot.*

"Our native rulers learned from masters," I commented, as I monitored the mute shock in Iris's eyes. Wars and tributes in slaves shipped to
Istanbul so depleted Romania that in 1866, arriving to sit on the young
nation's throne, the German prince Carol I of Hohenzollern exclaimed that
he was being offered the crown of a desert; yet, when they finally broke
the Turkish yoke, and drove victorious towards Istanbul, the Romanians
did not rape or burn the Turkish lands. Large Muslim communities were
left behind in Romania; they suffered no more than the Turkish vendors
did today. That the Romanians were less violent than their neighbors was
a sad merit, for goodness was always relative out here, always measured
against the cruelty of others. But even if they were spared, most often out
of an odd mix of pity, corruption, and practicality, still, they were saved.

Among those were four hundred thousand of her own people who survived the Holocaust *here*—I had that figure from books by American historians, the Commies had never published such figures.

I concluded bitterly that just as Romania's cycles of development were never fully played out, so it was with its the moral healing. Most of the culprits, and they were many, whether local tyrants or invaders' tools, were hardly ever made to stand trial. History was pressuring again, breathing down the country's neck, hurrying it into the next stage of development. There was no time for justice, just as there was so little time for building and consolidation. On to the next cycle.

I had finished, with my own words ringing in my ears, strange in the setting of my hometown, because they were in English. Iris was staring at me. I waited for her to speak, with suspense, almost with alarm. She mouthed softly, "I can understand that you want to defend this place, to find reason to be proud of it. That makes me feel close to you. But could you ever live here again?"

I put myself in her place: trying to figure the unknown inner springs of a spouse whose past I'd never really known, until today. Scary. I hugged her. "No, not anymore. It's too late."

She walked on, next to me. I looked around, feeling that I was getting a bitter strength from the streets of my childhood. This was the present, and maybe it signalled the end of suffering. Out of the present came another taxi. We got in, and I told the driver to circle University Square, so I could show it to my wife.

Along one whole side of the University of Bucharest, my alma mater, there was a sort of freedom wall, like in Peking. It was still full of graffiti from last year, when, for weeks, hundreds of students had camped on this site, asking for a students' free TV station, for the provisional government to resign, and for Iliescu not to run in the first free elections.

After a few weeks, the giant sit-in degenerated into a kind of latter-day Woodstock. Street speculators made little fortunes selling the squatters food, blankets, and alcohol. Dirt piled up. The streets stank of urine and feces. Endless speeches and endless chanting finally exasperated the common Bucharesters, usually party animals who loved a good excuse to break off from work, and gape and shout; when the Bucharesters began to find the students too much, a vigilante force of workers arrived to strengthen the hesitant police and evict the students. The workers were coal miners shipped in from southern Transylvania, allegedly by the government. Chanting slogans like "We Don't Think, We Just Work," they beat on the students and scattered them. University Square was hosed clean, traffic was reestablished, the stench dissipated. The miners went home; but their raid, remembered sarcastically as the "Mineriad," gave ample ammunition to the opposition and outraged the foreign press (I, for one, protested it in the *Los Angeles Times*). But then things simmered down again, and Iliescu did run for president, and won 85 percent of the vote, thanks to the workers and peasants voting freely for the first time in half a century.

But the student body remained a giant firecracker, ready to reignite. The graffiti we were passing proclaimed: *Zona libera de comunism* (Communism-free zone), and *Ultima solutie, o noua revolutie* (the last solution, another revolution). I didn't know what to think, whom to side with in my mind. With the students? They equaled purity, fervor, and . . . immaturity and incompetence. How could they govern a country? Their rule would disintegrate in a week. But who was left? The inexperienced opposition, and the others, the professional politicians, the "realists," the schemers of all ilks. As usual and as everywhere.

A receptionist greeted us at the Flora. "Mr. Popescu, you had four telephone calls."

One was from George Arion, publisher of the *Flacara* group of newspapers (new, independent, opposition-oriented). Another was from my friend Gusti, with a brief message: he hoped we had settled in satisfactorily; if we needed anything, he was ready to help. A third was from another newspaper, *Adevarul,* semigovernmental. A fourth was from my uncle Petre, who knew the day of my arrival, but not where I would be. I figured that he probably called from hotel to hotel, there were not that many in this city of over two million, until he found us. But it was too late to call him back now.

Soon we were in our room, between sheets that were clean but had holes from overuse. The quiet darkness smelled of dust, even though the suite had been vacuumed: the furrows of a heavy, Soviet-made vacuum machine could be detected on the carpet. There was no sound of traffic, though two main thoroughfares intersected just a few hundred yards away, but I heard a hazy echo of dogs barking. Barking sleepily, like hundreds of years ago, when Bucharest was just a caravan station, on the route to those legendary Eastern empires.

woke up in darkness, at 5 A.M. Careful not to awaken my wife, I slipped out of bed. I'd slept little, but I felt energetic. Cool-minded and logical. Today, I would start doing my journalist's job. In a few hours I would make phone calls, asking to interview the main political figures, including the president.

I tiptoed into the bathroom and shaved, listening to an invisible radio broadcasting in another suite. I could hear it clearly: broadcasting a political commentary, acidic and anti-government. So unlike the Communist radio I used to know, it shook me to my core. There was a totally different Romania around me, and I, obsessed with the past, had only noticed it in its shallowest aspects, the messy streets, the moonlighters. This boost of hope was welcome.

At six, I slipped out of the room, walked down to the main lobby, and found a lone receptionist dozing behind the front desk. The restaurant and the bar were closed. My footsteps woke the receptionist, and I asked her if I could persuade anyone to make coffee. I'd pay for it. She gave me a hurt look: pay? What kind of boorish American attitude was that? She herself would make the coffee. I asked for the morning papers, which were in already. After a few moments of chat, the receptionist realized my greed for Romania's news, so she dug around the office, and brought me the papers from the last two days.

With those stacks, I sat in the bar next to a steaming pot of Romanian coffee, which, like Arabic coffee, is prepared by boiling the ground beans in water, and then is poured in the cup unfiltered. I had several cups, thick and strong, leaving on the cup's bottom a finger of dregs that looked incinerated. The punch of that super-espresso was beyond imagination. My ears buzzing, I read the press.

It was as stimulating as the coffee. Well-written, but verbose, as if drunk with the freedom of using as many words as possible. Between the words, the present reality pranced free. The impression was sharp, vital, hard to reconcile with the depressing city I'd seen. Novac was right, this kind of press would not tolerate a return to Communism. Many papers' names contained the words "free" or "freedom": *Libertatea* (Freedom), *Tineretul Liber* (Free Youth), *Romania Libera* (Free Romania). I read the political commentaries. One particular commentator who threw grenades at the government was a certain Petre Mihai Bacanu. He was unknown to me, but not to his readers, for his byline surfaced often. My only query was, a lot of this journalism was very high-end: how many readers could follow it?

There were plenty of pieces about the revolution and its unanswered questions, mostly from revolutionaries on the outs with the "power." Over and over, they accused President Iliescu of having appeared with an organized apparatus behind him, some of which would necessarily be Securitate. I knew many of those witnesses, they were from my generation, a few were national celebrities. Ana Blandiana, who had been with me at Iowa, had briefly served as vice-president of the FSN, right next to Iliescu. Ion Caramitru, a stage and film star, and poet Mircea Dinescu, president of the Writers' Union I once belonged to, were among the original thirty-seven who gave birth to the FSN. Not all opposition leaders belonged to that initial core, and sore who did separated from it later. Nicolae Manolescu, Romania's leading critic, had formed his own movement, the Civic Alliance (acronym AC, meaning "needle" in Romanian). Manolescu was today the number two in the CDR, the umbrella assemblage of the opposition; number one was a leader of the old national peasant party, Corneliu Coposu, who had spent almost twenty years in a Ceausescu prison. Coposu was a staunch promoter of the return of the king. For these people, the question was not whether the revolution had been "stolen," but when and how. They kept reminding the public of the unsolved mysteries: Why were so few terrorists captured? To which special branch of Securitate did they belong? Right after the revolution, the Securitate's archives had caught fire; that might've happened from the explosions rocking the area, but more likely it was an attempt to destroy the lists of the Securitate agents. Without those lists, the agents would've had no difficulty vanishing and reappearing with fake identities.

There was no doubt that the revolution's original leaders had been thrown together by accident, first in the exploding streets, then in the crowded Studio 4 of Romanian television, cold (its heating system was not working at the time), chaotic with shouts, and soon to be blasted from outside by the gunfire of terrorists. Ceausescu, who had fled by helicopter, had not yet been apprehended, but the transfer of power to the amorphous new democracy was already happening on the tube. The army had joined the revolution, and infantry units had been deployed around Studio 4. As the terrorists attacked, inside, Caramitru, Dinescu, Iliescu, and other leaders of the first hours crawled on all fours under shattering windows and peeling plaster. It was a drama that should've cemented their alliance. But it didn't.

The terrorist attacks were repulsed, and the army became master of the situation. In the next few days, the initial thirty-seven leaders grew to over a hundred, turning into a noisy crowd, and beginning to fracture along the most predictable lines: those of class. The intellectuals, traditionally the cream of Romanian society, began to differ with Iliescu, a former Communist, though by most accounts an untainted one. In the revolution's first hours, Iliescu's name had been spontaneously (or by orchestration?) shouted by people in the crowd. The man had been called to Studio 4 from virtual house arrest to be welcomed live on the air as an anti-Ceausescu patriot. The audience knew that he had been a Communist, and at the time no one found that inappropriate or unsavory. Iliescu voiced the themes of free elections, the right of the people to have the essentials of life, and punishment for the still-unapprehended tyrant. He also talked of a "democratic socialism," while the intellectuals would soon begin to press for out-and-out capitalism, and some for the revival of the monarchy.

And that was the beginning of a house divided. The Ceausescus were soon caught on a provincial highway, driving in a little Dacia hijacked for them by their one remaining bodyguard. They were taken to the closest military garrison, tried by an extraordinary court hastily sent over from Bucharest, and executed. In the next few weeks, other former party activists began to appear around Iliescu, most of them not prominent and relatively untainted. With them, Iliescu took over the FSN. The intellectuals broke off, accusing the FSN of being invaded by crypto-Communists, and declared themselves the opposition.

The first free elections were five months later with foreign observers present. Iliescu won by a huge margin. The elections should've put a stop to the conspiracy theories, and generally quelled the recriminations. But the "stolen revolution" scenario resurged with a vengeance. Although it was documented that Ceausescu had Iliescu watched around the clock, now the opposition declared such evidence not to be trusted. In the first hours, star poet Dinescu and star actor Caramitru, who had uttered the first appeals to the people ("calm and solidarity, the tyrant has fled, we seem to be winning"), stood next to Iliescu, but visibly allowed him a major part, and soon the leading part. Did that have to do with the fact that the revolutionary crowds comprised a majority of workers, viscerally more responsive to someone like Iliescu than to a bunch of "artists"? Probably. Certainly, there was no trust now between the former allies. *Romania Libera* (Free Romania) accused Iliescu of being a master puppeteer, while the semi-governmental *Adevarul* (the Truth) gave it back to *Romania Libera,* belittling Iliescu's critics as complainers and defeatists.

Turning a page, I came to a spread of excerpts from a diary attributed to Elena Ceausescu, just published in Paris. One read, "The Securitate delivered to me a group of criminals, all ethnic Hungarians, denounced by their neighbors for having listened to Radio Free Europe. Nic gave me carte blanche to do with them as I please. Cute, no more flies, I've got some real stuff to experiment with." Elena was then the dean of Romania's Institute of Chemical Sciences. Other highlights: "In Valea Jiului, the miners went on strike. We'll show them, without us they would've been nothing but losers." The miners had once surrounded Ceausescu when he arrived for one of his spot-check visits, and forced him to descend into a mine shaft, to show him their work conditions. Ceausescu promised improvement, then arrested the "instigators." Some ended up as rabbits for Elena's experiments: "I dissected the brain of a miner. It's the brain of an inferior individual, doubtlessly responsive to imperialist propaganda. I'd like to examine some of his family, but Nic wants me to put off tests for now. Pity, though." With work on brains momentarily stopped, Elena focussed on more traditional torture: "Interestingly, when you break the legs of an enemy of the people, he stops answering to the investigators' questions! I wonder what would happen if his arms were torn off? I'll research the matter." Mixed with her scientific notations, there were bits about her husband: "Nic sold two oil refineries to the 'bedouin.' I ordered two minks." Their marriage wasn't smooth: "I haven't talked to Nic for three days, in the bedroom I turn my back on him. I want a nuclear bomb, how can you get along nowadays without one?" If the diaries were apocryphal, they kept in step with the events, and with the couple's deepening dementia.

Among the miners who beat the students in University Square, there were some who had dared challenge Ceausescu. Iliescu had welcomed the miners to Bucharest; then, faced with world criticism, he had scolded them. The problem was that the miners wanted the cradle-to-grave security they'd had under the Communists; so did all Romania's workers. It was as if Communism, conceived for the workers but never implemented to their liking, was now a ghost whispering to them to cling to the past, even to beat and kill for it.

Another page: pictures of the runners-up for the first Miss Romania contest. Aged from eighteen to twenty-two; their height in centimeters and weight in kilograms were noted, along with the color of their eyes. They all looked rather full by Western standards, and older than their declared years. They wore dresses and high heels, and sat or sprawled alluringly, with much cleavage. Their eyes were lusty, impatient.

I connected with a larger feeling of impatience, which rose from those pages like steam. The impatience of a breed that hadn't had its chance. I related it to what I'd seen the day before the grass growing tall around the buildings, to the decrepit Elisabeta Palace, the mangy hotel, with its threadbare towels. And the people: the robotic stewardesses, the taxi driver who pined after Ceausescu, the *bishnitsari* yelling after customers, "Hey, sefule!", the Miss Romanias with their cleavage and dresses forced high on their thighs to show flesh. And the bar I drank my coffee in, the grounds outside, this whole space, this cosmos. The cosmos of Communism, as these people knew it, as I knew it too, Communism without pretense. Even the morning sunlight, travelling in from the East, lighting up long tracts of Russia before it touched Romania, felt anxious and painful.

Pain, everywhere. More than in the fragmentation of Prague, with black marketeers next to the saintly statue of Jan Hus. There was far more pain here, more confusion, missed opportunity, regret, and scrambling. So the impatience felt good, active. An almost animal will to survive, to make up for lost time, and win. The Miss Romanias wanted to win their contest, and the opposition wanted to win the power. I smiled alone, next to the nearly empty coffee pot; just then the receptionist walked in and asked if I wanted some more. I thanked her, no, but asked where she was from. A little village south of Bucharest. She had been in the hotel business for three years. While we chatted, a bartender showed up to unlock the bar and count the supplies, then a waiter strolled in; until, little by little, a small crowd of youngsters, all employees of the hotel assembled around me. Dora D. had done a good job of spreading her enthusiasm about the visiting native son, but they didn't want to know about me, they wanted to know about America. What was it like. Could it be conquered. They had the involuntary charm of their age: unblemished skin, clean eyes, an unoffensively direct manner. Moderately critical of the government. As I served them bits about America, I noticed a waiter, young too, standing alone by the bar's door, unwilling to join the group. He was handsome, and his hair was built up in a shiny wavy deck—how I envied that kind of hair when I was young, for mine was stick-straight. I forgot him, enjoying the others, enjoying not the least the fact that my Romanian had not lost its fluency, or humor. They'd be fine, they'd be cured from the past all right, I kept telling myself. I finally parted with them and walked up the stairs with a bounce in my step, from them and from the fierce native coffee.

"Are we going to meet your family?" my wife asked me as I walked into the suite. She was drying her hair. She was amazed not to have heard me leave the room, for she was usually a very light sleeper. She had been exhausted.

"Yes. I'll call them."

"Are you putting it off?"

"Absolutely not, but . . . there's a lot of other stuff I have to do. Here, I'll call Uncle Petre right now."

Did I nurture a submerged hope that the phone might have one of its breakdowns? It felt that way, but I bravely picked it up, and dialed. Someone picked up on the second ring. "Heeey," said my uncle Petre, "what's with you, you appeared and redisappeared like a meteor!"

"No, Uncle, I've been busy." I explained quickly that I was here to write about Romania for the American papers. So, how were they all? Good, his son and daughter were at the medical school, one of Bucharest's best academic institutions, his wife was out battling the shopping lines, still in existence despite the revolution, he alone was guarding the phone, waiting for my call. "We made ourselves free all week, when are you coming over?" As soon as we could, I assured him, most likely tomorrow if nothing intervened. "Your uncles Nicu and Tudor and your godmother Puica can't wait to meet your wife," he said, bringing out the strength of numbers. Yes, of course, I gurgled, clearing a knot in my throat, she was impatient to meet them too, gotta go now, Uncle.

I hung up, braced myself for my wife's inquiring look. But the phone rang. Dora D., from her station downstairs, thanked me again for the autograph, and warned that there were very few tomatoes left for breakfast, so if we wanted to have any, we should come down to the restaurant now. How nice of Dora, I told Iris, with the subtext: See? They're nice people, my people. From where I stood by the phone, I could see a copy of *Amazon Beaming* in my open suitcase, peering out from under a stack of shirts. The brand-new cover combined in my mind with the raggedy cover I'd signed my name on yesterday, and a sense of continuity, of unexpected meaningfulness hit me. I was continuous. So was this former homeland of mine, despite the appearances. I basked in a brief and secret happiness: the good, the stable, the continuous existed, all I had to do was keep my eyes open and recognize them. My Romanian family was part of what was continuous. We would meet them soon.

Down in the restaurant, we were served by the young waiter with the impressive hair. Iris made the mistake of asking him about one, two, three dishes on the breakfast list. *"N'avem,"* we don't have, he hit back at her. "What do you have?" she asked. *"Nimic!"* (nothing). I glared at him and told him to bring us tomatoes and feta cheese and coffee, a Romanian peasant breakfast. There were no more tomatoes, he announced with a scowl. I argued: Dora just told me . . . *"Nu mai sint!"* (no more), he cut me off. I told him to send me another waiter. He ambled away, stopped to chat with a waitress, and checked his reflection in a mirror. Finally, another waiter arrived, older, less curt. We ended up eating feta cheese, on old bread spread with yellow, runny butter, and drinking thick coffee and mineral water bottled in southern Transylvania, in a region of spas once enjoyed by the Austro-Hungarian nobility. Iris was outraged: "Eat this junk that even your monks, I'm sure, would despise, and be snapped at too?"

"In fact, my monks always made up for their sexual chastity with great food, way above the level of Bucharest restaurants. And they certainly had better manners."

She was silent, absorbed in her desire to like my land and people. I tried understand, but there was nothing to understand about gratuitous hostility. We ate without appetite, and looked for our waiter to pay the bill. He was nowhere, the restaurant was totally empty.

When we stepped out into the main lobby, we found the waiters and the guests of the hotel massed in a crowd in front of a black-and-white TV set. Dora was there too, and all the women from the front desk. The rude young waiter was there as well, standing aside from the others, his arms crossed in the same hostile pose. The crowd watched with tense attention, eyes shining as if witnessing an incredible event: the monitor showed a kind of jammed convention hall, decorated with Romanian flags. On a podium, a bunch of burly, sweaty men, with old-fashioned moustaches. One read a kind of proclamation; I instantly guessed its content from the reader's accent: slow, deeply palatal, the accent of the Romanians in the Soviet Moldovan Republic.

The Soviet Moldovan Republic was declaring its independence from Russia. Cheers broke out in the convention hall, the flags were waved, the men and women present hugged tearfully. Outside, other crowds danced the Romanian hora. In the hotel lobby, the little crowd of onlookers broke up. Their eyes were glowing, but their body language was a mix of excitement and uncertainty. Dora spotted us, charged towards us: "Thank God, the Moldovans did it. At last!"

She looked dizzy. As if behind her enthusiasm lurked a silent question: Now what?

I explained what all that meant to Iris, while the television played footage shot at the Romanian/Moldovan border: Romanian and Moldovan peasants waving at each other across the lazy river Prut, throwing flags and flowers into the river. The river's slow waves pushed the flowers and flags together into one flow. Boatfuls of Romanians, boatfuls of Moldovans rowed towards each other, crossing into each others' territory, sharing the symbolic bread and salt, and bottles and flasks of peasant wine. People who had never met, families the Russians had never allowed to visit with each other after 1945, smiled to the cameras now, united. They hugged, they danced on the Moldovan shore, where once the Soviet soldiers had levelled their rifles at them. The TV cut back to ecstatic crowds celebrating in Chisinau, Moldova's capital.

There were now two free independent Romanian states.

I took a look around me. The people in the lobby acted excited, yet their voices, their gestures seemed stilted compared with the abandon of those Moldovan crowds. Someone uttered the ancestral words of well wishing, *"Sa fie intr'un ceas bun"* (may this hour be blessed), while the crowd became fluid, strolling into the restaurant or settling into the lobby's chairs, back to conversations interrupted by the TV, back to their immediate concerns. I noticed again that curt young waiter, heading back towards the restaurant, hands in his pockets, a very unwaiter-like stance, face stony with reflectiveness. He would have been a great Securitate, I thought silently. Unless, who knows, he was still one.

"That's it, back there." I pointed out for Iris a seven-story-high rectangle of columned limestone, carrying on its flat top a smaller rectangle, only five stories high, upon which sat another four stories. The three boxes were streaked vertically by rows of cold, inexpressive windows. It was Ceausescu's master edifice, Casa Poporului (the house of the people). "He started building it in 1984. When we get close, you'll see that it's still not finished."

I'd hired another taxi, and asked the driver to take us to that part of Bucharest which Ceausescu had intended as a symbol of his era. The Victory of Socialism Boulevard, longer and wider than the Champs Élysées, leading to the Casa Poporului, whose inner square footage surpassed that of the Pentagon. I told the driver to stop the car at the start of the monster boulevard. Iris and I stepped out, and stared at the building. Its facade was flat and inexpressive, but there was something in it that was deeply disturbing: the windows looked like vertical strings of eyes. Maybe what Ceausescu wanted as a symbol of his era were eyes, open, staring, missing nothing.

This morning, Iris was wearing a cream-colored pleated skirt, of silk, with a black short-sleeved silk top, and cream-and-black sling-back heels. She looked striking and out of place. I was wearing ironed jeans, a khaki shirt, a light gray Armani jacket, and my reporter's gear: a shoulder bag with a tape recorder, a pen and pad, and my Canon camera.

The boulevard ran up to Casa Poporului between a double file of apartment buildings a dozen stories high. They had been left unfinished. They were empty shells, unpainted see-throughs, like a double file of movie sets. To build them and that thousand-eyed sphinx, Ceausescu had knocked down the heart of old Bucharest: Arsenal Hill and Spirii Hill, which included some of the city's most ancient streets, including Sfintii Apostoli, on which stood the old Popescu house. The birthplace of my dad, and of most of his brothers and sisters—in good Romanian fashion, my grandmother had given birth to most of her children at home.

I'd learned that the old Popescu house was no more by accident. In 1985, digging in the heaps of a used bookstore in New York, I found a little tome on Bucharest, complete with a city map. I opened it, and Ceausescu's picture grinned at me. The book documented his plans of giving Bucharest a new "spine," modern and in keeping with the other achievements of his "golden era." On the map, more than a fourth of downtown was a blank with the legend *"ansamblurile noului centru politico-administrativ"*—the grounds of the new political/administrative center. The blank swallowed Spirii and Arsenal Hills. A piece of my childhood had been bulldozed. The Sfintii Apostoli church, one of the oldest in Bucharest, where all my uncles and aunts had been baptized and some had wed, was gone too. On one of the two vanished hills, Spirii, a battalion of Romanians had died back in 1848, battling Ottoman forces four times more numerous. Dealul Spirii was Bucharest's Alamo; now that Alamo was no more.

Between picking up that book, and lining up at the bookstore's register to buy it, my mind had experienced a storm of thoughts. I thought of Dad, who had recently died and had been buried without my hand throwing a palmful of earth on his coffin: I thought of Communism's borders, which had been part of my earlier loss: when Pavel was sick, those borders were sealed and he couldn't get the Salk vaccine. Then, when Dad died, those borders were still sealed. Communism had defeated Pavel, and Dad, and me.

And I thought of the old Popescu house and the Sfintii Apostoli church, for I knew them intimately. In an attempt to describe my youth, I had told Iris about a family ritual enacted every spring in that house: *"Bataia halvitei,"* a fun Romanian custom whereby a piece of halvita was suspended by a string from the ceiling, and swung back and forth, with two youngsters standing at opposite ends of the room, trying to catch it in their mouths. For those who don't know, halvita is a candy made of crushed sesame seeds, soaked in honey and hardened. The candy was usually "beaten" by a man and a woman, or a boy and a girl; in the Popescu house, it was the custom that only those unmarried would participate. And try to imagine a joyous crowd of Popescus, still sipping drinks or finishing dessert, for the beating followed dinner, and laughing and cheering while two players lunged forward to bite at the hard sweet stuff. I was among the players, swinging one spring night against a paramour of one of my cousins; her lips left pink imprints of lipstick on the halvita, which I found sexy, for my hormones were running. I was surrounded by the warm presence of kin, my dad was in the other room, talking politics with his brothers, and in thousands of other Bucharest homes the same custom was being enacted. Our world was little, and quaint, and our own. Soon after the day of the halvita came Orthodox Easter, which in Romania is observed on the eve of Easter Sunday, at midnight, in a spectacular ceremony. The priest appears at the altar with an armful of lit candles, calling out loud, "Come share in the light!" And the whole congregation, packed tight inside the nave, leans forward to light their candles from the priest's. In less than a minute, the light travels out of the church and into the street. The service ended with the light travelling out to worshippers who hadn't found room in the church, who then got into cars or boarded busses with their lit candles in their hands, their fingers seared with hot dripping wax. And for a few hours into the night, the whole city of Bucharest was crisscrossed by flickering candles, as the worshippers took them home, the belief being that if a lit candle survived the trip into the home, that was a sign of God's good will. All that was wired into my childhood, for our little church, always small, always modest and under attack, symbolized our soul and nationhood.

Dare I say it, I who was never a regular at mass: the Romanian church was all right. It was cool, with its melancholy chants, strange cylindrical tiaras, black garb, and big gray beards. Rural, poor, folkloric, it went on within dark naves smelling of wild flowers and melting wax, with danging clocks in stooped belfries, with itinerant priests travelling on donkeys, from a baptism in one village to a funeral in the next. Throughout Romania's history, the church was a positive institution, with one glaring exception: under the Iron Guards, there were priests who acted against the faith, standing in the pulpit to ask for Jewish and Communist blood, leading cohorts to loot and kill. After the war, they were not brought to trial. The Russians engulfed the country, and bore down on the faith itself. The whole clergy was persecuted.

So when I grew up, I only knew the church as a victim. Monitored fiercely by the Communists, I crossed myself with my tongue, and felt secretly connected to the first Christians, hiding in Rome's catacombs. I didn't really believe in God—after my twin brother was killed by disease, how could I still believe? But when I stepped into churches alone, at odd hours, peering over my shoulder to check if anyone had seen me, I felt peace come over me, and I was thankful.

Well, in his last years, Ceausescu almost destroyed what was left of the Romanian church. He, who had been born to peasants for whom the church had been school, solace, and sacrament, decided that both the religion and its buildings would be his next target. On the excuse of building a new Bucharest, he razed a third of Bucharest's 350 churches. Orthodox ones mostly, but also a few Catholic and Protestant, and one synagogue. Many of the Orthodox churches were historic and architecturally irreplaceable.

The much-oppressed Bucharesters tried to protect their churches in a rather pathetic way: they stayed inside them for hours, while the priests sang interminable masses, thus trying to hold back the wrecking ball. Vacaresti, an old and impressive monastic complex, was cordonned off by Securitate so that the demolishing crews could do their work. Vacaresti was so valued, so central to the soul of old Bucharest, that eminent personalities, most notably the chief rabbi of Bucharest, wrote to Ceausescu, begging him not to do it. In vain. It happened to be in an interfaith area: the church of Sfantu Gheorghe Vacaresti rose practically next to the Choral Synagogue, seat of the land's chief rabbinate. Ceausescu ignored the letters (the Securitate visited the writers and warned them not to do it again), and Vacaresti was destroyed, first the Christian, then the Jewish part. But, sensitive to potential flak from the Jewish American lobby, Ceausescu spared the Choral Synagogue, which stands today in absurd isolation, next to the open end of the Victory of Socialism Boulevard.

I had taken long walks in Vacaresti, in the summers when I researched *Burial of the Vine.* Slipping from the Christian side to the Jewish and back, I felt at ease in each; both were lively, picturesque, and economically poor. Vacaresti was another piece of my youth that the dragon had destroyed. And now, I took the arm of my American wife, and guided her up the unfinished but already cracked sidewalk, towards the thousand-eyed sphinx.

I'd made arrangements that morning to visit one of those sad orphanages on whose discovery the Western press feasted for the last two years, without explaining why Romania had so many orphans. Here was the reason: walking towards the mammoth building, we were walking on money. Staring ahead at its obtuse rectangles, we were staring at money. The driving lanes, the gaunt unpainted apartment buildings, the fancy lamps on high poles—money, money, money, denied to young mothers and their infants, to the impoverished Romanian schools, to the farmers, to the burly, hirsute miners ("We don't think, we just work"), to country folk and city folk who ate meat once a month, and went to bed in winter in their overcoats. Money. Somehow, history always came down to money.

Incredibly, our latest taxi driver was a fan of the dragon's. The worst he would admit about him was that he'd unsuccessfully tried to acclimate polar bears to Romania, so he could hunt them with his foreign guests. He told us that the two Ceausescus had designed the giant building together: "He and she came here every week, to look at the work's progress. Sometimes they ordered it torn down, and done another way. But they never quarrelled when they disagreed. They went home, worked it out, came back in agreement. And you know, he buried a parchment at the building's foundation. Like the Romanian princes of yore did, to their endowments."

"I know," I responded. I'd seen the parchment photographed in that book I'd bought in New York. The driver asked me if I knew about it "from satellites." The Americans recorded Ceausescu's every move from satellites. I burst out laughing: "D'you believe we'd waste our time and money on him?"

"Absolutely, he was one of a kind. You in America never had one like him."

We passed the unfinished buildings, empty, like huge sets ready to be dressed up for lights, camera, action: Romania's golden era under the "genius of the Carpathians." We came to the end of the sidewalks, and stood in the shadow of the sphinx. "Ready to enter Ceausescu's brain?" I joked.

"Why are you asking? If I said we shouldn't, would you stop?"

No. I wouldn't stop.

"I don't know why you need me as a witness," she said. "I hope this helps you. Let's go in."

We climbed an incline of plain earth. Heaps of unmixed cement and other construction material lay about. Past a small garrett, empty, we approached the main entrance. The building was supposed to be under guard, but there was no one around. The main entrance was sealed with wires tied around the elaborate and rusted door handles, but only a few yards away, a side entrance was open. Again, no guards.

We walked inside.

This was a very large brain. The proportions of everything inside it, stairways, rooms, landings, were breathtaking.

There was more unmixed cement, and pipes, new but already rusting, and wood slats lying on the floors, and dust and dried-up mud marked by footprints. And graffitti: *Ceausescu nu mai e!* (Ceausescu is no more) defaced a whole wall. We walked with echoing steps, up stairways that would dwarf giants, let alone Ceausescu, who was five foot four, and very careful to surround himself only with people of equal or lower height. We made it into a huge hall, perhaps designed for signing international treaties. There was no furniture, just chandeliers larger than the ones in the Vatican, anchored to the ceiling by giant chains—I couldn't repress a fantasy of one chandelier tearing off and crashing down, flattening in one strike Ceausescu and some visiting world leader. Perhaps the Queen of England, who gave Ceausescu a knighthood, and took it back a few hours after the revolution triumphed. She owed him a return visit.

The brain was built of first-class material. Beautiful marble, from Italy. The doorknobs and door handles were gilded, a sign of restraint—in the private residences there were door handles and bathroom taps of pure gold. Everything around us was thought out with such grandiosity, designed and executed with such desire to impress, that the effect was achieved. We were impressed. The village idiot from Scornicesti, the hopeless stutterer, had a wish to imprint himself upon history like no one else in this land. He fulfilled his wish.

But he couldn't finish this palace, in which he intended to bring together every single institution of power in Romania. He wanted to box them all inside this mountain of stone, the ministries of economy, transportation, agriculture, communications, culture, army, all around his own office. He wanted to monitor them at all times, rein them in all at once, bring them to a state of such coordination that working inside this monster would have led to a kind of collective telepathy, each henchman reading all the other henchmen's thoughts, and all anticipating the wishes of the leader. The heads of the various departments would have spent their days riding the elevators back and forth, reporting to his office. Most people get sloppier with age, and stop caring, but he became more and more demanding and obsessive. Like an aging peasant kept in bed by disease, but bringing his gaggle of children to his bedside every few minutes with hoarse impatient calls.

I extended my arm and knocked on a wall, in one spot and then in another. We both could hear the difference in sound: dull, and then deep, rich with echo. Behind the walls the building was said to be a Swiss cheese. Tunnels connected it to an underground maze that included other key administrative buildings, the main Securitate command posts, the private residences, and several airfields. Iris asked why, on that morning of December 22, he hadn't escaped by the tunnels, instead of taking off from the roof of the RCP building in a helicopter whose pilot immediately put him down on a country highway, claiming that he'd run out of fuel.

I didn't know. "I guess he wasn't thinking clearly anymore. Things were moving too fast."

I'd been determined to see Casa Poporului, and now I felt an interesting disappointment. It was connected to a personal memory. I'd felt let down when I'd seen Ceausescu in the flesh. My meeting alone with him, unique in my life, granted to so few other Romanians, had amounted to an insignificant two minutes, after which I found myself alone, trying to remember the dictator in more detail, and failing. Small, stilted in his speech, monotonous in his aggressive stance, was all I could muster about him. When I went home after the meeting, my mother asked me countless questions about him, and then, frustrated that I hadn't said anything memorable, or at least colorful, she asked me about the building of the RCP, in which he had his office. About the stairways and hallways, the furniture, what was his secretary like, was the security tight. I could say nothing extraordinary. There was nothing extraordinary.

I felt the same now, even though the palace was impressive. But without him, it was meaningless. And he was meaningless too, in relation to the obsession he had generated. Maybe this was it, the truth about tyrants, and I'd glimpsed it by coming close to one of them, by peeping through the myth. Tyrants were mechanical. Predictable. Rarely did they regale the visitor with the flamboyant variety of character of a Napoleon or Mussolini. Most often they were dull and orderly, and when they yelled, they yelled one-liners. Now I knew what they were about: recreating reality according not to dreams, but to blueprints.

Not surprisingly, they insisted on control and order. It was what they understood, for inside they were like that, controlled and orderly. Hitler had designed a hell as dull as Germany on a gray fall day. In that hell, death was meticulous, and mass-produced. The Holocaust was a machine. The only human thing about it was the victims.

Not surprisingly, all tyrants have been obsessed with architecture. With towers, monumental dams, and pyramids. As if knowing that everything else they imposed on humans was superficial and short-lived.

"This would have been a fascinating experiment," I said to my wife. "I'm so glad that the revolution interrupted it."

I told the driver to stop at a pay phone, so I could call Gusti, as I'd promised him the day before. He came on the line, and sounded very up. "You know, our foundation has a publishing house. Would you give us any of your books in English, to translate and publish?"

Whoa. This was so direct. "Gusti, the young here don't know me. They haven't heard of my books, they haven't seen the movies I made in America. . . ."

"They'll want to read your books. And see your movies."

"Gusti, now they can read anybody. Why would they want to read me?"

"Why wouldn't they? I discussed you with our editorial board this morning, and everyone said that we could make money with you. Writing in English, living in Hollywood. You're a success story. Now, do I have to contact your agents?"

We could make money with you. . . .

"No, Gusti, you don't have to contact my agents. You and I will talk about it."

I wanted to show Iris the balcony from which Ceausescu denounced the Timisoara revolutionaries, only to be booed and frightened into fleeing by helicopter. I told the driver to let us off on Victory Avenue, next to the Kretulescu Church. Minutes later, I showed Iris the steps I once climbed with my mother, returning from one of our cemetery pilgrimages. I told her how I saw Ceausescu in the window of his office: a peasant gnome with exploding hair.

Then we walked to Victory Avenue. The movement on the street was brisk, most people storming along as if beating the air into submission. I sought on their faces anything I could connect with the news of Moldova's independence; I found nothing. I stared at the youngsters, who cut the air with the frail aggressiveness of skinny hips, flat stomachs, light legs. Some wore T-shirts with logos in English. They drank Cokes from bottles, tilting their heads back, uncaring, with their lives still in the future. I too, as I passed Ceausescu back then, had my life in the future, a future I didn't want to live. I was struck by the thought that if the world's young suddenly decided not to mate, our two-million-year-old race would simply disappear. A stop of one generation. Ahead of us, there was a big trampling of feet, as people started running. A bus approached, overloaded, with people hanging in heavy clusters out of each open door, fighting each other as they hung on. It slowed down, two or three people dropped out, others jumped in from the sidewalk, working themselves with their shoulders into those hanging clusters. The bus hurtled off, a fleeting sight of humans fighting for space, eyes hard and lips tightened as they pressed against each other almost intimately. A few hundred yards ahead, before the RCP building, the same people had acted like one, booing Ceausescu out of power. I felt like yelling out, patience, my brothers, manners, my brothers! I turned, and found my American wife gaping from the sight of that bus. "Like the New York subway, huh?" I quipped.

"Kind of," she agreed.

And I saw it in her eyes. She, the straightforward one, was being careful today. She watched what she was saying. Because she loved me.

All right. I wrapped my arm around her waist. "This was the route of Richard Nixon's motorcade, remember him?" "Yeah," she smiled, "we hated him, and marched against Vietnam, and were paranoid about being infiltrated by the narcs. What about you? You marched in praise of the Leader and his guest Nixon, and were already infiltrated by the Securitate?" "Right on. Smart girl." We laughed, drank Cokes bought from a Turk, and then I guided her, feeling like I was moving in a dream, into Palace Square, surrounded by the monumental royal palace, the Central University Library, the Atheneum concert hall, and the building of the RCP. On the second floor of that building was the office where I won my passport from Ceausescu. We walked slowly, because the pavement was pitted. All the buildings around were damaged by the gunfire exchanged on the night of December 23, when the so-called terrorists tried to retake the square we were in, the television building, the Ministry of Defense, and the airport. The terrorist attacks failed, and ceased completely after the radio and TV announced the Ceausescus' execution. I looked at the Central University Library, where I'd studied for finals many times, and cringed: its walls were black from smoke, and so riddled with bullets, they looked ready to crumble. During the night of the twenty-third, an unidentified crowd broke into the library, and smashed it shelf by shelf, with crowbars, axes, and chains. Who were those thugs? There was still no answer. The former royal palace was poxed by bullets. On that same night, the mysterious terrorists broke into it and aimed their fire through its windows, onto the building of the RCP, occupied by the revolutionaries since midday December 22. The army, already sided with the revolution, responded from positions below, in the square.

At the same time, one of the most amazing episodes of the revolution took place. General Vlad, head of the Securitate, and General Guse, deputy minister of defense, had not followed the Ceausescus in their flight out of Bucharest, even though both were among the Leader's top aides. But where were they at this time, in hiding? No, they were hanging around freely, inside the building of the RCP. When the terrorists' attacks started, they volunteered their services to the one-day-old Council of the National Salvation Front. Instants later, both generals were on the phone with the commandants of Securitate and army units, instructing them to join the revolution, and to protect the phone connections—had those been cut, the Council would have been paralyzed inside the RCP. Unarmed and still ignorant of Ceausescu's whereabouts, the Council accepted the generals' hasty conversion to the people's cause. Almost undoubtedly, Vlad and Guse rescinded on the phone orders of repression they had issued earlier. In the acceptance of their services lay the seed of their forgiveness. The terrorists stopped their attacks, and vanished. Vlad was later arrested but given an insignificant sentence. Like countless times in Romanian history, once the top rogue's head rolled off, most other henchmen were ignored, or even quietly welcomed back.

I told Iris about all that, and was surprised by her reply: "What a male culture, Romania. Do the women like it here?"

I smiled. "Within limits. When it's like storming that bus, they don't."

"But if they're not trampled, and get their hands kissed now and then, it's all right?"

Hmm. Romania's women were not a cowed lot. Yet, the power of American women was in their convictions, while that of Romanian women was in their maneuvering skills. The Romanian women had not discovered the benefits of uniting in a movement. They maneuvered alone, to be desired females when young, to be the queens of their circle when old. They were great flirts and teases. The ambiguity of their status gave them a texture rare in the West, where everything was so direct, so on the level. In my time, that ambiguity was exciting. But then, nothing else was exciting.

"There must be an enormous fear of change in these people," said my wife.

I nodded. Yes, yes. Fear of change was as deep in this country as the need for change itself. Yet Iris astounded me again, reflecting aloud, "But maybe the backwardness, the slowness, was what kept you surviving one invasion after another."

Was it? If that rugged wilderness was what kept Romania distinct and continuous on the map, how did that bode for becoming a democracy? Tribalism was out. The world was made of malls and airports, all compatible and interchangeable. The Yurts of Mongolia had TV. And yet, if so many cultures' strength had come from tribalism, what would they have if they lost it? Democracy, and malls? Was that it?

We stopped before the Atheneum, home of the Bucharest Philharmonic. During Ceausescu's last years, the Philharmonic played in winter with hats and coats and mittens on, to an audience equally attired. Past the Atheneum, a narrow street led to the Lido Hotel, the first in the Soviet bloc to install artificial waves in its pool back in the sixties. Bringing a girl to the waves of the Lido meant scoring for sure. Some guests of the Writers' Union, whom I piloted around as an interpreter, stayed at the Lido, which bristled with Securitate bugs. We crossed the street, past a beer garden shelled into a blackened pile of twisted wrought iron and charred tables and chairs. And here we were now, in front of the building of the RCP. Entrance A, the one which Ceausescu's guard abandoned to the crowds on the day of the twenty-second, was the same one through which I walked once in to ask for my passport.

The entrance was guarded now by an armed soldier. I made a quick decision. "We're going in to take a look."

"They're not going to let you in."

"You'll see."

She trailed behind me as I approached the sentry and asked politely if I could speak to his commanding officer. My name was so and so, and I was an American journalist on assignment in Romania.

The sentry, a young conscript, gave me an amazed look, then walked inside. Meanwhile, I pointed up to the balcony: it was from here that he had condemned the invasion of Czechoslovakia in 1968, and that of Afghanistan in 1979, each time earning himself America's accolades. I was a puppy in the crowd cheering below in 1968, and I would have been there again in 1979, had I not fled. And again in 1989, as a revolutionary. Iris listened with her eyes narrowed. "Awful, a life wrapped around politics, timed on the pronouncements of a strongman. Awful."

"You're beginning to get it," I chuckled. "And yet the people were happy when there was a pronouncement, because that got them out of their coma. They cheered him madly in 1984, when the Soviets boycotted the Olympic games, but he sent Romania's team to Los Angeles, and Reagan stood up in tribute when the Romanians marched by. Yep, that's how we lived. A few years of darkness, and then a flicker of light: a show."

A pair of boots and one of shoes stepped out of entrance A. The soldier was followed by a lieutenant. The lieutenant marched up to me and asked me my name. I told him and prepared to pull out my assignment letter, but he stopped me with a raised hand: Was I the one who wrote *Honey-sweet Bullet*? I nodded.

A little clumsily, he stepped aside. *"Poftiti,"* he said. Come in.

I knew that after I'd left, *Bullet* had gained a cult among the military. I knew it from another defector to America, Adam Soch, whom I met by chance in L.A. Soch, now a documentary filmmaker, told me that two years before he defected he served his army time with an artillery regiment at the province town of Botosani. An avid reader, Soch swapped books with an officer in the garrison, a certain Captain C. Captain C. lent him my novel, which had already been banned, with the enigmatic comment, "This is a great book, you'll see why." A Securitate officer found it in Adam's locker during a spot inspection, and Adam was incarcerated and questioned for several days. He claimed that he'd owned the book for a while, and was unaware that its author had defected. The book was confiscated and he was released, with punishment to be determined by his superior officer.

Thus, I learned years after that incident that while all my books were part of the black market, to the younger military *Bullet* was a specific patriotic manifesto. Captain C. could have been court-martialled for owning it, let alone recommending it for its content. Adam Soch's determination not to rat on the captain won him favors in the regiment, and the prime favor was receiving the book itself as a gift. He managed to take it out of Romania, and I autographed it in Los Angeles, enjoying the screeching of my pen on the tough Romanian printing paper. I was photographed on the back cover, in uniform, with my hair cropped regulation size, half an inch long. We were a cult piece, my book and me.

And now, this lieutenant felt bound by my book to let me inside the building, but he wanted my word that I would not describe it detrimentally. He said it in a fashion that touched me, it was not out of a military manual, it was something he believed in. He was wide-shouldered but skinny, and looked chaste from the slight acne that peppered his shaven jaw.

Very well, I gave him my word. Iris realized how unique this instant was for me. When she stepped inside she moved as if into a giant reliquary. The colors of the furniture, wall paint, and rugs were subdued, beige and gray. The damage inflicted by the angry crowds had been repaired. The lieutenant told me that the building would house one of Romania's brand-new parliamentary chambers, the Senate. We climbed the stairs, while I tried to recapture the feeling I had when I came to request my passport.

But it was impossible: I was too filled with the thought that this was where the revolution had chased away the dragon. On November 27, not even three weeks before the uprising, the Romanian Communist Party had held its 14th Congress at Bucharest's Palace Hall, right behind the former royal palace. The Berlin Wall had collapsed already, but in Bucharest the Congress decided that nothing in Romania's system should be altered. Yet even Ceausescu sensed that his constituents needed something: out of the blue, pathetically, he denounced the Nazi-Soviet pact of 1939, voided this morning by Moldova announcing its independence. His tirade was hollow. When, on December 15, crowds in Timisoara protested the banishment of a dissident local priest, a Hungarian, Ceausescu again tried to press the nationalist button: the priest was a foreign agitator. But the protesters started shouting: "Down with the Ration Cards!" and "Down with Dictatorship!" Ceausescu formed an emergency commission chaired by his wife, ordered the army and Securitate to shoot, and flew to Iran.

No record of these last days in the Ceausescus' lives has been pieced together yet, but their visit to the former Persian empire was in itself a climax of absurdities. It went like clockwork, filled with what Ceausescu had come to like best: official nothing. In the meantime, on the seventeenth, the army and Securitate fired on the crowds in Timisoara, killing almost a hundred demonstrators (including several children), and injuring over two hundred. A woman was bayoneted by soldiers. The dead bodies were dragged from the streets and piled into trucks headed to Bucharest. The enraged crowds looked for the bodies of loved ones in cemeteries, and that was where they dug up those homeless paupers' corpses which were photographed by the Western journalists.

The shooting in Timisoara resulted in two developments that complicated Ceausescu's plans. The crowds became enraged and continued to march and battle the armed columns. And the chaos helped the news of the uprising spread to the rest of the country, not by phone or radio, but by word of mouth, like in the Middle Ages. After a few days of cooperating in the slaughter, the army stopped taking orders from the Ministry of Defense or from the Securitate, and started to side with the revolution. When Ceausescu came back, Timisoara was still in full insurrection. He ordered massive reinforcements sent there, and prepared a giant "solidarity" rally in Bucharest, to denounce an invasion of "foreign imperialists." Based on the example of Timisoara, Ceausescu's aides should never have let him call that rally, but by this time some were already thinking about how to depose him, and save their own skins. More than likely, they decided to ride Bucharest's own uprising, and possibly aided it by slipping their agents into the crowds, to yell "Timisoara!" and "Assassin!" The crowds would have done it without instigation anyway. The solidarity rally turned into a mass mutiny, and since the television was there, as usual, to glorify the boss, the whole scene was captured on tape.

Hearing himself called assassin, Ceausescu reacted as if thunderstruck. He stood mute for a second, his waving arm frozen in the air. Then he babbled about an increased allowance for large families and students, an offer so puny that the boos and catcalls continued. As all the cameras and mikes were trained on the balcony and the Ceausescu pair, one mike caught Elena whispering urgently to Nicolae, *"Mai da-le ceva!"* (Give 'em a little extra!) More in touch with reality, she knew how pathetic his offer was. But he couldn't think of a little extra, and was whisked from the balcony by his aides, back into the building which we were now visiting.

From this moment on, he and his wife had only four days to live. Ceausescu called an emergency meeting of the executive bureau of the central committee of the party, which decreed a state of siege on Romania's entire territory. Troops, both Securitate and army, moved to cordon off the RCP building. In the city, the crowds swelled, and the Securitate snipers started shooting from roofs, while columns of tanks began to labor towards downtown.

The lieutenant was now describing to us the furious unleashing of the crowds: "They kept coming, in waves. Beaten out of Palace Square, they flowed back towards the Intercontinental Hotel and the University. There they regrouped, and flowed down Balcescu and Magheru Boulevards, with soldiers and tanks in pursuit. Other crowds swelled and flowed behind the soldiers and tanks, so that although the soldiers had beaten a wave, now they had to turn and face another one. The waves seemed to always flow back towards the building of the RCP, because the people knew that he and she were still in there. They yelled a spontaneously coined rallying cry: 'Nu plecam acasa! Mortii nu ne lasa!' (We won't go home, the dead won't let us!) They passed several bookstores with windows crammed with Ceausescu's works on 'building of the multilaterally developed society.' They broke the windows, trampled the books, and set them on fire. As the hours passed, the crowds' chants became more confident. Now they felt that they were masters of the streets. Already some soldiers had taken the magazines out of their automatic weapons, and showed them to the crowds, signalling that they wouldn't fire."

Before midnight, however, Securitate troops mounted severe attacks on the crowds, sweeping the streets around University Square, using tear gas and then live bullets. They narrowed the area occupied by the demonstrators, shooting at them (forty people were killed within an hour), pushing them into the subway station, beating them with rubber truncheons, and finally arresting hundreds of demonstrators, who were hauled away in army trucks. Meanwhile, city workers who had been bussed into the area started spreading paint over the anti-Ceausescu graffiti and cleaning the pools of blood. Revolutionaries fleeing from the charging tanks caught glimpses of their martyrdom already being erased. "Some people told me," said the lieutenant, "that seeing the city workers inspired them not to leave the streets. Not another whitewash, they thought."

I interrupted him. "Where were you that night?"

"That night and the next, when the terrorists launched their last and heaviest attacks, I was at Otopeni Airport, guarding the planes. The first night, there were no attacks, but it was clear that something unusual was going on downtown: helicopters kept flying out from the airport, and our officers were constantly on the phone with their military commandants in Bucharest. The first day of the revolution, the papers published pictures of Ceausescu's visit to Iran, and the radio broadcast its standard program, as if nothing happened. The next day, around 10 A.M., the radio announced the state of siege. A half-hour later, the news broadcast that the defense minister, General Milea, had committed suicide, after "betraying" Romania by not ordering the troops to open fire. Then, at eleven, a "bomb" exploded: General Stanculescu, one of the deputy defense ministers, ordered the army back to the barracks."

That meant that the armored shield between the RCP and the demonstrators was no more. Thousands of people flowed back downtown, realizing that the tyranny was collapsing. They saw the army units deployed around the RCP withdraw. Then there was the last and most amazing appearance of Ceausescu himself. As if out of history's box of tricks, he popped onto the balcony again. Pale from sleeplessness, hoarse, with a megaphone in his hand, he tried to address the crowds. But he was incoherent. The crowds were already bursting in through entrance A, practically under him. He was pulled in by the Securitate. Ceausescu himself decided that they would leave the building by helicopter—one was already revving up on the roof. As the crowds stormed up the stairs, the Ceausescus and their bodyguards stepped into an elevator and rode up to the top floor. In an ironic coincidence, there was a sudden power cut, and the elevator jammed between two floors. The crowds were in the building, and would have captured the Ceausescus, had they known that they hadn't left yet. Elena panicked, realizing that if they were found, they would be lynched; but the power came back, the elevator hurtled up to the top floor. Then the door to the roof wouldn't open. A bodyguard gave it a volley from his automatic, and the Ceausescus made it onto the roof, and into the helicopter.

Later, it was discovered that Ceausescu had ordered four helicopters, for himself, the politburo of the party, and choice government members. That only one was there proves that someone made sure that only the Ceausescus could leave; most henchmen were ready to turn themselves in, and hoped to be spared. The Ceausescus went up in the air, but flew only a few minutes before the pilot claimed that his machine was low on fuel. Besides, he told them, it had been spotted by radar. They had to land. In a few more minutes, the Ceausescus and two Securitate were standing by a freeway, hitchhiking. They commandeered one car, and drove off quarrelling over where to go, finally heading for Tirgoviste, the royal capital of Vlad Dracula. There they were captured by the local military, and held until an ad hoc tribunal formed by the National Salvation Front arrived to put them on trial. The trial was brief and superficial, and its videotape showed only the defendants, while the voices of the prosecution were heard offstage. Were the prosecutors afraid that surviving Securitate forces would target them? Perhaps. The tape of the trial ended with a still shot of Ceausescu and Elena lying by the wall of an army building, dead. And that was the end of "Romania's golden era under the wise leadership of the most beloved son of the people, Nicolae Ceausescu, and his devoted comrade in life and work, academician Elena Ceausescu."

Thus ended Europe's strangest first pair. They were a most rapacious and illiterate duo, and also one of the most durable: in this century, Ceausescu and Elena reigned longer than any European king or queen, twice as long as Hitler, three years longer than Mussolini, and only five years less than Stalin.

And now, we were looking at some of their trappings of power, and they seemed shockingly mediocre. The RCP building had been built in the thirties, in that square *stile fascista* that had swept all over Europe, mixing cubism with vestiges of Greek temple. It was all square shapes and surfaces, apart from its round bulky pseudo-doric columns of gray cement. The doors were big square glass panes framed in metal cases, the windows more square panes, blindfolded from inside by stiffly hanging white curtains. That so many famed leaders, from Nixon to Chou En-lai to Golda Meir to Gorbachev, had been here was amazing. The lieutenant led us out onto the balcony where Ceausescu had uttered his last speech. A floor of square tiles, a square stone bannister with little columns absurdly shaped like miniature amphorae. A rain gutter of dark square holes. This building was a hymn to the square. Ahead, Victory Avenue, now without crowds, was a shapelessly wide street streaked by traffic. The midday heat was heavy. Across the avenue, atop the royal palace, a tricolor flag without the Marxist hammer and sickle hung limply. That undistinguished sight spelled freedom.

"Now, I can let you step inside his office," said the lieutenant, using that indescribably explicit "he." "But only for a minute."

I nodded. A minute was all I needed.

He went ahead. I remembered the hallway to the office as darker, and maybe it was. Now, I was intensely aware of its squareness. Its paint was peeling. He opened an unexceptional door, into the little antechamber before the office, and I suddenly remembered a plain middle-aged woman in a gray two-piece suit who sat typing in that antechamber fifteen years ago: his secretary. There was no one in there now. The lieutentant opened the door to the office.

I stepped inside, hearing Iris's footsteps behind me. I was shocked to see how well lit it was. The furniture was the same as I remembered; it hadn't been torn by the crowds that had broken inside, it wasn't even distressed by time. I faced a square room with an indifferent carpet, a large conference table, a big desk set at the room's other end, perpendicular to the conference table, and a book rack behind the desk, with two doors set evenly on each side of the book rack—table, desk, book rack, doors were all absolutely square, of course. The conference table had six chairs on each side and two more at the ends, twelve in all, and was enlivened by a vase with flowers: yellowed, droopy gladiolas. Like in a principal's office. The drooping flowers looked like an insult to the room's geometrical regularity.

I stepped towards the desk. So. This was the big desk behind which "he" sat on the day he received me, correcting a book he had not written. The desk seemed very low now, as if buried in the floor by the passage of time. On the wall behind Ceausescu's desk had been a shield of the Socialist Republic of Romania. Now it was replaced with the shield of the young democracy, a heraldic quarter held up by a vulture with a cross in its beak. The man who X-rayed me with his eyes from behind his desk was gone.

For a few seconds I experienced the crassest, basest satisfaction that I was here and he was not. That he had croaked, while I, alive, moved around freely in his old territory.

Then I realized another deep, yet simple fact.

The man I was then, when I stood in front of Ceausescu's desk, was also gone. I remembered him, but he was gone.

* * *

What exactly was the feeling I was experiencing? Was it a brusque liberation, for the old me was not in me anymore, except as a trove of memories? Was it a sense of loss, a sadness, a reflective nostalgia, a pensive strength, what?

I could not analyze my feelings but my new self took a step forward. And talked in my mind to Ceausescu, about the very different ways in which we were here no more. He was dead, while I was alive, and had changed. That difference threw a harsh spotlight on both of us.

I had changed, become a new individual. Before he died, he had never changed, even though his life encompassed such a spectacular rise, to a nation's pinnacle, and then into the club of the world's major players, even though in that club he was always second-rate.

My mind recalled every single memory I had of him, and they combined into an increasingly more accurate picture, until I saw him sitting in that empty chair—I saw him clear as day, in his most typical stance, that of a monotonously self-interested zombie. From various recesses, pouches, and creases of my memory, like from the folds of an old gunny sack, I remembered his face, poses, expressions. I remembered his gestures, inhibited and stiff, but above all so very few. His words too were incredibly few: just the party slogans, which he spat out over and over, and a few key phrases with which he handled other humans, like the one he'd thrown at me at our first encounter, on that lawn with journalists scrambling about for chairs: You don't like working? To a casual observer that might've sounded straightforward and directed to the core of the matter, yet it was actually simpleminded, indeed stupid: he'd asked me to that lawn to get acquainted with a journalist, not to see me working carrying chairs. The memory of that encounter rammed home something else, which I'd always known but never quite formulated: everything about him was scant, insufficient, numerically low, poor in variants, barely there. What you saw was what you got. Despite his peasant shrewdness, he was an open book. Had it not been for the system's fixation with secrecy, everyone would quickly have realized that this leader's linearity was not a mark of character, nor were his brief utterances deep, let alone oracular. He was short in stature, brief in speech, unvaried in expression because he was primitively simple. He was a one-trick pony, a two-tone portrait, a three-note speech. He was lacking, sterile, uninventive. He was inadequate.

But his fundamental inadequacy was compensated for by an ego as exaggerated as it was incapable of understanding reality. In a flash, I remembered him with the leaders he'd met on his South American tours. With Castro. During one of Castro's interminable speeches, I'd watched Ceausescu waiting for his turn to speak. His face had an air of mute skepticism, and of patience; but that air was illuminated now and then by a very brief and hard to spot inner smile, and a tiny jerk of the head. Something cracked his features, stretched his lips, gave his eyes a pale glint, and made him nod. Then back to patience. Then again the glint, the crack, the nod.

Had that reaction not been so brief, I would've recognized it sooner as a self-satisfied confirmation, a kind of "I told you so, didn't I?" As if Ceausescu had seen through Castro. Or through Nixon. I'd noticed that grin and nod during Nixon's visit too. The much taller, self-assured American stood next to the Balkan dwarf, and it wasn't the American who grinned seeing through the dwarf, it was the other way round. Ceausescu saw through other people, or thought he did. He thought he saw their weaknesses. His "I told you so" was based on an enormous conviction that no human was smarter, or more powerful, than him. It was the conviction of an illiterate Balkan goatherd, that he, the shepherd, was the center of the known and unknown universe. So, he waited for some kind of flaw to show in that other human, and if he thought he'd glimpsed it, there came the I told you so. In between, he was patient.

Amazingly, two years after his death, over fifteen years after seeing him last, I understood him.

I remembered clearly now that he'd shown that little grin and nod after I told him that I was ready to spread his Marxist thought in America. Till then, he couldn't figure me out, or my desire to go to America, and treated both with his natural hostility. But when I gave him the most transparent, most obvious line of adulation, he chuckled to himself: I told you so. Here was the key to my persona: I was one of his fans. Why did I want to go to America? Because as one of his fans, I was dying to promote his importance in America. Great. Done. Give him his passport.

In the light of that scarcity of character, I saw his life as a series of lucky misunderstandings, all based on an initial misunderstanding of his own importance. Put in power along with the whole RCP by the Russians, then hoisted to the top by Gheorghiu, the stuttering peasant had found himself in the stratosphere of importance, and that had been too much for his reasoning abilities. He had decided that he was ordained by fate. From then on, as illustrated by the fallibility of others, by the loyalty, by the servility and adulation of others, he would be ever right, ever victorious. No wonder he'd had the nerve to stand up to the Russians.

And no wonder that he ignored the imminence of the revolution to the very end. When it did occur, his self-preservation instincts, awake in any sane individual, repeatedly malfunctioned.

He could not change with the times, because he had never changed. He was always an ego making up for all other adaptive functions. In his functional blindness, he thought himself the most beloved son of the people, the genius of the Carpathians, the chosen of fate, truth itself, and all the other hyperboles sung to him by his court poets. Those lies filled his life, which, though busy with political action, was on a certain plane totally static, just as his stiff movements seemed not so much lived, as simply performed by his body.

Back then, as I stood in his office and groped for something to win his favor with, I sensed that blowing the thickest, grossest puff up his rear would be precisely the move to turn him around, and that in just a few seconds. I got his number then, better than he would ever get mine, and the proof was this day, when I stood in his empty office, not just alive, but a survivor in a totally new set of circumstances, a victor in a new game.

If ever there was triumph, I felt it now. I'd done it against his programming, in spite of my late start and distant birthplace, in spite of everything. And not by luck or chance. I'd done it by human endeavor.

I started tittering silently, as I stood in front of his vacated desk. Yes, I did like working, Comrade Secretary General. You died without ever finding out how much I liked it, but then, you never even found out that people like me existed.

I heard a man clear his throat behind me. That young Romanian lieutenant. "Mr. Popescu . . ."

"Yes, yes."

I answered, but did not turn. For I was afraid that this incredible moment would be finished, that this incredible connection beyond time could be broken. I had him right here in front of me, the boss. And he couldn't escape my reckoning, he couldn't in any fashion deny that I'd tricked him back then, I'd beaten him. Of the two beasts he and I were, I was the stronger, because even then, sweating, scared, acting powerless and prideless, I had elasticity and adaptability. Of life's solutions, a whole variety were available to me even then. I could choose, and improvise, and that made me smarter, and smarts meant power. My triumph was not that I had outlived him, but that I understood him.

I had tricked the boss, and that said something about bosses. Bosses of the world, beware, you're only powerful thanks to the system, and that's your infirmity. That makes you forever vulnerable, and unprepared.

"Mr. Popescu, you've been in here ten minutes. I must do my duty . . ."

And I must do mine.

I turned, made eye contact with our guide. Then with my wife. There was a slight paleness of concern on her face. She realized that I was all right, and turned to walk out ahead. I followed her, through the square door, out into the square lobby.

The lieutenant ended our tour by taking us into the elevator in which Ceausescu had fled to his helicopter. We stood in a small, padded, upholstered box, which rode up smoothly. I felt like I had tripled in size, as if gravity's pull no longer effected me. Without feeling the floor under my feet, I walked out of the elevator. There were segments of new masonry, patches of fresh paint, on the wall right by the door. The door itself, of metal painted a light oceanic gray, was new. The holes left by the bullets fired by that Securitate bodyguard had been repaired, and the door had been replaced.

A quick flight of steps led upward. At its end was the door to the helipad on the roof, now sealed by a brand-new grating.

The lieutenant explained that the city had put that grating here, to discourage vandalism. Right after Ceausescu's escape, the crowds had stormed out onto the roof, and torn off the roof slabs. Some had taken them home as souvenirs. More people showed up in the following days, even after the Ceausescus were executed, to try to carve up pieces of the helipad, as if they were bricks from the Berlin Wall.

Now, the grating prevented that. The slabs of the roof had been replaced as well, and washed repeatedly by the Bucharest rains. Now, the ever-present grass, tall, sun-bleached, sprouted from between the slabs. The sign of this new era, which started, paradoxically, with neglect.

And now it was my turn to satisfy our host. The lieutenant came from a family of professional soldiers, and was a fan of *Bullet,* so he had some very specific questions to ask. For instance, was the book's raisonneur character, my uncle Nicu, patterned after some important World War II commander? Who was hiding under the modest portrait of my uncle? No one famous, I replied. He was an actual uncle of mine, a simple captain in the corps of engineers.

"Just a captain?"

"Captain Nicu Tudor Popescu, royal corps of engineers. Fell prisoner in 1942, and spent the next eight years in Soviet gulags."

He gave it some thought. "That's commendable," he said, though I could tell that he was a little disappointed. "That was a great book. Did you ever write another one as good?"

"I hope so," I said, touched yet a little alarmed by the myth growing around that old book: did it leave enough room for the new writer I'd become? "Did you read *Burial of the Vine*?" I asked him. He blinked, trying to remember. "The one with a youngster who after being expelled from the party couldn't find a job, so he ended up a clerk in a cemetery, a Jewish cemetery?"

"Ah, yes. I heard about it, but didn't read it. You must write another one like *Bullet*. Another one about us." I found his stare hard to take, it was so passionate.

He took us back to the entrance hall, where we thanked him and shook hands. He gave my hand a healthy tug, then shot his own up to his cap—and though I was not the man I once had been, something in his gesture touched me, a sense of impossible fraternity, an honor which the old army had, which my uncle had. Maybe that honorableness was reborn when the Romanian army sided with the revolution.

Iris thanked him in English. He bent a little stiffly and touched his thin lips onto her hand. And with that chivalrous send-off, we were back outside.

"What the hell happened in there, that you're grinning like the Cheshire cat?" Iris asked me.

I tried to explain, and she understood and didn't understand, but said that she was happy to see me relieved of any pains from the past. So, where to now? I asked her how she was doing on her high heels, and she answered that if her toes started bleeding, that would be her small offering to the local history. We walked back to Magheru Boulevard, where I stopped at a newspaper stand and bought the special editions about Moldova's independence. Other people were stopping, buying, walking, and reading the papers en marche, something I'd never seen in my time, the newspapers were never that exciting. Iris glanced at the papers over my shoulder, and I had the feeling that she understood every word, and how could she not, out here the makings of life were so obvious.

"Look at this," she exclaimed.

"What?"

Black and white photos of movie stars, Hollywood movie stars, among the screaming headlines about Moldova, the political editorials, the diatribes against the "crypto-Communists." "I can't believe it," laughed Iris, "we land on Mars, and who do we find? Harrison Ford, Sharon Stone, Mel Gibson!"

I laughed too. "Actually, this Mars was always open to Hollywood." I pointed across the boulevard, to Bucharest's biggest movie theater, Scala, the first to be equipped with a cinemascope screen in the late fifties. In there, through clouds of cigarette smoke, sitting on creaky old seats, for only the cinemascope screen and projector had been up-dated, other schoolboys and I watched faded copies of *The Vikings, Spartacus, Trapeze, Fantastic Voyage*—American movies came to Romania in strange sequences, out of synch with when they were made and with what they meant as social statements in America. People queued up at the box office at six in the morning, for the lines were often two blocks long, or paid three times the tickets' price to street speculators, and in the evening gaped at *Love Story, Guess Who's Coming to Dinner,* or *In the Heat of the Night,* movies described by the Communist state as self-indictments of capitalism. Even *Whatever Happened to Baby Jane?*, released years after it was made, was billed as Hollywood's own admission that capitalism drove people to psychosis. But somehow, we stupid Romanians who went to the movies to laugh and cry and kiss and feel each other up, and eat sunflower seeds and oohh and aahh at the clothes the stars wore and the cars they drove, we were not appalled by capitalism for an instant. Or by America seen on celluloid. On the contrary, we loved that America was bad. Give us, say, *The French Connection,* or *Coming Home,* each fitting the Communist propaganda perfectly; we loved the grittiness of New York, loved that Jon Voight's character, the impotent paraplegic, went down on Jane Fonda. At its worst, America could do no wrong.

The censors knew that the propaganda had failed, they knew it from those movies' phenomenal box-office grosses; yet they continued to release Hollywood movies. Why did they do it? Because Hollywood worked magic even on the Communist censors, and if the Romanian crowds walked out of the theaters sighing "Oh, Hollywood . . . ," well, it was just Hollywood, it was unreality, and it was less threatening than Milos Forman's *The Loves of a Blonde,* or other dissident Czech movies. The big Hollywood fantasies were safe, and great to point out as tokens of freedom to visiting U.S. secretaries of state.

And thus, pell-mell in terms of genre or initial date of release, I saw *Stagecoach, Seven Brides for Seven Brothers, Cleopatra, Last Train from Gun Hill, The Poseidon Adventure, Planet of the Apes, The Seven-Year Itch,* and *Judgment at Nuremberg.* Some of those movies arrived long after their stars had already aged, and their messages had long lost their edge. But many were contemporary enough to give us images that reshaped our understanding of the world, inevitably towards an idealistic infatuation with capitalism. No wonder that once Communism fell, Eastern Europe's population would prove totally unprepared to deal with capitalism's problems, which, alas, turned out to be nothing like in the movies.

In my time, a whole nation and I sat petrified with awe and revelled in the Hollywood product, mostly shown in black and white because the regime bought one color print from the American distributor and made cheap black and white copies from it. There were never enough copies: the outer districts of Bucharest and the smaller Romanian cities had to wait their turn for a copy, which finally arrived, weeks later, months later. The films filtered down to smaller and smaller localities until they ended up in the "cine caravans" which shlepped mobile projectors and screens to every corner of rural Romania. There, in the hamlets of the Carpathians, Kirk Douglas or Julie Andrews made the same mythical gestures and uttered the same memorable lines, but by this time, the print "snowed" with stains and scratches, the admission might be paid in chickens, and the soundtrack had to compete with dogs barking and cows mooing.

When my dad took Mom out to see Humphrey Bogart, Rita Hayworth, Fred Astaire, and Ginger Rogers, they and other viewers waited outside the movie house, in the rain if it was fall, under snow if it was winter, till a man on a bicycle brought the film cans over from an earlier performance in another theater. Yet, in my parents' time as in mine, Hollywood made it to Romania. Under the Nazis, under the Commies. Nothing could keep Hollywood out.

As we lingered by the old theater, a news vendor, sixtyish, short, bulky, walked towards me. "You from America?" he asked in Romanian. Surprised, I nodded. "I can tell by your shoes," he grinned, "all Romanian Americans wear light shoes, shoes for driving." I glanced at his shoes; a heavy Romanian brand, from the times when the Danube peasants wore shoes made to last a lifetime, and was buried in them too. "You like our free press?" I nodded, and asked him if he had *Flacara,* whose editor had called me again at the Flora; I had agreed to give a press conference at his editorial office. *Flacara,* the news vendor volunteered while handing me an issue, was a press trust already, with a daily paper running four hundred thousand copies every day (I gaped at the figure), plus several weeklies, and a daily for Moldova. *Flacara*'s editor was probably a millionaire. I asked if the opposition press was distributed freely. It was, in Bucharest. In small towns and villages, news vendors pressured people to subscribe to the semigovernmental *Adevarul* or *Dimineata.* The printers delayed printing the opposition papers, and the post office forgot to deliver them. He made a disgusted face: they were paid off by "the power." Everyone knew that the fight for freedom was the fight for the media. The vendor was impatient to switch the subject: "Mr. Bush, what's he got in mind for us?"

"You mean the U.S. president?"

"Yes. We were on your side in the Gulf War. With you at every turn, bang! bang!" He imitated the pounding of a gavel.

That was true. As the U.S. built its anti-Saddam coalition, the secretaryship of the United Nations rotated to Romania. Romania's ambassador at the UN sat on the imposing rostrum, and sided with every American-sponsored resolution. "I don't know," I said, truthfully. "But the Americans sympathize with the Romanians, they know you had it hard."

"What do you do for a living?"

"I'm a teacher," I lied.

"Teach them about us," he said. "Teach them that *fara noi, nu se poate*" (without us, it won't work), he insisted with a depth of feeling that was physical, I smelled it on him. "Without us, it's not possible—and that's what he did well; he annoyed everyone into knowing that we existed."

I blurted out, "He annoyed everyone into knowing that *he* existed! And that's what the world knows about: his corruption, his cruelty, his orphan children."

The news vendor, the same one who had just complained that the power interfered with the distribution of the free press, blurted back, "So? Did the world ever know something different? Did it ever stop treating us as the worst? He at least was not taken in! He saw through them!"

"He saw nothing! Nothing that helped us Romanians!"

Here I was, plunging into the "we"!

He lowered his jaw, giving himself a gross double chin, and drilled me with his eyes. Unbelievably, he looked like a twin of that little man, five feet of adipose Balkan flesh. Sizing up the queen of England with that knowing glint in his eye: I know how you got there. Yet I remembered that I too, piloting around the likes of Snodgrass, thought angrily: Good, sock it to them, pay them back smirk for smirk and attitude for attitude! But now was not the time to reminisce. The vendor was bearing down on me bodily: "Why are you coming back here?" His eyes swept my bag, the camera strapped to my shoulder. "To take pictures of our misery, and show them to the world? Shame on you!"

I stood to full stature, swelled my chest. *"Mai moale, batrine."* (Cool it, old man). I gestured to Iris to get away from him, then walked past him, cheeks blazing. I wondered what I would do if he hit me, would I hit back at a old man? I lifted the camera, and snapped several shots of him, vindictively. And uselessly, with the lens I had on, I'd have to enlarge the shot to get the rage crusted up in his face. He showed me his fist.

We walked off, I explaining what had happened. Excessive sense of isolation. Confusion about the dead tyrant. "Your dead tyrant will gain a lasting myth," Iris said quietly.

"As what, as an architect?"

"As a first-rate, larger-than-life badass. You'll see."

We were suddenly deafened by shouts. An uneven column of young boys and girls, by all appearances students, marched with interlaced arms, shouting, *"Moldova libera! Moldova libera!"* (Moldova is free). And then, that opposition slogan, *"Ultima solutie, o noua revolutie!"* (the only solution, another revolution), and *"Monarhia salveaza Romania!"* (the monarchy will save Romania).

I snapped a picture, and they waved at me, amused. I hurried into the street, fell in step with them, started talking: I was a Romanian who hadn't seen the country in years, so why another revolution? The youngsters shouted without slowing down, "We want something new!" I argued that the monarchy was not new. "It's better than the old party clerks," a freckled youngster shouted back, "how many people would the king bring with him if he returned, perhaps a hundred? The party clerks are a few million, and they are everywhere." I asked where they were going. To University Square, the freckled one answered, to a meeting with students from Moldova. Moldova was free and wanted to unite with Romania. All that was holding her back was the presence of the Russian 14th army. I asked one last question: where were they on December 21, 1989? Several shouted that they were here, in the exploding streets. And off they went, leaving me with a fleeting physical sensation of what it was like when the streets rang with the same words, shouted repeatedly, in unison. What power.

When I joined Iris on the sidewalk again, she was angry: what was I doing plunging into that crowd? Emotions were too close to the surface here, anything could happen to me. One more episode like this, and she would get on the next plane out. I put my arms around her. "I feel so old," she whispered. "I just realized it. I used to march against Vietnam, I shouted at cops, I got hosed down, and I was never afraid. Now I am."

I hugged her. "Guess what? They'll be fine, these people."

"So tell them that. It's one thing you can do for them."

Down narrowing streets, past shady gardens and turn of the century homes, we walked to the Armenian Church, whose bells tolled through my childhood, for the church stood one block from our elementary school. Romania's Armenians came here in massive numbers after World War I, some from Turkey, others from Russia, all deeply imprinted by the killing of those two million Armenians. They settled in Bucharest, and worked, and prospered, and dreamed about a free Armenian homeland. They liked the Russians, because the Russians, compared to the Turks, had been good to the Armenians, and so they welcomed the Russians with flowers when they invaded Bucharest. The Russians, on orders from Stalin to liquidate the "bourgeoisie," arrested a number of prosperous Armenians, including all the leaders of their community.

So, years later, in Los Angeles, a certain Ara Ghemigian, formerly a Bucharest photojournalist, told me this amazing story: his father, a lawyer in the Armenian community, was deported by the Russians to Siberia, just because he was a bourgeois lawyer and an ethnic leader.

In a small Siberian village, so isolated that the deportees never tried to escape from it, he met a young Jewish woman from Lithuania who had been deported for having militated for a free Lithuania a poor Jewish girl who had mischosen her cause. The result was that in the loneliness of Siberian nights, Jew and Armenian got together, and my future acquaintance Ara was born. When the couple had served their sentence, Ara's father chose to bring his woman and son to Romania. Of three potential homes, Russia, Romania, and Lithuania, Romania was the kindest to minorities.

Thus, Ara, born a Siberian and a Soviet citizen, but ethnically a mixture of Armenian and Jew, grew up in my hometown of Bucharest. Stories he told me about his childhood played now in my mind: "My parents almost never mentioned that my mother was Jewish. My father had family in Bucharest, and friends who had known him for years, so he couldn't hide that he was Armenian. But my mother had no one. So she never told me about her holidays, and I was raised as an Armenian. It was easier, you know what the Romanians are like. I mean, they don't like Armenians either, but at least the Armenians are Christians like them."

"Ara, Romanians *say* that they don't like the Armenians. When they fled from the Turks, Romania took them in without asking questions. And you yourself said that of those three countries, Romania was easily the kindest . . ."

"Well, that's true. Don't get me wrong, Romanians are nice people. But it's best to be one of them."

So. Ara ended up in the United States. An American.

I thought of that Jewish-Lithuanian woman, who followed her husband to Romania and learned yet another language and another identity. She was often sick, Ara told me. Her body had taken too much. She died when Ara was fourteen. His identification was not with her, but with his father.

The sight of the Armenian church had reminded me of that story. Even though I was hot, the sky was cobalt blue, the temperature ninety degrees, I felt a cold breath on my flushed face. The breath of history's deception. Cold from history's cruel cheats, inflicted on so many people, who suffered, hoped, expected . . . what? A certain flag? Some did get to live under the flag of their choice. What did that bring to their lives? How much was lost, how much gained?

I felt that cold spreading, as if signalling that the chasm of nationalism gaped right under these sidewalks. How many of the bones rotting in this soil were not touched by it? Not many, I tell you, not here. And I made a vow, silent and fierce. My kids, they would be Americans. Disneyland and turkey. The Oregon Trail and the supremacy of English. That's what they would be, and I would watch to ensure that they remained that. I wanted them living wrapped in that super-nationality, America, inside which we were all something else. That was the world I'd chosen. I felt like turning towards The House of the People, to swing my fist at the ghost of that absurd little man and shout: You lost! You lost!

I gathered myself, caught a sentence uttered by my wife: "Your people have to do something about how they see themselves. They are far too negative and discouraged."

"That's what that maniac turned them into, neurotics en masse."

"It's coming from much farther back. Look at these lovely old buildings. How could the people in them let them peel like this? I know," she raised her hand as I started to object, "there was no government money, but these are their homes! They could've banded together in tenants' associations, and bought brushes and paint—they can't cost a fortune! If they couldn't pull down that ridiculous little man, because . . ." she took a breath, continued fluently, as if she'd thought this over, "because they'd told the world that they supported him, then they should've truly supported him, instead of cheating him and themselves behind his back. The Cubans are doing a better job backing Castro."

"Yes. I guess not one Cuban in four is a member of their Securitate."

"How do you know that one Romanian in four was Securitate? It was a rumor, wasn't it? Didn't you tell me that the Securitate itself started all the rumors? I'm not surprised that even the revolution is said to have been arranged!"

I took her hand. "Sweetheart. You care."

"I care because you care. This place could look good! And all these people, why are they in the streets? Why aren't they working?"

"They're in a rut. They'll get out of it, they did it before."

"They lack confidence, and social cohesion."

"Don't tell that to my family, they're such patriots."

She threw her arms up. "Oh God, don't worry, I'll behave myself, whenever we meet them. . . . By the way, is something holding you back from meeting them? I mean, it's like everything else is more important, this street, that street, Ceausescu's office, Romania's fate. . . . Why? Are you for some reason not ready to see them?"

I thought about it. And I thought of the pictures of my kids, which I carried in my wallet. Their pictures told me that I was safe here. Safe to meet anyone, to do anything. For even if something did happen to me, my genes would be alive and well, in America.

"I guess we'll see them tomorrow. I'll call Petre. I guess I'm ready."

"It's so strange," said my wife, "to meet your family for the first time years after we were married."

"Are you nervous?"

"No. But I want to like them."

I grinned. "Me too."

I wasn't joking. I hadn't seen them for so long, and I was going to appraise them with such different eyes. Also, I'd left so many, and now I would find so few. When I was growing up, ten of the thirteen Popescu boys and girls were alive. The sisters, Mia, Rodica, my godmother Puica, and Lena. The brothers, Sandu, Nicu, Dinu, Mircea, Radu, my dad, and Petre, to whose house we were now driving. The others, Stefan, Mihai, and Mitu, I didn't remember because they died before I was born or when I was still a baby.

When I had left, the brothers and sisters were still active, still in good shape, still gathering on Thursday nights in the old house, occasionally taking group pictures in which they stared straight at the camera with those haunting Popescu eyes. Now, Uncle Nicu, the soldier, the second oldest, was the family's dean of age. All the other brothers were gone, except Uncle Petre, a retired stage director. Of the girls, Rodica and Lena were no more, Mia was ailing in New York City, and Puica, my godmother, didn't leave her apartment, so we would have to visit her separately. Of course, there were still the children of those, the cousins, but not so many as you would expect, for a lot of the brothers did not have kids. Today, we were to meet Nicu, Petre and his wife Ella, their daughter Riri and son Tudor, who were my first cousins, and an older first cousin, whose name was also Tudor, son of my late aunt Rodica. Rodica was older than my father and had married quite young, so the older Tudor was now in his sixties. When I defected, the younger Tudor was six and Riri was four. Between the surviving relatives there were big jumps in age, typical of large families strung across several decades and generations.

We were getting close. An army of impersonal high-rises streamed past the car, and I narrowed my eyes to decipher the addresses. This was it, number 116, building 58. They lived up stairway A, in apartment 12, on the third floor. The madman that razed their old neighborhood forced them into this forest of numbered concrete. It was his dream to count his prisoners. He succeeded.

Stairway A was on the side of the building. Behind it, we glimpsed the bleakness of rows of overflowing garbage cans, and rows of identical parked Dacia cars. If this building complex were new and high tech, its regularity would have the hip look of science fiction. But the complex was gray and crumbling. Wherever the eye landed, there were timid improvements added by the tenants: one balcony had bars that looked homemade; a window had been walled up except for a hole to let out the stack of a wood stove; there were loaded clotheslines on virtually all the balconies, and demijohns of country wine, kids' tricycles, mops and brooms, homemade TV antennas. The curtains were made of all sorts of materials, from embroidered doily to old newspaper. The whole place had the look of an American prison: a barrenness of stone and iron animated by the junk of the inmates.

As we climbed up the stairs (I called the elevator, but it never came), there was a spill of life in front of each door. Doormats of all shapes and sizes, some with "Welcome!" woven into them; mud boots, waiting to start service again in winter; steel hoops and chains for anchoring bikes. A few doors carried cards with the names of the tenants. There was no air conditioning anywhere in the giant complex, but there were countless radios and TV sets, we heard them from behind every door.

Here it was, apartment 12.

I rang the door bell.

I heard the quick vigorous footfalls of a young male: young cousin Tudor, I guessed, zooming to open the door. So in keeping with the dutifulness of the clan's younger members.

Tudor opened the door, revealing a dark hallway—almost all Romanian hallways were poorly lit, and overpacked with clothes hanging from old-fashioned trees, even in the middle of summer. This one was no exception. Tudor's silhouette loomed lanky but muscular, and his eyes glittered in the shadowy light. I realized that I didn't know him, he was a child when I left. He had the true Popescu eyes, deep brown and sharp, and yet somehow retractive and dreamy.

"Petru!" he said in a voice that to me sounded inimitable. It had a warmth and energy that went right through me. Like we had parted yesterday. And he exuded youth almost like an aura.

I kind of lost it, pushed Iris forward, babbled something. Tudor spoke English. "Welcome, how do you do?" he greeted my wife. In that Britannic greeting, I recognized his English teacher: my uncle Nicu. Iris hesitated, then leaned as if to hug the cousin from Romania, but it was too early for a hug: they shook hands. I found Tudor so handsome, he looked almost miraculously harmonious to me, after the twisted streets and the decayed city. I hugged him, feeling a body like a rail, and wiry muscular arms.

Behind him, there was movement: his sister Riri, also my cousin, came forward.

Riri. She had been a plump little girl who loved reciting poems at Christmas and making a show of herself, while Tudor hated that. She was a young woman now. She had her mother's hair and features, and the Popescu eyes, and she smiled with utter confidence. After hugging Tudor, a rigid male squeeze, Riri's hug was graceful and fluid. Behind them, Ella, their mother: barely changed, but grayed and with glasses on. And then Petre, once tall and skinny, now tall and bulky, and almost bald.

I didn't know how we had moved from the hallway into the apartment. We were now in the living room, under the lit bulbs of a wrought-iron fixture. The living room was furnished with sixties stuff, touched up with bits of Romanian folklore: the tablecloth was in bright red geometric patterns, and there were country napkins under the flower vases. I spotted a sepia photograph of Grandpa Tudor and Grandma Riri, taken back in the twenties, and remembered that I'd seen it in the old Popescu house. I saw a table that vaguely reminded me of the family Christmas dinners. Deeper into the apartment, I saw two older men seated on chairs, with the reserved expressions of family elders waiting for youth to exhaust their greetings.

I hugged Petre. His hug was warm and sloppy. Moved, he looked at me with my father's eyes. I swept my eyes back to Iris: she was just breaking away from hugging Ella. I heard my name, Petru, Petru, Petru, and *"Ce faci, mai?"* (how are you?) repeated endlessly with a dazed wonderment that expected no answer. I repeated the same thing, *"Ce faci, mai? Ce faci, mai?"* endlessly.

Finally released from the hugs, I felt that I understood yet again. What else could we do to make sure that we were real, after all those years? That we were not ghosts, not dreams? We hugged. We got knots in our throats, started sentences, did not finish them, swallowed, stammered, babbled. And hugged.

Now they were hugging my wife. "We're so happy that Petru has a family," said Ella.

Finally I was free to face the two older men. One was my cousin Tudor, who stood with difficulty, shaking, acting reserved, frail. I'd learned from a letter from Petre that Tudor had developed Parkinson's disease some ten years ago. He had been a handsome knockout of a man, muscular, with bedroom eyes. Never married. I shook his trembling hand. I hugged his body and felt its frailness: all those beautiful muscles were gone. He had been a sportsman. He talked to me in sentences shaky like his body: "You have children, Petru, yes? Two, I hear?" Genuinely glad and interested, as men become when disease or loneliness reveal to them what they missed in life.

And finally the other old man rose. Uncle Nicu, the one I saw in so many earlier episodes of my life, starting with that childhood memory of his return from the war. Uncle Nicu, who swapped camp stories with my father-in-law when he came to visit us in California. Uncle Nicu had aged the most and yet the least. He had the same stocky allure, strong round cranium, and thoughtful eyes. Yet, his eyes belonged now in a world that I never thought he would enter. The world of thanking fate for every added day.

"Welcome home," he said solemnly. I heard him—and heard Dad, to whom he was so close. He advanced his hand, a rather small one for a soldier, an artist's or writer's hand, like my father's. I saw my father's hand in his, my father's holding a pen, writing at night in our old apartment, on that desk lit by candles. And I started to cry.

"Can't you see?" said Uncle Nicu. "Can't you see that *this girl has the typical features of the Romanian race?*"

Uncle, my dear old uncle. What made you say these emotional words? What made him say them were the pictures of my daughter Chloe.

We'd been through several rituals already. The ritual of hugging. The ritual of declaring to my wife, in English, that she was welcome, and the picture of what they would have wanted for me. She mentioned that she was of Czech descent, Jewish Czech. Followed by the ritual of declaring how friendly my kin always were to Jews. My dad was notorious for it, wasn't he? I heard the subtext: he was such an original. My folks had never been in such a situation, of welcoming a Jewish, or an American, spouse. They were clumsy at giving reassurances that were not needed, and I knew why they were giving them: Romania, Romania. They wanted Romania to have a good name.

My wife spoke very softly. "I'm glad you are my family," she said.

And we returned to the pictures, pictures of our son and daughter, of our house, of our life in California. They were examined, passed around. They elicited aaahs of wonder, and questions. Several pictures included my mother. There was an outburst of interest, those pictures were torn from each hand, accompanied by the same endless: *Ce face Nelly? Ce face Nelly?* She lived alone, and still drove a car? I responded that she no longer lived alone, that she'd had a partner for a while, that American who came to see her after they were pen pals for several months. Came to see her, and moved in with her. The exploits of the gutsy old girl left my family dreamy.

Back to the ritual of asking questions. How did Iris and I meet? What was our wedding like? How did we make money? How many books had I published, how many movies had I directed or written, did I still write in Romanian? Only letters now and then? No literature at all? What about our children, did they speak Romanian? Not at all? Iris came to my rescue, our kids don't speak Czech either, the language of her parents. Nor did she.

"America . . ." sighed Uncle Nicu, with an intonation made of dream, awe, disappointment, and yearning. My kids spoke no Romanian, that was sad. My kids spoke only English, and that was proof of the strength of America.

"Do they *know* they are Romanian?" asked Uncle Nicu.

"Of course they know. It's one of their heritages."

"How do they say Popescu?"

I pronounced our name American style. Poe-pess-que.

"Amazing," said Petre. He sat right next to me. Throughout the afternoon, he'd kept himself close, smiling each time I looked at him. He was always one of the family's extroverts; it was no wonder that he ended up in the theater. I smiled back, revelling in a closeness that hadn't been interrupted by time, or tinged by jealousy or attitudes. He was not the one who asked the questions about my kids' Romanianness. He wasn't concerned about making Romania look good. He was a big six-foot-tall tower of affectionate curiosity, my uncle Petre, and I ate him up.

Throughout all this, the TV set was on, volume low, broadcasting incessantly from Chisinau, the capital of now independent Moldova. The Popescus had been watching the Moldovan celebrations while waiting for us to arrive. I asked them their feelings about a possible union with Romania. They were skeptical. "It will take a long time, and I don't know if the Moldovans really want it," said Nicu, the soldier who fought for uniting Moldova with Romania back in '41. "Because we didn't treat them very well when we had them with us, in the twenties and thirties. Bessarabia (Moldova's historic name) was viewed like a kind of Siberia. Nobody wanted to go there."

"They're different, the Moldovans," said Ella. "They're too Russian. But it's good that they are independent. It's good to have another country between us and Russia."

The older Tudor asked if we planned to hop over to Chisinau. I answered that there was no time, I had to interview the current leaders, including the president, and visit the orphanage of Nicoresti. That produced shock: Why would we want to waste a day driving out there to see those orphans wallowing in their own filth? That's exactly the point, I explained. Those children were an international concern now, a consciousness issue. Uncle Nicu made a face: I should take Iris to Sinaia, to show her the royal castle at Peles. I slid off the subject, asked my two younger cousins if they liked medical school. "As much as I can like something second best," said Riri. "You know that Dad forbade me to become an actress."

"I crushed that foolishness like a true Balkan father," laughed Petre, while Riri's eyes glazed over, as if after the loss of a dream. Iris scanned her with curiosity. "You're not serious. Did you really not do it because your father said no?"

"That's what daughters are like back here," responded the future doctor. "He said no, they said no," she looked around to include her mother in her reproachful stare, "and I listened."

"You can go back to it, Riri," said Iris. "Anytime you want, you're so young."

"After medical school? It's all right, I'm over it now," she said, looking like she wasn't over it at all.

"I made dinner," said Ella, as if to kill a dangerous subject. "Iris, I hope you are hungry. Petru, you still remember Romanian food?"

We ate. Taste this, Petru; good, huh? Have more, you haven't had it for so long, we can tell, you must've forgotten its taste. Have more, Iris, you didn't eat anything. You mustn't be afraid of Romanian food, it's light. I felt the soul that Ella had put in the cooking, I imagined the talk in the kitchen: Let's make this, and this, Petru hasn't had them in years. I found myself unable to mention that I took Iris to Romanian restaurants in L.A., restaurants where the food was better than anything we'd eaten the past few days in Romania. I mentioned that we had a Romanian cookbook, that Iris made *mamaliga* (Romanian polenta), that my kids, at Easter, painted Romanian Easter eggs with me, out of respect for Dad's culture. Yes, we did that, colors to paint Easter eggs were sold in many stores in America.

I'd forgotten what this Romanian food tasted like. It was good, and heavy, basic, essential, to fill you up, to last you through an unexpected famine. I washed it down with red Pietroasa wine—its taste was not as smooth as I remembered, but it went with the food. I experienced another realization: my senses were back home, finally, and they loved it. An enormous part of this need to revisit was sensorial—I needed the colors, the smell, the touch, even if they were not pretty, refined, sweet, that didn't matter. I remembered my mother-in-law, saying, "I'd like to go back to Zhdenev, and put my hand in the river." Now I knew what she meant.

"You're drinking a lot," my wife whispered to me.

"Am I?" I reached under the table and took her hand.

"Kind of. I don't care, you're not driving." Her eyes reviewed the table. "Your folks must've spent a little fortune to prepare this meal."

"They did."

Petre was seated to my left, and Nicu across from me. From their combined features, *Dad's face* floated forward. I closed my eyes, and saw him at the table, listening to the others, kneading in his fingers a piece of bread, a habit that annoyed Mom. Dad, why did you have to leave Mom? Had you not left Mom, I might have not left Romania. I rose and asked where the bathroom was. Once in the bathroom, I locked the door and turned the sink tap on—a good Commie tap ought to make plenty of noise. This one didn't let me down. It splashed like a spring flood, while I cried.

I got myself together and examined the bathroom. No, there wasn't an old soap box by the john, with squares cut from Commie daily papers. There was toilet paper, factory-cut, in little folded squares held up against the wall by a wire holder. The paper was a pale pink, and its graininess was apparent to the naked eye. The toilet was the old European type, flushed by a chain ending in a porcelain pommel yellowed by the many palms that had rubbed it as they pulled it down. The aged mirror's edges were invaded by an irregular greenness that made the sharp focus area in its midst look gothic, like an ancient looking glass in a vampiric castle. The tiles shone, scrubbed too many times, the bathtub sparkled, scrubbed too many times. I recognized that scoured cleanness, I recognized it with my senses: the spic-and-span unaffluent cleanness of a Romanian family determined to maintain its standards against any historic barbarities. Ella, the unsung hero of this household, taught school (French, the second language of civilized Romanians), and scrubbed and cleaned and cooked, and joined Petre in disapproving of cousin Riri's plans to become an actress. They didn't want to lose her to the chaos of an artistic life. They did the right thing, cousin Riri. And if you didn't rebel and run from home to the nearest drama school, it means that you agreed with them. I could tell by the way you and your brother sat next to your parents today, that between the four of you ran that blessed fluid of a normal family life. It was there, connecting you. We, my father, my mother, and I, lost that fluid, lost it with the death of my brother. It came back into my life many years later, with marriage, with fatherhood.

I jumped: the sink was brimming. I imagined it flooding Uncle Petre's water bill. I turned off the tap, washed my face, combed my hair.

As I walked back into the dining room, Tudor finished saying something in English. The Popescus were laughing. Tudor turned towards me: "You heard this one? Maggie Thatcher visits Romania. Chatting with Ceausescu, she comments that the Romanian language is wonderful, but so hard to learn. 'Tell me about it,' sighs Ceausescu."

I started laughing hard—laughter and nervous release mixed together. The Popescus were telling their new in-law anti-Communist jokes.

Telling those jokes was the juice of Romania's social life—thousands of times, my friends and I stood at parties, in dance halls, in the streets, and while a few of us spied over our shoulders so as not to be surreptitiously joined by some Securitate stool pigeon, one of us told a political joke. We listened and laughed, incorporated in the "we" in its most tolerable form: anti-government humor. All of us waited our turns to tell our jokes; each of us had a practiced technique of modulating our voices suspensefully towards the punch line, which we usually spewed hard and fast. Each joke was a plunge into absurdity or self-deprecation, each encapsulated years and years of Communist life, not to speak of Marxist economics, sociology, and history. For telling such jokes, or listening to them, untold numbers of people were jailed, or lost their jobs, in some cases even died. So let's hear them, and laugh. Laughter was our special form of reverence towards the suffering that these jokes symbolized.

"Two Romanian housewives meet. One carries an empty shopping bag. The other asks: You going to the market? No, I just got back, the one with the empty bag replies."

Iris didn't get it, then she did. She smiled. I could tell that her smile was strained. The Popescus went on. Shaving, a Romanian asks his image in the mirror: of the two of us, which one is Securitate? Iris still didn't laugh. They went on: Adam and Eve were Romanian, only two Romanians could go naked and barefoot and with an apple for lunch, and claim that they lived in Paradise. Iris got a look that worried me: her forehead was wrinkled, her cheeks pale, her body tense on her seat. I laughed at one joke after another, and they kept coming. What was Hitler's punishment in hell? To translate Marx's complete works into Hebrew. Were there thieves in Communism? No, for there was nothing to steal. Since the revolution, Romanian optimists learned English, Romanian pessimists learned Chinese, and the ones in the know learned Russian. American prohibition tried to put an end to drinking; Communism tried to put an end to eating. A Securitate brought in a suspect. What did he do? asked the commandant. Nothing, the Securitate replied, I was so vigilant, I got him before he could do anything. Nudist colonies were multiplying in Romania. The reason? No one could afford clothes. What were Romania's economic prospects in '92? Worse than in '91. But better than in '93. A sign at the Intercontinental Hotel read: Don't water the flowers, it makes the bugs rusty. Could a Romanian dog have a coronary? Yes, if he lived a Romanian's life. My wife took a deep breath; I wondered if the unfamiliar food had upset her stomach. She caught my glance, gave me a brief smile: I'm okay. So what's happening in Romania, now that the political opposition is legal? Everyone's in the opposition party, so we still have a one-party system. A Briton, an American, and a Romanian bragged about which one of their nations had more courage. The Briton claimed the honor: one Briton in ten died at sea, and they were still sailing. The American topped him: one American in seven died in a car crash, and they were still driving. The Romanian topped him: one Romanian in four was Securitate, and they still told anti-Communist jokes. The reason why the Securitate was not disbanded after the revolution? There would've been millions of unemployed. I was not laughing at the jokes anymore, but Iris looked better—the color was returning to her cheeks. What's a dictatorship? A society in which all that's not forbidden is mandatory. When were the world's first free elections? In Genesis 2, when God made one woman and then told Adam, "Choose a wife." Late one night, after the revolution, citizen Popescu heard a knock on his door (I explained to Iris that our name was so common in Romania, most characters in jokes were named Popescu). Who's there? asked Popescu. A gruff voice replied: the Free Romanian Securitate!

That one was terrific. A nation's feelings packed in one punch line. All the Popescus laughed. I spoke across their laughter. Great jokes, all of them. But let's stop now. Enough.

We ate Romanian preserves, served with iced water and thick Romanian coffee. The preserves were a meal in themselves. Some, made from quinces or from bitter cherries, tasted like nothing Iris had ever had. Now we were discussing Romania's image in the West.

Uncle Nicu was leading. When Ceausescu sold Jews and polluted rivers, hung out with Arafat and put orphans behind barbed wire, his marquee value in the West was unaffected. To support our man in Bucharest was correct political thinking. The West loaned him millions of dollars, of which today's Romania didn't get a fraction. Romanian dissidents were confused: how could they be against Ceausescu when Carter loved him? Now the West wanted Romania to have dissidents again, because of the assumption of crypto-Communism. Today, the Romanians were the West's favorite barbarians, and they in turn saw the West as a bunch of hypocritical moralists. A serious situation. "Why are we treated so unfairly?" the old soldier asked over and over. "We lost a thousand people in the revolution; the other Communist lands lost not a soul. And now to be treated like this?"

Dear beloved uncle. Whose voice reminded me so much of my father's that I had to grit my teeth to stay cool. A debate about the country's image, oh how my dad would've plunged into it. You fought the Iron Guards, Uncle, and then the Russians, and after being a prisoner for years you returned, and were thrown out of the army, and humiliated and persecuted, but still you picked up your engineer's ruler and went back to work, helping Romania's construction needs, if not the Communists. And you never complained, and never took a penny more than your salary. Can I tell you what I think? Do I dare?

Iris had been distracted into a conversation with Riri. Grateful for her inattention, I leaned over the table and imparted almost conspiratorially that it wasn't the Western papers, or the Western lobbies that gave us a doubtful name, at least not them alone. There was this sense that the Romanians hadn't come clean as yet, though they suffered so much. Because, look: even the army that crushed the Iron Guards, the army that was your life, Uncle, it also had units that slaughtered Jews in that slice of Russia called Transnistria. Marshal Antonescu, now remembered by many Romanians as a tragic anti-Russian hero, he resisted the final solution in Romania, but the soldiers who killed in occupied territories were still under his command. Most Romanians didn't know that those killings happened, not even now. The king's government didn't come clean about that tragedy after it took power in 1944, and the Communists didn't come clean, though they found proof, and records, and names of executioners and victims and witnesses—because now it was time for something else, the building of Communism. And the nation had suffered so much already. Coming clean would've meant even more suffering. But let me put that one aside, let me not sound like a fresh zealot. Always, the sense of our suffering overcame that of our errors. I'm not being original when I mention the disappearance of the Securitate—where are its legions, in what court of law are they being tried? In the court of bitter jokes? I don't buy that the Securitate still pulls the strings, but I'm convinced that the new democracy could debunk them en masse if it wanted to. But . . . there are other things to do, more pressing things. So that piece of history, again, is to remain unclean.

And what about the ex-Communists? The opposition is crying that the infrastructure is full of ex-Communists, and the Western press echoes their cry. So? Big fucking revelation, we all know that. Over three million former party members cannot be erased from society, and the competent ones must be allowed to go on, to work. I've heard their explanations, their recantations, they are convincing or not convincing, it doesn't matter. What I've heard so little of is true regret. No one says I'm sorry, truly sorry. No one feels sorry, not towards the world, but about themselves, within themselves. *That* is the problem. Everyone's sealed up in an armor of aggressive or defensive historic excuse. Just like at all times in our history.

"Wait a minute," protested my uncle Nicu.

But I was too far gone. In 1907, Romania's landless peasants rioted against work contracts that were obscenely ungenerous, and killed scores of landlords and overseers. The army, the nation's *army,* Uncle, the shield of the land's freedom, attacked the peasants with sword and cannon, and killed eleven thousand of them without arrest or trial, in punishment for a few hundred lynched landlords. And no one came clean about that either. The king wasn't deposed. The political life remained the same. The peasants, those who survived, bowed over the plow again, and that was the end of it. Old story. Plenty of Romanians fall, few conclusions are drawn.

Uncle Nicu understood. He looked back at me as if from the depth of his being. Petre, my voluble and affectionate younger uncle, listened to this with concern. He didn't want the dean of age to feel bad, or me, the returning son, to feel bad. Don't worry, Uncle Petre, I'll wash this off in pain of my own. I defected, I cheated on hell, and won my great new life on the other side, but up to a few years ago, I kept my roots buried. Deep inside, under constant denial. So really, I'm not judging now. I'm suggesting.

"You're suggesting," said Uncle Nicu, "that we should feel even more shame than we do?"

"Not shame. Responsibility."

"By digging up a bloodied horrible past? And who would do that? And who would be interested in listening?"

I knew what he was saying. That was my question too: who would be listening? Perhaps no one. The Romanians, the Bulgarians, the Russians, the Poles, they were interested in something else. In catching up with the post-industrial age, in leisure, money, power. Let's skip over clearing our conscience like over a muddy stream. My uncle Nicu was as much a survivor as anyone worth that name. An hour earlier, I'd offered to send him medication from America, to pay for it; his monthly pension was 60,000 *lei,* equivalent to sixty dollars. He turned me down with the soft dignity I remembered: "Thank you, Petru, I have all I need, right here." Honor above all. Even now, in his well-preserved clothes— an old-fashioned blazer, brown trousers, and a dark tie, he looked good, showed no loss of standards. When I wrote to him that I was marrying Iris, he wrote back to congratulate me, adding a brief P.S.: "Remember! Children!" It was a loving order. I breathed in relief, as he put his hand on my arm.

"Petru, you're one of the family, so you'll understand what I mean. If we Romanians weren't so few . . ."

"We're not that few, Uncle, that's precisely the issue. We were always numerous enough to stand scrutiny, we just felt we weren't. But now the family's enlarging. The world's the family, Uncle, and it wants responsibility, not excuses."

Petre stared from me to Uncle Nicu and back. In the silence, I heard Iris talking with the old Tudor, who complained that Bucharest had become a crime jungle, and it was all over the papers, the radio, the TV. Iris laughed softly, gave an imitation of America's evening news: There was a drive-by shooting in this neighborhood, an abduction in that one, a hostage situation in a third. There are fires upstate, a virus outbreak was traced to a restaurant chain, a serial killer is at large, and a rapist is returning to his hometown. And that's it for tonight, sleep well, folks, you got off.

I said, "Petre, doctors make good money in America. Are Riri or Tudor interested in practicing in America?"

"I don't think so," said Petre. "Riri's getting very serious about a boy, a colleague from medical school, I wouldn't be surprised if she decided to marry him. Anyway, please, Petru, don't put ideas in their heads."

"Don't worry, you tyrant Balkan dad. If they don't want to leave, they won't leave. I don't want them to leave either. I fled because the land was Communist, remember?"

"A Communist land," grumbled Uncle Nicu, "which had dignity, wouldn't you say? Culture, safety of the streets," compliments of the Securitate, I commented silently, "the charm of our old-world manners, inexpensive service, and the respect of the big powers."

"Uncle!" I was appalled. "Stop!"

He stopped. This had been too much for him. I got up, tied my arms around his torso, and pressed, to hug out the past, to squeeze out from between us that invisible border made of time spent apart, of life lived differently. Was it vanishing? I couldn't tell. I stepped back. He panted. When he spoke again, his voice gurgled emotionally. "You look so much like your father."

We said good-bye when it was almost time for dinner with that Mr. B. who had appeared so incongruously at the airport; he was probably already waiting for us at the hotel. There was the ritual of Iris and me hugging, Iris and me being hugged, plus assorted handshakes, pats on the back, smiles, wishings of see you soon, you're not disappearing again, Petru, are you, oh no, we're here for the whole week—what an immensity of time, after over fifteen years of absence. We descended the stairs escorted by almost the whole family. More hugs outside, on the sidewalk. The older Tudor waved shakily from the balcony. The younger Tudor stepped into the roadway to flag us a taxi.

So we had dinner with Mr. B. at Bucharest's only Chinese restaurant—one of the two worst Chinese meals in our lives (the other had been in Canton, Communist China). It was an inhibited, though interesting affair. All the themes discussed with feeling by my family were brought up again by Mr. B. from the government's position. He was ingenious in his facts, and almost convincing. I felt like stopping him, and confessing that I both saw through his words, and cared. He gave me the impression of an intelligent man caught in events that had disappointed him. He also mentioned several times that the Romanians abroad had to "do something," their homeland was desperate.

The dinner was brief, because we were tired. He dropped us back at the Flora, where Iris took off her high-heeled shoes, which she had worn today against my advice; her bruised feet made me wince. She didn't care about them, though her threshold of pain was usually quite low. She told me that she'd found my family's political jokes painfully self-deprecating, they reminded her of ghetto humor, which she hated. My people, from the Popescus to Mr. B., had to change their thinking. Putting themselves down, then blaming the put-down on others. They had to change their act, and by themselves. The West could not save them nor could I. "They think you and others like you can," she went on, "and that's the danger: they want others to do their job. And you'd be so flattered to be asked!" Bingo there, Wife. "They have to stop pretending, their stuffing shows anyway. But they're not worse than others, and by that same token, they're not so damn unique." Bingo again. "And I don't care if it sounds corny, they have to put some *love* in their lives." Bingo, bingo, bingo. She walked with her bruised feet, over to me. "I was so sad the other day. When I asked you if we would have married, had we met here. And you said no, because we're different."

"I never said that."

"You did." She looked at me with the special anxiety of certain married moments, when reassurance needs to be given even late and against credibility.

I took her in my arms. What the hell did she think I was, a weakling? I braved the censorship, I snatched my exit to freedom from Ceausescu himself, I was a toughie. I would've married her anywhere any time. We kissed, a long kiss, eyes closed.

During that kiss, my cousin Sandu from New York, the building contractor, appeared in my mind. He didn't know his father while growing up, he wasn't allowed an education, he did his army time in a work detachment with political offenders and criminals. He had one simple piece of advice for me, when we reconnected in America: Cousin Petru, be tough. He gave himself the same advice, and made it in the union jungle of New York City construction work, got an ulcer, survived the ulcer, made money, married a blonde, had a strapping son. When he visited Romania—rarely—he stayed like a lord at the Intercontinental Hotel.

I'll be tough, Cousin Sandu. I'll be tough.

I wanted to remember this day, so I looked at the date showing on my wristwatch: It was August 27, 1991.

The next morning, my picture (an old one) was in the early edition of *Free Youth,* with an almost sentimental tag: "Back visiting the place where he grew up and became a writer." Then Riri called—the Popescus had seen my picture, and were excited. Riri offered to show Iris more of Bucharest. So we parted. Iris off sightseeing, me on my way to my press conference at *Flacara.*

Flacara was in the Casa Scanteii, that other Communist sphinx. I faced a room packed with journalists, mostly very young, some were in kindergarten when I defected. They asked a lot of questions about my career in America. When I told them how hard it had been, how hard it still was, I got blank looks of disbelief, even disapproval. They asked why I defected. I'd pledged to myself to be honest. So I answered that I did it for freedom, yet might not have been desperate enough to do it, had the dementia of Ceausescu and his inner court, glimpsed on that trip to South America, not signalled to me that Romania was on the road to disaster. The disbelief was still there, I felt it. Then I told the story of my hoodwinking him in a two-minute meeting, promising to spread his Marxist thought in America. That went over a little better. I guessed one reason why our dialogue was hard: when speaking Romanian, I no longer talked in grand pronouncements and intellectual arabesques. I was being real, and to that extent baffling. They wanted a star talking, stars don't have dull lives, or workdays of fourteen hours. I was puncturing their fantasies.

They wanted to know about commercial success, and my personal recipe for it. Here, whatever I said was listened to like in church. I mentioned power agents, executives with thirty-second attention spans, hype, high concept. Hard work didn't impress them, but hype and high concept won the day. All throughout, people kept walking in, and standing on tiptoe to see above other people's heads; soon I felt the pressure of all the bodies in front of me like a mass of physical warmth. The women asked questions, acting deliciously direct, not at all like the fuss-ing flirting females of my generation. "I first read you this year," a twenty-year-old female reporter addressed me. "You hold up. Are you as good in English?" *Flacara*'s editor George Arion seized that moment to announce that his publishing house—I didn't know he had one—would like to publish *Amazon Beaming* in Romanian. That stirred other questions: How would I feel being translated into my mother tongue?

Most of these journalists had cards, which they proudly slapped into my palm. I stuffed a stack of cards into my pockets. George Arion whispered to me, "They're acting like they like you, but let's see the papers tomorrow, they might tear you to pieces. Want to meet some old friends?"

"I didn't set any meetings."

"They'll see you without set meetings. This isn't America."

So on I went, from meeting to meeting, what an ego feast for a former traitor. The Casa Scanteii, designed as a beehive for Stalinist workers, housed dozens of rival publications, so the atmosphere sparked, while the johns reeked unflushed and the paint was peeling. Many publications had simply declared themselves owners of their offices, so now they had equity in the Stalinist mammoth! My friend Arion piloted me into the office of the minister of culture, who turned out to be Andrei Plesu, a former schoolmate of mine, once as fast as quicksilver, today unrecognizably slow and overweight. In Plesu's office, we were joined by Mircea Dinescu, Romania's poet *en chef,* and tribune of the revolution in the early hours. Dinescu told me that he wanted to leave the presidency of the Writers' Guild, which he currently filled; today's cultural vulgarity was too hard to take, especially at the helm of a once-respected institution. I asked him why he was no longer an ally of Iliescu's. He answered that he was too much of a poet for politics. Very likely the truth. Arion kept making phone calls to friends in the building, and telling me that everyone, well, most everyone, wanted to see me. Including Nicolae Manolescu, doyen of Romania's literary criticism, in his office at the weekly *Romania Literara.*

Manolescu was now a key opposition figure. He led his own movement, Alianta Civica, acronym AC, and chaired his own party, PAC, "whack" in Romanian. I reminded myself that I was a reporter, and rushed. In my time, Manolescu was the subtle terror of the literary world; writers prayed to get a B or C from him. Me, he refused to grade, I was too unorthodox, so I got my accolades from other critics. I found him aged but still handsome, and exuding a cosmic skepticism about the government in power.

"All this vulgarity, in the papers, in the streets, is a kind of self-purging of the last forty years," he told me. "It's a crude growth, with the dirt hitting everything and everyone. These are the dregs of Communism, totally exposed. This phase has to pass, and it's good that the opposition chose not to share the power. Thus, we will not be guilty of prolonging this period of history."

"You're opening yourself up to the accusation of sitting on the fence," I remarked.

"I'd rather sit on the fence than have the opposition, the first one in fifty years, make deals and become morally objectionable. It's better to have fewer votes than opportunistic ones."

"But aren't you helping the power entrench itself?"

"We would help it entrench itself even more, if we participated."

Hmm. I had my doubts. But I admired his radicalism. His cooperation with the rest of the opposition was not smooth. A very strong opinion-maker, poet Ana Blandiana, had parted ways with Manolescu after being his literary darling for years. She was now pushing Emil Constantinescu, former rector of the University of Bucharest. The other opposition leaders were far from Manolescu's radicalism or intellectual class. He was handicapped by his own excellence. Nonetheless, he, a literary critic, was now in the game of power. I loved it.

"Are you coming back to live here?" he asked. I explained that it was impossible, I had two children in America. He smiled. "Very well, you were always too Anglo-Saxon for this place."

A little jab? Probably. In his way, he too was a nationalist: he decided who was a valid Romanian writer, and who wasn't. I let it pass, and realized that he wanted to see me just to size me up. Not unlike Mr. B. last night. When I was a best-seller here, I was what he claimed he was waiting for, a talented rebel against the system. But to heartily recognize the rebel was to abandon control, so he approved of me in pinched little mouthfuls and carefully worded phrases. Too bad that we always played on different fields. I asked him why he reproached the ruling party. He responded, intelligently, "They rushed to depict capitalism as a threat to savings, jobs, pensions. To do that to an electorate so brainwashed by Communism is a crime. Unfortunately, it worked. The workers, especially the miners, became totally manipulatable. Iliescu, as you know, welcomed the miners to Bucharest. He only distanced himself from them after they beat up and savaged the crowds."

"All right. I heard the conspiracy scenarios. If the Securitate and other dark forces are still pulling the strings, what do you think their purpose is?"

"To make the West give up on this part of the world."

"Then why shouldn't you share in the power? Why scuttle your own access to shaping the new society?"

"Because we need to be a moral example."

"Wait just a second." I was getting all heated up. "If Romania remains isolated, the moral example at home will not be enough. The oligarchy in power, irrespective of its background, will become authoritarian and paranoid. We've seen it too many times. The yes men will be promoted, the others silenced."

"*They* don't want to share the power," he interrupted me. "Caramitru, Dinescu, Blandiana, the intellectual revolutionaries, they were forced out of the NSF."

"Forced physically?"

"No, not physically. There are other ways to make a climate intolerable."

"True enough. But do *you* want to share the power?"

He smiled thinly. "No. Not in these conditions."

"So, what's to be done?"

"Wait. Things will change, consciousness will grow."

All right. The air felt empty between us. I had a copy of *Amazon Beaming* in my strap bag. I took it out, and autographed it for him. He gave it a fleeting look, put it in a drawer. We spent another few moments chatting, feeling superficially similar. I walked out deflated, and in turmoil. Which was the right way: to share the power, not to share it?

On to meeting other old friends, or making new ones. At *Romania Libera,* I was introduced to a top editor, a man with a small dark moustache, and movements that were so vivacious and snappy, he almost seemed able to ignite the air around him. Petre Mihai Bacanu—I remembered the name from seeing his byline so often in the papers I'd read the day before. Bacanu completely jolted me from the depressed mood Manolescu had put me in, by asking me if I was connected enough in

America to put him in touch with any existing Marshall plan for Eastern Europe. No? Too bad. So what else was I doing here? I asked his opinion about the political situation. Those brooding miners could reappear in Bucharest any time, he said, to fix anyone not to their liking, or not to the liking of those who maneuvered them. For him, that was a far bigger threat to democracy than the presumed survival of the Securitate. Yet without minimizing that threat, Bacanu spoke of the power as of a paper tiger. He was confident that the opposition could accomplish a second revolution, if necessary; in fact, at times he sounded as if he himself could accomplish it solo. About Moldova, he fearlessly assured me that the Russians would never use their vaunted 14th Army to hold the Moldovans back, the Russians were "finished." So that made Moldova a promising new addition to the power game. Tongue in cheek or not, I couldn't tell, he wondered if he might find in Moldova a politician who could successfully run for president in both countries, forging a de facto union under the same president. Like the Romanian principalities united under Prince Cuza. The speed of his mind, the casualness of his speech made me dizzy. We parted, I with the impression that he'd forget about me in the next five minutes, as his mind played with the new polities and potentialities of a renascent East.

The buzz of my presence in the building had been spreading. I kept hugging friends and friends of friends, and the traditional *"ce faci, mai"* echoed over and over in the monumental Stalinist lobbies, so loud, in a place where till 1989 people practically whispered. No walls were said to have better electronic ears than these. Finally, I secured Arion's promise that my statements at the conference would be printed verbatim, passed on lunch in the mammoth's cafeteria, and called the Flora, to see if Iris was back.

She was there, and wanted us to eat together. She told me that a certain Pavel Manole had come to the hotel looking for me around nine this morning. According to Dora, who now chatted freely with Iris, he carried a copy of that *Free Youth* with my picture. He was not there now, but had left a phone number.

"Are you sure the name was Pavel Manole?"

"Pavel Manole," she responded, accenting the Romanian name. "What's the matter, is something wrong?"

"Not at all. Stay there, I'll meet you for lunch."

* * *

I hurried back, digesting what she'd just told me.

Pavel Manole was that tenant in our little vineyard who paid no rent for the last two years of Mom's residence in Romania. After she left, he took over the property as if it was his own. Why was he looking for me? How did he know I was staying at the Flora? How did he know I was in Bucharest at all?

Ten minutes later, at the hotel, I verified the information. Yes, a visitor by that name was here at 9 A.M.

"He probably saw your picture in the paper," Iris offered. "Dora said that he had a copy of the paper . . ."

"I know, the paper said I was in Bucharest, but it didn't say where. Let's say *Free Youth* is delivered in the village of Balotesti, where my vineyard is. Which I find odd, because it's a city newspaper of relatively low circulation. Anyway, let's say Manole's a subscriber, so his paper is delivered at 8 A.M., at the vineyard. Balotesti is half an hour by car. So, this guy gets the paper at eight, and in the next half hour he somehow finds out that I'm staying at the Flora, so he steps in his car, if he has one, and is at the Flora at nine, missing me by minutes?"

"What are you implying?" asked Iris.

"I'm not implying. I'm saying it's utterly bizarre that this man discovered where I was staying so quickly. How did he do it? By calling hotel after hotel, and asking if I'd checked in?" I backtracked towards Dora, who was at her station at the reception desk. "Is it possible to find out," I asked her, "if there were any phone calls this morning, asking if I was staying here?"

"Had there been such calls, we wouldn't have given out the information, it's not our policy," Dora said firmly.

"All right. Did anyone ask for me this morning, and not leave a name?"

"Just a second," she said, and stepped into the office behind the reception desk.

"What do you think happened?" Iris examined me closely. "Someone else knew we were here, and gave your tenant the information?" I shrugged, that didn't seem impossible. "Why d'you think he came looking for you?"

"To talk about the vineyard. I'm the lawful owner of a place he's occupying illegally, and I'm in town. Perhaps he wants to offer a settlement. But how did he find out where I was so quickly?"

"Maybe he saw you. For the last two days, we've been riding all over town."

"That's true. But he is supposed to be out of Bucharest, in Balotesti . . ." I realized that I knew nothing about my tenant—did he live at the vineyard, did he use it as a summer home? Anyway, if he did find out what hotel I was staying at, that was enterprising, but perhaps not sinister. Still . . . I smiled to Iris. "Forget it, let's go to lunch."

"Fine. Don't be so paranoid."

I hissed, "I'm not paranoid!" That word wouldn't make me blink in America, but I found it so insulting here.

Before Iris could act amazed at my behavior, Dora reappeared. "Mr. Popescu, all the people that called for you this morning left their names. And now you have another call. You can take it in the booth."

"Who's calling me?"

"He said a friend."

Blast that mysterious friend. The phone booth was an old-fashioned, heavy wooden enclosure, just like in Prague. I tore the door open. Just like in Prague, a fibrillating light bulb came on above me. I picked up the phone. "Who is this?"

The caller identified himself as an aide to President Iliescu. The president would like to speak with me. Despite my surprise, I shot right back, "Just a second, how did you know I was here?"

"We asked the office of Mr. Augustin Buzura. They told us that you were at the Flora."

The president came on the line, and he and I spoke very briefly. He wished me welcome to Bucharest, and asked if I was busy. I told him we were about to have lunch. He suggested lunch at the new seat of the presidency, the Cotroceni Palace.

Soon we were in a cab headed for Cotroceni. Another big manse in Brancovan style, with Byzantine stained windows, Cotroceni was rebuilt on the site of an old Romanian monastery. Its exterior had a monastic feeling, but inside it was sumptuous. We had little time to appreciate the architecture. As we started climbing an ornate stairway, we saw Ion Iliescu descending towards us. An aide respectfully tagging three steps behind him reminded me of someone I knew, and I realized that he was a sometime activist in the youth Communist organization; I couldn't remember his name, but here he was, working again for the former minister of youth. Iliescu wore gray slacks with a gray jacket thrown casually over his shoulders, smiled broadly, and looked to be in strikingly good shape for a man over sixty. He gave me the Romanian welcome hug with swift kisses on both cheeks (Manolescu had not), and acted genuinely pleased that we were there.

Minutes later we sat down for a simple lunch of vegetable soup, grilled fish, and pastries, washed down with Romanian mineral water.

For the first time, my wife was meeting an East European head of state. She was throbbing with curiosity. As for me, I noticed how at ease Iliescu was, and how much his English had improved—there was no interpreter present. He clearly wanted to charm Iris, behaving with the marked courtesy older European men show to younger women. He also wanted to show off that he knew me well and was an old literary fan. I liked that, but I was not disposed to easy social seductions; as for Iris, not knowing how defensive Romanians could get, she had no notion of how far she was straying in her direct remarks and questions.

As for me, I went in all guns blazing, asking about the real implications of the miners' raid on Bucharest, and why did he waffle, first welcoming them, then keeping his distance? Also, who exactly had called them in? And why had the top intellectuals left his team, and constituted themselves in the opposition? How exactly did he see Romania as a market democracy? How many Securitate were employed in the new intelligence agency, the SRI? What did he expect the Romanians outside Romania to make of this confused situation? What was his role in this transitional period, as he himself perceived it?

Iliescu had probably prepared himself for the blizzard of questions; he answered unhesitantly, uninhibited by my tape recorder, which I set rolling right on the lunch table—later, we moved to his office to have coffee and I set it on the coffee table. I was staring at him voraciously, and he kept smiling, as if silently urging me to take it easy. Answering in order, he denied categorically that he had called the miners; he had welcomed them at first because the situation in "Tiananmen Square II" (University Square) had become untenable, with mounds of human refuse rising daily, and squatters of a very dubious nature adding themselves to the protesting students. Meanwhile, the Bucharest police, intimidated by potential cries of "assassins," very quickly uttered these days, did nothing to solve the situation. Most of the time, he repeated my own family's view of the events.

At this time, an aide slipped his head in. The president was wanted on the phone. He excused himself, leaving us momentarily alone. Iris turned a plate bottom up, to read the brand, then examined the flatware. "This is *Christophe,*" she commented appreciatively.

"It might be from the previous regime."

"Absolutely not, I can tell it's new. The prez has good taste."

The prez came back. Where were we? Oh yes: who called the miners to Bucharest. To Iliescu, that was an insignificant issue—the miners were the same who had forced Ceausescu down into the mine shafts to show him their work conditions. They were the rednecks of Romania, panicked about their security and needing no instigators to be politicized. If there were instigators from the old Securitate among them, which was possible, they found a ripe terrain. Iliescu seized the opportunity to criticize the opposition's naivete not just in Romania, but in most of Eastern Europe. Their hopes of quick Westernization didn't take into account the real problem: a huge population of workers rendered unneeded by the switch to a market economy. What was to be done with them? How fast could they be recycled? Could they be recycled at all? He was being criticized for his go-slow policy. But what would a full fast-forward bring, apart from more miners' raids? The Eastern countries that could afford to plunge forward had loans from the West. Romania was being denied such loans, which was absurd, for Romania had no foreign debt.

I started to understand why he'd won the elections with 85 percent of the vote, and according to the Western observers without rigging. He had a personal, reassuring quality, folksy and unhurried, and he acted confident. His analysis was patient and commonsensical. He told me that the intellectuals had left him because they differed with him not just about the pace, but also about the reach of the reforms. He wanted a free-market social democracy, with its social safeguards in place, not a capitalist free-for-all. He had written a book and several essays, in which he puzzled the same dilemma: how to bring back a free-market economy, without completely destabilizing a poor country.

It was clear that he labored under enormous pressures, and often saw his convictions overturned. Was he still optimistic? Yes, he answered. The Romanians were too capable. But he was very concerned that the

333

Visegrad nations, Poland, Hungary, Czechoslovakia, the ones with a more civilized image, would be invited to join NATO, while the "less civilized" Romania, Bulgaria, and others would be left to the Russians. There lay the big gamble, the big suspense, the potentially historic tragedy. Romania, which was swapped off to the Ottoman Turks, to Hitler after Munich, to Stalin at Yalta, might now be swapped out of Europe again, at some Yalta 2 imposed by a regrouping Russia.

"But if so much turns on that civilized image," interjected my wife, "why, for instance, was it necessary to execute Ceausescu so quickly?"

Iliescu turned with the fierceness of an aging tiger. "Because we were at war with an enemy whose strength we didn't even know. In fact, the fighting only stopped after we announced the dictator's execution. But putting that aside, on the very day, December 24, when the NSF created an extraordinary tribunal to try Ceausescu and his wife, James Baker, then U.S. secretary of state, declared on NBC that the U.S. would not object if the Russians intervened in Romania. That was suggested by Baker in the spirit of stopping the bloodshed; in other words, we were to be saved from Ceausescu through an invasion! Thank God the Russians called the idea stupid. Shevarnadze told Baker that any Soviet intervention would transform Ceausescu into a martyr."

I jumped in. "But the Russians didn't turn down an invasion out of principle. The U.S. had just invaded Panama. The Russians would never have given the Americans the gift of a parallel invasion."

Iliescu turned to me. "Of course. The powers have their agendas. Meanwhile, we Romanians live *here*."

My wife cut in. "Mr. President, I think that what you need is PR. What you need is a lobby in Washington."

Iliescu reacted with surprise, almost with suspicion. This man, insightful about national and global politics, didn't know about lobbies and special interest groups. "Don't we have an embassy in Washington?" he wondered aloud. Iris chuckled, I smiled. Everyone had lobbies in America, every big business, or foreign nation, or ethnic group that could afford it. It made sense to have one. Iliescu nodded, as if the idea merited thought.

"We'll stay in touch, right?" he asked as I turned off my tape recorder.

We rose to have our picture taken together outside, on the ornate Brancovan balcony of Cotroceni. I watched Iliescu's profile as he smiled at the camera, and thought: Eugene Ionesco, Elie Wiesel, Hollywood star Edward G. Robinson, flutist George Zamfir, Brancusi the famed sculptor, they were all born in Romania. Yet the world still didn't know where Romania was, or what it was. Iliescu had won the elections by a landslide. If he took Romania out of her isolation, he would win his place in history.

"So they seem to be down to sentimental expatriates like you," Iris commented on the way back. "You going to roll up your sleeves and start organizing the native sons in America?"

"Whoa, I'm waiting for Romania's next elections. If those are not rigged either, then maybe I'll do something."

Back at the Flora, I found a message from Dana Nistor, legal counsel for the Free Romania Foundation, a Boston-based organization that raised money for the Romanian orphans. Accompanied by Nistor, we were to drive tomorrow to Nicoresti, 150 miles north of Bucharest, to a hospital for "irrecoverable orphans," in other words children with great physical malformations or mental deficiencies. Many of them had survived coat-hanger abortions during Ceausescu's ban on abortions and contraceptives.

We'd been bracing ourselves for this trip for a few days. Over and over, we had been asked. "Why are you going to see them? Do they have to be part of your story? Very well, don't be surprised if they spit at you, bite you, or hit you. They're like little beasts."

They were not like little beasts.

Dana Nistor, a respected figure of the Romanian bar and an ex-defender of dissidents, arrived to pick us up at the hotel in an old Mercedes 400, weathered, its interior a little frayed, but still a Mercedes 400, and with a driver. A friend had loaned it to her for the day. We left Bucharest before nine in the morning, to allow plenty of time for the twisted Romanian roads.

Half an hour later, we passed Balotesti, site of my vineyard. On the spur of the moment, I asked the driver to take the exit to the village; I wanted to peek at my property, perhaps to find out my tenant's intentions. Minutes later, we were slowing down in front of it's wooden gate and fence. The place was empty, except for a not terribly aggressive dog. Iris was shocked by the size of the land; it was barely larger than our Beverly Hills backyard. The initial Dom Perignon domain wasn't much bigger, I responded, and strolled about, looking at the lopsided little house, at the vine posts, not particularly well tended, although my tenant was an agronomist. Where the hell was he? The dirt preserved the dips of tire tracks, likely from his car. I chatted with a neighbor, a certain Monica, who remembered my mother and inquired about her health. No, Mr. Manole was not here, she hadn't seen him in a few days, but he always came and went.

I pushed the experiment further. We got back in the car, drove to the adjoining village of Saftica, and stopped at the town hall. I got out and so did Iris, who had to use the bathroom. The waiting room was full of peasants, some barefoot, waiting to present their problems to the mayor or the clerk. The clerk had just arrived. I stepped ahead of the waiting line. My old class reflexes were intact—I didn't have time to wait in line, I was a foreign guest with a busy schedule. As no one protested, I identified myself with my passport, and asked the clerk to dig up the file on my property. Iris came back from the bathroom with a strained face (I could guess why), and found us looking at the file. It was supposed to contain a copy of my certificate of ownership, and a record of the agreement of tenancy. Both were missing. The file was empty.

I talked tough. "I'm here to take possession of my property. Who just stole my ownership certificate?"

"What do you mean, just?" asked the clerk.

"It was in the file two days ago," I improvised haughtily.

And whether or not it was there, and, as I assumed, my tenant stole it before coming to look me up at the hotel, the clerk turned pale. But, he explained, he wasn't there the last two days, and there was more than one key to the records room. Someone else might have taken my file.

I took down the clerk's name, announced that I'd be back, and we left. I didn't know when I'd be back, I didn't know if I'd ever fight for that little slice of Romania. After all, that other guy had worked it for the last seventeen years. But his appearance at the hotel, and the disappearance of the documents, were part of the old Balkan soap opera. I had just verified that the soap opera hadn't changed its plot.

"This is very typical," commented Nistor. "You can imagine the frustration of being a lawyer in this country where no one upholds the law."

Off we drove. The pre-Carpathian hills, a bluish rampart to the left, gave the landscape a dreamy unreality. Ceausescu's ugly agro-complexes gave way to real Romanian villages: thatched roofs, storks nesting atop chimneys, fences and doorposts dripping with woodcarvings. *Schituri* (small monasteries) dotted the landscape, cutting the sunlight with svelte belfries. Then oil refineries showed on the horizon, like crashed alien ships. A lake: in a boat, a monk fished standing, his black *anteri* ruffled by the breeze. In another boat, three village boys, stark naked, fought over shares of bait. Men in city suits pedalled on bikes, leaving their villages heading for their desk jobs in the nearest little town. In a yard, a girl practiced a trombone. We stopped for a wedding marching in the middle of the freeway. The groom was dark-skinned and handsome, the bride was invisible under her doilied veils. More villages, more porches, more wood sculptures. Peasant women selling clay pots. A completely different Romania, unhurried, ignoring the world and ignored by it, except . . . everywhere, there were fleets of TV masts.

"Now the peasants watch CNN," said Nistor.

We crossed the Siret River. The fields were increasingly lush. Almost every peasant home had huge wine barrels lying about in its yard: we had entered the Odobesti-Panciu-Nicoresti triangle, containing Romania's oldest vineyards, some older than Roman times. Their wines had won countless gold and silver medals, but today they were so poorly marketed that they sold in Los Angeles at three dollars a bottle.

We had brought two sacks of presents for the orphans, one with crayons and drawing paper, the other with bubble gum and candy. They were hurtling along in the back of the car.

They'll hit you, they'll spit at you, they'll bite you.

Film footage of those orphanages had been shown on American TV over and over. I recalled a shot of nude teenage girls, identifiable as females only because, as they hunkered in a filthy little room, one could see their budding breasts. Otherwise, terrified, their heads shaven, their bodies unbelievably skinny, they didn't seem to have a gender. They barely looked human. I knew we weren't going to see such an extreme scene at Nicoresti, this particular orphanage was part of a hospital, and had already been visited by experts and do-gooders. The hospital had an infantile neuropsychiatry section, so the orphans who were mentally disturbed (I wondered what criteria were used to decide who was and who wasn't) were given much better care there than in other orphanages, or *leagane* (cradles). But there was only one doctor for every ninety orphan beds, and four nurses per shift, plus six freshly arrived volunteers from

Ireland. Nistor told us that there were some American volunteers en route too, trained by the Free Romania Foundation.

Nistor was impressed that we had lunched with the president. "If you see the prime minister too, can you remind him of a document he's supposed to sign for us? It's a license for our foundation to operate in Romania. We applied for it nine months ago."

"In nine months, the prime minister never found the time to sign it?"

"Or his aides never found the time to show it to him."

"But that's outrageous, you're helping Romanian children."

"Tell them that, I told them too," said Nistor with a tired little smile.

I began to feel nervous about what we would find at the orphanage.

The day before, I'd mentioned to George Arion that we would be going to Nicoresti. He immediately formed a reporters' team to go there as well, to see if it was worth a story. Thus, when we pulled in front of the orphanage gates, wide doors of iron, with bars topped with sharp spikes, we saw the car of the press team from *Flacara* parked at the curb.

The journalists were not inside the orphanage, they were in the street smoking and chatting. A dozen orphans perched perilously on the spiked tops of the gates, like birds on a telephone wire, were staring at their car. They looked normal, apart from shaven heads and drab sweaters and pants which reminded me of the war orphans in my elementary school. They looked at us, and many were cross-eyed. When they laughed and shouted, their teeth showed, crooked, imploded, and brown from the wild carobs they chewed on, spitting the skins and seeds in the street. The girls had a strange male look from their short hair and absolute absence of fat. They seemed between six and ten. They started chanting loudly, "Goo-may, goo-may!" rattling the gates' old shaky bars, pulling at them with clangs of loose metal. They had to be speaking Romanian, but for my life I couldn't figure what "goo-may" meant. The stronger ones shook the gate so hard that one kid fell off in the yard, and only by the way she started crying when she hit the concrete did I realize that it was a girl. She yelled loudly from a mouth without teeth. The others didn't give her a look, they were too interested in the visitors and probably witnessed such falls all the time. Before I could think of what to do, Iris flashed in through the little doorway by the gate. She rushed past me so fast that she dropped her sunglasses and didn't even notice it, for she was already in the orphanage yard picking up that girl.

Yelling GOO-MAY all the more, the other kids jumped down onto Iris and the girl she was helping to her feet, so both were knocked to the ground again. Like a zombie, I noticed how out of place Iris's clothes looked in this gray/yellow/brown drabness: today she was wearing a chic white suit with a shiny zipper on one side, and sunglasses. She should've put on something else. And she had jumped right in anyway, what if they bit her, what if one or several were HIV positive? But there she was, so I couldn't stay behind. I rushed in. I stuck my arms into that pulsating mass of kids fighting over Iris and the crying girl, to try to pull them aside, and rescue my woman. When I touched the little huddle of bodies, it broke upward. I was surrounded by them. Iris surfaced holding that girl, who was so confused by the closeness of this stranger that she forgot to go on crying; trails of tears shone on her dusty cheeks. To her, the first impression of Iris was smell—I saw her flaring her little nostrils; then, noticing the zipper on Iris's suit, she grabbed it and pulled, revealing nothing, the zipper was purely ornamental.

I saw no scratches on Iris, but there was no way she could step out of the kids' grip, they all pushed and pulled till she stumbled and then sat on the dusty pavement, with the kids all over her. Several little hands were now pawing me. I grabbed them and held them, to make sure they were not going for my wallet—then I was ashamed of the thought. They looked at me, leaning their heads on one shoulder, on the other, then they exploded into laughter, ugly, hoarse. I raised a hand to stroke a shaven head, noticed that my hand was shiny, one of them had drooled all over it.

"Usurel, copilasi" (easy, kids), I muttered repeatedly, and looked back towards the street. Through the gate, I saw Dana Nistor talking to one of the journalists; the others stared through the bars, watching how Iris and I performed with Romania's orphans. But they were not coming in.

And I still couldn't understand what the kids were saying. Iris was sitting on the ground, still pulled at by the kids, yet impatient and clumsy as they were, I realized they wouldn't hurt her. I went over, with several kids hanging on my clothes, to talk to my wife: "You all right, babe?" From inside the dirty-faced little circle, she called to me, yes she was, and could I run back to the car to get the crayons and bubble gum. I untangled myself and zoomed out, past the journalists, noticing among them the young woman reporter from yesterday, the one who had told me at the press conference that my writing held up. Today she wore a cute semi-folkloric outfit, with colored ruffles and bangles and beads, and she was just lighting a cigarette.

I got the two bags of presents out of the car and rushed back with them. The kids plunged for the bags, and Iris was left alone for a second. Her face was shiny with tears, hers or the kids', or both.

The bags exploded under prying hands. Bits of plastic flew up in the air. The kids found the bubble gum. And the crayons and drawing paper. I turned at random, and found myself being watched by a constellation of dark eyes peering over a low wall. Beyond that wall was the yellow two-story building of the hospital proper, with a sign: MATERNITY WING. I was being examined by six or seven Romanian women holding wrapped-up babies. Brand-new mothers.

They were staring at me with that curiosity out of place and time which I had noticed in so many Romanians; I'd felt it wrapping itself around me ever since the customs officers looked at my passport, and then at my face and clothes, at the airport. Over and over, the same look, curiosity and a kind of confused disapproval. Why? Was I weird? Was I not doing the right thing? I saw one lean to whisper a comment into another's ear. I felt like checking to see if my fly was open, but I knew that wasn't the reason. I, we, were paying attention to the orphans, that was the reason.

I turned back to the little prisoners of the irrecoverable clinic. A young man, very blond for these lattitudes, was just stepping out of the orphanage's office.

By this time, the children had destroyed almost half of the crayons and paper, and were fighting over the gum. Hitting each other, pretty viciously too. No way to share this equitably. The bigger ones grabbed a load and ran away with it, like ducks on a pond flying off with the best crumbs thrown by Sunday strollers. One bumped into that blond young man. "Kay-vay, kay-vay, kay-vay!" the kids started shouting, again in that language which I couldn't figure—was it perhaps Gypsy? The young man lifted one kid and set him on his hip with a well exercised movement, then walked with his charge towards us.

"I'm Kevin," he said. "From Cork, Ireland. I'm a volunteer. Welcome."

I asked the question foremost in my mind. "Are these kids just learning how to talk?"

"No, they're talking. They're saying my name. Kevin."

Now I got it: Kay-vay = Kevin. "And you," said Kevin, "they're calling *gume* (goo-may), Romanian for gum. Because the visitors usually bring them bubble gum."

I got it. I was a piece of gum.

"But some don't speak so well," pursued Kevin. The kid on his hip had laced his dirty hands around the young man's neck; Kevin looked barely twenty. "And some didn't speak at all when the first Irish team came here."

"When was that?"

"About eight months ago. You want to take pictures?"

"Uh . . . I don't know, I guess not right now."

"You want to see the place?"

I could smell the kid in his arms: he smelled like he had pooped in his pants. Or like his clothes hadn't been cleaned in quite a while. The others smelled the same. I glimpsed two kids picking up Iris's sunglasses. One rushed ahead with them, the other followed; blushing with excitement, they handed the glasses back to Iris.

Kevin noticed the mothers peering at us from the maternity ward. "They always do that, like we're a circus or something. A bit strange, those Romanian women. Sorry," he caught himself, "you Romanian too?"

"Yeah. I am."

An older man, round around his middle, bald, in a doctor's frock, put his head out of the office building. Dana Nistor told me his name. He was Dr. Preda, the medical director of this establishment.

They were not like beasts. More like abused puppies, who only yesterday figured out that these new owners won't beat them.

And, we were told, these kids were doing great compared to kids in other places. Back in 1968, when, by banning abortions to build up the population, Ceausescu forced several generations of Romanian mothers into coat-hanger abortions, no one was prepared to deal with the infants who survived them, for many did even if the mothers died of post-delivery infections—some while in jail, waiting to be charged for having aborted illegally. Those, however, were few. It was to the population's credit that while everyone looked for loopholes against the law, and some illegal obstetricians got rich, few mothers or doctors were turned in by malicious neighbors, or even by Securitate. The monstrous plan of producing assembly-line babies was tacitly sabotaged. Still, some 125,000 children (some sources said 300,000) were born crippled or brain-damaged, or became ill when abandoned by parents who couldn't support them.

Typical of Ceausescu's impractical plans, there was no increased production of *anything* for this overpopulation of babies, no diapers, no pacifiers, no baby powder, let alone school books, classrooms, or teachers. The morbid baby boom hit only a few years before the dictator decided to repay the foreign debt, slashing social services even more. Thus, the boom was on a collision course with the mass starvation caused by the paying of that debt, which only ended with the revolution. Without proper food and medication, orphans and non-orphans died and died, and Romania's mortality rate shot up. Some clever brain in Elena Ceausescu's circle (she was credited with that genocide even more than he was) devised an incredible bureaucratic trick to conceal the mortality rate from UNICEF and other world organizations. All infants were to be officially registered not at birth, but two months later. Thus the infants who died during those first two months from lack of incubators, from the cold of unheated hospitals, from shortages of baby food, left no record of their brief passage on earth. They did not exist. They were part of no tabulation. No one will ever know how many infants died in Romania under Ceausescu. On those who didn't die, academician Elena performed yet another scientific experiment. She decided to fatten up the emaciated kids. But where to get the food? At that time, Romania was exporting its last tomato and pint of milk. Instead of protein, Elena ordered massive blood transfusions to be given to the weakest orphans. That was how, from a tainted blood bank, hundreds of them acquired AIDS. And the opposition continued to insist that even those crimes did not justify the Ceausescus' hasty execution. One still should have given them the opportunity to confess (or not confess!) all their gruesome acts. One still ought to have shown the West how Westernized Romania could act towards her dictators. If the Ceausescus were killed, it was because the crypto-Communists were in power.

Iris and I were here, with some of the kids who didn't die.

* * *

The ones who had managed to get crayons and paper scattered about the yard to try them out. We followed a few into a kind of classroom, which, due to some colored charts and drawings thumbtacked to the walls, looked somewhat more normal, almost like a regular kindergarten.

We'd been here an hour. We'd been drooled on, and punched now and then by a friendly little fist, and stared at cross-eyed, and giggled at from little mouths with harelips and imploded teeth. It was obvious that many kids here were at least a few years behind in development. They expressed affectionate curiosity by rushing unexpectedly at us, to bump into our knees and thighs. As we walked around, we were regularly hit by these small meteors of frail and dirty flesh. They all wanted hugs, yet got scared and fought them off. But when they saw others accept our embrace and survive, they clustered back, and there was nothing more heartrending than this enormous need for *contact,* it was in their eyes, in their babble, in their frantic gestures, in the way they trailed around after us. Unless momentarily busy with something we handed to them, they wouldn't miss a second of our being here. We were fantasy becoming fulfilled, we were a dream of another world, happening now, so they sucked us in greedily, to coast on us later, for weeks or months, till some next visit.

They were dirty, and there was nothing one could do about that. They were kids, and the water supply was low and the shower facilities indescribably rudimentary.

"But there's some money coming," said Kevin, "to improve the plumbing. At least, we hear it's coming." I saw that the boy he was holding had a club foot. He was cross-eyed too. In between our chat, the two nuzzled each other, looking absurdly like an older brother and a younger one.

"Where's that money coming from, Kevin?"

"From the Romanian government."

"Is it really coming?"

"We keep hearing that it is."

"How long are you going to be here?"

"Three more months, then I have to go back to Ireland. But I'll return soon, for a whole year."

Jesus. This place offered no entertainment, unless perhaps he had some local sweetheart. The food was coarse and unvaried, the shower archaic. Why would you come back here? "Because I'm making a difference. You're a nuisance, a nuisance," he turned affectionately to the Romanian kid, who was trying to stick his fingers into Kevin's mouth.

Every few minutes, I felt as if this place were changing, becoming something else—because every few minutes, or at least it felt that often, the kids became less inhibited, and wanted to establish some new contact. They zipped and unzipped Iris's suit, and played with her sunglasses. Iris and I guided their dirty fingers, pushing those crayons over paper, drawing; some, it appeared, did it for the first time. We took out the things we carried in our pockets, those that we could afford to see pawed and scattered onto the floor, and showed them. I talked Romanian to the kids, and no matter what Kevin said, most of them did not speak an intelligible version of that language. Iris spoke English, which caused amazed stares and giggles.

The kids finally had lunch, and we got to see the Romanian nurses, all of them old. Their presence transformed the place into a jail again because they acted like wardens: dour, casual, tired. Today's lunch was a kind of oatmeal. We watched how the kids ate it with their hands, smearing their faces, often wiping their fingers on their hair. Most of them ate the oatmeal to the last scrap, no spoiled kids here.

We left them still at the table. With Kevin and Dr. Preda, who looked like they had learned to tolerate each other, we visited the rooms. Few kids were lying in the beds: most were doing well enough to be out. But those in the beds were frighteningly skinny, and screamed in terror when they saw us. The beds had no mattresses, just sheets; Preda explained that the kids soiled their beds so often that it was cleaner to take away the mattresses and have them lie on thin plastic covers, which barely covered the beds' springwork. In an upper ward, a female Irish volunteer attended to a six-year-old who looked two. She wouldn't eat, and banged her head against the bed. Plastic gloves on, the young Irishwoman tried to feed her a Romanian version of Similac.

Preda had been here thirty-six years. He told me that he'd done some psychiatric observations of the kids. "You don't know what this place was like a year ago," he said. I translated for Iris. "I wonder what *he* was like a year ago," she whispered with a dark look—one of the volunteers had told her that Preda used to let medicine sent in from the West outlast its expiration date in the storage room. Not out of malice, out of sheer passivity. When I asked him what the future of these kids would be like, he shrugged: how was he to know?

I asked, "Do the doctors of Romania have no professional associations, no ties to politics, no concern about this situation? A lot of these children cannot be irrecoverable, even if they were classified that way. That classification came from the old regime."

He shrugged. "The doctors in Bucharest are very excited about reopening their private practices," he said.

"So? Most of these kids will live another forty, fifty years. What is being prepared for them?"

He popped his lips, ppfft. Not even pretending. He didn't know, he'd never cared to wonder. I was talking to the wrong guy. He asked how much longer we were going to be there. Iris muttered through clenched teeth, "He wants us out of here, so that these kids don't get too comfortable being hugged and stroked by us . . ."

She'd been touching and stroking. I'd been touching and stroking too. They say you don't get HIV from sweat or saliva. To hell with it, this old geezer hadn't gotten it, so most likely we'd be fine too. Kevin's little friend ran around on his club foot, nimble, prancing. A kid with both knees bent not forward but *back,* and stiffened at that impossible angle, moved quickly and vigorously also, by sliding, kind of, on his rear and on the hardened backs of his knees. I asked what had happened to him.

"Possibly polio years ago, before he was abandoned," said Dr. Preda.

"Polio?" I jumped, ran to the kid, frightening him. He started scurrying in that strange fashion, but I was faster. I caught up with him, bent down, touched his deformed and dirty legs. They were warm with young, normally flowing blood. I let him go, turned to the doctor: "He could have corrective surgery. Did you make a report about him, about any of the kids here that could have corrective surgery, from bad knees to harelips?"

He finally lost his patience. "Is that your business? Are you teaching me my profession?"

Your profession. I made an impotent gesture, and strode off so as not to give him a good kick in the ass. Dana Nistor quietly approached me, told me to leave the scared old man alone. Too many things needed to be changed and all at once. These orphans were not even under one authority. Some of the orphanages and cradles belonged to the Ministry of Health, others to the Ministry of Labor, others to various local authorities. What was needed was a whole change in administrative practice, plus one in the surrounding population's mentality. The very villagers next door wouldn't help these kids, because they didn't have enough for their own, or so they said. They called the orphans mooncalves and Gypsies.

Yes, a few were Gypsies. Only a few. Yes, you could call them mooncalves, they looked and acted like mooncalves. So, was that enough to ban them from the human race?

Funny, just instants before I would have defended the doctor to Iris—no, sweetheart, he's not a criminal, he's just a standard nomenklatura man, like a million others, faceless mayors, agronomists, postmasters, rural police, clerks, doctors too. He may not even be a doctor; those who were not admitted to the Romanian medical schools, which had rigorous high standards (Ceausescu couldn't destroy *everything*), could opt for three-year internships as medical technicians in the provinces. Later, they were promoted to doctor status for "experience in the field"—nobody ever asked to see their degrees. Now I felt like tearing this old idiot apart, because . . .

He was here. Pavel, my brother. He was here, a little piece of him in every one of these kids. And almost every one of them had his eyes.

My cousin Sandu from New York popped up in my mind: Be tough, cousin Petru. Be tough.

I better be, for love is not yet in the Romanians' political vocabulary.

"I'm going to ask to see the prime minister, to interview him for the *Los Angeles Times,*" I told Dana Nistor. "I'll ask him why your foundation's license to operate in Romania was never signed."

As we left, they stared after us, sticking their noses and mouths, their whole faces out through the bars of the gates. Our fairy-tale visit was over.

I stepped into the maternity ward next door. I walked across a hallway, past some of the mothers who had watched me being mobbed by the orphans a few hours earlier. The ward was visibly modest, but it was all right, in the realm of the normal. The peasant women looked all right too. Funny, several of them *were* Gypsies; one, a dark strapping beauty of twenty or so held a big baby. They all stared back at me the way they'd stared at me over the wall.

I stepped out into the street again.

Iris was talking to the journalists. I could tell that she had cried. The journalists had spent only a fraction of their time inside the orphanage.

They'd been outside again a long time now, smoking and talking politics, and watching us with curiosity. Hmm, the fierce new free press, just now it didn't act too different from those peasant women. I asked them if they would write about this place, and they said that they would. The young reporter with beads and bangles approached me and asked, was it true we'd had lunch with Ilich? That was what she called President Iliescu, Ilich, after Vladimir Ilich Lenin. I confessed that we had, and she looked at me with deep disappointment, and told me that she hadn't expected that from me. I explained my interest as a journalist on assignment. She countered that he was a crypto-Communist. I mentioned that in my time Iliescu had dared Ceausescu more than Gorbachev had dared Brezhnev or Andropov. He had called the miners to Bucharest, to beat on the students, she responded fiercely.

"I protested about the miners' raid in the *Los Angeles Times*. I'll send you my article. As for Iliescu, he was elected . . ."

"I didn't elect him!"

"Don't you take any responsibility for those who did?"

"Why should I? They're workers and peasants, primitive and disinformed!"

She was probably so incensed because she'd enjoyed my appearance at that press conference. I represented a yardstick of Western sophistication, which I had debased, first by talking to the strongman and then by arguing with her. In her passion, she talked to me as if I were a member of the family, whose transgression was unforgivable.

I was back in the family all right. From these days on, I was to be treated with the unforgivingness that Romanians reserved for those they appreciated.

It was almost sundown. The peasant women looked on, and the orphans giggled and waved as our two cars turned and headed back for Bucharest.

The next day, a brief notice about the Nicoresti orphanage appeared in *Flacara,* saying in essence that the orphanage was there, and not much more. I called the office of Prime Minister Petre Roman, and Iris and I were granted a meeting at the Victoria Palace. The corridor leading to the prime minister's office was guarded by armed soldiers. We met a strikingly handsome man in his mid-forties, sure of himself and friendly, and quite surprised that the first thing on our agenda was the orphans and the operating permit for that American charity. In a corner of Roman's office burned a votive candle, a reminder that this man was a practicing Christian.

Two days before, riding around downtown, graffiti on a wall had caught my eye: *Roman nu e Roman*. Which meant literally, Roman isn't Roman. At first I didn't get it, how was the current prime minister not himself? Then I got it, this was a nasty little play on words. Roman also means Romanian. So Petre Roman was not Romanian.

I refrained from pointing out that graffiti to my wife. Petre Roman did have a father who was a Jew and a Communist. His father fought in Spain on the republican side, and was later a member of Romania's Commie elite, one of the smartest, may I add. The young Roman grew up in nomenklatura comfort. He received a good education, and could travel when countless other young Romanians couldn't. But it wasn't the Commie perks for which this graffiti reproached him, it was his "foreignness of faith," which wasn't even there: Roman's mother was a Catholic, and he himself was baptized. A college professor till 1989, Roman surfaced politically in that first tide of revolutionaries that soon split into power and opposition. He became Iliescu's second in command, and was now prime minister. Criticized by the opposition, he was also blasphemed in Nazi-style attacks in Eugen Barbu's *Romania Mare*. Meanwhile, he was at odds with Iliescu over the pace of the reform, Roman being an advocate of radical, sweeping changes.

He sustained a very smart conversation, and seemed born for politics. I imagined what deep envy he stirred in his rivals; he spoke excellent English and handled himself like a Romanian Pierre Elliot Trudeau. He promised to look into our request, but never had a chance to do it. Three weeks later, the miners were to return to Bucharest—this time not to scuffle with the students, but to demand a freeze on the rising prices, a stop to market reforms, and the resignation of reform-minded Petre Roman. For Roman, that fall from power was a blessing in disguise. He moved into the opposition, and became one of its brightest stars.

My own story about Romania was published in the *Los Angeles Times Magazine* two months later. It was ten thousand words long, and the orphans' situation was its longest subchapter. I received a number of letters from compassionate readers, some offering to help. What were the Romanians themselves doing about that issue? several letters asked.

But all that was still in the future.

"I'll come with you to the cemetery," said Uncle Nicu, ever the stoic soldier. "Otherwise you'll never find the family plot."

That might have been true. I hadn't been to the rambling St. Vineri Cemetery in over fifteen years.

Uncle Nicu had wisely brought his umbrella. As the three of us got into yet another taxi, a huge clap of thunder started, like a whip cracking somewhere at high altitude, and then descending into the Danube plain like a ramifying avalanche. It finally died in a giant coughing fit. I looked up. Huge clouds were hanging down like the grotesque udders of a mythical cow. The thunder kept cracking, tearing up the sky. In a few minutes, it would start raining as it rains in Bucharest, flooding the sewers, inundating the roads.

The people in the streets started running. Bucharesters never carried umbrellas, but took shelter in entryways and under bus-stop roofs, fighting for space like the Titanic's passengers storming the lifeboats. Uncle Nicu, Iris, and I sat in the rolling taxi, and our breath turned to steam. Outside, the Bucharesters who had made it under various shelters stopped pushing each other. They philosophically lit cigarettes, struck up conversations, and waited.

Bucharest was built on sandy soil. Bad anchorage for high-rises, hence the devastation of earthquakes, and poor absorption of rainfall—the drainpipes always maxed out and started spewing back muddied water that flooded the streets. It was the same this time. As we drove around the Casa Poporului, even more monstrous and ugly in the rain, the water had already covered the driving lanes. We followed wide peripheral roads cut across plain empty fields. I glimpsed a street sign: Sos. Orhideelor (Orchids') Highway. No orchids that I could see, just depressed suburbs peeping through the vertical deluge. We were sailing. We came to an arched bridge, the only unflooded piece of roadway. We passed over it. Underneath, dark fascicles of train tracks. Seconds later, we splashed into a flood lake on the other side, gurgling up from hundreds of stopped-up drainage holes and sewers.

We were on Calea Grivitei, which I recognized by a yellowish row of storage buildings to my left. Beyond them were the train tracks, and the North Railway Station, the scene of thousands of my family's departures and reunions. I heard my heart: it was pounding. No, it was the car, hitting potholes. The rain was easing; a feathered rainbow showed in the northeast. Right under it rose the bell tower of Sfînta Vineri Cemetery, with the entryway I knew so well.

The taxi driver helmed the car across another flood lake, and into the cemetery's entrance. The gates were open, with scaffolding hanging right above them: the tower was being repaired. I looked at my watch. Seven P.M. exactly. The bell should be tolling. But it was not. I panicked, I was at the wrong cemetery.

No, this was it, and the bell wasn't tolling because of the repairs. Ahead, I saw the central alleyway leading to the chapel. Here were the chestnut trees past which Mom and I walked towards Pavel's grave so many times. They were still daubed waist-high with that white insect repellent. I remembered a trick from childhood: when I didn't want to feel pain in my heart, I bit my tongue behind my sealed lips, almost drawing blood. I bit it now. Iris watched me wide-eyed—I wondered how my behavior compared with hers in the Prague cemetery. I wanted to tell her something reassuring and loving, but I forgot about it as I noticed that we were well inside the cemetery.

Then the car stopped. Uncle Nicu opened his door. Iris opened her door, and commented, "I don't think I can walk through this."

I opened my door.

"This" was mud.

I'd forgotten about the Romanian mud. It mired the Roman legionnaires, and the Nazis' and Soviets' tanks. The rain turned the packed earth of the alleyway into mud that bubbled from the thinning raindrops and rippled from the movement of the car. The rain was stopping. But the mud was everywhere, and I was wearing expensive shoes.

The mud was reddish brown, specked with cigarette butts and wilted flowers and bits of wax. I thought urgently: candles! I must buy candles!

The taxi driver said something to Uncle Nicu. Uncle Nicu said something to me which translated into: there were no candles, this cemetery was closed for work—even though we had driven in as if into an abandoned ruin. Never mind the candles. I turned to Iris, asked her to please stay in the car because the mud was too perilously thick and widespread.

"You want to visit your brother's grave first? Or your father's?"

Those words came from Uncle Nicu. He was already out and sinking in the mud. His shoes had almost disappeared. The mud touched the bottoms of his pant cuffs. He fought to open his umbrella, which seemed stuck. Straggler raindrops landed on his shoulders. His umbrella finally opened. I stepped out in the mud, and it sucked me in.

"I want to go alone," I said, amazing my uncle and myself.

"But you don't know where to go."

"Just give me the directions, and I'll find it."

I remembered the cemetery's layout. The family plots were clustered left and right of that central alleyway, from which branched scores of smaller access alleys. Uncle Nicu reminded me that the second and fourth alleys on the left led respectively to the Popescus' family plots, including my father's grave, which I'd never yet seen, and to my twin brother's. I asked him to stay with my wife, and took the umbrella from his hands. Splashing in the mud, I followed the second alley to the left.

I was to see my father's grave in a few seconds.

What thoughts cross a human mind, when something so meaningful but so long delayed finally happens?

The one thing I was aware of just now were the pictures of my kids, in my wallet. You don't know that I'm a father, Dad, I thought. And then my latest book, lying on the bottom of my suitcase, at the hotel. You don't know that I'm an author again, Dad. Then came the next thought, swallowing up the other two: you always knew so little about me. If I believed in an afterlife, and that the spirits of the departed were all-knowing, it would only be so that Dad would get his chance to know who I was now. Not only as a writer, Dad, but as a son and as a man. Due to your constant war with Mom, to Pavel's death, and to your leaving home a few short years later, you never learned who I was.

He had not. Suddenly, memories rushed to illustrate that thought. I am six foot two, and he was five foot six, a midsize man as Balkan sizes went. Almost two years passed after he left Mom, before I agreed to see him again. Inside that time, I grew tall and skinny as a pole, and when I saw him again, I was more than a head taller than him. Dad, who used to loom big, had become little. Dad, who used to be so handsome, had been ill (this was the beginning of a long battle with a recurrent ulcer), and had started to lose his looks.

That change in him haunted me. It felt like his punishment, for he had left our home without talking to me, without giving any explanation or warning to his son, no, nothing at all. He left. Then I saw him again for only a few minutes, at the hospital. Then a lawyer came to talk divorce terms with Mom.

Whether tearing himself from Mom was more an ordeal for him than a liberation, I didn't know. He never told me why they didn't make it, not even later. Mom, with energy comparable to that which she had put into Pavel's loss, reviled him loudly for his betrayal. Time passed, until Dad sent over Uncle Nicu, of course. Uncle Nicu, who pleaded with me that Dad had had no choice, and I had no right to judge him, he was still Dad.

So, when I saw him again, his shortened stature seemed like a symbol—he was a different person, a stranger. I looked at him, smaller, older, and tasted the bitter taste of demystification, about him, and about the woman who had replaced Mom, an actress substantially younger than my father. Before he left Mom, they'd had a long affair, the woman made no secret of it, she almost boasted about it. So I'd had to stare at the fact that even before Pavel's death, the marriage had been fraught with conflict, estrangement, and adultery. Pavel and I had been no binding power between our parents.

Naturally, my perception of my mother had also changed, but as she and I had shared the same home until I left Romania, there was only one gap in my memories of her—between my defection and her own. With Dad, there had always been gaps, big, small. He always came home late he hardly ever played with us, preferring his friends who smoked up his study and wasted hours in intellectual gobbledygook. He rarely joined us on our vacations. It all made sense now—he had another life, separate from ours.

So when I defected, I sensed that he would fall behind along with my old world. So I buried him before he died, in oblivion. And then he really was gone, and I was forbidden from going to his burial.

Reversing our long separation, this visit, even if it was one to a graveyard, now felt so real that I was choking.

* * *

I'll see him, I kept thinking. Even though I'll only see a grave and a tombstone with his name on it. That was as much of a meeting as one live being and one dead could have. Rare lingering raindrops fell on my uncle's umbrella, an umbrella that had been in this cemetery before, I was sure. The sky towards the northwest was now bleeding red between retreating clouds. From the east, a fast-sweeping wing of darkness advanced, inky and menacing. I glanced down. My shoes looked like two animals, two gross, mud-splattered amphibians. The time of the day, the rain, the work in the cemetery had precluded all other visitors but me. Being so alone here made my hair crackle. I needed to say something, and it passed my vocal cords so painfully that when I heard it muttered by my lips, I was aghast:

You too, Dad. You too didn't come clean.

And I realized it, right then, as I trampled the mud.

That was what I always wanted to tell him. My last message long held back. The one which, if uttered face to face, would've turned a live encounter into a healing experience, at least for me. End of a cycle, start of a new relationship, but above all forgiveness, face to face.

But wait a second. . . . What was this? I thought I'd forgiven him already . . .

Confused, I treaded the mud, while the small Romanian grave plots slid by, enclosed in rusted wrought iron, with old oval photographs above narrow carved lettering, some of it gilded, and low beds of earth which the rain had turned into pools; on some of those pools floated withered store-bought flowers. In little lamps of iron or tins affixed to poles, candles and votive lights had been drowned by the rain.

Dad, it's me. Dad, it's Petru. I'm here.

I'm here . . . and if you ever asked yourself . . . if you ever asked yourself why I truly fled . . . if you ever wondered where you went wrong . . .

I stumbled over a lip of concrete hidden in wet and muddied grass. I lost the umbrella and almost crashed down. Straightening up, I cursed loudly, in the cemetery, what a sin. But I didn't care. I called back to my mind the involuntary solemnity that had surged in the Strasnice Cemetery a few days ago, out of the gestures of two strangers, my wife and me, ripping weeds to find the grave of Martin Davidovich. Our little procession, headed by that survivor with a number on his arm, with the innocent taxi driver bringing up the rear, so impressed by my wife's tears.

That encounter between the living and the dead was sad, but pure. Iris carried no angry unspokens, just clean grief. But here, I was alone, I'd even asked to be alone. So that no one would see my shame and confusion. Because things were not clean between my father and me, not resolved, not done.

I hadn't known it. But I knew it now.

I knew what I wanted to say to you. You didn't come clean, Dad.

I was in front of a line of graves. There were five of them, the main family plot. Only five graves? How surprisingly few for our little army. But in the fashion of old Europe, where space was fiercely fought for, even in cemeteries, a family's dead kept being buried in the same graves, on top of each other. In these tiny lands that fought so fiercely over territory, this was the custom. There were two types of graves—the "seven year" plots, and the "eternal" ones. An unexpected death made a family scramble: if there were no family burial spaces available, money was spent to secure a seven-year one. When the seven years were up, either more money was paid to make that grave "eternal," or the bones were disinterred, to be moved or cremated. Most often they were buried again on top of kin who had died already. That explained the names of the Kafkas, all three, on one tombstone in Strasnice. Franz mingled in one grave with the people he wanted most to get away from: his domineering father, his passive unsympathetic mother.

We too had that custom, but in even more extreme form, for we were Romanians, and everything about us was extreme. Here was the tall tombstone of Vlad Popescu, my older brother whom I never met. Under his name was carved that of Tudor Popescu, my grandfather who had fathered all thirteen Popescus. Grandad died after Vlad, in 1955, and after the custom (but over my mother's objections, as I learned later), the Popescus opened Vlad's grave to lay in his grandfather. I knew how it was done. The old bones were dug up, washed, sealed in a sack—they didn't take a lot of space—and put in the casket of the new dead. Grandad carried Vlad back below with him. The other Popescu tombstones also showed several names each. Here was my grandmother Riri, after whom my cousin Riri was named, and another cousin Riri, who died in infancy, and the uncles, our most plentiful item: Sandu, Dinu, Mihai, Mitu, Stefan. Stefan died at thirteen, after having been a schoolmate of King Michael (the once and perhaps future king). To make sure the boy king knew his subjects, his classmates were drawn from all walks of life and regions of Romania (no minorities, of course). Stefan was selected to represent the Bucharest of the thirties—what joy and honor for the Popescus! He died long before I was born, but he remained in the family history, talked about, quoted as an example—the straight-A student who rubbed elbows, literally, with the king!

So many uncles. The ones I didn't meet at Petre's dinner table, I could find here. And on one side, the last in the row . . .

The last in the row was Dad, Radu Popescu, *scriitor*. Writer.

Dad's tombstone was carved from a kind of grayish granite, with darker chips of rock imbedded in the stone face. A round bronze plaque, pleasantly brown and warm in the grayness of the stone, showed his face in relief. Staring with dreaminess in his eyes, his appearance had been excellently captured by the sculptor. The face had an amazingly realistic carnality. The shock of rich hair on his forehead was as I knew it. The lips were his, the contour of the jaw and neck were his. It was Dad.

I felt pain.

A very special kind of pain. An ugly, embarrassed pain.

Dad, the pain I felt now didn't make me cry, for it was more about me than about you. It was sad that, standing before you, I thought of myself. After all, you too suffered, Dad.

I took a step closer. The features I knew were even more at hand, more accessible. This was hard. Did it have to be done? Should I rather run back, through the mud? Plunge into the safety of that taxi, next to my American wife and your beloved brother, who ought to know about this, as he ought to know about everything. They all should've known, but they didn't. They took you here, and paid for this beautiful stone and well-replicated bronze face, and *didn't know*.

There was another grave not two yards from Dad's, the grave of Vlad, his older son. And two alleys away, two minutes of splashing through this mud so much like the land we were all born in, there was Pavel's grave.

So I told him why things were not finished between us. You lost two sons, Dad, but had a surviving one, me. Me you chose to leave, a few years after Pavel died. Only a few years, but you were hardly at home those years, so it felt like you left right away. You split. Out of our lives. And when, resigned to the fact that our family was no longer whole, I met you again, you didn't come clean, Dad. You never told me, father to son, man to man, why you left.

I know it wasn't because you were sparing my feelings. I had the right to know what went wrong between Mom and you. But you didn't have the guts.

So you thought it would be easier if you didn't talk. It was easier for you, but not for me. The other thing that you never told me was that you were sorry. Sad for my dead brothers, especially for Pavel. Never showed your pain for them, or for me, the one left alone. Had you shown it, I would've forgiven you, for I would've had a measure of comfort. I would not have been alone in my pain, alone, alone, exactly as I am now.

Why did you not show your pain? How could you not, Dad? What bizarre compensatory mechanism worked inside you, that we could meet thereafter and talk of art and politics and books, my own books included, and eternally of Romania, Romania, her fate, her image—but never of what had happened to us as a family? Meanwhile, Mom talked about it incessantly. You abandoned me to her voracious need for an audience, but you, you said nothing. *You never said anything anymore, about my twin brother.* It was as if he'd never existed.

Would you imagine, Dad, *could* you imagine what comfort it would have been for me if we had taken that old tram to this cemetery once, just you and I? And visited Pavel's grave, without my mother? Two men, giving homage to a fallen man, fallen ahead of his time, not much younger than those students who died two years ago in the revolution. Pavel was ours both, Dad, but you didn't share him. You acted as if he was forgotten, when he wasn't. You left me the whole burden of that sadness, as you left me the whole burden of consoling Mom.

That made you both weak and heartless. I realize it now, I realize it fully, there is nothing more meaningful for a son, than to know that his father can shed tears. We had so many reasons to cry in our unlucky family, but I did not see you get teary-eyed once.

So I can't cry now, for I'd be crying for us both, and excusing you yet again. And that's not right.

I can only ask, what happened? How could someone so insightful about literature, philosophy, and Marxism, oh Marxism, your generation's damned obsession with *scientific reason,* be so unfeeling about normal human things? How could you not realize that hundreds of times I knocked on your door because I missed Pavel, or was confused by growth, or was plain scared. And you, without guessing it, took immediate refuge in listening to Bach, or arguing about Sartre or Lukacs, late luminaries of the Marxist movement, thus exiling me into loneliness, from where I tried to decipher *what you felt,* by watching your enigmatic intellectual act. It always remained enigmatic—there was the twitching of your eyebrows, the absent-minded doodling of your hand with a pen, and your talking lips, talking talking talking about ideas ideas ideas. Intellect. Not feelings, never feelings.

I had been standing several feet from the tombstone. I moved closer.

I finally put my hand on the stone, and felt the cool round rim of that bronze plaque.

The place was silent, the stone was lifeless, so I felt like I was forcing my thoughts on a reluctant interlocutor: Dad. God, what a fool I was not to do it before, while he was still alive. Not to ask him: What the hell did you find in that intellectual nonsense, more dead than the people we had both lost, that I, a young live human being, was not enough to arrest your attention?

I talked some more to that silence and that lifelessness. I realized that no one heard me, yet I talked. It was amazing how much I needed to talk.

So now I'm back, Dad. And sadly, I haven't forgiven you.

Because you were not honest. You held back the reasons of your behavior from the one man who needed most to understand you. You were selfish, and a coward. It would have been so much easier, for both of us. Certainly for me—I stepped into life, and then into America, without guidance, without models. And with so little to be proud of.

You left our home, in which Pavel had died. His real dying place was not in the hospital, his real grave was not in the cemetery, they were in our home, and you left them. Perhaps, had you not been unfaithful to my mother, to me, and to Pavel's grave, I would not have been unfaithful to this land. I'm not unfaithful to women, it's not my style, but I became unfaithful to this land, to which by my trade I was to be irreversibly wedded. You sought your happiness in a second spouse, I in a second homeland. You hurt me by leaving us, and yet I feel strangely grateful, because you taught me that one can leave, that one can take loss and guilt, even the guilt of hurting loved ones.

You taught me freedom in your own way, Dad. But why did your lessons have to be so painful?

You also taught me something about patriotism, and pride in one's roots. It doesn't come from ideas, Dad, nor from place, or language. It comes from *family,* and if it's tortured and incomplete, it means that the family was tortured and incomplete. The symbol of these Romanian bones buried together is wasted on you. To stay in this land, to suffer in this land, takes loving parents. I know that my younger cousins, Riri and Tudor, will stay here. I might have stayed too, had you been a loving parent, not just a sporadic intellectual friend.

But you weren't. So, aside from the issues of freedom, of escaping Communism, it's you who taught me to *leave,* as you yourself left.

And that brings me to the Romanians. Why do we never come clean, and even when we try to, it's not complete, it's always circumstantial and full of excuses, always under the pressure of history, always without an honest face to face? Why so much pride in not admitting, in not confessing? And is that pride really pride, since deep down we do know the shame, and our part in it? That cannot be pride, it's simply self-defense and oblivion, and excusing everyone if he's *our own,* so we ourselves can be excused. I hear everyone here, even myself, excusing, excusing. But I hardly ever hear anyone in this land blurting out: Enough excuses, let's look at ourselves. Let's not be forgiving and soft and soothing, let's be hard on ourselves, let's be extreme on our own foibles. It will be all right, we'll survive.

And maybe that is the way to break the cycle, to stop being victims, and to stop being secondary in the fate of the world. We have to question our actions, and we have to answer for them. Someday even this land has to start answering, for everything. Do you hear me? Do you hear me, Dad? I live now in a land where there is questioning, and answering. Are we better people, over there? Hardly. Are we honest and just to everyone? Not yet. But we are questioning, and answering.

I felt exhausted. My shoes had sunk in the native mud. I pulled them out, stepped back, and bumped into a stranger's tombstone. An old one, so old that its letters were almost erased. I sat on it, and stared at the bronze face of my father.

I was not crying. I could not cry. My crying on my graves had been that first evening, in the Novacs' apartment.

I rose and stepped up to my father's tombstone, closed my eyes and swept my hand over my father's bronze features, as if over a death mask. Then I walked away, found a mired footpath, and followed it two alleys over, to Pavel's grave.

This grave I knew so well from our countless pilgrimages that when I saw it, I experienced a shock. There were two names added to Pavel's on the tombstone. One was Agripina, Mom's mom, who stayed with me while he was in the hospital. And Constanta, Mom's older sister, the one who married an English theater producer and went away and was an actress in England. She came back years later, when she was in her seventies, and died in Bucharest after my defection. Mom had buried her in my brother's grave. And Mom buried my grandmother here too. I started laughing. Mom, you the enlightened soul, who found the Popescus' burials together so barbaric. You wanted Pavel away from Dad's cohorts, but had no problem mingling him with your own kin! I kept laughing, Mom, this is so you. But it's real, it's so much better than Dad's indifference. A betrayed woman grabbing back whatever she could, even ashes.

Well, here was the truth: she and Dad were not a family. Life didn't unite them, nor did death. But they were what this country with an illiterate past always admired: a pair of brilliant intellectuals.

Rare, slow tears, like the lingering rain, started finally. My eyes blurred. Tears fell on my muddy shoes.

A thought made its way into my fogged-up mind. Iris. I'd been here almost an hour.

I had to trample back.

But I couldn't trample back without passing that bronze face again. As I made it to the brief and almost soldierly row of Popescu tombstones, the crying from the other plot carried over, and I was happy in the bitterest way, happy that I had tears for Dad too. And so as not to spoil them by some brusque memory of hurt, I bubbled into talk. Dad, let's talk about politics in this land. I've seen the people, they're free now, but they're deeply traumatized and full of negative emotions, enduring fear of the Russians, slowness in accepting responsibility, defensiveness, belief in conspiracies. I'm afraid that the politicians more adept at exploiting those insecurities will win the game. Old story, in a new time. So what's to be done, Dad? What shall I do, Dad?

I felt that my plea of concern brought us together, a little.

I walked around a big marble mausoleum, a memorial to one of the grain or oil barons of the past, and dead ahead, like a shock cut in a movie, I saw my wife walking carefully through the Romanian mud. Looking for me. When she saw me, she smiled her best bravest warmest smile.

Out of the car peered Nicu. When I got closer, he said something flatly sensible: "Let's go. Enough."

On the way back to the hotel, we dropped off my uncle. He had lost his stiffness and chatted freely with Iris, about Bucharest's uncharacteristic dirt. She told him of Beverly Hills' manicured lawns, on which well-fed dogs pooped steamily, with their owners looking on—five percent of them, if that many, cleaned up after their dogs. If you drew their attention, they flipped you the bird. How was that for social cohesion? I listened and nodded contentedly: life was tough in America, we paid for our advancement. And we admitted its limitations.

Iris kissed him on the cheek; the old soldier timidly inhaled the scent of this pretty American woman. "We see each other again, no?" he asked me, with the gasping breathing of an old man. A touch of insecurity in his voice. After I walked back from the graves, I hardly spoke, I was deep in thought.

"Sure, Uncle. Every day that we're here."

"W e're going to miss you two so much," said Ella. "Petru, we missed you all these years, and now we saw you a few times, so we're going to miss you even more. Don't forget us again." She turned to Iris. "Don't let him forget us again."

I smiled. Before this trip, Iris was apprehensive of this unknown mysterious place, Romania. Now she was asked to keep me connected to it. I glanced at my watch. Two hours till take-off. Seven thousand two hundred seconds. I found it as unbelievable that I would leave as I'd found it unbelievable to be here again.

All the Popescus were here, in the narrow apartment of Aunt Puica, my godmother. Widowed, she lived alone. It was amazing that she managed, for she no longer saw with one eye, no longer went out, and barely walked. She and I spent a long time holding hands and not talking, while the other Popescus made conversation with Iris and among each other. Then Puica (a name that meant "sexy" in Romanian, and that she was, over fifty years ago) held up her gray head and asked, "How's your mother?"

"She's well, Godmother," I said. "Enjoying Los Angeles." Puica's frail old hand was in mine, and it squeezed mine without power, and felt hot, feverish. I feared that her breathing might give out right then, with Iris and the Popescus looking on.

"I hear it's a big city."

"One of the biggest in the world, Godmother."

"Your mom will conquer it," whispered Puica, and in her whisper there was such admiration for my bohemian, iconoclastic, unvirtuous mother, from a female who was herself a paragon of virtue, that I struggled not to get choked up again. Be tough. But I couldn't be tough, because I was feeling something so terribly strange—how many countless times before, when people asked me how my father was, how my mother was, my mind kind of jumped over an inner snicker, bitter and always there:

oh, *them*? Those two who called themselves my parents? I swallowed the snicker, and answered the question, no sense in confessing to strangers how unparentlike those two had been to me. Well, this time that silent snicker was not there.

It was not there. I was looking forward to seeing Mom, back in America. Home.

And I felt at peace, pretty much, even with that bronze face in the cemetery.

I felt whole.

I was a little frightened that the feeling would prove deceiving, that it would go away never to come back.

"You're not going to leave this beautiful meat pie uneaten?" asked Petre. "Ella worked her fingers to the bone. Petru, we want you to take it with you."

"I'll wrap it in plastic for you," said Ella.

I met Iris's eyes: she found the meat pie too rich, its scent too strong—and now we were to bunch it in my camera bag, and stick it under one of those narrow plane seats? But she said nothing. So I took along the wrapped meat pie, and ate it the next evening in a hotel room in London, while Iris had room service.

We took some other little gifts. A couple of napkins woven in folk-loric red. And a few of those sacred family pictures, black and white, on the back of which were printed the names of photo studios long non-existent. The fact that the Popescus entrusted the pictures to me meant this: Be one of us, out there. Perpetuate us. Make us last, make us known. And, bless them, they set no conditions as to how exactly I should per-petuate them. They left that up to me.

Uncle Nicu took me aside, and said solemnly, "Remember, you're a writer. You've always been a writer."

"How the hell can I forget that, Uncle?"

"Just in case movies and what-not mess up your mind."

I didn't have the time to explain that they couldn't mess up my mind, even if I wanted them to. I'm too wedded to the inner truth of words. As for being one of the Popescus, I was that already, had always been that, even at my times of deepest denial. Thank God that America's roots were in other countries. Carrying my roots with me was all-American.

One more Bucharest taxi. How many more seconds? Some two thousand.

I still felt at peace.

We were flying Lufthansa, to Frankfurt, and then to London. We climbed the steps to the plane, and for an instant the sight of a German stewardess, blond and large, seemed strange—she was smiling so sweetly. Where was the fierce intentness I'd seen on so many faces in my homeland? She led us to our seats with jolting courtesy, and brought us Western newspapers. We saw our first American paper in days. I glanced at the headlines and felt that America's problems were so tame, so manageable. America was powerful, and young, and had money.

We took off and rose into the skies, sharp and fast, until we glimpsed Romania below, through scattered white clouds. Its plains and roads, mountains and mountain passes, places of glory that were paid for in blood, too much blood, became as small as toys. The continent that gave us to the world fell away below. This flight was too short for one movie, but I wanted to see a movie, a Hollywood movie. Maybe we'd go to see one in London. But first we would call the kids, my mom, Iris's parents. We would tell them that we did it, we conquered our roots. I didn't know how exactly we would express that, but I was sure we would find a way.

I saw the Carpathians from the plane, curving across Romania. I'd cried too much these days, so this time the land spreading far below only made me smile. What did I achieve? I understood. Who was I now? A man born in that land below, but rooted in himself. I leaned into the plane's window, to treasure this instant of looking at my birthplace as I left it again, this time with a clear soul, and in peace.

Epilogue

There is no story of success in America without a pot of money at the end.

At seven o'clock in the evening, on a Tuesday in September of 1995, the four Popescus of Beverly Hills were eating hamburgers at a fast-food restaurant called Johnny Rocket's. The place looked like a fifties' diner, complete with period napkin dispensers and juke boxes. A few minutes after seven, Iris and I excused ourselves to the kids, and paced up to the public phones, to make a call to Richard Green and Howard Sanders, a hot young duo of film agents who specialized in selling books to film. We made the call with high trepidation. Since ten in the morning, the two agents had been selling my latest novel to the Hollywood "industry."

The secretary told me that the two couldn't talk to me just now, they were on the line with a major studio. One, however, broke off and spent twenty seconds with me, advising me not to worry. "They're seriously interested, we're in good shape." He hung up.

I'd been through fire all day, but it was still not over. "Seriously interested" didn't guarantee that they'd buy my new novel, which I hadn't even finished, though I'd written over four hundred pages of it. Or that the sale would be concluded today. This could extend into tomorrow, and the day after tomorrow, and the rest of the week.

We looked at each other disappointedly: we had hoped to get solid good news. Then we walked back to our unfinished hamburgers and our children, who were aware of our tension. This new book had invaded our family life. The last nine months, I'd worked ten to twelve hours a day, seven days a week. After years of being easily available—when I worked, I did it in an office which my wife and kids traversed when they pleased, the kids trampling the research material scattered on the floor—this book absorbed me so much that I became a zombie able to utter only one line: Sorry, what did you say?

The book was a scientific thriller which I'd meant to write for a long time, about an anthropologist meeting our apemen ancestors in the African wild. I wrote it with the great passion of childhood fantasies: seeing man at his zero hour, piercing two-million-year-old mysteries of how we came to walk upright, and hunt lions with spears, and make love face to face. Now, Richard Pine, my literary agent in New York and the hot Hollywood duo had decided to "go out" with it even before I finished writing it, because everyone they'd had lunch with in the last three months had instantly become dreamy about the beginnings of man. This was "auction material." I feared to agree or disagree with them. I only thought of how a major sale would change our lives. I thought of five (5) other novels heaped on my office floor, unsold. None, in my view, inferior to this one. I thought of *real success,* which, before good reviews, fan mail, or surprised nods from usually indifferent relatives, consisted of being able to say screw you in your mind to all those who rejected you over the years (I had a very long list), while knowing that this time you could also say it out loud. I thought of college funds for the kids, a better computer for me, a better computer for Iris, jewels for Iris if she wanted them. I remembered other people's rags to riches stories, and my envy of them over the years. For all those reasons, I said yes to "going out" with a partial manuscript.

The literary agent and the film agents huddled together, took New York's and Hollywood's pulses, and came up with a daring strike: sell simultaneously to both media, movies and books. If the movies bought first, so much the better.

I hadn't lost sleep over this, because I didn't believe it possible. Thus, the previous Friday, when the film agents outlined the plan, and read me the companies they would submit the material to, I heard names like Disney, Twentieth Century Fox, even Steven Spielberg, as if they were uttered in another world about another writer. Let them sell to anyone at all, I thought. Let them sell at whatever price, I just didn't want this novel to become the sixth yellowing on my office floor.

So, last week all this was still abstract. To me, to us. To the agents, it was already real. They were out there already, in the outer space of a dazzling future, predicting who would "bite." My wife, usually the skeptic, was out there too, even ahead of them. She and the agents compared figures fetched by other novels sold on "partials," and she countered each time with an inflection of surprise: But Petru's stuff was really better than this or that top sale, wasn't it? Hopefully, they said, but those who had to see it that way were the buyers, and you never know what can happen to change people's minds at the last minute; now, let's look again at the submission list. Through all of Friday, the submission list shrank and expanded and shrank, as two agents and an excited spouse felt in turn ready to take on the world, or cautious, or ready to take on the world again. When they felt ready, they wanted to submit the piece to just a few well-garnished pockets. When they didn't, they felt like throwing the book at everyone, to see who would be blinded by it.

I wished I could act cool, or with humor. The closest I could come to holding my composure was to smile at the unreality of this. I thought disjointedly of the sun of Africa on the nape of my neck when I did my research, of the old typewriter I used in Romania, of the word *scriitor,* writer, on my father's tombstone. The film agents' office was in a little unassuming house in Beachwood Canyon, totally offbeat location, but out of that unlikely lair the two fire-eaters had sold a number of books for six and seven figures. Their quirkiness worked for them in the best Hollywood way: people didn't know what to expect from them. Which would be excellent, because the buyers would scramble not to be left out of the auction.

Mom lived less than a mile away from the agents' office. She and I had had a major reconciliation. I'd written her a ten-page letter about the past, and after hesitating a few days, she had read it. From the priceless amazement on her face, I felt that the child I was once had finally been heard. Writing to her about the past was perhaps childlike in itself, but I could not do otherwise. So she read, and accepted. And I felt, now that this little ritual had been completed, that other things could happen too. Like, even a big sale. Why not? I did not allow it to enter my adult mind, but I hoped it with a child's heart.

"Damn," said my wife, and it showed how caught up she was in this waiting and hoping, for otherwise she never said a bad word before the children. "What does it take for those guys to make a decision? What guarantees do they need, to buy a good book?"

"It's not finished yet."

"So? You gave them a complete storyline. They hardly ever read more than a storyline."

"Let's hope they're reading the manuscript this time," I chuckled, yet without humor. "That's what's taking so long, the mental effort for film executives to read a manuscript."

Last Friday at noon, as we returned from meeting with the agents, I had found at home a handwritten note from a top film executive I knew from way back. He used to work in television; now he was the president of a major movie company. In his note, he reminded me of what good friends we were, and asked to be the first to read the manuscript. I called the agents. "Nice move," one of them commented. "You call him after we sell it, and tell him you did want to give it to him first, but we didn't let you. You make us the heavies."

I thought: I'll probably never have a reason to make that kind of phone call.

Monday passed in preparations. The agents xeroxed the four hundred pages twenty times, enough copies for twenty submissions. They made or returned phone calls, to juice up this and that hopeful. They told us that there were plenty of hopefuls. I asked why. "They want to know how man came about," explained one of the agents.

I tried to laugh. "I'm so glad. I've been wanting to know how man came about for the last twenty years."

"Well, they've wanted to know why only for a few weeks, and that's enough for a sale."

Now, at past seven in the evening, long after most Americans returned home from work, my agents were still in their office, the execs of several big movie companies were still in their offices, and if I was to believe that any of this was happening, the heads of the business affairs divisions of the respective companies were in their offices also, waiting for a deal to be closed. But it might be closed tomorrow, or after tomorrow. Or not at all. Things could sour. I'd asked my agents what could kill a sizeable sale. "Passing on an offer for a potentially bigger one which, for some reason, does not materialize," Howard Sanders explained. "You tell a buyer: You're not giving me enough, and he may well tell you: Fine, go look for someone who'll give you more. Now, if you don't find that someone, it can get tricky. You don't want to find yourself going back to an offer you rejected, because most times, that offer's not there anymore. Or it's substantially reduced."

"Which is why you want to include enough people in the race," said Richard Green. He had pretty eyes, and was always smooth and cheerful. A born diplomat and finder of solutions.

"But not wimps," said Howard Sanders. He was direct, built like an athlete, intense. He'd struck off the list some "wimps" whose names cut my breath. The cheerful one later convinced him to put a few of them back on.

"So, what's your basic strategy?" asked my wife.

"We both get on the phone Tuesday morning, and call a bunch of people, not too few, not too many," said the cheerful one. "We tell each of them: we have this material here, ready for you to have it picked up. It's very special, cancel all your meetings and read it today, we want an answer by tonight. Some will answer tonight, some not. Some will pass."

"Some will not read," I offered.

"They'll all read. Everyone wants to see what the big fuss is about. So they'll all read, even if some won't read all four hundred pages, but hand them halfway through to an assistant."

I tried to picture top executives cancelling all their meetings, to read my stuff, the juice of my brain, inked into four hundred pages. I tried to picture them not taking phone calls; in Hollywood, phone calls are the oxygen of the business.

"We'll have fun," said the athletic one.

I could tell why. When they mentioned the "going out day," it was as if they mentioned D-Day. Their eyes started shining, their features tightened with a hunter's thrill at glimpsing the prey. But the thrill was high-risk. Being an aggressive agent is like being a kamikaze: they would plunge their planes at the targeted battleship, the "industry," and the plunge would end with a score, or with a crash. Repeated crashes put their status in danger. Repeated scores made them top agents, edge players, authorities in what should sell high and what shouldn't. Sales are the bottom line of Hollywood life. Which is why writers feel important only at times like this; in between, they work behind the scenes, unheard from, unknown.

And I, who had built my independence on my books, felt that during these tense few days I'd been surrendering it. I felt that years of research, of travelling to Africa, of dreaming about what made humans human, a personal obsession since I first saw bits of fossils under glass in Bucharest's Antipa Museum of Natural Sciences, were being surrendered now to the quick and hurried eyes of people who would read and appreciate only in terms of casting and financing and domestic and foreign distribution. Was I nervous? Of course I was. Those people would react impressed or indifferent, pleased with what they read or confused by it, and from their unpredictable reactions would be woven a kind of magical rope from which would hang, for a few days unlike most other days, my writer's achievement. My writer's life. Me. No false bravado about that, no posturing. The way they would respond would influence not just the fate of this book, but my fate.

And I didn't write this book for the movie executives, because I couldn't. I didn't know them, I couldn't tell what made them tick. I wrote it for me first, then for my son, who inspired its main character. Then for my daughter and my wife, they were my first readers, the first ripples of a stone I'd be throwing in the mysterious pond of a population's reaction to a new book.

We paid for the hamburgers, exited Johnny Rocket's, and drove home. I chatted with my daughter and son, trying to hide my distraction. I got into it, and felt happy with my wife and my brood around me. I felt complete. What did I need this nerve-racking assault on success for? I consoled myself that if it didn't happen, I'd still be my old self, still uphold writing standards I always upheld, and still talk with an accent. I'd continue on, as a certain kind of American author, equal to the natives but never to be confused with them. There was some pride in that stance, and some pain, and that showed in my heroes, and in the choice of my stories.

But now my latest story lay under the scrutiny of the world's biggest cultural machine, and I remembered when my Romanian books lay under scrutiny inside that mysterious sphinx of publications, in Bucharest. Much had changed, and much was the same. I was pierced by my old Romanian insecurity. It wouldn't happen. It couldn't happen. I wasn't scripted to go that high. I was born under Communism, I cleaned my rear into adulthood with party newspapers, I typed on a typewriter registered with the Securitate, the same Securitate who slapped me around. I still had nightmares about being kidnapped back to Romania now and then, and still ordered in restaurants not quite the cheapest items on the menu, yet hardly ever the most expensive ones. I'd seen the world, but I hadn't really changed.

And yet I had.

We arrived at home, and the kids begged for another half-hour of TV before being put to bed.

They sat on the floor to watch, and I sat behind them on the couch. The backs of their heads blocked off the screen, but I didn't want to watch TV, I just wanted to peer at the dark fluffy shape of their heads and fantasize about the minds inside that shape, about the thoughts synapsing through their brains just now. Experiences, discoveries. They were transforming, these minds, they were *becoming,* right this second. They were achieving unseen steps of growth.

I too was achieving unseen steps of growth, and realized that at all ages, I was still young, and even immature.

In the four years since I'd first travelled back to Romania, a lot had happened. I organized a Romanian lobby in Washington, and became one of its leading members. Under Iliescu, Romania made some big strides, especially towards regaining international acceptance. It entered NATO's Partnership for Peace. It was granted several major loans, and it won back the most-favored-nation clause, lost during Ceausescu's final dementia. The situation of the orphans improved substantially, and more broadminded legislation about adoptions was passed by the Bucharest parliament. But the economy continued to barely creak through. Though personally popular, Iliescu was accused of allowing the old cadre to prosper from shady deals. Prime properties were sold preferentially to cronies, who in turn contributed to the "power's" war chests. The industrial workers resisted privatization. The disgruntled miners raided Bucharest again, bringing down Prime Minister Petre Roman—Iliescu was accused of agreeing to sacrifice Roman in order to protect himself. Roman went on to form his own political party. After some loud infighting, the opposition united under that former geology professor at the University of Bucharest, Emil Constantinescu. Romania's dream of being led by an intellectual would finally come true in 1996, when Constantinescu, with critical help from Roman, would defeat Iliescu and win a presidency finally no longer suspected of "crypto-Communism." Poet Blandiana, once my colleague at Iowa's International Writing Program, was now a big power wielder, and the columnist I'd met at *Romania Libera,* Petre Mihai Bacanu, a top opinion maker. Romania had grown several scores of local millionaires. The press continued to be raucously free, and the country gained a strange popularity in America as a place of fascinating and yet frightening contrasts, a once and always Draculaland.

I published two books I'd written in English in Romania, experiencing the odd feeling of being translated from English into my original language. They sold out their first printings in days. In America, I stood in the midst of conflicting perceptions of Romania, many as passionate as the country that stirred them. Over and over, I explained the area's history to congressmen, or argued to Jewish organizations that the Romanians were not a breed of xenophobic rascals—I was a case in point! I did a silent, thankless job of "righting the image," which made my mother nervous: "Don't help them too much, they'll turn against you."

"Why would they do that?"

"They'll think you're too important and start resenting you, it's in their nature."

"So," I joked, "the Romanians are an extreme illustration of the human nature."

My in-laws went on their own trip to revisit their roots, which included Budapest, Prague, and Zhdenev, my mother-in-law's home village. Listening to the itinerary of their trip, I smiled, because it had more to do with Blanka's memories than with Carl's. Carl strolled around Prague, stopped at the National Theater, which had been a cover in his sabotage work, and photographed it out of focus. He did not ask to go to his own hometown of Slatinske Doly. But Budapest was prominent on the itinerary because Blanka lived there as a young girl with Gentile papers. All the more so was Zhdenev. In order to visit the city, they had to cross the Slovak border into what was now the Ukraine; in honored tradition, that slice of the former Jewish pale had again changed hands.

"Zhdenev was wonderful," Blanka told me. "We walked down Main Street, and I was recognized by someone, a girl who knew me back then. She asked: Blanka Davidovich? and I said yes. So she took us to the church; it was Sunday and almost everyone was there. We entered and they stopped the service and gathered around us, and then we all went outside and we talked and laughed and cried . . ."

"They cried?" I asked.

"Well, I cried. Yes, a few of them cried too, maybe because we were so old now, and we were so young then. Anyway, it was just wonderful. For them too."

"Did you do everything you wanted to do?"

"I wanted so bad to go to the river and put my hand in the water."

She didn't explain why and I didn't ask, I needed no explanation. "But it got late and we had to leave. Anyway, it was wonderful."

Wonderful.

What makes the human soul feel that its deep traumas can be reversed, or at least alleviated by revisiting a certain space, usually not larger or more imposing than a house or a street, and by spending a few minutes there? Those hours in her hometown, that visit to the church (the church, the sanctuary of the "other"), were Blanka's belated reversal of fate. That reversal continued, when she and Carl went to Muhldorf, Bavaria, for a reconciliation with the Germans of today, most of them children of Nazis. Muhldorf, an ancient little country town, had a concentration camp attached to it, and that was where my in-laws were liberated by the U.S. Army. Two-thirds of Muhldorf's citizens voted to erect a monument to that liberation, and to invite fifty survivors to the dedication, at the town's expense. Carl and Blanka went, and were put up in German homes, one belonging to a doctor whose father was the Nazi mayor at the time of the liberation.

After those journeys, they acted changed. Not healed, perhaps that was too big a word, but restored. They saw the past differently. A certain haunting loneliness of being survivors had been pierced from outside, by a gesture of manifest respect from the other side. No matter how small. It worked.

I understood.

I'd made peace with Dad, somehow. I made peace with his grave, and therefore with him. I even made peace with Communism, somehow. My memories were not erased, but I moved on.

And now, I got up, and I made a call to my Hollywood agents.

"Fox studios is going to make a move to preempt," said Howard Sanders. "To buy your novel before the others have a chance to make their offers."

"You kidding?"

"No."

"Who's read it over there?"

He gave me the name of a top executive. "He locked himself in his office this morning at ten o'clock, and was done by five. It really looks good."

I lost my breath. "That's . . . that's . . ."

"Yeah. Stay by the phone, it won't take long now."

I hung up. My wife came down the stairs, read the excitement in my face, and said like in a comedy, "I hope it's the right amount, I just bought a new car."

"You what?"

"In fantasy, dummy."

We went up to put the kids to bed. As we stepped down the stairs again, I told myself that this was not happening. Too much like a movie: years of hard work, then the big stroke of luck, and a sappy ending. Too mainstream. I was not a mainstream guy. Just to give reality to my feelings, I called my literary agent in New York, the one who had started all this. It was almost midnight in New York, but Richard Pine was up. "It looks good," he said; he'd just talked to the West Coast agents.

So this *was happening*. Richard Pine was a svelte, fit man with graying hair, very confident, straightforward and realistic, the opposite of the agent who snows you with talk. I'd seen him in person only twice. But he kept seeing me in the manuscripts I sent him, that was my real person for him—my writing. He told me of three publishers who were reading the manuscript over the weekend, and he expected them to call him first thing Monday. I wished him luck with the editors, thereby wishing myself luck, and hung up. The phone rang again instantly.

"Fox wants to buy the book tonight," said Richard Green.

I waved my wife over. She picked up another phone. Told the news, she asked for how much.

"You'll be almost rich," said Richard Green very cheerfully.

She didn't flinch. "What do you mean, almost?"

He started laughing. "Well, you'll still have to pay us our commission."

Before 10 P.M., the deal had been closed.

I called my mother and Iris called her parents. We had a quietly hysterical family gathering on the phone, they wondering at how quickly it all went, Iris telling and retelling the details, which were very few as yet, I wondering silently what, if anything, could happen for this not to materialize, to remain a fantasy. But it wasn't a fantasy. In a few days, the contracts would be written up and ready to sign.

We hung up with our parents, and kissed. I suggested that we drink a glass of champagne, but we had none, and Iris didn't want me to drive out to a liquor store, didn't want a celebration yet. Let's see it on paper first. I didn't feel like drinking champagne anyway, I felt like thinking, like making a new plan. Where did I go from here? What was the real end of this happy story?

There was no end, really.

Glancing out the window, I noticed a soft bluish light shining in the converted garage I used as an office. My computer, I forgot to turn it off. That hardly ever happened to me. I stepped into the office, didn't turn on the overhead light, but just lingered, lit by the blue glare from the computer's monitor, wondering what thought was appropriate now. What words could express a new sense of direction.

I swept the darkness of the room with my eyes, making out on the shelves the spines of books and dictionaries, all partners and allies in my writer's journey. I bought many of them in used bookstores, when I had no money to buy new books. I read them after unknown other readers. I liked them like that, battered, alive. They reminded me of my books in Romania, still being read, still alive. And the words came all by themselves, ordinary, happy: *I had so many more stories to write.*

Petru Popescu
Los Angeles, 1993–1996

Acknowledgments

I must first thank my family for generously allowing me to describe events and memories that included all of us. My wife, Iris, in particular showed great patience, selflessness, and humor. The next such accolade goes to Nelly Cutava, my mother. Then to the Popescus of Bucharest, with special mention for Nicu, Petre, and Ella. And finally to my in-laws, Carl and Blanka Friedman. They each deserve the deepest gratitude from me, who played alone with memories dear to us all.

My mother also provided my childhood pictures, while my cousin Alex Galdau helped procure the group photo on the cover.

I owe thanks to a large number of people who helped me research this book, or helped me shape its thought over the years. Often they did it by reminiscing out loud about the past, while I listened, planning to write it all down one day, yet doubting that any American publisher would want to publish it. While those people were sometimes unaware that they were helping my research, as I myself was unaware that I was pursuing it, they all gave me access to their experiences, which are always better than facts dug up from computer banks. Some were or are leaders in the Romanian community in America: the late Miron Butariu, the late Reverend Florin Galdau and Mrs. Maria Galdau, and Ion Cepoi. I also had help from a number of Romanian journalists in exile: the late Noel Bernard, for years with Radio Free Europe, Aristide Buhoiu, editor of Los Angeles's Romanian publication *Universul,* Liviu Floda, Horia Puscariu, and Andrei Brezianu. I checked certain facts about Romania's Jewish minority with the late chief Rabbi of Romania, Moses Rosen, with Radu Ioanid, a historian at the Holocaust Memorial Museum in Washington, D.C., with World War II contemporaries and survivors Yakov Bodo, Regine Lazar, Marcel Zingher, and Enrico Modiano, but first and foremost with the late Filip Brunea, Romania's top social reporter in the thirties, and a friend of my father's.

Mihai Sion, Romania's Consul General in Los Angeles, read the manuscript to help me check my data about Ceausescu's last years, and about the revolution. Others, including Robert Arakelian, Sorin Zarnescu, and Ara Ghemigian, read either the whole book or just parts, and helped with suggestions and constructive criticism. On the academic side, I found excellent political analysis in the works of Vladimir Tismaneanu, Matei Calinescu, Nestor Rates, and Daniel N. Nelson. About minorities specifically I learned a lot from a thesis on "Postwar Romania and the National Question," by Jonathan Bradley Rickert. Concerning Romania's press and arts after the revolution, I got updates from Bucharest from literary critic and publisher Magdalena Popescu. Finally, my friend Joyce Rappaport reread the manuscript for me, pointing out both its strengths and its repetitions.

Still, this book would never have been published without the help of two Americans completely unconnected with Eastern Europe or with Romania. Back in 1991, agent Anthony Gardner insightfully introduced me to Morgan Entrekin, who alone among New York publishers declared interest in such a subject. When the book was finally delivered to Grove/Atlantic, senior editor Anton Mueller convinced me to "declutter" the manuscript, at that time 700 pages long, to lift its themes above the ever-creeping-back nostalgia of memoirs, in short, to make the book better. To them all, and to others not named for reasons of space or faulty memory, goes not only my gratitude, but my sense of wonderment.